Mission

AT THE DAWN
OF THE 21ST CENTURY

A VISION FOR THE CHURCH

ALLeluia

PAUL VARO MARTINSON, EDITOR

Kirk House Publishers
Minneapolis, Minnesota

Mission at the Dawn of the 21st Century

A VISION FOR THE CHURCH

Cover design: Karen Walhof

Library of Congress Cataloging-in-Publication data
Mission at the dawn of the 21st century: a vision for the church /
    Paul Varo Martinson, editor.
        p.   cm.
    Conference proceedings.
    Includes bibliographical references.
    ISBN 1-886513-30-9
    1. MissionsCongresses.   I. Martinson, Paul Varo, 1934-
BV2020.M54 1999
266—dc21   99-33588
                                                                  CIP

Kirk House Publishers, PO Box 390759, Minneapolis, MN 55439
Manufactured in the United States of America

Contents

Preface

The Congress on the World Mission of the Church: St. Paul '98 is now a little over a year away. It is time that the papers feeding into and energizing this Congress now be made widely available to the church.

The heart and soul of the Congress was the eleven colloquia—mini think-tanks one might say—composed of twelve to thirteen persons chosen for their special competence in specific areas that would contribute to the overall goal of each colloquia. Six of the colloquia were geographical; five were topical.

In preparation for each colloquia a Status and a Vision paper were prepared by two carefully selected persons—in the case of China one paper served both purposes. In the volume these papers for each colloquia appear in the order of status and then vision. These papers were meant to serve each colloquia as resource, not to control an agenda. The freewheeling colloquia were to come up with their own "Idea Packages", which they did (see the *Proceedings of the Congress*—http://www.luthersem.edu/Congressideapackages/). But as resource they retain their value and inspiration. Without them the Congress would simply not have been what it was.

While these papers form the main body of this text, also included are papers that were made available to Congress participants as a whole. First are four papers that were distributed to participants prior to the Congress. These touched on broader themes related to mission. At the end are four presentations that were made in plenary at the Congress. Altogether these and the status/vision papers present a remarkable summary of the status of mission as we enter a new century and set forth an agenda for the future that is both specific and comprehensive.

It was desired that the papers and presentations should convey their own flavor. Indeed, a cardinal principle throughout was that each paper and presentation should freely express the convictions and priorities of the writer without reference to a pre-cooked Congress agenda. Thus, also, in editing there was little effort to make them all conform to a single format. This of course applied to language, but one will also see a variety of ways that matters of reference, for instance, are handled.

Many persons are to be thanked for making this publication possible. First, of course, are the writers and presenters themselves who made their work available for this volume—some having to write out oral presentations already made. Many were consulted in the course of this project, including members of the follow up committee. Ann Foltz kept a firm and competent hand on the tiller—without that this could have taken much longer. Tom Ewald did yeoman's work in editing. Raymond Rosales kindly translated some portions of the Latin America Status paper that were in Spanish. Alice Loddigs and Phyllis Engebretson were called upon for assistance in a variety of matters. Craig Moran helped keep a channel of communication going in several directions. Leonard Flachman and Kirk House are to be thanked for their cooperative spirit in design and production.

This volume consists of words. It is the church that will put vision into acts.

Paul Varo Martinson
Fredrik A. Schiotz Professor of Missions and World Religions
Luther Seminary, St. Paul, Minnesota

Foreword

Roland E. Miller

The Congress on the World Mission of the Church: St. Paul '98 took place on June 23-27, 1998, at Luther Seminary in St. Paul, Minnesota, U.S.A. It drew together 148 participants from various nations and denominational backgrounds in an intensive think-tank on mission. Two contemporary mission realities provided the raison d'être of the Congress and were its primary issues. The first was the vast number of people who have not yet heard or fully heard the gospel. The second was the basic and unresolved question of the nature of the continuing responsibility of North American Christians in regard to that fact. These fundamental issues in turn attracted a series of other themes and questions that were considered at this historic event.

Prior to the Congress, selected participants prepared papers that were distributed in advance, while other papers were presented in plenary sessions. This volume offers a compilation of these important materials as a potentially primary resource for mission reflection.

The Congress was set up in eleven colloquia related to specific geographical and topical areas. The colloquia included: Africa, China, Former Soviet Union, India, Latin America, North America, Theology, Service, Structures, Education, and Information Technology. The members of each colloquium received a status and a vision paper related to their area. The status paper outlined the current state of the mission enterprise and the vision paper, as the term suggests, pointed to new possibilities. These original reflections provided the grist for the Congress mill. The four general pre-Congress papers by Paul Martinson, Mary Motte, Alan Neely, and James Scherer, and the plenary papers by Choong Chee Pang, Tom Houston, Timothy Lull, and Andrew Walls brought great enrichment of thought. For example, the questions raised in Professor Scherer's paper will always require addressing and answering by those concerned about and involved with the global mission task of the church. In the end, all of the 29 major papers delivered became available for publication!

The ethos of the Congress may be described by the term "think-tank." It was a call to fresh thinking about the mission of the church, to be responded to in freedom and with courage. The fresh thinking would not have been easily possible without these materials from the hands, minds, and hearts of a very knowledgeable group of individuals recognized for their long association with the mission of the church. It is hoped that their appearance will provide stimulus for a wider and ongoing reflection on that task, at a crucial time in its history.

The papers are not the only product of the Congress. The planned outcome of the Congress was a series of Idea Packages that were developed by the respective colloquia. In addition, various homilies, theological reflections and Bible studies were presented. All these materials, together with programmatic and participant information, are incorporated in a volume entitled *Proceedings of the Congress on the World Mission of the Church, St. Paul 1998*, published by Luther Seminary and available to the general public. The volume also contains the formal Message of the Congress.

The title of the Congress' opening service sermon was "The Desire of God," based on 1 Timothy 2, 3-4:

> This is right and is acceptable in the sight of God our Savior who desires everyone to be saved and to come to the knowledge of the truth. For there is one God; There is also one mediator between God and humankind, Christ Jesus, himself human, who gave himself a ransom for all.

That expressed desire of God was, in fact, the meeting point of all the papers. Broad in scope and varying in approach, the papers are held together by a common "theology of desire," the same spirit that held together all the participants in a great mission congress. The papers gathered in this volume, therefore, do not only provide the basic documentation for a significant event, but they also mark a united effort to suggest how the salvific desire of God may be best served by God's people in the first decades of the new century. It is in that light that I recommend this volume to the reader. The distinguished authors would wish me to close with a word of thanksgiving and praise to the Lord of the mission: Alleluia!

GENERAL
PAPERS

ALLeluia

Key Issues to Be Considered in Global Mission Today:

Crucial questions about mission theology, context, and expectations

James A. Scherer

What lessons does mission history teach for tomorrow's mission?

A generation ago the World's Student Christian Federation (WSCF) published a volume of essays entitled *History's Lessons for Tomorrow's Missions*. These essays examined earlier mission epochs with a view to discerning lessons for the present. This Congress, standing at the threshold of the third millennium of the Christian era, and contemplating the form of future missionary obedience, would do well to consider lessons from recent mission history for our global mission practice in coming decades. Given the ending of the older era of western missionary expansion, can there be a new and different, but equally faithful and valid, era of global mission in the next millennium?

Roughly one hundred years ago, the Protestant mission enterprise from North America embarked on a greatly expanded and historically unprecedented movement of missionary outreach into Asia and Oceania, Africa, and Latin America. That movement laid the foundation for the worldwide Christian community of today. It rode the crest of a rising tide of American global imperialism, and took advantage of the convergence of student revivalism, western paternalism and popular support for a benevolent foreign policy. The movement that gave rise to John R. Mott's slogan "the evangelization of the world in this generation" was thus born out of a buoyant sense of optimism and self-confidence. This was reinforced by the firmly held conviction of western moral, spiritual, cultural and religious superiority. But such a context clearly does not exist today.

Fifty years ago, following World War II, there occurred another great outpouring of missionary personnel and resources from North America into what was coming to be known as the "Third World." This new wave reflected a positive response by North Americans to missions affected by war (the so-called "orphaned missions"), the emergence of newly independent churches in countries liberated from colonialism with their special needs, ecumenical missionary concepts such as "partnership in obedience," and the influence of newly created organs of international missionary cooperation such as the National Lutheran Council's Commission on Younger Churches and Orphaned Missions (CYCOM), and later LWF/CWM and DWM. The beginning of the "cold war" and the closing of China to western mission activity lent added urgency to mission planning, recruitment and sending from North America. The war's end released pent-up energies and resources for mission both at home and abroad. But this is not our context today.

The present historical moment seems to lack those positive catalytic elements which provided the impetus for earlier waves of missionary outreach which took place one hundred years ago or fifty years later. Today we live in a post-colonial global era in which the dismantling of western colonial empires is virtually complete. Independent churches with "three-self" marks of autonomy have emerged throughout the non-western world. The cold war has suddenly and unexpectedly come to an end, and with it the near collapse of the communist world empire. Christianity's religious rivals, above all Islam, are demonstrating new missionary vigor. Market capitalism has become the order of the day, and autocratic regimes face resistance from newer democratic movements. Nationalism, tribalism, and ethnicity in various places burst forth in fragmentation and genocide.

In the West, secularism pushes religion to the margins, granting religious convictions a narrowly confined private and personal sphere. Our "post-Christian" society dabbles in "new age" spiritual discoveries and experiments, while post-modernist assumptions undercut faith in traditional beliefs and values. A troubled and confused western Christianity finds itself, in spite of the collapse of atheistic communism, in spiritual decline. Suffering from loss of membership and declining participation, it anxiously seeks ways to maintain its own relevance and viability. Church movements that seem to be numerically successful are often marked by dubious entrepreneurial initiatives that ignore deeper theological issues. Mainline churches, disturbed by media caricatures and criticisms of mission work, suffer from a guilty conscience and are prone to engage in self-recrimination over alleged past missionary failures. They seem to have little real energy or vision for new mission ventures.

The question that naturally arises is, "what can provide the spiritual impetus for a new era of global mission from the West? What will motivate western missions in the next millennium?" The question asks not merely about the what and how of mission activity but preeminently about the why. Pope Paul VI raised this question earlier in his 1975 Apostolic Exhortation on evangelization in the modern world (Evangelii Nuntiandi):

> In our day, what has happened to that hidden energy of the Good News which is able to have a powerful effect on man's conscience? To what extent and in what way is that evangelical force capable of really transforming the people of this century? What methods should be followed in order that the power of the Gospel may have its effect?

Paul VI's query thus raises questions about the *medium* and the *message*, and certainly also about the identity and motivation of the *messengers*. These are questions which would-be missioners from the West must answer today.

What will motivate and guide efforts of western Christians in the new missionary era? Will it be a faithful response to the overwhelming biblical witness that the church is *missionary* by its very nature, and therefore not to engage in mission is to deny Christ and to misrepresent the nature of his church? Will it be an attempt to maintain institutional continuity with past mission endeavors, or to carry out church constitutional requirements which mandate mission at home and abroad as part of the church's comprehensive mission in the modern world? Will it be an effort by Lutherans or others to retain or extend their market share of global mission prestige in a day of shrinking denominational commitments to mission, thus maintaining a competitive edge for their particular group? Will it be a concern to spread western and specifically American culture and values among developing nations in the era of globalization, thereby helping to establish a dominant *pax americana* as a replacement for cold war ideology? Or will it be simply a desire on the part of affluent western churches to provide inter-church aid in the form of personnel and project assistance to partner churches as these churches struggle to carry out mission in their local areas?

Whatever the reasons, western Christians will not be able to play a worthy part in the new missionary era unless they understand their own motivation, and have a valid biblical and theological basis for their contribution. It is crucially important that western missionary agencies have a clear sense of their own missionary identity, role, and function within the ecumenical mission of the global church. The new missionary era calls for a profound rethinking of all essential missionary relationships.

What are some major elements of a biblically based and theologically sound mission practice? Is there agreement on basic marks of global mission practice?

In 1982 a statement of "common convictions" about mission, entitled "Ecumenical Affirmation: Mission and Evangelism," was adopted by the WCC Central Committee, and commended to the churches for their study, inspiration, and guidance. Along with other statements that might be considered, it offers valuable benchmark criteria for thinking about mission practice in the emerging mission era. The Ecumenical Affirmation received widespread approval from conciliar Protestants, Evangelicals, and Roman Catholics. It opens with an urgent renewed call to mission at a time when many Christians in the West apparently assume that the missionary era has already come to an end. The statement proposes seven "common convictions" concerning which it is claimed that wide agreement exists. The Congress may wish to examine these convictions to determine whether they provide a blueprint for common missionary action in the new millennium.

Conversion: "the proclamation of the gospel includes an invitation to recognize and accept in a personal decision the saving lordship of Christ."[1] This bedrock conviction obviously includes baptism and justification by grace through faith yet it cries out for further clarification of the meaning of conversion in the mission context of witness to non-believers. This is especially necessary because the western sending church has for centuries operated with no clear understanding or definition of conversion, measuring growth in terms of infant baptism or adult membership transfers (rather than "conversion"), and preferring to speak of "church members" (rather than "disciples"). Do we have, and do we need, a more consistent understanding of the meaning and practice of conversion in the missionary situation, especially when dealing with non-believers or members of other faith communities? What would it mean to speak meaningfully about a threefold conversion to God in Christ, to the Christian community, and to God's work in the world?

The gospel to all realms of life: this means that the Lordship of Christ is to be proclaimed to "all realms of life"[2] in the whole creation, thus not merely as a private or personal message, and not simply with a view to planting the church. In one eloquent sentence the statement declares: "The Church is called to announce Good News in Jesus Christ, forgiveness, hope, and a new heaven and a new earth; to denounce powers and principalities, sin and injustice; to console the widows and orphans, healing, restoring the broken-hearted; and to celebrate life in the midst of death." Given the general acceptance today of what is called "holistic" or comprehensive mission, and the astonishing multiplication of "mission" activities (e.g. such areas as human development, advocacy of justice, human rights, women's leadership, etc), the question must be asked: what is our understanding of "mission to all realms of life"? What are its limits or parameters? Are all activities of equal importance? Among the many things to be done, what should be designated as "priorities"? How do various mission activities relate to each other and to the overall task of evangelization?

The church and its unity in God's mission: the practice of ecumenical mission or "joint action for mission,"[3] long accepted in mission circles, has resulted in some united churches and many cooperative or united institutions (e.g. Christian medical centers and theological seminaries). The practice has been grounded in both ecumenical convictions (e.g. John 17:21) and economic realities. A new challenge arises with the ratification by the ELCA, the Presbyterian Church USA, the Reformed Church in America and the United Church of Christ of an ecumenical agreement that calls for "full communion." A similar bilateral agreement on "full communion" is expected to be adopted by ELCA Lutherans and Episcopalians, with others on the not too distant horizon. These groundbreaking agreements cry out for clarification of their missiological significance, since they generally appeal to John 17 and similar texts as their ultimate rationale. It is urgently necessary that concrete steps on the road to "unity in God's mission" be spelled out and enacted, lest "full communion" be downgraded to the level of pulpit and altar fellowship at the level of the local parish. What are the ramifications of the wider recognition of baptism, shared participation in eucharistic worship, mutual recognition of ministries, and common confession of our apostolic faith for mission practice in the future? The discussion must quickly move beyond theological agreements to include consideration of integrated mission structures, joint control of finances, and joint strategizing and planning if the agreement is to have any validity. Issues of power, money and patronage cannot be avoided, and the negative legacy of "dominance and dependence" in church-mission relations must be taken into account. Because the church's mission is God's own mission and not simply an enterprise of the churches, nothing can be declared "off limits." In the light of our koinonia in Christ, how do we envision missionary interdependence and "mission in unity" missiologically, and how do we give concrete expression to it?

Mission in Christ's way: "The self-emptying of the servant who lived among the people, sharing in their hopes and sufferings, giving his life on the cross for all humanity—this was Christ's way of proclaiming the Good News Our obedience in mission should be patterned on the ministry and teaching of Jesus."[4] This conviction calls for a serving church in every land, willing to be marked with the "stigmata" of the crucified and risen Lord. Issues raised by this central conviction, which calls on us to pattern our mission attitudes and relationships on the model of Christ, go well beyond shedding the habit of colonial dominance. Western mission agencies must ask themselves whether their use of money, power, prestige, and influence in relation to mission partners but also the outside world actually does represent "mission in Christ's way." Glaring disparities between western mission executives and their less well endowed overseas mission partners in terms of access to funds, travel opportunities, training, housing, and other amenities, including modern technology and communications, must be seriously examined from a missiological viewpoint. Expatriate missionaries are the ongoing front-line representatives of western churches abroad, and their ability to model "mission in Christ's way" locally may well be the ultimate test of koinonia in Christ between people at different economic and cultural levels. How can mission structures which express "mission in Christ's way" be developed, and how can mission candidates be identified, nurtured and freed to transcend their own background and limitations?

Good News to the poor: the church is called to follow the example of the Lord Jesus who lived as one among them and gave them the promise of God's kingdom. This discovery of God's "preferential option for the poor,"[5] initially made by Latin American Roman Catholics, is now widely accepted as a guiding principle of mission. It invites more affluent Christians to rethink their economic priorities and lifestyles both in the local congregation but also in relation to mission practice. It means a movement from condescension and mere charitable giving to pro-active involvement with the poor. Concretely, it means developing strategies to share the gospel with the poor, the marginal, and the powerless, to give them new identities in Christ, and to empower them for service. For middle-class churches, taking the poor seriously calls for revolutionary changes in attitudes, strategies, and methodologies of evangelism. It requires discipline and focus, and the recruitment of persons willing to sacrifice status and to view mission as ministry among the poor. Institutionally, it would undoubtedly mean questioning patterns of ecclesiastical wealth and property, equalizing salary scales for professional workers, and rethinking pension, endowment, and investment arrangements. The issue before the Congress is: how do we in our mission practice hold ourselves accountable to Christ's love for the poor and the outcast?

Mission in and to six continents: this is generally taken to mean that global mission is "from everywhere to everywhere."[6] It means that western Christians recognize that we are both the agents and the objects of mission; that we as evangelizers also need to be evangelized, and to recognize the right of others to evangelize us. Mission goes on "from everywhere to everywhere": at our own doorstep, at the ends of the earth, and in all places in-between. With the de-Christianization and secularization of the West, mission must now be viewed as a worldwide activity, not one confined to the "non-Christian world."

Re-evangelization of the West now becomes no less important than the evangelization of the former (but now non-existent) "non-Christian" world. Those we evangelized now become our evangelizers! No longer is there a valid theological distinction between mission at home and abroad, and the structural separation between agencies for mission within the United States and beyond our frontiers becomes increasingly artificial. Although united agencies for mission at home and abroad do not appear likely, it is interesting to speculate on what benefits might flow from such a reorganization. Short of full amalgamation, greater interchange of personnel, resources, information, and methodologies should be undertaken between home and foreign mission units. Application of the principle of "mission in and to six continents" will mean greater mutuality, respect, sharing, and inter-dependence between churches engaged in mission in different places, as anticipated in the discussion of mission in unity. Consultative processes and structures will still be needed at the local, national, regional, and global levels. Missionary consultative organs such as WCC-CWME, Lausanne Committee, LWF-CCC (now DMD), and NCC area and functional committees need to be reshaped to play a more effective catalytic role in the new millennium.

Witness among people of living faiths: this conviction affirms that "Christians owe the message of God's salvation in Jesus Christ to every person and every people."[7] Christian witness follows Jesus in respecting and affirming the uniqueness and freedom of others, fully aware that God has not left himself without some kind of witness in the faiths of other people. "Life with people of other faiths and ideologies is an encounter of commitments." Witness among people of living faiths is a two-way process in which "Christians are able to bear authentic witness" to their commitment to Christ, even as they receive the witness of others to their own convictions. It follows that western contributions to global mission cannot be offered simply as a form of diaconal service to partner churches (i.e. medical, educational, or development services) but must specifically be dedicated toward the evangelization of people of other living faiths or no faith. Simply put, the justification for global mission cannot simply be inter-church aid, though it includes that, but looks toward the completion of the "unfinished task" of world evangelism. For this reason, mission efforts which seek to reach "unreached" or unevangelized peoples are not simply one approach among many; but may be especially necessary when local churches prove unequal to the task of evangelizing their neighbors of other faiths. Expatriate missionaries have traditionally brought a boundary-crossing gift to the task of gospel witness, and this charism needs to be encouraged. It should be obvious that taking the frontier of other faiths and ideologies seriously means not simply dedicated study and development of expertise in those faiths and their traditions, but an actual witnessing encounter with living representatives of those faiths in daily life situations. Programs designed to foster Christian witness among Muslims, Buddhists and others should be evaluated in terms of their actual effectiveness in bringing about this result. What this might mean for actual conversions to Christianity needs to be addressed in terms of a cross-cultural understanding of conversion.

Authentic witness within each context: Although this point is not one of the seven original convictions of the Ecumenical Affirmation, it seems appropriate to add it to this list in light of discussions at the recent CWME meeting (Salvador, Bahia, 1996).[8] The relationship between gospel and culture, and between church and culture, has been approached in terms of various models for "contextualization" and "inculturation." It is acknowledged that there is an inseparable relationship between gospel and culture, and that witness to the gospel is never culturally neutral. "Authentic witness to the gospel takes a particular contextual form within each local setting." Yet human culture, although part of God's creation, has an ambiguous quality. Local cultures can be transformed and enriched through the gospel; at the same time, the gospel can become captive to demonic elements in local cultures. Syncretism develops when the gospel is too closely assimilated, or subordinated to, the claims of culture. Discerning God's Spirit at work in various cultures is an ongoing process that requires missiological sensitivity. Consideration of what constitutes "authentic witness" to the gospel can best be done in an ecumenical context where various Christian communities come together in mutual respect to understand, examine, and criticize one another. On one hand, each local community must be free to develop its witness to Christ within its own cultural context, without having alien forms imposed on it. Yet the final product must be recognizable as a true expression of the universal faith in Christ and the Triune God as witnessed to in scripture and creeds. This approach welcomes a diversity of cultural expressions while at the same time setting limits on diversity.

Other recent statements of missionary basis, policy, and objectives, including the 1974 Lausanne Covenant, could also be introduced as points of reference and examined for their contribution to the discussion of global mission in the third millennium. While few of these convictions are new, time and changing circumstance highlight their contemporary relevance and their need for reinterpretation. Most have been inadequately realized up to now, even when recognized as faithful expressions of Christian mission. Such convictions represent ideal or ultimate goals to be striven for in mission, not program descriptions.

How do we envisage the next stage of missionary advance? What is our understanding of the relation between the church in mission and the coming of the kingdom of God? What role does eschatology play in our mission planning and expectation?

It goes without saying that mission strategists cannot predict with certainty the unfolding shape of *missio Dei* (the mission of God), since the Triune God is and remains the ultimate author of mission. The church's calling is to remain faithful to God's plan disclosed in scripture. Yet mission policy and strategy must be shaped by some notion or understanding of God's purpose for the final outcome of the *missio Dei*. The mission of the church is, after all, an eschatological activity, that is, an activity of the "end-time" of salvation history. "The good news must first be proclaimed to all nations" (Mark 13:10). Accordingly, the mission of the church must continue to the end of time and to the ends of the earth until Christ returns in judgment and glory. The Holy Spirit is poured out following the Resurrection at Pentecost as a gift for the completion of the apostolic task of witness (John 20: 21-22). The mission of God, and of the church, can be understood only within a Trinitarian understanding of the saving work of Father, Son and Holy Spirit.

Missiology in recent years seems to be in agreement that the kingdom of God, rather than the planting of a universal church, is the goal of the *missio Dei*. Two changes in missionary thinking since the IMC Willingen Conference (1952) have led to this conclusion. First is the recognition that the older nineteenth century "church-centric" mode of missionary thinking, which saw the goal in terms of planting churches in all nations and the expansion of Christianity throughout the whole world, literally filling the world with congregations of believers, suffers from limitations. The second is the reluctant conclusion that the conversion of the entire world's population to belief in Jesus Christ as Lord and Savior is not likely to be realized. Luther himself understood that universal proclamation of the gospel, rather than the conversion of all people, was the goal described in scripture. Missiology that sees movement toward the kingdom of God as the goal of mission, with the servant church as the privileged instrument of the kingdom, but also its foretaste and forerunner, opens up new dimensions for the church's missionary planning and strategy.

Even when it is affirmed that church expansion cannot be taken as the final goal of mission, there is as yet no general agreement on the kingdom-oriented missionary goal that should replace it. Such a goal must take into account God's salvific purpose for the entire creation and embrace the redemption and reconciliation of all that God has made, including peace, justice, economic relations, ecology, cultural development, and the achievement of human unity across lines of race, religion, sex, or nationality. This final expectation for a redeemed creation finds its initial expression in the covenantal promise made by God to Abraham: "In you all the families of the earth shall be blessed" (Gen. 12:3b). Its ultimate expression is suggested by the description of Christ's saving work in Ephesians 2:13-14:

> But now in Christ Jesus you who once were far off have been brought near by the blood of Christ. For he is our peace; in his flesh he has made both groups into one and has broken down the dividing wall, that is, the hostility between us.

Mission can be described in one way as the manifestation to the world of "the plan of the mystery of the ages hidden in God" (Ephesians 3:9), made known through the church for everyone to see in its rich variety (Ephesians 3:10), in accordance with God's "eternal purpose carried out in Christ Jesus our Lord" (Ephesians 3:11). While this is only one among several scriptural images of the goal of God's mission, it is not merely theoretical but has important consequences for ecclesiology and missiology. The church is obligated to engage continuously in the task of hermeneutical research and reflection on God's saving purpose for the world in the light of scripture but also of contemporary global conditions and challenges. For only so will it be possible to design a missionary strategy for the church which approximates God's purpose to bring blessing and reconciliation to the whole creation through a covenant people gathered in Christ. Facing this challenge must be one of the tasks of this mission congress.

References

Called to One Hope: The Gospel in Diverse Cultures. Edited by Christopher Duraisingh. Geneva: WCC Publications, 1998.

Let the Earth Hear His Voice: International Congress on World Evangelization, Lausanne, Switzerland (1974). Edited by J. D. Douglas. Minneapolis: Worldwide Publications, 1975.

New Directions in Mission and Evangelization 1: Basic Statements 1974-1991. Edited by James A. Scherer and Stephen B. Bevans. Maryknoll: Orbis Books, 1992, 1998.

"The Evangelization of the Men of Our Time." (Evangelii Nuntiandi = EN): Apostolic Exhortation of Pope Paul VI. Rome, 1975.

World Mission Conferences in the Twentieth Century

Mary Motte

Introduction

If we think of the course of the twentieth century as a trajectory moving from 1900 to 1999, we can image a series of missiological signposts spanning from 1910 to 1996, from Edinburgh to Bahia. Edinburgh marks the beginning of the modern ecumenical movement, and each of the signposts that follow has contributed to an emerging ecumenical tradition. This tradition, which has thought about a more commonly shared understanding of mission among Christians, has been crafted by a search for what it means to be church in mission, and by historical awareness which has consciously interacted with events in a theological way.[1]

There are several parameters to keep in mind as one reflects on this ecumenical tradition. The first is perhaps the most obvious, namely that the conferences on world mission and evangelism are part of a larger series of signposts spanning much of the present century, and this is especially true since the World Council of Churches (WCC) came into existence, and has held regular assemblies.[2] Likewise, Faith and Order has held regular meetings since its first world conference in 1927.[3]

Both the academic and juridical processes that have accompanied the journey of the ecumenical movement offer other parameters. Here one is reminded of the work of Faith and Order as well as of the various bilateral dialogues that are also part of the ecumenical tradition. These have contributed a body of literature that helps us to measure as it were the progress of the movement.

In this paper I want to look at that aspect of the ecumenical movement which gives a place to a dialogue of life.[4] While the world mission conferences have not been conducted in a non-academic or non-juridical way,[5] one of their greatest contributions stems from the gathering of Christians periodically from different places in the world in order to reflect on mission. It is important to give more attention to this dialogue of life within the ecumenical movement. It is this manner of relationship, consciously acknowledged, that permits the recognition "that we need one another across the spectrum of Christian memory and cultural experiences and that we are actually part of the growth towards koinonia of worship."[6]

Such a dialogue of life in the framework of the ecumenical movement and specifically in the framework of the world mission conferences, can be seen to function in two ways. First of all, through this interaction, one can show how missionary understanding and engagement has come to be situated within a dynamic conception of church. Second, the dialogue of life in mission has engaged the historical process in a way that is continually reshaping the concept of mission. As we approach the end of this century, profound changes are challenging both of these emergent understandings in ways perhaps not even dreamed of in 1910. Bringing both of these concerns together, the ecclesial and the missiological, a word needs to be said about their foundational relation to unity among Christians. This unity cannot be separated from engagement in mission. Unity and mission share an identity within the Christian community, and while this shared identity is not always easily realized in practice, the conviction about their ultimate inseparability remains the inspiration and motivating force of the ecumenical movement. The world mission conferences arc among those instances representing this deeply rooted conviction.

A Search for What It Means to Be Church in Mission

Development of mission within the colonial framework, a period of time that began in earnest around the sixteenth century with the voyages of discovery and lasted until around the middle of the present century, was somewhat separated from the daily life and self-understanding of the church. This was true for both Protestants and Roman Catholics, although with some varying nuances due to different theological understandings, especially about the church. For both, mission was something confined to specialized groups who went out to places where people had not heard the gospel message and where the church was not present.[7]

A more interactive and integrated understanding of the relation between church and mission has been developing over the past several years. Anderson has noted that one of the ways in which the theology of mission has developed in the present century has been through the "progressively deepening confrontation of the Church and mission with theology."[8] While this observation was thirty years ago, subsequent events have borne out the continuity of this process.[9] Edinburgh certainly gave this unfolding process a strong initial impetus. As Latourette noted, this gathering in 1910 marked a "new sense of fellowship among Christians. . . the growing realization of this fellowship was to be one of the most significant characteristics of the ecumenical movement."[10] Faith and Order, which has done so much to develop theological discernment in the interest of developing and strengthening the ecumenical tradition, traces its original inspiration to Edinburgh.[11]

This first world mission conference intended to focus on practical collaboration in mission among its Christian participants, and therefore had ruled out "discussions about differences of opinion in doctrine and ecclesiastical structure and practice."[12] However, concern was expressed from within the conference that cooperation among separated Christians was insufficient to address some of the fundamental issues facing Christians.[13]

Yet, preparations for Edinburgh stemmed from a deep desire for unity. J. H. Oldham, who was largely responsible for the preparations, included among the participants some of those who were rooted in the Anglican tradition.[14] Bishop Gore was among this number, and he, with others, insisted that Latin America not be included as a mission field in the purview of the conference out of respect for the Roman Catholic Church.[15] Attention to the sensitivities of the different traditions, rather than criticism or excluding them from consideration, provides an opening towards building an ecumenical tradition.

After the experience of Edinburgh, those who had participated saw the need of continuing their collaboration. From this, the International Missionary Council (IMC) was formed in 1921, and prepared the way for the next world mission conference to be held in Jerusalem in 1928. While the participants at Edinburgh had been largely of western origin, those of Jerusalem were more widely representative, having come not only from the West, but also from Asia and Africa. Their churches were the fruit of earlier missionary labors. However, the self-understanding of these new church leaders brought about the beginning of a new way of perceiving the relation between church and mission. S.C. Lueng, from the Church of Christ in China, insisted on the subsidiary relation of mission to the church. He stressed that missionaries should be inserted in the life of the church rather than continue as representatives of missionary boards. David Yui, also from China, noted that "missionaries ought to have a permanent place in China, just as we hope Chinese missionaries must in future have a permanent place in America."[16] Among the other contributions of Jerusalem in relation to its concerns about the kingdom of God, syncretism and *diakonia,*[17] a changed perspective concerning the relation between church and mission emerged around the question of relations "between younger and older churches." This, in fact, was one of the volumes in the final report of the conference.[18]

The next world mission conference was held in Tambaram, India in 1938, under the theme "The World Mission of the Churches" focusing on the church as "bearer of the Gospel."[19] Participants from the younger churches were present in increased numbers, and their experience of mission and church impacted the thinking of the conference. In fact, "mission had become increasingly the realm of the indigenous churches and their life and development was therefore central towards its understanding."[20] Of course, Tambaram is perhaps best remembered for its discussion of how the church relates to persons of other faiths. This continues to be a missiological concern, as "Tambaram Revisited" illustrates.[21]

Experience of being a community of faith in mission was strengthened, especially through the contacts and relations built up during these gatherings. Yates notes the significance of this growing sense of being a world community in the experience of Karl Hartenstein, a participant from Germany at Tambaram. Facing conscription to fight for a cause with which he profoundly disagreed, he wrote to William Paton, also a participant, about the hope he experienced at Tambaram as "the communion and fellowship by all Christian churches of the world."[22]

The World Council of Churches was formed in 1948. The existence of the International Missionary Council outside the WCC, once again posed the question about the relation between mission and church. While mission was understood increasingly as belonging to the nature of the church, an inherent temptation remained to view the church as the end of mission. J. C. Hoekendijk led in challenging a church-centered concept of mission, citing such an approach as an obstacle to evangelism. Willingen took up this challenge and examined the nature and source of mission. It concluded that the saving action of God precedes the church and mission; the church is not the starting point nor the goal of mission; the church is the one sent on mission.[23] Studying the missionary obligation of the church, the conference had concerned itself with questions about the authority of faith, the growing church, evangelism, the life of the church, the economic basis of the church, and church-state relations.[24] Mutiso-Mbinda notes that a shift occurred at the Willingen conference from "emphasis on an ecclesiocentric mission to a mission-centered church."[25] Now the way was open to explore more deeply the relation between a church sent in mission for the ultimate Reign of God. In Ghana, 1958, the shift became clearer: mission belongs to the very nature of the church, there are no geographical boundaries to mission; mission is to be carried out in partnership rather than in a model suggesting any kind of domination of one Christian community over another.[26]

The International Missionary Council and the World Council of Churches met jointly at New Delhi in 1961. The IMC was integrated with the WCC, and became the Division on World Mission and Evangelism (DWME), later to become the Commission on World Mission and Evangelism (CWME), in 1971.[27] The integration of the IMC into the World Council of Churches, while it did not resolve all the questions surrounding the relation between church and mission, symbolized the process toward a deeper insight into the place of mission at the heart of the church.[28]

The DWME prepared the next world mission conference, which was held in Mexico City, 1963. Another dimension of the church's participation in mission was realized at Mexico City. The Orthodox Church, as member of the WCC, participated in the conference; and there were three official observers from the Roman Catholic Church. The Second Vatican Council, which had opened in 1962, proved to be a major ecumenical event in the life of Roman Catholics. In a practical way, this extended participation of the Christian community reflected the ecumenical vision of the conference, which stressed that mission is to be carried out by the whole church because the mission of God takes place in all six continents.[29] Mission was understood as God's mission, *missio Dei*; the church participates in this mission.

At the end of 1972 and the beginning of 1973, the next world mission conference, the second under the direction of the CWME, met in Bangkok. The theme of the conference was "Salvation Today" which was studied under the aspects of 1) culture and identity, 2) salvation and social justice, 3) churches renewed in mission. The contribution of Bangkok to the developing integral understanding of a church sent in mission was chiefly in the discussion about relationships among churches across national, confessional and continental boundaries.[30] This thinking resulted in what became known as the moratorium on sending funds and personnel from Europe and North America to other parts of the world. This discussion, which originated at Jerusalem in 1928, had become more urgent in the light of the events reshaping the world in its various ethnic and cultural self-understandings that emerged in the aftermath of the end of colonialism in the late 1940s.

Melbourne in 1980, with its theme of "Thy Kingdom Come: Good News to the Poor," represented a deepening and an extension of the reality of the whole church coming together. Both Orthodox and Roman Catholics wrote preparatory studies of the themes. The number of Roman Catholics present as observers increased about threefold over those present in Mexico City. Bible study, another important aspect of the conference, centered on a different text from the Lord's Prayer each day. The experience of shared faith around this central Christian prayer significantly deepened the participants' awareness of being part of a gathered community.

San Antonio, 1989, continued a missiological reflection on the Lord's Prayer around the theme, "Your Will be Done: Mission in Christ's Way." Much preparatory work was done to enable the participants to enter into worship in a way that brought into sharp focus the meaning of being a community gathered in the name of Christ to worship the Triune God.[31] This was ecumenical worship that reflected dynamically the "impulse to a common witness" the source of which is "the personal and community experience of Jesus Christ."[32] Both worship and Bible study, as at Melbourne, were integrated into active participation at the conference. While it is difficult to assess how such an experience affected each participant, and while it is likewise appropriate to assume that some were left unmoved by it, there remains the evidence from a number that this experience brought about "awareness of the communion with Christ and with each other (which) generates the dynamism that impels Christians to give a visible witness together."[33]

This evolution in recognizing and deepening the relationship between church and mission, from Edinburgh in 1910 to San Antonio in 1989, is principally missiological. That is, it is concerned first of all with communicating the gospel message to peoples who have not heard the good news, or have not heard it in a way that they can either accept or reject it. (The latter situation is particularly that of the western countries that have traditionally been thought of as Christian.) This foundational missiological concern first of all drew Christians together from a number of different confessions, recognizing that division among Christians was a missiological contradiction. This awareness, over time, grew to a greater inclusiveness among the various confessions. The engagement is still incomplete. The words of *Common Witness,* written in 1980, are still true, "the tragedy of our divisions remains with us at the focal point of our testimony to Jesus: the Holy Eucharist."[34] Melbourne captured the urgency of this tragedy in the image of *Eucharist as Bread for the Missionary Journey,*[35] an idea developed in *Baptism, Eucharist and Ministry* by Faith and Order in 1981. The strength of the worship experience in San Antonio prepared the ground more proximately for a witness that can move to another level of unity. This is not to suggest that there are no difficulties, nor is it to suggest that this path alone is sufficient to find the reconciliation and unity of the church. However, this experience of a gathered people, even a pilgrim people, symbolized in the participants of the conferences who came from so many different places in the world and who represented such a great diversity of gifts in the service of the gospel, is likewise an essential element in the search for unity among Christians.

In summary, the world mission conferences have recognized that a separation between mission agencies and local churches is yet a further contradiction. Mission is not seen as activity limited to the formation of Christian communities but is seen much more comprehensively as God's communication to all peoples—an activity in which the church is called to participate. Therefore, mission is not focused solely on the church, but the church is sent in mission. Mission is at the heart of the life of the Christian community; it is the dynamism that enables its members to go out to those who have not heard about God's infinite love for them.

As one stands on the threshold of Bahia, one can ask how the journey will go ahead. Will the participants in Bahia have the courage of those who preceded them in Edinburgh, Jerusalem, and Tambaram, and take significant steps toward unity from the missiological conviction that "what we have in common, and the hope that is in us, enable us to be bold in proclaiming the Gospel and trustful that the world will receive it?"[36] The heritage of the world mission conferences have enabled us with a vision of mission that is integral to the life of the Christian community, a church sent in mission. This has happened in a number of ways, but especially in and through the lived dialogue of Christians coming together from an increasing diversity of cultures and ethnicities. It has happened particularly in and through the lived experience of faith expressed in worship and Bible study. The reflection from the WCC Faith and Order consultation *Towards Koinonia in Worship,* illustrates a significance that also seems to apply aptly to the world mission conferences: "Within the giving and receiving we held together experiences of the unity of worship without which any appreciation of koinonia would be impaired: church and world; word and sacrament; gospel and creation; Christ and culture; life and faith. We recognized that we need one another across the spectrum of Christian memory and cultural experiences and that we are actually part of the growth towards koinonia in worship."[37]

Toward a Deeper Missiological Awareness

We have just considered how the world mission conferences, over the course of this century, have brought about a clearer perception among Christians about the missionary nature of the church. These conferences, as alluded to in the beginning, have also taken place in a stream of historical consciousness that has shaped missiological awareness. Since mission is primarily and foundationally about communicating God's good news, it has become increasingly evident that while the content of the message remains the same, the way it is communicated, the language and style used, must be in relation to the context or situation in which one is communicating.

The earlier conferences were not so explicit about contextualization; but caught, as it were, in the movement of twentieth century history, they gave expression to Christian experience of unity in God's love that transcended national enmities. It is somewhat of a sad paradox confirming elements of Christian unity that this present century has given occasion to prove more than once that national and international wars cannot completely destroy those elements.

When the conference on world mission and evangelism met in Jerusalem in 1928, the participants were keenly aware of the spiritual poverty of the West, which became evident after World War I. As compared with the gathering at Edinburgh, there was significantly less triumphalism.[38] At the same time, a new sense of national identity was emerging in Asia and Africa. As noted earlier, leaders who came from these churches reflected this new political sense and brought their thinking to bear on the conferences. Initially, they questioned the relation between mission agencies and church; in time they would ask about the relation between being Christian and being of a particular nation, and how to express Christian identity within different ethnic, national, and cultural contexts—the central question for the last world mission conference of this century.

When the participants gathered for the conference in Tambaram in 1938, they did so in the midst of a rapidly increasing international conflict. Some countries were already at war with one another, and yet delegates from these countries in conflict prayed together and witnessed to the universality of the Christian community and its foundation in the love of God.

The IMC met at Whitby in Canada in 1947, in the immediate aftermath of World War II. As the participants gathered, they experienced a profound awareness of the significance that their Christian relationship in the gospel had survived the war. They were also aware that tremendous changes were reshaping the world, although they probably could not have foreseen how profoundly. Their understanding of mission challenged them to discern what meaning these changes held for communicating the gospel. The theme of the conference reflecting this conviction and concern examined partnership in obedience in an effort to understand the momentous changes and what they implied for mission. Attention was given to the effect of environment and context on the church and its mission, as well as the meaning of Christian witness in this situation of a changing world order.

Context continued to challenge missiological insight, and by Willingen in 1952, the world was recognized as the horizon of mission, since this world is the place of God's activity and communication. A global concept of mission grew in the context of a rapidly shrinking world, due to new means of travel and communications. Theologically, this globalization was undergirded by the concept of *missio Dei,* especially at the conference of Mexico City, 1963, with its agenda of mission on six continents. The theology of *missio Dei* provided a way of seeing that God's mission in the world is growing. An increasing international perspective in mission thinking accompanied this perspective.

As new countries became independent, liberation was a theme that gradually took hold in theology. Missiological praxis became immersed in liberation struggles, and mission theology engaged with liberation themes. Biblically, new insights emerged about reading the Word of God in the midst of present day contexts and conflicts. All of these currents were present at the world mission conference held in Bangkok in 1975. Its theme, "Salvation Today," opened up new spaces for missiology with its direct challenge to purely eschatological views about the meaning of salvation. The conference studied the relation between salvation and human liberation, and the relation between the kingdom of God and the liberation of the poor.

Focus on the poor, those who live in the places where need for liberation is most clearly defined because of the extent of material deprivation and oppression from outside forces, took on greater importance. It became a central theme of the next world mission conference in Melbourne, Australia in 1980, as can be seen from its theme, "Thy Kingdom Come: Good News to the Poor." Oppressed peoples, struggling for liberation, challenged those concerned about communicating the good news in new ways. They were the starting point for mission, they were the majority of peoples who had not heard the gospel message. The poor became the leaders who summoned missionaries to new ways of communicating the gospel. They called for non-dominating models, they challenged those who would speak to listen first; those who would lead, to walk with, to accompany. The conference itself often became a situation of struggle as the voices of the poor, audible through the dynamics of the conference, probed, and at times provoked. Out of all of these liberation developments, new approaches and understandings in mission emerged. Melbourne was not solely responsible for these developments, but it symbolized in an intensive way, the process operative in the world in the late seventies and into the eighties.

In retrospect, 1989 became one year that marked a cataclysmic change in the world. Already in May 1989, when the world mission conference met in San Antonio, Texas, a number of the participants from eastern Europe had experienced liberation. The theme of the conference, "Thy Will be Done: Mission in Christ's Way," was studied in terms of 1) Turning to the Living God, 2) Participating in Suffering and Struggle, 3) The Earth is the Lord's, and 4) Towards Renewed Communities in Mission. All of these dealt with various missiological themes, such as mission and unity, dialogue and witness, the question of secularized society and the gospel message, solidarity with the poor and suffering, prophetic witness. Ecological awareness as a missiological question was given attention for the first time, with affirmation by the conference that "mission in Christ's way must extend to God's creation."[39] Missiological concern for integration of theory and action led the conference planners to call for a way to continue the conference beyond its actual time of gathering. Each of the working sections formulated "acts of faithfulness" which accompanied its report.[40]

The theme of the conference, "Thy Will be Done: Mission in Christ's Way," was intended as a process of discernment to understand more clearly how we are to carry out mission today in Christ's way, rather than to further define mission.[41] With the events that led up to 1989, especially in eastern Europe, but which had repercussions around the world, major shifts were occurring right at the time of San Antonio. In fact, at that very moment, the students were gathered at Tiananmen Square, Beijing. The conference itself was too close to analyze the meaning of these shifts, yet a brief comparison of the messages from Melbourne and San Antonio, illustrates how the participants in these two world mission conferences experienced the meaning of mission in the context of the world.

From Melbourne:

> We meet under the clouds of nuclear threat and annihilation. Our world is deeply wounded by the oppression inflicted by the powerful upon the powerless. These oppressions are found in our economic, political, racial, sexual and religious-life. Our world, so proud of human achievements, is full of people suffering from hunger, poverty and injustice. . . .[42]

From San Antonio:

> Concerned with the discernment of the will of God in today's world, the representatives of the churches gathered in San Antonio, and spoke about shared signs of hope and renewal. . . Communities, and even entire nations, in unexpected ways, are involved in self-examination, repentance, renewal and struggle for justice, turning to the Living God, stressing the infinite value of human dignity, and turning to one another to make peace. . . .[43]

Melbourne was deeply conscious, as noted earlier, of the plight of the poor and the underlying relationship of this reality to engagement in mission directed toward the realization of God's kingdom or reign. The image of the poor—those who suffer injustice, at "the periphery of national and community life," enabled the conference to image Jesus Christ "exercising his healing authority on the periphery."[44] The conference launched a call in its message, taken up later in "The Ecumenical Affirmation," to direct missionary proclamation toward those on the periphery, because the poor and oppressed in the world are often "the people who have not heard of the Gospel of Jesus Christ." At the heart of this call to mission, however, there is the conviction that Jesus Christ goes to those on the periphery. The call to mission, "Your Kingdom Come," is a call which "brings us closer to Jesus Christ in today's world."[45]

Conscientious commitment to solidarity with those who suffer was clearly present among the participants in San Antonio. It had become rooted in a deeply ecclesial and spiritual vision:

The two most significant trends of this Conference were the spirit of universality (catholicity) of the gathering, and its concern for the fullness of the gospel, namely: to hold in creative tension spiritual and material needs, prayer and action, evangelism and social responsibility, dialogue and witness, power and vulnerability, local and universal.[46]

Awareness that the signs of the times carry "a new call to faith" and "a new challenge for mission and evangelism" marked San Antonio as a further development in understanding mission as a process of communicating the good news in today's very different world. A little over a year later, at the end of 1990, John Paul II issued his encyclical letter, *Mission of the Redeemer.* Speaking of "new worlds and social phenomena," he notes that "rapid and profound transformations . . . characterize today's world, especially in the Southern Hemisphere, . . . having a powerful effect on the overall missionary picture."[47] The sense of new call to faith and new challenges for mission, finds a new expression in the modern equivalents of the Areopagus (cf. Acts 17:22-31).[48]

Images of new spaces for mission in a world that continues to experience profound and unforeseeable change characterize the moment of mission on the threshold of Bahia. "Called to One Hope: the Gospel in Diverse Cultures," the theme of the conference, will be examined under four aspects: 1) Authentic witness within cultures, 2) Gospel and identity in community, 3) Local congregations in plural societies, 4) One gospel—diverse expressions. It is not appropriate to try to forecast the outcomes of Bahia. However, given the record of the world mission conferences to date in efforts to develop a pattern of inclusive participation, and in developing a tradition of ecumenical worship and Bible study, one can hope that, out of the dying and rising experienced in such a diverse and committed gathering, new hope will be born, new spaces of mission will be discovered, and new challenges to unity among the disciples chosen to communicate the good news will emerge.

Notes

[1]   Cf. Roger Haight, sj. "Jesus and Mission: An overview of the problem" in *Discovery*, No. 5 (December 1994), pp.1-23. The author emphasizes the bearing of historical consciousness on theology and the understanding of Jesus Christ, the church and mission. He proposes that historical consciousness constitutes the framework within which we must

think today. If our theology is to be intelligible in our world, it has to be correlated with and inculturated into a historically conscious world. Historical consciousness describes the context within which our questions arise. It describes the intellectual culture or world into which theological answers are appropriated, p. 5.

[2] A poster, *Highlights — 20th Century Ecumenical Movement,* from the World Council of Churches, illustrates this idea of signposts marking the ecumenical movement.

[3] G. Gassmann, Faith and Order, *Dictionary of the Ecumenical Movement,* N. Lossky et al., eds. (Geneva and Grand Rapids: WCC Publications and William B. Eerdmans Publishing Company, 1991), p. 413.

[4] This term has been used originally by the Federation of Asian Bishops Conferences (FABC), to describe the inter-relations between Catholics and persons of other religious faith traditions; it is a concept that attempts to capture the dynamic process of human relationships in the context of lived experience rather than starting with theoretical assumptions. In this way it opens new space for persons to live together and share in common pursuits.

[5] The earlier world mission conferences may have produced more academic style documents, while the latter, following developments in conference style generally, have emphasized more relational styles of meeting, and briefer reports, along with a number of papers both before and during the conferences.

[6] Faith and Order Commission, "Towards Koinonia in Worship: Report of a WCC Faith and Order Consultation on the Role of Worship Within the Search for Unity," *Midstream: The Pluralism of the Ecumenical Movement,* 34, No. 2, (1995): pp. 197-229.

[7] Cf. G. H. Anderson, ed. *The Theology of Christian Mission* (New York: McGraw Hill, 1961), p. 4; A. Dulles, sj. "John Paul II and the New Evangelization," in *America,* Vol. 166, No. 3, 1992, pp. 52-59, 69-72.

[8] Anderson, op. cit.

[9] It would be too lengthy to include all the various examples that one could cite since 1961, but a simple indication of some of the more influential moments suffices, e.g. Vatican II with its insistence that mission is at the heart of the church; the integration of the International Missionary Council with the World Council of Churches; the *Ecumenical Affirmation* of the World Council of Churches; *Baptism Eucharist and Ministry* — the document of the Faith and Order Commission; the study of Gospel and Culture presently being carried out by the World Council of Churches.

[10] Cf. K. S. Latourette, *Christian World Mission in Our Day* (New York: Harper and Row, 1954), pp. 360-61.

[11] Cf. Gassmann, op. cit., pp. 411-412.

[12] Cf. Latourette, op. cit., pp. 360-361.

[13] Cf. Latourette, ibid.

[14] Cf. T. Yates, *Christian Mission in the Twentieth Century* (Cambridge: Cambridge University Press, 1994), p. 29.

[15] Cf. Yates, ibid.

[16] Cf. Yates, op. cit., p. 67.

[17] Cf. Yates, op. cit., pp. 67-70; also J. Mutiso-Mbinda, *Concepts of Mission in the World Council of Churches 1961-1991* (Rome: Domenici-Pecheux, 1993), pp. 16-18.

[18] Yates, op. cit., p. 67.

[19] Cf. Mutiso-Mbinda, op. cit., p. 18.

20 Yates, op. cit., p. 120.

21 *International Review of Mission*, Vol. 77, (1988).

22 Yates, op. cit., p. 12.

23 Cf. Mutiso-Mbinda, op. cit., p. 114.

24 Cf. Van der Bent, *Dictionary of the Ecumenical Movement.* Lossky et al., eds. (Geneva and Grand Rapids: WCC Publications and William B. Eerdmans Publishing Company, 1991), p. 327.

25 Cf. Mutiso-Mbinda, op. cit., p. 112.

26 Cf., ibid., p. 114.

27 Cf. K. Nissen, "Mission and Unity: A look at the integration of the International Missionary Council and the World Council of Churches," in *International Review of Mission*, Vol. 63, (1974), p.543.

28 Cf. T. Stransky, International Missionary Council, *Dictionary of the Ecumenical Movement*, Lossky N. et al., eds. (Geneva and Grand Rapids: WCC Publications and William B. Eerdmans Publishing Company, 1991), pp. 528-529.

29 Cf. Mutiso-Mbinda, op. cit., p. 115.

30 Cf. Mutiso-Mbinda, op. cit., p. 37.

31 Cf. F. Wilson, ed., *The San Antonio Report: Your Will be Done in Christ's Way* (Geneva: WCC Publications, 1990), pp. 9-12.

32 *Common Witness: A Study Document of the Joint Working Group of time Roman Catholic Church and the World Council of Churches* (Geneva: WCC Publications, 1984), No. 7.

31 Ibid.; this kind of experiential transformation was evident in the sharing about the conference on various occasions, as different images that touched deeply into one's experience of being part of a church sent in mission were highlighted in a variety of conversations and reports in the weeks following the conference.

34 Note 31.

35 CWME, *Your Kingdom Come: Mission Perspectives* (Geneva: WCC Publications, 1980). pp. 205-206.

36 *Common Witness*, op. cit., no. 30.

37 Faith and Order Consultation, op. cit., p. 197.

38 Cf. Yates, op. cit., pp. 67-70.

39 Cf. Mutiso-Mbinda, op. cit., pp. 44-45.

40 Cf. Wilson, op. cit.

41 Ibid., pp. 4-5.

42 CWME, op. cit., p. 234.

43 Wilson, op. cit., p. 21.

44 CWME, op. cit., p. 236.

45 Ibid.

46 Wilson, op. cit., p. 20.

47 See No. 37.

48 Ibid.

References

Anderson, G.H., ed. *The Theology of Christian Mission* (New York: McGraw Hill, 1961).

CWME. *Your Kingdom Come: Mission Perspectives* (Geneva: WCC, 1980).

Dulles. Avery, sj. "John Paul II and The New Evangelization," *America,* Vol. 166, No.3. (1992): pp. 52-59; 69-72.

Faith and Order Commission. *Towards Koinonia in Worship: Report of a WCC Faith and Order Consultation on the Role of Worship Within the Search for Unity. Mid-Stream: The Pluralism of the Ecumenical Movement,* Vol. 34, No. 2, (1995): pp. 197-229.

Flannery, Austin, ed. *Vatican Council II: The Conciliar and Post Conciliar Documents* (Northport, N.Y.: Costello Publishing Co., 1975).

Gassmann, G. Faith and Order. *Dictionary of the Ecumenical Movement.* Lossky, N. et al., eds. (Geneva and Grand Rapids: WCC Publications and William B. Eerdmans Publishing Company, 1991), pp. 411-413.

Haight, Roger, sj. "Jesus and Mission: An Overview of the Problem." in *Discovery* 5(1995): pp. 1-23.

John Paul II. *Mission of the Redeemer* (Boston: St. Paul Books and Media, 1990).

Tertio Millenio Adveniente (Boston: St. Paul Books and Media, 1994).

Latourette, K. S. *Christian World Mission in Our Day* (New York: Harper and Row, 1954).

Mutiso-Mbinda, John. *Concepts of Mission in the World Council of Churches: 1961 to 1991. A Study of the Historical Development in the Understanding of Christian Mission in the Documents of the World Council of Churches from New Delhi to Canberra* (Rome: Domenici-Pecheux, 1993).

Nissen, Karsten. "Mission and Unity: A Look at the Integration of the International Missionary Council and the World Council of Churches," in *International Review of Mission,* Vol. 63 (1974): pp. 539-550.

Stransky, T. International Missionary Council. *Dictionary of the Ecumenical Movement,* Lossky, N. et al., eds. (Geneva and Grand Rapids: WCC Publications and William B. Eerdmans Publishing Company, 1991), pp. 526-529.

World Council of Churches. *Common Witness: A Study Document of the Joint Working Group of the Roman Catholic Church and the World Council of Churches* (Geneva: WCC Publication, 1984).

Wilson, Frederick R., ed. *The San Antonio Report: Your Will be Done in Christ's Way* (Geneva: WCC Publications, 1989).

Yates, Timothy. *Christian Mission in the Twentieth Century* (Cambridge: Cambridge University Press. 1994).

Reproduced with permission from the *International Review of Mission,* Vol. 84, No. 334 (July, 1995) pp. 211-222.

Religious Pluralism:
Threat or Opportunity for Mission?

Alan Neely

Recently a news director for National Public Radio wrote, "In America, it is more and more evident each year that diversity has replaced unity as the underlying assumption of our national culture." What he labeled euphemistically as "an underlying assumption" is, however, frequently portrayed in more graphic, disturbing terms as "culture wars"[2] or to use *Time* magazine's more vivid metaphor, "America's Holy War."[3] In either case, it should be clear to any perceptive observer in this country today that encounters between peoples who share neither a common culture, religion, or identity often engender anxiety and fear, resulting in misunderstandings, conflicts, and even violence. Conflicts of this kind are always lamentable, often avoidable, and they can be exceedingly dangerous for anyone perceived to be different.

Religious Pluralism in the United States: A Brief History
In the past, even when I was a youth, it was matter of pride that the United States was a religiously pluralistic society. But ours was a very limited pluralism. From the time the Puritans arrived and established themselves in what they called "New England" and later in other colonies along the eastern seaboard, their communities—and later the nation as a whole—were overwhelmingly European and Christian in terms of the culture. This is less and less the case today. The roots of the change can be traced to at least five centuries ago, but only in the last forty years has the change become conspicuous to most of us.

The roots of change. Prior to the sixteenth century, Christianity was predominantly—though not exclusively—a faith concentrated in eastern and western Europe. Enclaves of Christians existed outside of Europe, the faith having been carried to such distant lands as South India and China well before the end of the first millennium. Forms of Christianity also survived the incredible seventh century spread of Islam that swept through the Middle East, westward across North Africa, into southern Europe, eastward through Persia, and into India. In most cases, however, Christians outside of Europe survived as struggling minorities, oftentimes closed and defensive. The vast majority of Christians were Europeans. In fact, virtually all Europeans were considered to be Christians, albeit inaccurately.

With the so-called discovery of the Americas in the last decade of the fifteenth century, followed by the rise of multiple European colonial powers (besides Spain and Portugal) and the modern missionary movement, Christianity was taken to peoples, lands, and cultures all over the world. Unfortunately, a tragic feature of this largely European expansion was the political domination and economic exploitation of non-European peoples often sanctioned or ignored by western Christians. Meanwhile, the religious impact of Christianity on non-Europeans ended the geographical confinement and cultural isolation of the world's religions and peoples. For whereas before the sixteenth century Christian and non-Christian peoples frequently intersected and sometimes clashed, since that time their contacts have increased even to the point of periodic intermingling and constant challenging of each other. Not only has the Christian faith penetrated previously closed societies, gained from them millions of converts, and established hundreds of thousands of Christian congregations in Africa, the Americas, and Asia, the increased presence of non-Christian peoples in the West—together with the gradual awareness of what these people believe and practice—have forced Christian theologians to re-think many long-held ideas.

As already implied, until this present century, adherents to these non-Christian religions—with the exception of Jews— were almost entirely concentrated in non-European areas of the world. India was the home of Hinduism. Buddhism was the predominant religion of the Far East, and Islam dominated the Near East, North and Central Africa, and spread eastward as far as present-day Indonesia.

Though most Hindus still live in the Indian sub-continent and Buddhists in East and South East Asia, Muslims dominate or represent significant minorities in many African and Asian countries. Moreover, a significant dispersion of Hindus, Muslims, and Buddhists to the West has taken place in this present century, especially since the late 1940s and the 1950s. Though it is impossible to pinpoint exactly when this non-Christian diaspora began, certain features of it are quite clear.

Islam in the Americas. Some African-American scholars contend that as early as the sixteenth century when hundreds of thousands of Africans began to be brought to the Americas as slaves, many are believed to have been Muslims. Some of them and virtually all their descendants became professing Christians. In the last half-century, however, a substantial number of African Americans in the United States have abandoned the Christian faith and embraced Islam. Whether this phenomenon can be explained as the result of genetic disposition, the slow impact of collective memory, or simply rebellion against one of the principal institutions of the perceived oppressor, I would not venture to say. But the growth of Islam among African Americans is not only significant in terms of numbers, it is crucial to understanding the rapidly changing cultural and religious makeup of this country.

Alan Neely   33

Before the end of the nineteenth century, some Turkish and Arab Muslims entered the U.S. as immigrants, nearly all of them settling in major industrial cities such as Detroit, Chicago, New York, and Philadelphia. Those who practiced their faith did so in homes, rented rooms, or in small, nondescript buildings. Early in the present century several hundred thousand Muslims from eastern Europe were allowed entry, and one of the first mosques built in the United States was constructed in Maine in 1915 by Albanian immigrants. Then, in1928, Polish Muslims opened a mosque in Brooklyn, N.Y., and slowly a few others began to appear. Then in 1947 the magnificent Islamic Center opened at the corner of Massachusetts and Belmont Avenues N.W. in Washington, D.C. Now there are mosques and Islamic centers—more than 1500—of every size scattered throughout the country.

Hinduism in the Americas. With the abolition of slavery in the British colonies in the 1830s, large numbers of poverty-stricken East Indians were lured to the British and Dutch colonies of the Caribbean to replace Blacks on the sugar plantations. Few of the East Indians returned to India, and eventually some of them and their descendants were among the more than a million immigrants from the West Indies who entered the U.S. between 1820 and 1970. Until after World War II, however, the number of Hindus in the United States was small.

In terms of public impact, Hinduism clearly emerged as a rival faith in this country during the 1893 World's Parliament of Religions meeting in Chicago. A small contingent of Hindus had come from India, and more than one gave major addresses to the assembly. No one, however, European or Asian, Christian or non-Christian, was received more warmly and enthusiastically than the diminutive Bengali ascetic, Vivekananda. Richard H. Seager in his recently published study of the Parliament notes that Vivekananda was "a favorite of the press and crowds," and every time he appeared "in his ocher robes and turban, greeting the audience as his sisters and brothers in America, he received several minutes of tumultuous applause."[5] Not only did this diminutive ambassador of Hinduism charm those attending the Parliament, he left the United States after having established a permanent Hindu presence in this country, the American Vedanta Society.[6]

Buddhism in the Americas. Earlier, in the mid-nineteenth century, thousands of Chinese, some of whom were Buddhists, were brought to the United States as indentured workers. A few temples were opened— two, for example, in Montana. But when the jobs for these Chinese workers were completed, many, though not all of them were returned to their homeland. Buddhism, albeit very weak, had a gained a foothold and was here to stay.

These Chinese indentured workers were first brought this country to toil in the California gold fields and later to work in the construction of the transcontinental railroads. In a book published early this year, two Alabama historians observe that within five years following the end of the Civil War, "nearly a thousand Chinese laborers" were brought to Alabama to construct a rail line linking Chattanooga, Tennessee, and Meridian, Mississippi.[7]

Like indentured workers in other lands, the Chinese were severely restricted and were not free to mingle with the society. In Alabama, for example, they were forced to live in camps set up for them outside the towns and cities. More than three hundred of these Chinese were bivouacked outside Tuscaloosa and their provisions were supplied by the railroad company. When in 1871, shortly after the work had begun, the Alabama and Chattanooga Railroad declared bankruptcy, these Chinese laborers were suddenly cut off from their jobs and support. They survived only because they were able to live "off the land" by catching crayfish and gathering berries they scavenged from the nearby creeks and fields. Eventually, the ever-roving labor agents managed to relocate some of them on the sugar plantations in Louisiana, but according to one southern historian, the economic collapse of this single railroad company "resulted in the largest dispersal of Chinese to occur in the South." Many southern U.S. Chinese families today can trace their ancestry back to this one economic incident when their forebears, by their own resourcefulness, were able to overcome what could have been a disaster.

In contrast to the Muslim African slaves who preceded them, the Chinese and East Indians who came to the Americas retained for the most part their cultures and their religious beliefs and practices, and therefore they represent the earliest Buddhists, Hindus, and Muslims resident in this hemisphere. Many others, however, followed: Buddhists from Japan and other areas of Asia, Sikhs from India, and Muslims from eastern Europe and Syria, Palestine, Egypt, and other African and Asian lands. As already indicated, most of them originally settled in the major industrial centers of the country where they found jobs, friends, and a degree of anonymity. Those who maintained and practiced their faith did so unobtrusively and, until the last half-century, relatively few mosques or temples were built. The worship centers that were opened were small and unimposing, and as already implied, they were for the most part found in the largest cities. Today, however, the situation has dramatically changed, and temples and mosques can be found in virtually every urban area of this country.

Moreover, until the 1960s few people outside the largest U.S. cities had contact with or knew any person whose culture and/or religion was neither Christian nor Jewish. Is this not one of the reasons why Bible reading and prayer in the public schools was commonplace? Few school administrators, teachers, or pupils were aware of the *Vedas, the Bhagavad Gita,* or the sayings of Buddha, though more did know of the *Qur'an (Koran).* The Bible was the only sacred text most North Americans had ever seen or knew existed.

Religious Pluralism in the United States: The Present Reality

Following World War II, however, especially in the late 1950s and 1960s, increasing numbers of Muslims, Buddhists, and Hindus—as well as persons of other non-Christian faiths—began coming to the United States as students, as business people, and finally as immigrants and residents. When they began settling in areas other than the largest northern, mid-western, and western cities, the cultural and religious scene in this country began to change, and this change has continued unabated. Until recently, religious pluralism for most people in the United States meant living and working with people whose culture and faith—if they were persons of faith—were either Roman Catholic, Protestant, or Jewish. Pluralism for some was exemplified in the multitude of *Christian* denominations and the ability of Christians to tolerate Jews. The presence of practicing Hindus, Buddhists, and Muslims was rare if not totally unknown in most communities in this country.

Today, because of the changes in the culture resulting from the increasing presence of peoples of many faiths—Christian and non-Christian—religious pluralism means something entirely different from what it meant fifty years ago. Furthermore, this dramatic transformation of the religious makeup of this country means that Christian hegemony so characteristic of the past has ended.

Daily contact with believing and practicing Muslims, Buddhists, Hindus, Jains, Sikhs, Zoroastrians, Confucianists, Taoists, and Shintoists raises complex social as well as legal questions. What is the legitimate role of religion in public life, for example? What rights do non-Christians have in this country? What are the ramifications of the linking of religious agendas to political platforms and parties? And what is the theological and missiological challenge peoples of other faiths represent?

The demographics. The dimensions or demographics of this profound alteration in U.S. society are not easily discernible, but there are some indicators. The English Pilgrims who came to North America in the seventeenth century and established themselves in this new land were professing Christians. The people who were already here—the Native Americans—were not Christians, nor was their culture. The Europeans, in fact, assumed that the Native Americans were devoid of culture, and their religious impulses and practices were routinely described as pagan or heathen. Cotton Mather (1663-1728), the well-known colonial clergyman, for example, summed up the prevailing opinion among the colonists when he declared, "The best thing we can do for our Indians is to Anglicise them," that is, make them like the European colonists.[9]

Many, though not all, the Native Americans were "Anglicised," as were most immigrants into the United States and their descendants—even African Americans— until the last half-century. The "melting pot" image was not therefore, as some regard it, pure myth. At least this was the case until the last three or four decades. Admittedly, numerous subcultures existed: Irish, Italian, German, Scandinavian, African American, Hispanic, Chinese, and Japanese, to name only a few—but most of these sub-cultures, with certain exceptions, lived in accordance with a generally accepted set of values influenced by the predominant Christian faith. Virtually all African Americans were professing Christians, as were a significant percentage of the Chinese.

As already noted, some Hindus and Sikhs—besides the Buddhists and Muslims who arrived earlier—managed to enter the United States in the early decades of the twentieth century, but they were few in number and largely went unnoticed until they sought U.S. citizenship.[10] It would have been regarded as a breach of the Constitution for anyone to have been denied entry because of his or her religion, but given the fact that a series of immigration laws were passed specifically aimed to keep Asians out of this country,[11] and given the additional fact that most Asians were not Christians, by severely limiting their numbers in this country the effect was a maintaining of the status quo.[12] When the Immigration and Nationality Act was amended by Congress in 1965, however, all the previously practiced national quota systems were abolished. The law which earlier favored immigrants from Europe and severely restricted Chinese, Japanese, and other Asians, as well as Africans and Latin Americans, was revised and the patterns of immigration into this country— and concurrently the religious configuration—began to change dramatically.[13]

Because we have no national religious census, however, no one knows exactly how many peoples of other faiths are now in the United States. Samplings and estimations vary widely. In a study published in 1988, for example, it was concluded that though the population of Jews in this country had remained stable for the previous thirty years, the number of Muslims had quadrupled. More than three million Muslims were said to be in the U.S. The same study estimated that there were at least 700,000 Hindus and 250,000 Buddhists then in the country.[14] James Davison Hunter, in his widely read *Culture Wars*, suggests that in the early 1990s there were more than four million Muslims, three-quarters of a million Hindus, and six hundred thousand Buddhists.[15] This part of his study, however, is replete with inaccuracies, and therefore the reliability of his statistics is questionable.

In 1989-90, a group of sociologists at the City University of New York (CUNY) did what they called a "National Survey of Religious Identification," and they published their findings in 1991. They estimated the number of Muslims then in the United States to be 877,000 of which 351,000 were Black Muslims (or 40%). Jews, they said, numbered 3,157,000.[16] The survey, however—like others of this type—was a sampling. The interviewers spoke by telephone with 113,000 adults in the 48 contiguous states, and the respondents were asked one question about their faith, viz., "What is your religion?" Like the two previously cited sets of data, the CUNY study is of limited value in terms of the religious affiliation of the respondents.

The National Council of Churches *1995 Yearbook* gives the following figures: 5,500,000 Muslims, 910,000 Hindus (1,315,000 in North America), 230,000 Buddhists (578,000 in North America), and 4,300,000 Jews.[17] But as you can see, the numbers are all "rounded-off" and clearly represent estimates, not hard data.

According to the Bureau of Census of the U.S. Department of Commerce, there were living in the U.S. in 1994: 625,000 foreign-born Chinese, 533,000 foreign-born Koreans, 496,000 foreign-born Vietnamese, and 494,000 foreign-born Indians.[18]

One can only guess how many of the 1,654,000 Chinese, Koreans, and Vietnamese are Buddhists, and how many of the 494,000 Indians are Hindus (or Muslims, Sikhs, and Jains)."

A number of scholars are attempting to secure more accurate statistics, such as Professor Diana L. Eck of Harvard, but to date one can only estimate the actual numbers.[19]

On the basis of my own study and observation, I am inclined to think these samples or estimates probably are less than the actual numbers, and most likely there are more than five million Muslims, more than a million Hindus, and more than a half million Buddhists living in the United States today. Like Christianity, each of these religions is divided into numerous subgroups. Yet virtually all forms of these religions can be found somewhere in the country. There are, for example, Buddhists from Sri Lanka, Thailand, Tibet, China, Cambodia, Viet Nam, Korea, and Japan, and they practice Theravada, Mahayana, Tantra, and Zen forms of Buddhism. The same is true of the other faiths. In addition, there are Jains, Zoroastrians, Sikhs, Baha'is, Rastafarians, worshipers of Isis, along with hundreds of other imported and homegrown varieties of religion. The United States has become, therefore, an irreversibly multi-religious as well as multi-cultured society.

A century ago when the first World's Parliament of Religions was held in Chicago, it was said that there were no Hindus living there. Those who attended the Parliament came as invited guests from India. Now there are at least sixteen Hindu temples in metropolitan Chicago, and scores of others have been constructed all over the U.S. Hindus, like Muslims, are also opening in some places their own parochial schools.

According to Muslim leaders, there are more than 1500 mosques in the United States and an increasing number of Muslim elementary and secondary schools.

Buddhists meanwhile have their own network of temples, house-temples, and store-front worship centers—many of which are located in mid-size and smaller cities of the country.

Unforeseen developments. One of the curious and surprising facts about these new religious communities is that many of the devotees were not faithful, practicing Hindus, Buddhists, or Muslims until *after* they arrived in the United States. But like other immigrants before them—including many of our European ancestors—their faith or religion has assumed a new significance in their lives. Obviously, it is a means of preserving their language and culture as well as a way for finding and being with others from their countries. It is also a readily accessible means of collective and individual security. Thus, their newfound religious ardor frequently has as much to do with their desire for community and for maintaining their sense of cultural and linguistic identity as it does with religious devotion. But was this not also true of many of our Christians ancestors who immigrated to this country?

Whether and to what degree these new non-Christian residents and citizens will be accepted by the majority of people in the United States and assimilated into the prevailing American Christian culture is yet to be seen. One fact, however, is certain: it will not be solely up to them.

Once again in our country emotional and political steam is building up regarding the issue of immigration—especially illegal immigration—and it is quite possible that further legislation inspired by neo-Nativists and passed by legislators both at the state and federal levels will ignore our history, distort our established values, and inflict, especially on innocent children, unnecessary hardship and suffering. That immigration ought to be legal is a given, but illegal immigration, says Richard Rayner, has become "America's most exaggerated threat."[20] The issue is of course complex, but it is not likely to be resolved in any just fashion if left solely to politicians.

These are nonetheless primarily sociological, economic, and political issues. For us as professing Christians, there is a deeper and perhaps even more crucial question, namely, what should be and what will be the theological and missiological response of us to the presence of peoples of other faiths in this land?

Christianity continues to be the religious faith with the majority of adherents in the United States, and Christianity continues to claim the largest plurality of followers in the world. But churches and Jewish temples are no longer the only centers of worship in Europe and the Americas. Moreover, despite nearly a century of institutionalized ecumenical endeavor, Christians remain divided into hundreds, even thousands, of competing and sometimes antagonistic camps. Complicating the picture is the fact that Christianity, in the West at least, is no longer the most evangelistic and aggressive missionary faith. In the United States churches now are having to compete with equally if not more passionately committed followers of other faiths who represent not only the other major religions, but also hundreds of new non-Christian religious groups. What this portends for the Christian and Jewish communities in the coming decades is not clear. But one thing is certain: the future religious scene in this country will be radically different from what it has been in the past.

Christian Responses: A Sampling

In the remaining pages I can only touch on the subject of how Christians and churches are responding to peoples of other faiths in their communities, and before giving some specific examples I want to make some general observations.

1. Most mainline denominations have someone or some office assigned to ecumenical and/or interfaith relations. A part of their assignment is to keep

abreast of the changing religious scene, issue statements, and publish and distribute accurate, attractively prepared, and useful materials. An example is the Presbyterian Church USA's excellent document "Interfaith Marriage," a 55-page guide which includes a discussion of the issues as well as practical suggestions and representative inter-faith liturgies.[21] Two other examples are the United Church of Christ's statement, "The Relationship Between the United Church of Christ and the Muslim Community," and the Evangelical Lutheran Church in America's "Report on Multicultural Mission Strategy."[22] In a class by itself is the Interfaith Network for the United Kingdom's pamphlet, "Mission, Dialogue and Inter-Religious Encounter," which includes a specific plan for "Building Good Relations with People of Different Faiths and Beliefs."[23] When I refer to these documents even in conversation with clergypersons, I discover that most of them appear to be surprised and unaware of the storehouse of resources available from their own denominations, and they frequently know nothing of what is available from other sources.

2. Attempts to do something positive and move beyond interfaith suspicion, fear, and antagonism are few and their impact mixed. Interfaith councils have been organized in some cities, but they are often composed primarily of clergy, and unless there is a crisis, the activities of these councils rarely are high on clergy agendas or garner widespread support. One of the most impressive of which I am aware is the "Partnership of Faith" in New York City. The group is composed of Jewish, Christian, and Muslim leaders and not only works to reduce ignorance and suspicion among the many religious factions and promote healing and understanding, but they also tackle the difficult questions such as Ayatollah Khomeini's death sentence on Salman Rushdie for writing *The Satanic Verses.*

3. Most Christians I encounter are unaware or only marginally aware of the presence of peoples of other faiths in their cities and communities. The next time you are with a church group, ask them how many Jewish, Hindu, and Buddhist temples and how many mosques are in their city. If one does not see these signs of change or chooses to ignore them, he or she is engaging in a kind of "disconfirmation" of our own reality.

4. Some denominations, congregations, and individual Christians speak boldly about "converting the world to Christ," and they openly target in their evangelization efforts Jews, Muslims, Hindus, Buddhists, and, I might add, even other Christians. Christ's followers, they declare, are called to announce the good news of the gospel to all people everywhere, and this surely includes people of other faiths. Moreover, the good news or the gospel, they say, is "salvation by the grace of God through faith in Jesus Christ as the only Savior and Lord."[24]

To encourage Christians to share their faith with others is, I believe, both appropriate and commendable. What is questionable is *when* and *how* such a witness is most appropriately and effectively made. Here one must decide what it means to be a Christian, a follower of Jesus Christ. Also, what is conversion?

Is Christian conversion the verbal or intellectual acquiescence to a set of theological propositions? Is conversion the submission to the rite of baptism and enrollment in a Christian church? Or does becoming and being a Christian mean accepting God's gracious invitation to a relationship of love, forgiveness, and trust in Jesus Christ? If it means the latter—and I believe it does—then how can one "witness" to a person of another faith without knowing the person, that is, without having established some kind of trusting relationship with him or her? Furthermore, how can one presume to tell another about the Christian faith without knowing something about the faith of the one to whom the witness is being made and having one's knowledge supplemented by that person's witness? Do we as followers of Jesus Christ not have something to learn from others in terms of God, faith, and religious devotion?

5. Interreligious encounters are a logical means for establishing an atmosphere where informal as well as formal dialogue can occur. We have nearly a half-century of accumulated experience in interreligious dialogue, and the ways and means are readily available.[25] Some dialogue groups continue for long periods of time; one of which I was a part went on for a decade. Some are formal; others are informal. Most dialogues, however, are of relatively brief duration. The problem is that interfaith dialogues have involved primarily clergy, and rarely have laypersons or grassroots believers been included. My concern is that congregation-sponsored interreligious encounters be on the agenda and calendar of all churches genuinely interested in peoples of other faiths, for they represent one of the easiest ways to foster better understanding, mutual respect, and community development.

Besides the examples already given, I want to mention some other models of Christian responses to peoples of other faiths.

6. Increasingly common are ecumenical, interfaith services of worship in the month of April commemorating *Yom Hashoah.* the day set aside to memorialize the victims of the Nazi Holocaust. Protestant congregations and judicatories, Roman Catholic dioceses, as well as the Anti-Defamation League and the B'nai B'rith, commonly sponsor these memorial events.

7. Then there are those interfaith events that bring peoples of good will together in times of collective tragedy or crisis. This past summer, many participated in services designed to raise public awareness of the church burnings that have occurred during the past few years. Most of the destroyed or damaged buildings belonged to African American congregations, and most were in the South. In the Sunday evening service last July held in the Witherspoon Presbyterian Church in Princeton, New Jersey, Jews represented one of the largest groups in attendance.

8. In Fort Worth, Texas, Protestant churches have established the Tarrant Area Community of Churches specifically to nurture community by giving "visibility to the essential unity of the church," calling one another "to witness and service" in the community and the world, and being a concrete "expres-

sion" of a common "striving for justice, peace and human dignity." Beyond this, the organization has established an Interfaith Resource Center for the purpose of making peace and doing justice by "alleviating interreligious and inter-ethnic conflict, promoting understanding of differences, and fostering cooperative service." A part of the Center is the Interfaith Peace Institute which sponsors interfaith awareness seminars, interfaith contact groups, interfaith dialogues, and interfaith conflict mediation.[26]

9. In 1990, in DuPage, Illinois, a coalition of religious and civic leaders began the "Interfaith Resource Network." Activities of the Network include an annual Interfaith Thanksgiving Commemoration, the DuPage Task Force on Diversity in Education (with Elmhurst College), "Women, Leadership and Religion" series, and other educational programs for public as well as private schools, libraries, and civic groups. The Network not only develops and provides curriculum materials, they also engage in teacher/leadership training. This has been one of the Network's most important contributions. They do this with one full-time employee, Ms. Deborah Levine, and an all-volunteer executive committee composed of a Roman Catholic sister and Roman Catholic priest, two rabbis, a Presbyterian pastor, and two laypersons.[27]

10. Five religious organizations in Minneapolis—St. Paul, Minnesota, with a sizable foundation grant recently launched what is called "Congregations in Community." The goal is to recruit and train 7,000 volunteers to facilitate and expand the efforts of religious organizations (including congregations) to provide support for children and families through child care, tutoring, after-school programs, homeless shelters, transitional housing, and other services, and bringing together people of different faiths to deal with the problems of their communities. The Council of Churches, the Jewish Community Relations Council, and the Masjid An-Nur/Islamic Centers of Minneapolis and St. Paul are all participating in what is a pioneering effort of interfaith cooperation.[28]

You may wonder why I have limited my remarks to positive responses Christians are making to the presence of peoples of other faiths in our land. One reason, of course, is the constraints imposed by a single lecture. But there is also a philosophical reason. The good things that happen and are happening rarely make the news, rarely are seen on the front pages of the papers. The tawdry, the ugly, and the mean or vicious responses, on the other hand, are often widely publicized. I have a folder full of examples of discrimination, threats, and violence, and they deserve to be mentioned, if for no other reason than to inspire persons of good will to go and do otherwise. But the "not-so-Christian" responses will have to await another lecture and another venue. Meanwhile, I would ask you to join in putting into practice the admonition of Kenneth Cragg, long-time missionary to Muslims:

> Our first task in approaching
>   another culture,
> another religion is
> to take off our shoes.

For the place we are approaching is holy.
Else we may find ourselves treading
   on another's dreams, [and]
More seriously still, we may forget that
   God was there before our arrival.[29]

Notes

[1] "One Nation? American Culture Wars: The Search for Common Ground" (May 9-15, 1995), Director's Notes of the printed text distributed by WUNC Chapel Hill, NC, prior to the airing of the series.

[2] James Davison Hunter, *Culture Wars: The Struggle to Define America* (New York: Basic Books, 1991). See also Robert Hughes, *Culture of Complaint: The Fraying of America* (New York: Oxford University Press, 1993), and Arthur M. Schlesinger. Jr., *The Disuniting of America: Reflections on a Multicultural Society* (New York: W. W. Norton. 1992).

[3] *Time* (December 9, 1991): p. 60.

[4] According to Alan Austin, at least 10% of the slaves sold in the Charleston, South Carolina market, for example, from 1711 to 1808, were "to some degree Muslims." *African Muslims in Ante-bellum America* (New York: Garland, 1984), 35. Austin goes on to say that his estimate of 10% is less than that of some scholars.

[5] *The World's Parliament of Religions*, The East/West Encounter, Chicago, 1893 (Bloomington: Indiana University Press, 1995), 111.

[6] Ibid.

[7] Wayne Flynt and Gerald W. Berkley, *Taking Christianity to China: Alabama Missionaries in the Middle Kingdom, 1850-1950* (Tuscaloosa: University of Alabama Press, 1997), 22-23.

[8] Lucy M. Cohen, *Chinese in the Post-Civil War South* (Baton Rouge: Louisiana State University Press, 1984), 92-95. Cited by Flynt and Berkley, 22, n.2.

[9] William R. Hutchison, *Errand to the World* (Chicago: University of Chicago Press, 1987), 31.

[10] A curious case was argued before the Supreme Court in 1923 when Bhagat Singh Thind appealed the decision of the Ninth Circuit Court which had denied him citizenship under the current immigration law. Some have mistakenly concluded that the Court of Appeals as well as the Supreme Court refused Mr. Singh's petition because he was a Hindu. According to the decision, however, Singh, though indisputably "a high caste Hindu," and thus "of the Caucasian or Aryan race," was rejected because, said the court, he was "not a white person within the meaning of the nationalization laws." In other words, Mr. Singh was not allowed to seek U.S. citizenship not because of his religion, but rather because of his race. The racial bias of the Supreme Court at that time is clear from reading the decision. See *United States Reports*, Vol. 261. *Cases Adjudged in the Supreme Court at October Term, 1922. From January 30, 1923 to and Including April 9, 1923*. Ernest Knaebel, Reporter (Washington, D.C.: Government Printing Office, 1923): 616-620. According to Robert D. Boyd, from 1920 to 1940 all people entering the U.S. from India were tabulated as Hindus by the federal classification system. "Census Categories Spark Renewed Debate," *The News and Observer* (Raleigh, NC), October 8. 1996, p. 2A.

[11] Exclusion Acts against "Orientals" were passed by Congress in 1882, 1888, and 1892. They prohibited Asians from entering the U.S. A so-called gentlemen's agreement was reached in 1907 between the U.S. and Japan which greatly limited Japanese immigration, but this was not satisfactory to the agricultural interests on the West Coast. Thus, the Immigration Act of 1924 prohibited altogether the entry of Asian laborers.

¹² *Immigrants to the U.S. & Countries of Origin 1820-1970:*

Germany	6,917,000
Italy	5,176,000
Great Britain	4,792,000
Ireland	4,302,000
Austria-Hungary	4,302,000
Canada	3,969,000
Russia	3,347,000
Mexico	1,593,000
Sweden	1,267,000
West Indies	1,090,000

Other countries sending more than 100,000 immigrants were: Greece, Norway, Turkey, Poland, Portugal, France, Denmark, Romania, Belgium, Spain, and Czechoslovakia.

¹³ The first law limiting the number of immigrants into the U.S. was passed in 1921. The number of immigrants allowed to enter the U.S. in any year after 1921 could be no more than three percent of people from that country who were living in the U.S. in 1910. Then in 1924 the percentage was lowered to two percent and 1890 was made the base year. Five years later, 1929, the national-origins law was passed limiting the number of immigrants to 150,000 per year and clearly excluding certain groups. The central restriction was aimed specifically against Asians, the rationale being to prevent any significant change in the racial composition of the population.

These provisions continued until the passage of the Immigration and Nationality Act of 1952, which established quota visas for all countries. The number of immigrants allowed from each country was based on the percentage of the white population living in the United States in 1920 who had originated from each country. The law, however, applied only to non-Oriental immigrants. Asians continued to be severely restricted.

The 1965 Immigration Act revised the 1952 law by abolishing completely the quota system based on national origin. The new law, however, limited the number of immigrants to 170,000 annually from non-western countries and 120,000 per year from countries in the Western Hemisphere. It also established a list of preferences based on criteria such as family relationships, education, occupational skills, and need for persons with those skills in the United States.

¹⁴ See *The Williamsburg Charter Survey on Religion and Public Life* (Washington. D.C.: The Williamsburg Charter Foundation, 1988), 35.

¹⁵ On pages 73-74 of his *Culture Wars* (1991), Hunter says: "Religious and cultural pluralism expanded after the war, as religious traditions native to Asia and the Middle East began to appear in the United States in greater numbers. For example, in 1934 there was only one mosque in the United States and fewer than 20,000 Muslims. By 1988 there were 600 mosques or Islamic Centers and more than 4 million adherents nationwide. These figures make Islam the eighth largest denomination in the United States—even larger than the Episcopal Church. the Presbyterian Church, U.S.A., the United Church of Christ, or the Assemblies of God. Just over half of these Muslims are recent immigrants from all over the world, particularly Pakistan, India, Turkey, Egypt, and Iran. The remainder are indigenous to America and belong to one of the branches of the movement formerly known as the Black Muslims. Some speculate that soon after the turn of the century, the numbers of Muslims will surpass those of Jews, making them the second largest body of religious believers after Christians.

"The growth in the size of the Hindu community is more difficult to assess because Hinduism tends to be a family religion in which a great deal of worship takes place in the home. Even so, estimates placed the number of Hindus in America in 1940 at about 150,000. By the early 1990s this figure had grown to about three-quarters of a million, with forty Hindu temples. Like Hinduism, Buddhism has no central bureaucracy, no single leader for its many different schools; worship is very often a private matter and, therefore, a difficult phenomenon to track. The introduction of Buddhism to America came as early as 1893 with the World Parliament of Religions in Chicago. At that time and throughout the twentieth century, virtually all the Buddhist immigrants were of Japanese ancestry. By 1909 there were just over 3,000 Buddhists in America. The number of Buddhists gradually increased until 1960 when, over the following decades, Buddhism experienced the most dynamic growth in the history of America. One of the largest of the Buddhist schools is the Buddhist Church in America (the Jodo Shinshu sect), which claimed in 1988 to have one hundred churches and 100,000 members. In 1960 it could claim only 20,000 members. The other Buddhist presence is the Nichiren Shoshu sect, which in the same year claimed to have forty-six community centers, six temples, and 500,000 members. For Islam, Hinduism, and Buddhism, the greatest concentrations of adherents are found in metropolitan areas, but in Hawaii, Buddhism competes with Catholicism as the dominant religion."

There are so many obvious mistakes in the comments above that one can only wonder about the credibility of the statistics Hunter offers. In endnote 13, page 332, Hunter says his data is from Richard Ostling, "America Facing Toward Mecca," *Time,* 23 May 1988, pp. 49-50. "For comparative figures," Hunter adds, "see Terry Muck, 'The Mosque Next Door,' *Christianity Today,* 19 February 1988, 15-17; and the *Yearbook of American & Canadian Churches* [National Council of Churches]."

16 "Surprises Surface in Religious Study," *Chicago Sun Times,* April 7, 1991, Microfiche: NEWSBANK 1991. Soc. 40:32; "Free-Form Freedom of Religion," *USA Today,* Nov 18, 1993, 2D. Nineteen other questions were asked by the interviewers, but they related to age, marital status, level of education, income, and race, not to religion. How reliable, therefore, are the data about the religions of the respondents when the questions are asked by telephone and no follow-up information about their faith is sought? Are the respondents candid? Is the faith they identify a faith they practice?

17 If there are 5 million or more Muslims in the U.S., they would represent the fourth largest religious group in the country. Only Roman Catholics and two Protestant denominations are larger, the Southern Baptist and the National Baptist conventions.

18 *The World Almanac and Book of Facts 1996* (Mahwah, NJ: World Almanac Books, 1996), 393.

19 Eck's undertaking is called "The Pluralism Project," a three-year research effort funded by the Lilly Endowment. She utilizes her students to gather statistical data on the presence and activities of peoples of other faiths during the last twenty-five years in designated cities and communities. The stated goals of the project are: (1) "To document and better understand the changing contours of American religious demography," (2) "To study the religious communities themselves," not only their places of worship, but also their retreat centers and informal networks, how they have adapted to the U.S. scene, their means of educating their constituents, especially their children, and how they interact with civic or non-religious institutions including the government, (3) "To explore the ramifications and implications of America's new plurality through case studies of particular cities and towns, looking-at the response of Christian and Jewish communities to their new neighbors, the development of interfaith councils," and assess the questions of church-state relations in this new context, and finally (4) "To discern, in the light of this work, the emerging meanings of religious 'pluralism,' both for religious communities and for public institutions."

In view of the fact that precise statistical data are not available on the membership of religious groups in the U.S., would it be wise to include on the federal census form a question regarding religious affiliation? I would be reluctant to advocate such a change for two reasons. It is the responsibility of the churches, synagogues, temples, and mosques to maintain this information—if they think it important—not the government. Moreover, information of this kind could be used by neo-Nativists and others to stir up fear and animosity against minority groups.

[20] "What Immigration Crisis?" *New York Times Magazine* (January 7, 1996): 26-31. 40-46, 50-56.

[21] Available from the PCUSA Distribution Management Services, 100 Witherspoon Street. Louisville, KY 40202, Phone (800) 524-2612.

[22] Commission for Multicultural Ministries, ELCA, 8765 West Higgins Road, Chicago, IL 60631.

[23] The Inter-Faith Network for the UK, 5-7 Tavistock Place, London, WCI 955.

[24] The Southern Baptist Convention's Home Mission Board, for example, says: "With America's growing multi-faith population in mind, the Home Mission Board created the Interfaith Witness Department. giving it the task of assisting Southern Baptist believers, churches, association and state/national bodies in their efforts to tell others about Christian beliefs and Baptist distinctives in the global village of the United States. The first object of home missions is to lead Southern Baptists in telling all Americans about Jesus; this includes, of course, offering each and every one an opportunity to respond." *Beliefs of Other Kinds* (Atlanta: Home Mission Board, n.d., 150).

[25] The Graymoor Ecumenical & Interreligious Institute, 475 Riverside Drive, Suite 1960, New York, NY 10115, a ministry of the Franciscan Friars, is an example. Also, "Seminarians Interacting," a biennial National Workshop on Christian/Jewish Relations, 71 Fifth Avenue, New York, NY 10003, is another of several well-known and tested efforts to promote interreligious dialogue. See also the pamphlet, "Interfaith Guidelines on Dialogue," PCUSA's Ecumenical and Interfaith Relations, 100 Witherspoon Street. Louisville, KY 40202. Tel (502) 569-5292.

[26] For the Articles of Incorporation and other information, call or write Dr. Henry N. Smith, Director, Tarrant Area Community of Churches, 801 Texas Street. Fort Worth, TX 76102. Tel (817) 335-9341.

[27] DuPage Interfaith Resource Network, c/o Bethany Theological Seminary, Meyers & Butterfield Roads, Oak Brook, IL 60521. Tel (630) 572-1400.

[28] "Interfaith Program in Community Service," *Christian Century* 113 (May 15, 1996): 538-9.

[29] I have altered slightly this beautiful statement. Other complimentary affirmations are worthy of note as well. Several months ago, for example, a Princeton Seminary student added to my collection of statements of mission by giving me a copy of one from the Plymouth Congregational United Church of Christ in Des Moines, Iowa. a portion of which is:

> "We are a people on a journey, witnesses for God and disciples of Jesus Christ—people of the church ecumenical and citizens of the whole earth. As pilgrims we are energized and led by the Holy Spirit toward "at oneness": with God and each other.

> "We have a common Story. We share that Story along with our own unique stories in openness and trust. Called individually to be members of the body of our Lord, we are made new by the creative power of God in Christ. Living our faith in relationship to our Creator and each other, we seek to make a difference in the quality of all life.

"We are called to be authentic persons in our worship, fellowship, teaching and service. Tension exists as we respond to this calling, but we regard it as creative and productive. We desire to enable each other to fulfill our mutual ministry with a vision of wholeness and peace.

"We invite all persons to join us in this pilgrimage."

Reproduced with permission from *Currents in Theology and Mission* 25:2 (April 1998) 102-115.

Alan Neely

Social Capital and the New Missionary Pragmatics

Paul Varo Martinson

To release the creative energies of Christian proclamation and to generate greater social capital, the practice of Christian mission needs to move beyond centrally controlled and bureaucratically defined pragmatics to a diversified model that includes mission as joint venture as intersection, and as parallel presence.

Called and Sent

Every Christian community has a mission that begins locally and does not stop until it embraces the world. This is so, because to be a Christian is to be called to participate in God's movement of love towards the world. This call makes every Christian community an apostolic community.

The theological institution at which I teach defines its mission as that of educating "leaders for Christian communities called and sent by the Holy Spirit to witness to salvation through Jesus Christ and to serve in God's world."[1] To my ears this sounds as if Christian communities are by definition apostolic— "called and sent." And if graduates of this institution are to be leaders in such communities then at the core of what we typically refer to as the "pastoral role" is an apostolic function that unites and integrates all other functions, including proclaiming, care of souls, leading worship, teaching, or whatever.

At least three dimensions of the community of faith are always present in its apostolic functioning:

First, such a community is always a community of gospel. That is to say, it is a community that preaches a gospel of repentance and faith in Jesus Christ. This gospel aims for conversion, a conversion from self-regard to other-regard. The gospel can do this, for it is the message that we have already been regarded by God, freed from the anxious need for self-regard, free to be other-regarding.

Second, it is a community of anticipation. Gathered around the Lord's table, we anticipate the community that God in the end has in store for us. "For as often as you eat this bread and drink the cup, you proclaim the Lord's death until he comes" (1 Cor. 11:26). Indeed, rooted in this fellowship, our whole lives become little anticipations of that final community, when "the home of God is among mortals" (Rev 21:3).

Third, it is a community of trust. If baptism defines the gospel and our participation in it, and if the Lord's supper characterizes the Christian life as an anticipation of the final community we shall have in Christ by the Spirit, then this defines our relationship with the world about us, our vocation. At the heart of this movement is God's faithfulness. God as Father, Son, and Spirit is the everlasting community of trust. We too are called to be such a community of trust. Trust is at the heart of vocation. Trust is active—"confidence in" someone or something. We have confidence in God. The other side of trust, its passive meaning, is "trustworthiness." Only the trustworthy is worthy of trust. Trustworthiness is reliability. God is reliable; therefore it is right and good to have confidence in God; indeed, it is at the heart of creation—a creation that sustains life and bears fruit in "due season" (Gen. 8:22). And so, in this created order, parents are properly reliable; spouses are properly reliable; neighbors are properly reliable, one towards another; governments are properly reliable; the good things of this earth ought to be reliably available[2] to all without regard to class, power, race, faith, gender, wealth, and all the rest.

Social Capital

To speak in this way of trust is to speak of what some in the social sciences term social capital. What is social capital? Capital makes it possible to accomplish something. To start a business, for instance, one needs capital, start-up money. One also needs a space. Property is a form of capital. One also needs intelligence, mental capital. One might need a government license, that is, legal capital. Many kinds of capital are needed to start a business. Social capital refers to certain social habits that make it possible for people to cooperate spontaneously, without coercion, and get things done. In its essence, social capital is trust, trust in one another.[3]

We have seen enough in this troubled century of grand proposals for the solution to our human problem of justice. The Nazis had their grand solution. Marx had his grand solution. Laissez-faire capitalists have their grand solution. Surely one of the most dramatic events of this century is the sudden implosion of communism in 1989. Who could have guessed it? But the collapse of communism has not solved all the problems of the former communist nations. Now, only the last of these grand solutions is left standing at the end of the century. But will capitalism bring justice? Development, yes, but justice? Can trust replace greed? The question of what kind and how much social capital is present will decide the adequacy with which the former communist nations determine their future. It is no different for us.

One of the most important gifts the church, as a community of trust, offers to the world is the way in which it helps to build up social capital—trust. The crucified Jesus is, for us who believe, the most complete expression of trustworthiness that we know. Jesus, trusting in God, gave himself for us in a public way. This gospel ignites within the people of God a sense of public responsibility. A responsibility that is not simply focused on family and friends, or business partners, or some other "in" group. Where the preaching of the gospel does not lead to such public responsibility, either the gospel is not rightly preached or it is not rightly believed.

One might speak of three kinds of freedom. One is "sovereignal freedom."[4] This is the power of an individual "to act as one pleases regardless of the wishes of others." This kind of freedom is, of course, destructive of social capital. Understood theologically, to be sure, such full freedom is quite a different thing. Sovereignal freedom becomes what Luther describes with the words, "Free lord of all, subject to none."

Another type of freedom is "personal freedom." This is "the conviction that one can do as one pleases within the limits of the other person's right to do the same." This appears to be the dominant understanding of freedom in our secular American society. it is a highly privatized ethic with few public values, other than those that guarantee my private preferences. It is under the banner of this freedom that each sector of society and every individual clamor for their own rights.

A third kind of freedom is "civic freedom." This is "the capacity of adult members of a community to participate in its life and governance." It is impossible for such an understanding of freedom to function without an ethic of public responsibility.

Theologically, Luther describes civic freedom with the words, "Dutiful servant of all, subject to all. "[5] The gospel fosters an ethic of public responsibility rather than an ethic of rights. Moreover, where there are responsibilities, there are also claims upon those responsibilities. If parents have a responsibility towards their children, then children have a claim upon their parents, and so on. If so, then the sick have a claim upon those who are well; the lame have a claim upon those who can walk; the deaf have a claim upon those who can hear; the dumb have a claim upon those who can speak; the weak have a claim upon those who are strong, the poor have a claim upon those who are rich.

Where social capital is absent, the public space becomes filled either with power—whether political, as in authoritarian states, or economic, where wealth defines privilege—or else by anarchy, as in our inner city streets.

We are "called and sent" for what? To be this three-dimensional community of gospel, anticipation, and trust, everywhere and all at once. Or, as we have seen in one institution's mission statement: "To witness to salvation through Jesus Christ and to serve in God's world."

The New Missionary Pragmatics

Mission is not a set of ideas, however fine. It has legs. My concern in this section is: Can we get walking? How shall we use our legs?

We began this essay by saying that every Christian community has a mission that begins locally and does not stop until it embraces the world. But it seems that both domestically and internationally we have problems in implementing such a vision. One writer informs us, for example, that the growth or decline of the Reformed Church in America (RCA) during the last century depended simply upon how many babies were born to its membership.[6] Perhaps it is no different for Lutherans. Perhaps the Catholic Church has the really correct growth strategy—no legal abortions! Another writer informs us that giving for benevolent causes in the once mainline protestant and evangelical churches has decreased by 33% as a percentage of income between 1968 and 1992.[7] Such dour statistics fill volumes.

In the once mainline traditions, the dominant model for mission—certainly for global missions—is for congregations to play an essentially passive role in response to a national church agency. Congregations react to national pleas for money, prayer, and personnel. For their reward, they get certain kinds of information, missionary visits, touring opportunities, and occasional inspirational gatherings. Over the years initiative and control have been centralized in a top-down model. One writer warns, "It is time for churches still functioning in [this] mode . . . to recognize that they are seriously out of phase with today's world mission realities."[6] The boomer generation that wants action, and indeed a piece of the action, is unimpressed.

Rather than centralized bureaucracies, we need dispersed networks that fit the communication realities of our day. And rather than functioning as centers of top-down control, mission agencies should serve to consult, inform, inspire, and connect, functioning differently at different levels, letting the energy of local communities of faith take shape in any number of ways, in many manners of configuration. It is with these and related assumptions that the following pragmatics is put forward. Initiative for action can and should come from any and every source— whether local, regional, or national—that carries a vision and can justify that vision.

I shall proceed by suggesting three phrases: mission as joint venture; mission as intersection; and mission as parallel presence. These ways of being in mission, I believe, are universally valid.

Two concerns govern these three phrases. One has to do with the goals envisioned; the other has to do with pragmatics. While the goal of mission is always multivalent, it can in the end be summed up as bearing witness to Jesus Christ. Take that out and the heart of all Christian mission has been excised.

By pragmatics I mean to point to that which the situation demands. Many things are desired; not everything is feasible. Pragmatics is the process of wedding the desirable to the feasible. It has to do with a means that is congruent with the end. Pragmatics engages word and world.

The three phrases I have suggested depend upon the way goals and pragmatics relate. In the case of mission as joint venture, all parties in the venture share a common goal. Pragmatics and goal are intrinsically related. In the case of mission as intersection, the goals of the parties involved are different (for instance, a church and a secular or perhaps other religious—but not Christian—entity); they may even be contrary to each other, but there is a common pragmatics. In the case of mission as parallel presence, the parties share a common goal (two Christian communities, for instance), but the pragmatics are separate. I will fill out what I mean with some illustrations.

A. Mission as Joint Venture

Mission as joint venture describes a situation in which the partners in mission share common goals and join in common pragmatics. Partnership is full and complete. But a joint venture is more than partnership.

Some years ago, a group of us felt that our church in the St. Paul area should be doing something for the increasing numbers of Chinese scholars and students in our midst. What had been, in the past, a long and fruitful relationship between the upper Midwest and China had been long sundered. But now, here were significant numbers of Chinese in our midst. Who ought assume responsibility for renewing this relationship? The Division for Global Mission? Well, their duties were defined by the church as outside of North America.[9] So that was that. The Lutheran Student Ministry seemed to have logical responsibility, but they lacked the expertise to relate to specific cultural subgroups. We thought maybe the local synods were the logical place.

We met with the two synod offices and shared something of our hopes and plans for a hospitality ministry to the Chinese scholars and students. After some time it became clear that the bottom-line question was whether this was to be a "ministry of word and sacrament." Well, no; it was to be a ministry of hospitality, in which we as Christian people would do our best to make the Chinese guests in our midst feel at home.

So, we went ahead on our own. One group gave us initial funding to get us going.[10] With that, we began on an entirely volunteer basis, and functioned in that manner for some years. The local Lutheran Student Center was gracious in making space available. We began our hospitality ministry: meeting and temporarily housing new arrivals when need arose; monthly hospitality meetings; classes in English and other practical matters; getting Chinese friends into American homes; providing opportunity to visit sites, churches, and cultural events; and occasional crisis intervention. Eventually enough people with enough skills and enough cooperating congregations were drawn together so that we had the funds to call a full-time director.

By this time it became apparent that it was the right time to explore a more direct gospel ministry. A coalition of persons from the Twin Cities, Taiwan, Hong Kong, and China drew up ideas and plans. The Hospitality Board then contacted several church agencies: the St. Paul Area Synod, The World Mission Prayer League, the Hospitality Center for the Chinese, ELCA Region III, the ELCA Division for Outreach, and St. Anthony Park Lutheran Church. We discovered that all in this diverse group could now share not only in a common goal—a direct ministry of the gospel—but in a common pragmatics as well. We became partners in a new joint venture. In September 1997 a theologically educated mainland Chinese Christian was called as a full-time mission developer. Today the ministry flourishes.

From an independent venture this became a joint venture.

B. Mission as Intersection

Mission as intersection describes a situation in which the participants have diverse goals, while the pragmatics can be shared.

Some years ago a small group of five people visited the Muslim regions of China, traveling to Beijing, Urumqi, Xian, and Kunming. We met with several of the leading institutions and scholars in China that dealt with Islam. We also visited Muslim institutions. In Beijing we met with researchers on Islam in the Academy of Social Sciences, China's premier research institution. We met with the regional counterparts wherever we visited. We also met with university personnel who dealt with Islam. At each of these places a lecture was presented to set the tone for our conversations. We discussed various possibilities for cooperation.

The upshot of the visit was a report, included in a larger report on Islamic regions to the Division for Global Mission.[11] When the division took action on the report, the recommendations with respect to China were set aside. One of these recommendations was that we cooperate with the Academy of Social Sciences in China to sponsor an International Conference on Islam in China that would help introduce the rest of the world to the Muslim community in China as well as remove some of that community's own isolation. Scholars in the academy were eager to cooperate with us in this.

That idea has been dead for some years now. Some time after the fact, this story was shared with a Chinese Christian friend in Hong Kong. He paused and said, "I have a crazy idea." He then told of a unique Muslim community near the borders of China made up of perhaps half a million people. Chinese, who fled from China during a period of persecution in the early nineteenth century, they retain the language, dress, and customs of an earlier era. Some Christians have begun a social ministry among them. However, greater understanding of both Muslim beliefs and pre-modern Chinese culture would be useful. China has an interest in these people and maintains good relations with them. China, of course, appreciates a group of friendly Muslims on their border while they face Muslim discontent within. This friend wondered if it might be possible and helpful to develop an international conference on Islam that would bring the right kind of people together to help all interested parties-the community itself, interested Christians, and scholars from both this country and China. Might we, he wondered, with the Islamic studies program at our institution, have any suggestions in this regard?

Is this an idea whose time has come? Maybe so, maybe not. Maybe in some other form. If something of this nature were to occur, there would be several parties participating, each with a different set of goals, engaged at the pragmatic level in a common venture. Rightly done, might some such thing lead to greater mutual exchange and understanding?

This would represent mission as intersection.

C. Mission as Parallel Presence

Mission as parallel presence refers to a situation in which the goals are similar but the pragmatics are different. I believe this to be one of the most important fresh ways to conceive of mission in our day.

Recently I visited a city in South China. In this city was a Doctor Zhong. Short, rotund, very dynamic, she was retired. Some years ago she had begun work at a social ministry carried out by a local church. It was a kindergarten for children infected with Hepatitis B. Because of this infection they were not allowed in other kindergartens or nursery schools. It was feared they could easily infect the other children.

In this city, kindergartens are really prep schools for first grade. Thus, children infected with Hepatitis B, when it came time to enroll in first grades were sent off to the poorest schools, for they were unprepared. This social ministry, religiously connected, was designed for the aid of these children. Dr. Zhong, a deeply compassionate Christian, bubbled over in the love she showed to these children. Tremendous social capital was being built up. The children trusted her; the parents had confidence in her. Her work was their hope.

They began with some 200 children. Some time later the government began inoculating infants to protect them from this infection. The inoculation program was very successful. Eventually the kindergarten was down to 50 infected children. One day it was simply announced that the ministry was to be discontinued. The reason given was finances—it appears the ministry was making less profit than before. She was heart-broken—what were those children still left to do? The trust and confidence the families had in her and this ministry— what would happen to that?

I asked Dr. Zhong what she would do. Could she start something in her home? Yes, she said, she was thinking of that. She could perhaps help eight or nine Hepatitis B infected children. But, she said, "I can't teach them. Others will have to do that. It wouldn't take much, but such persons would have to have a little remuneration." So there she is, wondering what to do.

What will happen? Nothing? Perhaps. In a later visit she said she was still thinking seriously of trying to do something on her own. Will one of the churches in Hong Kong take an interest? Perhaps the Lutheran church, where I worship when in Hong Kong? It is possible, if the right person presents it to them. Will the church that canceled the program reconsider its move? There is little chance of that. If something does happen, it will not be in cooperation with that church, but will be a distinct and separate venture. It would become a parallel presence, alongside other church-related ministries—not a competing presence, but a parallel presence in the witness to the gospel. There are endless situations in China today, not to speak of our own nation, where what is needed is parallel presence in as many forms as possible. The only conditions are that the gospel is served, and that the ventures are not competing in nature. Beyond that, things are wide open.

After Deng Xiaoping's death, Li Peng, often considered to be the evil genius of Tiananmen, gave a speech. He drew attention to the extreme gap between the urban and rural economies. This gap between wealth and poverty is a potentially serious destabilizing factor. As a result, a much greater effort must be directed towards helping the backward rural areas, which is most of China, to move forward. For this, every kind of cooperation from resources both within and without China is needed. Li Peng wants to focus on the grassroots needs. Is this perhaps a rich opportunity for Christians from around the world to share in a multiplicity of ways in ventures that will build a healthy and enduring social capital for China's future?

Mission as joint venture, as intersection, and as parallel presence can move in any direction—into American, Chinese, or any other society; it can provide patterns for both local and global mission.

Beyond Partnership to Network

A. Partnership yes, but . . .

During the last three or more decades partnership has become a well-established metaphor governing the understanding of mission. In its original use by Paul it was certainly a very fluid concept.[12] In present parlance, "partnership" has gained very specific institutional connotations.[13] There are at least three reasons why we need to keep partnership but move beyond it. We need to do so to de-parochialize mission, to shift the focus from structure to function, and to foster innovation.

We need to de-parochialize mission. I use the word "venture" to describe mission because it keeps the focus on the church's call always to reach beyond its own boundaries, whether geographical, cultural, institutional, or generational. Too often, it seems, when Christians look out upon the world, what we see first are other Christians. We take a particular interest in other cultures, for instance, when we find Christians within those cultures. Why be so parochial? "Look around you, and see"—not other Christians, but the "fields . . . ripe for harvesting!" (John 4:35).[14]

Function must rule structure. I use the term "joint"—as in venture—instead of "partnership" for a reason. The word joint is a descriptor; it can't stand alone. Partnership is a noun, and, as all nouns do, tends to draw attention to itself. Partnership as an idea has an internal bias towards structure rather than function. It uplifts one particular way in which the pragmatics of mission is done. Moreover, it can readily become focused upon the issue of jurisdiction.

When in my territory you are under my jurisdiction; when in your territory, you are under yours. Jurisdiction sets up boundaries. But which are the really important boundaries? And boundaries are far more complex and fluid then can be defined easily by ecclesiastical interests.

We need to foster innovation. Because of the bias in the concept of partnership towards the institutional and ecclesiastical structures of mission, these structures themselves tend to take on the status of norms that control and govern function. A way is needed to allow, instead, unstructured gaps and spaces where new envisioning, new initiatives, new ventures germinate and take place.

To move towards a timely pragmatics there is a better way.

B. Networking

In a recent article, Stanley Skreslet has made a case for networking as one useful metaphor to understand the mechanisms of ecumenical mission today.[15] I agree.

Networking indicates the way in which people can cooperate in interactive and decentralized ways for the accomplishment of some larger purpose. Such networks might be short-lived or longer lasting, and they can readily grow and shrink in response to the demands of the context. Skreslet identifies three qualities of networking that have a particular attraction as a metaphor for mission. First, networking is "inherently flexible." It is a highly adaptive way of human interaction and cooperation, enabling partnering relationships of a great variety. Second, it is "essentially egalitarian." There is no fixed, stable center, and relationships have no need of hierarchy to function. It is therefore a rigorous horizontal and interdependent form of relationship. Third, it is "wholistic in orientation."[16] Since networks keep close to the ground of human need and participation. they foster the embodiment of multiple human experiences in constructive and interactive ways and assume a communal social reality, rather than one that is isolated and individual or programmed and rigid.

Skreslet argues that networking has its natural basis in civil society. This essay emphasizes this point, arguing that the Christian gospel—by its very nature—encourages social capital, perhaps the most important ingredient of a genuine civil society. Skreslet suggests that NGOs (non-governmental organizations) represent one model of the way in which such networking can function. His essay offers other grass-roots examples.

While drawing upon important ecumenical thinking at this point, Skreslet, after giving some concrete examples of networking, brings forward some important cautions with respect to the current ecumenical discussion of networking. He suggests that "efforts by ecumenical leaders" tend "to harness the power of networking and to direct its flow toward fixed structural ends,"[17] thus contradicting the inherent adaptive character of the approach itself. In the effort to mobilize churches and peoples for specified ends, bureaucratic means replace the informality and spontaneity of networking. Whether it be churches or ecumenical organizations, the tendency is to follow a statist solution that mobilizes from the top down. This draws so-called networking relationships into a hierarchical mode. But networking is a free-form web, and not a centralized system.

C. Concluding Comment

I have suggested a minimum of three mission models. Networking, as defined by Skreslet, easily becomes the common coin through which all of these models can take effect.

One final word. Throughout the history of Christian missions, mission by parallel presence has been one of the most important modes. It has brought the greatest innovations and achieved the greatest breaching of pre-set boundaries.

Someone has spoken of mission as a perpetual "orphan." Yet, it is the orphan that more often than not has set the agenda for the future of the church. The early church began in Jerusalem and would have sidelined Paul's mission, had it been able to do so. "It was clear," says David Bosch, "that the Jerusalem party's concern was not mission, but consolidation; not grace, but law; not crossing frontiers, but fixing them; not life, but doctrine; not movement, but institution."[18] Yet it was the gentile mission that made possible the survival of Christianity.[19] The spread of Christianity to the Goths and Irish was marginal to Rome. But when Rome collapsed the center shifted to Europe. And so it goes. Now today, as Christianity seems to be dying in Europe, the center is shifting to the non-western and southern world.

Paul's mission was a mission of parallel presence. Jerusalem wanted to control all mission. Paul presented his case, and so it was that the parallel missions of Peter to the Jews and Paul to the gentiles dominated the early church. They shook hands in fellowship, but not the fellowship of institutional partnership. It was a fellowship that acknowledged a common goal while keeping the pragmatics distinct. It was a fellowship of parallel presence. In that spirit Paul writes to the presumably petrine church of Rome on his way, he hoped, to Spain.

In the establishment of a ministry among Chinese students and scholars here in our neighborhood, it is clear that the partnership we now enjoy in a joint venture was necessarily preceded by mission as parallel presence. We were on our own. We had to innovate. We were orphans. The small initial networking steps gradually evolved into the more mature—though structurally temporary—joint venture that is enjoyed today. Only thus did this mission begin. It is possible to design mission structures that fully foster and do not inhibit such innovations at various levels in church and society.

Notes

1. *The 1997-1998 Catalog.* Luther Seminary (May 1997)15:6.

2. Reliably available is not to be confused with equally available. The concern here is for the conditions necessary for life, not the degree of excess consumption that might be enjoyed.

3. On the importance of social capital in contemporary society see, for instance, Francis Fukuyama, *Trust: The Social Virtues and the Creation of Prosperity* (New York: Simon & Schuster, 1995).

4. So suggested by the political scientist Orlando Patterson in Freedom, Vol. 2, *Freedom in the Making of Western Culture* (New York Basic Books, 1991). Cited in *China News Analysis* 1528 (February 1, 1995): 2, 8f.

5. Martin Luther, "The Freedom of a Christian," trans. W. A. Lambert and Rev. Harold Grimm, in *Luther's Works,* Vol.31 (Philadelphia: Muhlenberg Press, 1957), 344.

6. See Roger J. Nemeth and Donald A. Luidens, "The Reformed Church in the Larger Picture: Facing Structural Realities, Reformed *Review* 47/2 (1993-1994) 94; cited in George R. Hunsberger, "Sizing Up the Shape of the Church," in *The Church Between Gospel and Culture,* George R. Hunsberger and Craig Van Gelder, eds. (Grand Rapids, MI: Eerdmans, 1996), 333.

7. James F. Engel, *A Clouded Future? Advancing North America World Missions* (Milwaukee: Christian Stewardship Association, 1996), 11.

8. Ibid., 16.

9. It is not without irony that my church, the ELCA, separates domestic and global mission, the latter referring to mission "in other countries"; This bifurcation depletes the global of its full meaning. See, *Constitutions, Bylaws, and Continuing Resolutions, Evangelical Lutheran Church in America,* April 30, 1987, article 16.31.C87a on p.85.

10. The Lutheran Literature Society for the Chinese.

11. Roland E. Miller, "Planning Proposal for a Focus on Islam" (Paper submitted to the Division of Global Mission of the Evangelical Lutheran Church of America, January 1991). For the China strategy, see 102-126.

12. We refer of course to Phil 1:5. The RSV translation referred to "partnership in the gospel." Other words are also used to translate the original Greek term *koinonia* such as "fellowship" or "sharing."

13. For a very clarifying analysis of the use of this term within contemporary Presbyterian mission theory and practice, see Stanley H. Skreslet, "The Empty Basket of Presbyterian Mission: Limits and Possibilities of Partnership," *International Bulletin for Missionary Research* 19/3(1995): 98-104.

14. Not many years ago, after having preached I was sitting at table eating my noon meal in a church basement. The businessman across from me said, "The most dramatic sermon I ever heard preached was. . . ." And he told of a pastor who, as he drew near to the end of his sermon, asked eight or so persons to come forward. He then asked them to mime the Christian gospel. After some thought they formed a circle, arms around each other facing one another much as in a football huddle. "That," the pastor abruptly declared, "is the problem with the church. We Christians like to look at one another while showing our butts to the world! In the name of the Father, the Son, and the Holy Spirit. Amen!"

15. Stanley Skreslet "Networking, Civil Society, and the NGO: A New Model for Ecumenical Mission." *Missiology* 25/3(1997): 307-319.

16. Ibid., 309.

[17]   Ibid., 315.

[18]   David J. Bosch, *Transforming Mission: Paradigm Shifts in Theology of Mission,* American Society of Missiology Series 16 (Maryknoll, NY: Orbis, 1991): 51.

[19]   Andrew F. Walls, "World Christianity, the Missionary Movement and the Ugly American," in *World Order and Religion.* Wade Clark Roof, ed. (Albany, NY: SUNY, 1991) 147f.

Reproduced with permission from *Word & World*, Volume XVIII, Number 2, Spring 1998, pp. 155-165.

Paul Varo Martinson

COLLOQUIA
PAPERS

ALLeluia

African Christianity Today

Paul Gifford

The Context

This paper considers what has traditionally been called sub-Saharan Africa, leaving aside North Africa and South Africa. I admit at the outset that Africa is a huge continent, and every generalization can be faulted, but I want to attempt some broad brushstrokes of a general picture. The first generalization is that the high hopes of independence have largely disappeared. Africa is in a state of crisis. The reasons are complex, and it is difficult to speak appropriately because undeniably at least one factor is the colonial legacy, and more recently many would want to argue that neo-colonialism in the form of the World Bank and the IMF have further contributed. But there is no denying the crisis.

Let us first mention the economic dimension. In Nigeria—and one out of every six Africans is a Nigerian—when President Babangida left office in mid-1993, the real income per head was one tenth of what it was when he came to power eight years before. According to the head of the UN Economic Commission for Africa, commenting on the failure of the UN Programme of Action for Africa's Economic Recovery and Development (1986-90), the African was generally 40% worse off in 1991 than in 1980. Per capita consumption in sub-Saharan Africa fell by one fifth in the 1980s. In the mid-1990s as many as 10,000 African children were dying each day from the effects of malnutrition and lack of rudimentary health care. It is estimated that Africa's share of global infant death will rise to 40% by the end of the decade. Between 1961 and 1995 Africa's food production per person decreased by 11.6% (by comparison, Latin America's increased by 31.4%, Asia's by 70.6%). The World Bank predicts that a third of all food requirements will have to be imported by AD 2000. Africa's share of world trade has all but disappeared—in 1950 it was 5.2%, in 1980 4.7%, and in 1999 only 1.9%. Returns on investment in Africa dropped from 30.7% in the 1960s to 2.5% in the 1980s. Not surprisingly, then, there has been considerable disinvestment, and external private commercial investment in the continent totaled only $504m in 1992, or 1.6% of the total private investment in Africa, Asia and Central and South America as a whole. The GDP of the whole of sub-Saharan Africa in 1992, at $270bn, was less than that of the Netherlands. There has been a general collapse in infrastructure. Spending on health care declined by 50%, and on education by 25%. While GDP growth in sub-Saharan Africa was in 1998 averaging around 4%, more than double the rate of the previous 15 years, lost ground has still not been recovered. Even if this rate were sustained over the next decade, per capita income would still be 5% lower than in 1974. By any standards of reckoning—statistics for life expectancy, child mortality, health, education, GDP—Africa has fallen well behind other developing areas of the world. In the words of one not unsympathetic observer, the continent is slipping out of the Third World and into its own bleak category of the "nth" world. The same observer balances this, however, with a very necessary rider: "Africa's problems, as pervasive and ghastly as they seem, are not the final scorecard on a doomed continent. They are the preliminary readings from the world's messiest experiment in cultural and political change."

The economic collapse is not unconnected with its political systems; indeed, since the 1980s the accepted wisdom is that it is the political system that has caused the economic crisis. Africa came to be characterized by one-party states, distinguished for patrimonialism and corruption. The one-party state, run for the benefit of a self-seeking elite, has understandably earned for itself labels like "the bandit state," "the personally-appropriated state," "the vampire state," "the extraction state," "the opportunity state," or "the predatory state." For a brief period around 1989-1993 Africa's crisis looked as though it might be addressed, and in that period of euphoria terms like the "second liberation struggle" and "democratisation" were widely used. Although multi-party systems have in many countries replaced one-party systems, and even in a few countries regimes were voted out, now that the dust has settled, it is obvious that much of that optimism was misplaced. In Zambia, where much was made of the "democratic transition" from Kaunda to Chiluba, the president has changed but the structures remain largely intact, and Zambians are perhaps even more desperate than before the 1991 election. And in a few cases, notably Madagascar and Benin, the leaders voted out in those heady years, have, because their successors could do little to better the lives of the people, been able to get themselves voted back in again. (I will return to the example of Mathieu Kerekou in Benin below.)

And Africa's tragedy is not merely a narrowly political or economic one. It is also social and cultural. In Liberia and Rwanda it is obvious that whole populations have been brutalized. In other places, too, the situation is forcing people to kill, steal, and beg, and get into drugs, prostitution, and alcohol. Economic hardship has profound effects on family life, as young men unable to raise marriage payments leave young women to raise children without husbands. Kenyan human rights groups say the level of violence in society is spiraling; deaths in mob violence have tripled within two years, far outstripping deaths due to ethnic clashes and banditry, and this communal violence is fast becoming acceptable. The two high profile examples of Liberia and Rwanda are of considerable importance for us, because Christianity was a large part of the self-image of both countries, Liberia essentially Protestant, and Rwanda Catholic. These tragedies constitute something of a watershed in writing about African Christianity, in that so much of what was glibly said about Christianity in Africa before Liberia imploded in 1990 and Rwanda sank into genocide in 1994 is now seen to need rethinking.

Christianization

The first issue to be addressed is the rapid Christianization of the continent. The context sketched above is crucial in considering Christianization; the relevance of the context will be patent in many points made below. Africa's Christianization is obvious and rapid, but it must be understood carefully. Ghana provides an insight here. The Ghana Evangelism Committee conducted a survey of all churches in the entire country, even remote rural areas, in 1986-87. The advantage of the survey was that it counted those attending services on a Sunday; it did not rely on numbers of alleged members or adherents given by denominations themselves, which are notoriously unreliable. The nation-wide survey was repeated five years later. A comparison of the two surveys allows us to track trends over that five-year period, and is most revealing. The traditional African Independent Churches (AICs) are losing members, the larger ones substantially: attendance at the Musama Disco Christo Church fell to 30,382, a decline of 17% over the five years; the Church of the 12 Apostles declined to 34,808, a decrease of 22%; the African Faith Tabernacle declined to 29,051, a decrease of 23%. Of the mainline Protestant churches, those attached to the Christian Council of Ghana, the Anglican Church fell to 29,354, a decrease of 2%; the Evangelical Presbyterian Church fell to 68,966, a decrease of 14%; the Methodist Church grew to 188,725, an increase of 2%; the Presbyterian Church allegedly grew to 178,870, an increase of 17%—it is thanks to the last that the mainline churches overall can be said to have held steady, though their small overall percentage growth of 7% in these five years is well below the 17% increase of the general population over the same period. The Catholic Church, though still Ghana's largest single denomination, saw its attendance fall to 343,957, a decline of 2%.

The growth in Ghanaian Christianity occurred elsewhere, and in two areas. The first was in those churches belonging to the Pentecostal Council, where the big winners were the Assemblies of God (up to 60,298, an increase of 87%), the Church of Pentecost (up to 259,920, an increase of 31%), the Apostolic Church (to 51,100, an increase of 27%), and Christ Apostolic (to 36,270, an increase of 36%). The second area was a group of churches that the survey categorizes as 'mission related,' where the most successful were the Churches of Christ (up to 20,170, an increase of 36%) and, above all, the New Apostolic Church (up to 20,508, an increase of 369%). Another church (in a category of its own) which showed considerable increase was the Seventh Day Adventist (up to 79,491, an increase of 15%). These changes, monitored over a five year period, would support the impression derived from so many countries in Africa: the AICs are in serious difficulty, almost free fall; the mainline churches are static if not decreasing; substantial growth lies with "mission related" and new Pentecostal churches.

The growth in these "mission related" churches indicates that Ghana is experiencing something more complex than a "Pentecostal explosion," because the most remarkable church here, the New Apostolic Church, with its headquarters now in Zurich (formerly Dortmund), is as un-pentecostal as it is possible to be. It shows enormous growth in Ghana. In the span of one year, between 1 January and 31 December 1993 (and thus after the period covered by the surveys discussed above), their Cape Coast District increased from 10,272 to 15,152 members (an increase of 42 congregations); their Accra membership increased from 7,631 to 11,065 (an increase of 33 congregations). In Zambia, the New Apostolics are the second biggest church, after the Catholics. Of the several reasons that could be adduced to explain this growth, let me draw attention to the resources available to it. Its Zambian headquarters are far more impressive than the offices of the Christian Council of Zambia or the Catholic Secretariat. It has an efficient administration, which has to be paid for—most of the money comes from the headquarters in Zurich. Lusaka's magnificent headquarters, the principal churches (indeed, a good part of all churches), the vehicles, are all funded from overseas. The New Apostolics have no formal training institutions, but the frequent seminars and workshops are paid for from abroad, too. Besides, the church has a considerable relief budget; this goes primarily to its own members. Thus at least part of the dynamic operating here is related to Africa's extreme dependence.

Africa's New Charismatic Churches

However, much more obvious is the explosion of new Pentecostal churches. Let us consider this Pentecostal sector at more length, because this is undoubtedly expanding (and, it must be said, expanding primarily at the expense of other sectors—RC, mainline Protestant, classical Evangelical, and AICs) and because a discussion of this pentecostalism is revealing of the dynamics operative within African Christianity.

Let us be clear what we are talking about. The new churches (which I would prefer to call charismatic, leaving the word "pentecostal" for the longer-established churches of the Pentecostal denominations like the Assemblies of God or Elim) are not the same as AICs. I have felt justified in clearly distinguishing between AICs and the newer churches. I am not arguing that all the new churches are identical, but would feel that they possess a set of family resemblances. I would further argue that these are tending to supplant the AICs, formerly identified by a clearly different set of family resemblances. The newer churches, though they depend on primal conceptions like deliverance (see below), do not represent a return to the past, or a bridge to traditional culture, in the way the AICs did. They are harshly negative of much of Africa's traditional culture—not just polygamy and practices like (in Zambia) the "cleansing" of widows. They repudiate the veneration of ancestors. The new churches reject all the ritual—candles, blessed water, white clothes, drumming, sacrifices—that has been associated with the AICs. These new churches spend a good deal of time attacking "spiritual" churches (the AICs) for precisely such things. (There is observable here an interesting boundary shift. Many AICs began by denouncing the mainline churches as not Christian; now in their turn, the same accusation is being made of them.) Sacral robes are nowhere in evidence. In the new churches the worship is exuberant, but it is less and less distinguished by the trances and possessions characteristic of many AICs. ("Possessing the gift of tongues" is not "possession" in the earlier sense.) Dreams have given way to a much more direct and unambiguous form of divine communication. The new churches maintain a preoccupation with spirits, but in a markedly different way from the AICs. Miracles are performed without instrumentality. All props are modern and sophisticated. Their language tends to be English or French, their music western. They emphasize their links with the wider world. Culturally they play a role different from that played by the AICs.

Various factors are adduced to explain this charismatic growth. First, it is claimed, in today's Africa these churches are something new and important: voluntary associations of true brothers and sisters with a new organizational style. This new community provides free social space. Here members find shelter, psychological security, and solidarity. In this new association they create a new world, a new existence for themselves, away from the harsh and brutalizing realities of their former existence. In this new world they can forge a new notion of self, for here they can begin to make personal decisions. In the small area they have marked out for themselves, they can be free agents, responsible beings. They develop a sense of their own importance. They interact as equals. Here they learn patterns of discipline and independence. They shed their passivity and entertain goals and ambitions. Some even find leadership and responsibility. Moreover, in their group they develop a whole support mechanism to reinforce them in their new values and new self-understanding. So the individual takes charge of his or her own private life. In this narrow sphere an individual can bring control, order, and dignity. This argument has been made most notably for the new charismatic churches of Latin America—and most tellingly by David Martin. There is no equivalent research for Africa (and even for Latin America it must be said that this hopeful argument is extremely speculative—note the qualifiers like "maybe," "perhaps," and "probably" at crucial steps of Martin's argument).

Secondly, one obvious attraction of charismatic Christianity is its harmony with primal religious sensibilities. In this new charismatic Christianity (particularly in West Africa) there is great stress on deliverance from demons of every conceivable sort. This deliverance thinking has led to the recent emergence of institutions which promote and cater for the needs it addresses: prayer camps, deliverance ministries, and public deliverance rituals. The primal worldview is evident in the spate of literature now appearing—most famously, Emmanuel Eni's *Delivered from the Powers of Darkness*. But that thinking is not the only factor in the increasing popularity of this Christianity. When a few years ago I asked Ghana's most high profile deliverance minister Owusu Tabiri if his preoccupation with spirits and demons derived from African conceptions, he demurred, saying he got it all from American authors Derek Prince, Marilyn Hickey, and Roberts Liardon, whose books he promptly fetched from his bedroom. Certainly, West Africa is awash with the demonology of Americans like Lester Sumrall, Kenneth Hagin, Gordon Lindsay, Frank and Ida Mae Hammond, even Rebecca Brown. The origins are therefore complex. The two strands, the African and the western, reinforce one another, even feed off one another, and in certain circles tend to coalesce.

Thirdly, most of these churches preach a form of the "faith gospel," or "health and wealth" gospel. The basic idea of the faith gospel is that in Jesus we have already been delivered from sin, poverty and sickness; Jesus has already won for us health and wealth. This obviously is in harmony with primal religious sensibilities (traditional religion focused on health, flocks, crops, and children), and not surprisingly a concern with health and material sufficiency has enormous attractions in Africa's current conditions. However, as with deliverance thinking, I regard it as a mistake to relate the prevalence of the health-wealth gospel exclusively to primal considerations. As an elaborated Christian vision this is an American development, linked in its origins to positive thinking, and perfectly suited to America's economic boom lasting from the Second World War until about 1974. In Africa this teaching is formulated in the way made famous by Kenneth Hagin, the Copelands, Jesse Duplantis, Jerry Savelle, etc. in the USA. Thus this element, too, has complex origins. This doctrine's profoundly functional role in recent American Christianity offers another insight into its appeal in Africa. For an essential part of the faith gospel is tithing with its inevitable returns (Oral Roberts "law of sowing"), which has proved a successful way of generating resources necessary for America's very expensive media ministries. In most African countries the leaders of the new churches, though most of them are hardly "televangelists," are entrepreneurs in a very competitive market. The faith gospel, through its fundraising capacity, has enabled them to survive in very depressed economic conditions (another instance of the context not just proving relevant, but even shaping the manifestations of African Christianity).

Before leaving this sector of African Christianity, the most high profile and fastest expanding sector of all, I would make two comments. First, although claims are sometimes made that these new churches will play a significant role in revitalizing the socio-political scene in Africa, I think some skepticism is in order. Martin's argument is that these churches will perform for Latin America the same role that the Methodist church played in Britain in the 18th century. I consider that the faith gospel, with its emphasis on divine intervention, is almost the polar opposite of the Protestant ethic. Thus its socio-political effects remain to be seen. Second, it is apposite to say a word about Africa's increasing Christian-Muslim tension, for it is this charismatic sector which tends to have a very negative attitude to Islam. According to this sector, there is no room for dialogue, and the only thing to do with a Muslim is to convert him. It must be said that one shouldn't rush too quickly to label as "religious" the tension in places like Nigeria, the Sudan, and Tanzania between peoples of different religions. In these places more research is needed before it can be said that these conflicts are religious in any hard or exclusive sense. As many commentators claim that the conflict in Northern Ireland is not religious in any meaningful sense, but is primarily economic or political, there are different dimensions to conflict in Africa. However, one of those who argues that the Northern Ireland conflict is religious, makes much of the concept of 'monopoly Catholicism' as a factor in the struggle. In the Irish Republic, the Catholic Church, through its exclusivist demands in the areas of education, law, and marriage practice (not presented of course as Catholicism but as simply "natural law"), seems so threatening to the Protestant culture of the North that the Protestants feel forced to resist in self-defense. I wonder if a concept of "monopoly Christianity" would be helpful in analyzing at least some instances of Africa's growing tension. An exclusivist Christianity that publicly pronounces its aim to eliminate every mosque from Africa in the shortest possible time must be at least one factor in the increasing tension.

At least part of this impetus towards exclusivism is an American influence, exemplified in bodies like "AD 2000 and Beyond" with its mission to evangelize the "Godless" nations of the "10-40 window." It seems to me that AD 2000 and Beyond has assumed an almost hegemonic importance in Africa, even among many mainline churches. It is the USA that has demonized Gaddafi, the Ayatollah, and has elaborated a "Christian Zionism." It is the USA that has produced academics who see the future in terms of the "clash of cultures," Christianity versus Islam. This new charismatic sector of Christianity is manifestly responsive to trends emanating from the USA; an increasing "Islamophobia" may owe something to this.

I have briefly looked at the appeal of the emerging sector of African Christianity in terms of personal development, deliverance theology, and the faith gospel. I have deliberately not used the word "fundamentalism" in relation to these churches, for I think that label confuses rather than clarifies the discussion in Africa. An element of reaction, though it may be a key aspect of many charismatic churches in America, is not a key strand of black Africa's new churches. In Africa, this Christianity does not involve a positive repudiation of modernity; nor does it connote some stress on purity of dogma; nor is there any idea of "nationalism"—indeed, in a sense, there is nothing more transnational in Africa than the "born-again" movement. Nor is there necessarily any idea of repudiating the secular state; in much of this movement there is little political awareness at all.

Nor have I used the word "sect." Even though the word is frequently applied to newer churches in Africa, the idea of turning one's back on the world is not necessarily involved at all. Quite the contrary, these churches may be for Africans one of the best available means of linking into the outside world. For this reason too, I have not stressed the idea of "exit option" or "walkout" in regard to these churches. In Uganda and Zambia, becoming born again actually brings one close to power; elsewhere though it may sometimes indicate some turning against the political elite, it may be a way of linking into other benefits.

Mainline Churches

Under this category let me link together RCC and the mainline Protestants. (It seems to me that Africa's classical evangelicals have receded enormously in recent years; for example, the Evangelical Fellowship of Zambia, originally founded for churches like the Baptists, is now almost totally charismatic). Most African Christians would still claim allegiance to mainline churches, but there is great change afoot. Can one even note a certain transfer of moral authority or legitimacy or confidence? Visiting various churches in many countries, one is immediately struck by a massive age difference in membership. (This was caught in a headline in a Ugandan church paper: "Youth Exodus from Big Churches," where "Big Churches" refers to the Anglicans and the Catholics, and the exodus is to the charismatic sector.) We must note not only a steady hemorrhage of members, but also a process of "pentecostalisation" within the mainline churches themselves—in Ghana, the new deliverance ministries continually receive requests from mainline churches for deliverance sessions.

I think there is a different dynamic within the mainline churches from that within the charismatic churches we have considered—so different that it is more helpful to avoid glibly talking of African Christianity as one easily identifiable entity—there are at least two African Christianities. Many things could be said, but in the space available, I will restrict myself to saying that the dynamics of mainline Christianity are to be explained with reference to another set of issues.

Of these the first is the nature of the globalization process as it affects Africa. Religion is one of the forces operative in the globalization process, and its role has been well analyzed by scholars like Beyer. At one level, new global industries have grown up catering for areas like economy, law, health, finance and commerce, technology and science, and higher education. Religious networks function on this level, and indeed it can be fruitful to see African Christianity in terms of plugging into these global religious networks, particularly since Africa tends to be bypassed by many of the others. But at a deeper level, so much of what Beyer has to say is not verified by Africa. One of his central theses is that the global system corrodes inherited or constructed cultural and personal identities; yet at the same time it also encourages the creation and revitalization of particular identities as a way of gaining more power or influence in this new global order. Religion has been and continues to be an important resource for such revitalization movements. Thus he explains the rise of Islamic fundamentalism but also religious movements in places as diverse as Ireland, Israel, Iran, India, and Japan. Because of their stress on socio-cultural particularisms, such religious movements often display their conservative nature by stressing the relativizing forces of globalization as prime manifestations of evil in the world. But Africa is not reacting to globalization by revitalizing African traditional religion; movements like Afrikania in Ghana and the Godian Religion in Nigeria have very little appeal. Africa is responding to globalization by opting into exotic religions. Even though much of Africa's popular Christianity incorporates a good deal of the traditional worldview, which (I have suggested) constitutes charismatic Christianity's attraction over mainline Christianity where this mentality is denied or at least bypassed. Moreover, so much of Africa's exploding Christianity is closely linked with a particular religious expression formulated in the USA. To me, the significant thing about Beyer's treatment is that his theory of globalization is worked out in terms of all the rest of the world, excluding Africa. It is another sign of the marginalization of Africa, that theories of globalization are worked out without reference to the particularities of Africa.

I have noted that religious networks are increasingly important, as others collapse. As western donors have become more critical of African governments, they have turned to non-governmental organizations (NGOs—in the USA, PVOs?), and more and more aid is channeled through religious networks, to some degree changing the nature of these churches. (A few years ago I heard the phrase "the NGO-ization of the churches" used at the All-African Conference of Churches.) This is particularly obvious in the case of the Catholics, with their access to resources and personnel, so that I prefer to see the Catholic Church as operating with a rather different dynamic even from the Anglican Church, with access to much less. Those with resources (the Lutherans, with access to Scandinavian, German, and North American resources, are nearer the Catholic end of the spectrum) are major players on the development scene; indeed, I suspect that if a visitor from Mars came to Africa he or she might primarily understand these mainline churches as development agencies.

The involvement in development, though increasingly urgent and necessary, given the plight of so many Africans and the rolling back of government agencies, brings its own problems—strikingly evident in Rwanda. The Catholic Church in Rwanda was very proud of its involvement in education and health. Undeniably, this constituted an enormous contribution—it also brought the church considerable power, prestige, and influence. But it was able to retain its virtual monopoly in development only at the price of colluding in the iniquities of the system, leaving unchallenged the "genocidal culture," acquiescing in the racist mythology in which everyone was wading knee-deep. "Development" in this sense obviously must be subjected to higher criteria.

The access to external funds must be seen as part of a wider dynamic. The French political scientist Bayart has shed considerable light here. According to Bayart, the maintenance of political authority in Africa has been constrained by the relative paucity of the continent's economic resources, which has made it essential for would-be rulers to gain control of such resources and to use them, notably through patronage networks of one kind or another, as a means of ensuring political subservience. Given the inadequacy of the resources available within the continent, moreover, access to the external resources made available by participation in global economic and political transactions has often been essential for domestic political survival. This use of external resources to retain internal power (which Bayart calls "extraversion") can in his view be traced from the slave trade through to modern economic development aid and military assistance programs. It contributes to a "governmentality" (another term of Bayart) or a set of attitudes towards authority which is widespread throughout Africa and which may infuse bodies other than the merely political. In Africa, it has been significant that elites of different fields tend to coalesce; journalists, top civil servants, academics, military top brass, judges, politicians, and higher clergy often went to the same schools and universities, attend the same clubs or lodges and churches and often have the same perspectives and interests (a phenomenon that Bayart refers to as "the reciprocal assimilation of elites"). There is no doubt that in some cases all these factors have affected the functioning of mainline churches, and the increased access to external funds has at times strengthened a governmentality that militates against a clearly prophetic Christianity.

Parenthetically, I have dealt with "extraversion" in reference to the mainline churches because of their enormously high profile in development, but one might argue that the concept is significant in all branches of African Christianity. I mentioned above that access to overseas resources is at least part of the phenomenal success of the New Apostolics. It might be argued that part of the explanation of the proliferation of new charismatic churches is their readiness to link with overseas (predominantly American) churches. Such is the economic plight of Africa, that subventions from even a quite small independent church in say Arkansas or Alabama can transform the prospects of members of an affiliated African church. I mentioned above that Mathieu Kerekou, the Marxist strongman who bankrupted Benin in his 17 years of dictatorship, was recently able to get himself re-elected President. It is significant that he ran for re-election no longer as a Marxist, but as a born-again Christian; by 1996 there was no mileage in Marxism, but plenty in Christianity. And he has since attended major Christian gatherings like the Global Consultation on World Evangelisation (GCOWE 97) in Pretoria, South Africa, seeking investment in his country. It is not impossible that many see more resources on offer from Christian networks than from former political networks.

In the early 1990s the public involvement of mainline churches (or should that be churchmen?) was evident to all. In five francophone countries (Benin, Togo, Gabon, the Congo, Zaire) Catholic bishops presided over national conferences. In Malawi, the Catholic bishops issued the pastoral letter that began the whole drive to oust President-for-life Banda. In Kenya the Anglican bishops were widely seen as the unofficial opposition. This activity has been diversely interpreted; as the churches standing with the masses and acting as "midwives of democracy," or as influential churchmen belatedly seeing the writing on the wall and changing sides while there was still time to ensure their retention of power (a "passive revolution" in Gramsci's terms).

Political involvement advocating justice and democracy is to be welcomed, and many mainline churches now see it as an essential part of their Christian identity. However, again, it is often perceived as a mixed blessing. Not the least frequently heard reason for leaving these churches to join the new charismatics is that mainline denominations are "purely political" churches—which I take to mean that the more narrowly spiritual element is lost sight of to some degree. Many Africans see their religious needs met best by the newer charismatic churches. How the mainline churches can raise their prophetic voice while catering for their members' spiritual needs is one of their most pressing challenges.

Partnership, Mission, and Cross-Cultural Sensitivity:
Old Patterns, New Changes and Fresh Priorities

Lamin Sanneh

In these theological reflections on where we stand today in relation to the vision of the church in the context of general disenchantment with the western missionary enterprise, I want to reappraise the role of Third World partnership as a successor to classical forms of Christian mission. In particular, I want to re- evaluate in this light the role of Christian missions in Africa and inquire into what structures might replace old patterns and forms. Although we cannot return to the past, or at least to one type of past with its structures of domination and control, we cannot equally behave as if there is no past, either, with its local promise and potential. People today in the West, for example, believe that simple evangelism, based on unilateral proclamation, is no longer valid in a religiously plural world, and that proclamation should instead be replaced with social projects based on genuine partnership, or else on trust in the coalescence of all religions in the service of a common humanity.

The western liberal tradition, consequently, has remained opposed to the claim that Christianity is the only way to God, or that Jesus is the way, the truth, and the life, as narrow-minded and contrary to humility in the face of global religious pluralism. Modern liberals, both religious and secular, feel that the classical missionary view of the necessity of salvation, embraced by people who grew up knowing only Christianity, is in fact an old pitfall based on an offensive theology of original sin which requires a tribal blood-feud between sinful humanity and a wrathful God who exacts blood sacrifice.

We may justifiably ask, however, whether partnership as a prescription for a guilt-laden West does not carry too heavy a baggage of western cultural priorities and their effective propagation in the Third World to have much promise. Is partnership a form of theological cold war in which a post-liberal Europe, reacting to the consequences of western missions, tries to contain the project of missionary world conversion that is now threatening to take root in the Third World? Does partnership mean total theological disarmament, a truth ban treaty in favor of secular non-alignment? Does its package deal of hospital supplies, good roads, good water supply, fertile land, liberated sexuality, literacy, and well-fed children also contain a safety catch against a return to missionary triumphalism, a kind of time-fuse set to detonate with material fulfillment? However, if partnership is promoted without provision for theological discernment, it may create more serious pitfalls than those it is trying to avoid.

However, the desire that drives projects of partnership is a wholesome one, and that is the need for Third World people to be left as masters of their own destiny, that the West should stop meddling in their affairs, that it is time for the West to stop behaving as Big Brother and instead march to the beat of resource sharing and reciprocity.

Two major strands are intertwined with the partnership question. The first is the unquestioned responsibility of churches in Africa, Asia, Latin America, and elsewhere to take responsibility for the gospel to their own people whose safety and advancement are priorities of the first order. In the nature of the case, the churches find their credibility with men and women whose roots are in the soil, and it is those people that the churches must serve. Yet the gospel is not the monopoly of any one nation or culture, so that, to introduce the second consideration, the reality of the worldwide, ecumenical fellowship of the church should prevent the domestication and nationalization of the gospel lest it become nothing more than an ethnic or tribal fifth wheel. Human dignity is not a cultural or temporal calculation, but a primary catholic truth and belongs as such with the mission of the church. Consequently, it is important to build networks of partnership into the exigencies of tribe, race, and nation to demonstrate that truth.

For these reasons, we need to shift from mission chiefly as the wrongs and injuries the western world perpetrated on non-white races, true as that may be. As it turns out, it was the missionaries' adoption of mother tongues for the catechism and scriptures of Christianity, their adoption of the local names for God as the name of the God of Abraham, Isaac, Jacob, Moses, and Jesus, their appropriation of the music of the people as the hymn of the Savior, and local rituals as vessels of God's Spirit—it was these actions that launched Christianity on its non-western destiny and produced consequences more revolutionary than anything imaginable at the time. A rather momentous shift of focus is involved in such massive projects of indigenous adoption and transposition.

For those interested in partnership, they can rejoin the enterprise at any of its demanding points: at the task of primary evangelism at points of growth; at responsibility for leadership training; in prospects of ecumenical collaboration; in educating and equipping of women and youth: in programs of health and social welfare; in schemes of fertility and reproduction; in research into AIDS; in the creation of co-operative societies; in agricultural schemes and animal husbandry: in providing shelter; in problems of migrant labor; in stemming the tide of refugee dislocation and disenchantment; and in opportunities for national reconciliation, social reconstruction, moral rehabilitation, and in the general effort to resist the forces of death with the forces of life.

Lamin Sanneh

Yet there is something more in addition to this grim catalogue of need. Pliny, the Roman historian, said of Africa that "it always offers something new," which, after 1945 took the form of what Lord Hailey described as "the manifestation of the spirit of Africanism which is one of the most distinctive features in the picture of post-war Africa. . . . It envisages the attainment of a government dominated by Africans and expressing in its own institutions the characteristic spirit of Africa as interpreted by the modern African."[1] It is also echoed in the statement of Pope Paul VI that "the African who becomes a Christian does not disown himself, but takes up the age-old values of tradition 'in spirit and in truth' (John 14:24)."[2] This African sentiment was opposed to the view that supported western colonialism on the continent, and it found echoes in the ideas of pioneer African nationalists. Thus did Ndabaningi Sithole, an African nationalist, observe appropriately that, "No thinking African can deny that Africa very badly needs western help. but no thinking African accepts this as justification for being European ruled."[3]

Tom Beetham has observed that in retrospect European opinion in both church and state failed to understand the quickening pace for change in Africa in the first half of the twentieth century, there being such a slow appreciation for the value of indigenous agents and institutions. Europeans equated right qualification for leadership with technological competence. "Neither in Church nor in State," he writes, "was there yet a grappling with the problem of giving authority in leadership to those who were a people's natural leaders even if they were not personally seized of the methods of western technology; maturity is too readily equated by Anglo-Saxons with an acquaintance with water-borne sanitation."[4]

African societies in fact carry much deeper marks and more enduring roots from the systematic exposure of their languages and culture to missionary attention than from the shock of western colonial overrule, here today and gone tomorrow. The close connection between language and culture in these societies meant that language study and development, such as occurred under missionary sponsorship, touched off a beneficial ripple effect throughout society.

One effect was the democratic leveling of scriptural translation. The vernacular languages of missionary interest were, of course, the property of ordinary people, yet in adopting them for Christianity, missionaries detached these languages from tribal taboos, from their cultural infection and their racial pride, and, with that action, enfranchised the men and women normally discriminated by force of custom, offering them ultimately a decisive role in the Christian movement. As the Minister of Education in an independent Zimbabwe explained to the British writer on African affairs, Basil Davidson, Christianity helped introduce the subject races of the colonial empire to the cause of national solidarity by bringing together on the school premises and in worship young boys and girls from across ethnic, tribal, and geographical lines, imbuing them with the spirit of oneness. Even if that was not the declared intention of missions, it was incontestably the consequence of what they did.

The second was that culture as a creative human attribute was assumed into the higher process by which God fashioned tribal populations into tribes of Jacob. This had a double effect on culture. For the one part, culture was purged of the sin of deification, and for the other, the mother tongues were employed in proclamation and witness. Tribal cultures were constituted into expressions of God's living purpose through the vernacular Scriptures. By the same token, these cultures were stripped of their self-sacralizing tendencies by being subject to the rule that regarding Jew and Gentile "there is no respect of persons with God" (Rom. 2:11).

In his account of Europe's resistance to African voices, Richard Gray has described how most missionaries trained in the scholasticism of the first half of the twentieth century were unwilling to entertain the possibility of an intellectual partnership with Africans. He described the example of Rene Bureau, "fresh from presenting his brilliant, if Eurocentric, analysis of the impact of Christianity on the Duala," disputing with the Zairean Catholic theologian, Vincent Mulago, the possibility of an African theology. "'Theology,' Bureau maintained, 'was a universal science, and one could not contrast African with western theology.' We were all increasingly part of a universal, technological civilization founded on Jewish thought and Greek ideas, and another western missionary maintained 'it was as unreal to talk of an African theology as of a lay theology.'"[5]

Such views suggest that the West had no intellectual incentive to contemplate partnership with Christian Africans, and I am not sure whether western social and development projects represent a change from Bureau's attitude or merely an evasion of it.

Whatever the case, we must attempt here a brief reappraisal. First, we should recognize the immense vernacular gains of today as springing from the translation ferment of the missionary era. In some of the most significant instances, Africans came to their sense of cultural and national self-awareness through the grammars, dictionaries and the vernacular literacy of Christian missions.

Second, in view of the accelerating pace of world solidarity we might investigate how ecumenical co-operation could advance the search for the new humanity. Whatever forms such cooperation might take, it would have to involve some retracing of the pattern of the cross in the demands for self-denial, humble service, public responsibility, and trust in divine providence. Christians should grasp as a matter of discernment the delineations of the new humanity in the role being assumed in our midst by new waves of refugees, immigrants, and other transitory elements, seeing how a new world is coming into being to challenge old certainties and authorities. Churches with any future must claim the role of the sojourner as the paradigm-filled condition of the emerging new world order.

There is, then, the issue of economic development and social progress. Global economic pressures are feeding the tension between urban industrial complexes and the sources of rural productivity. Consequently, rural development projects might look attractive to churches whose social base is predominantly rural. Yet rural development might only result in reducing villages and farms to structural dependence on urban industrial forces, with local produce liable to sequestration by the export or urban sector. There are forms of appropriate technology and the requisite education that churches might undertake in partnership to ameliorate the distortions of urban industrial projects.

Two basic problems have held back people. One is the fundamental truth that life is more than meat and the body more than raiment (Luke 12:23), and losing sight of that has driven leaders into irrational greed. There is a spiritual hunger on the continent far deeper, even if also less inchoate and less tangible, than the famine or AIDS crisis, though those are real enough. The new waves of conversion that have threatened to overwhelm the churches and disorganize their priorities signify an extraordinary awakening, and demand bold structures to harness their force. Such new Christians, with a scandalous lack of resources, face daunting tasks of nation building, social reconstruction, and the pressures of the AIDS epidemic.

The second problem has to do with the substitution of the promise of material abundance for God's promises. Ordinary people who were taken in by the rhetoric of economic salvation felt betrayed as corruption ate away at the spiritual foundations of public life. As a frustrated highly trained African professional put it to me once, "Nyii gomun yalla" (these [our leaders] do not trust in God), the context being open and persistent economic corruption. The apparent intractability of material deprivation has compelled a fundamental stocktaking in both the material and spiritual sense.

These two problems are exacerbated by the crisis of the national secular state, with its dogma of the political kingdom preceding and superseding the heavenly kingdom. As Africans have become disenchanted with economic promises, they have been in incipient rebellion against the national secular state, more and more persuaded that people must work out their own salvation unfettered by state supremacy. In the meantime, Non-Governmental Organizations (NGOs) have stepped in to fill the breach, although even NGOs seem now increasingly to take on an international character rather than a local one. Pope John Paul II, addressing a gathering of Muslim youth in Casablanca in August, 1985, spoke in similar vein about the importance of religious freedom and the spiritual life vis-a-vis state power: "We desire," he said, "that all may reach the fullness of the divine truth, but no one can do that except through free adherence of conscience, protected from exterior compulsions which would be unworthy of the free homage of reason and of heart which is characteristic of human dignity. There is the true meaning of religious liberty, which at the same time respects God and man."[6] The churches have been drawn into playing an increasingly active public role, and to carry out this task effectively, they need a large cadre of trained leaders equipped with the requisite tools, something at present completely beyond their means. Avoiding old pitfalls is inadequate in the face of such urgent need. New theological priorities must be built into the logic of partnership.

Notes

[1] Lord Hailey. *An African Survey Revised 1956* (Oxford: Clarendon Press, 1957), p.252.

[2] Pope Paul VI. *Message to All the Peoples of Africa* (Vatican Publication, no date), p.19.

[3] Tom Beetham. *A New Order in Africa.* Beckley Pamphlets, fifth series, no.2 (London: Epworth Press. 1960), 7-8.

[4] Beetham, 1960, p.5.

[5] Richard Gray. *Black Christians and White Missionaries* (New Haven: Yale University Press, 1990), 72.

[6] "The Speech of the Holy Father John Paul II at . . . Casablanca," *Islamochristiana.* (II. Rome, 1985): p.203.

Giving Account of a Vision:
China and the Christian Community in Relation to North America Today

Paul Varo Martinson

Introduction

A vision interprets a context; an illusion distorts. While any given context allows for a variety of interpretations, an interpretation must in the end be accountable to that context; an illusion accepts no such constraint. Let us try to interpret Chinese society in the midst of enormous transition. In the long term, China is still seeking to define a political, social, and economic order to replace the long defunct imperial order of the Qing. That order has not yet been fully discerned or secured. It is, however, the short-term scale, measured in two or three decades, that is of more immediate interest in this paper.

In these terms, the current transition in China is dominated by the forces unleashed by the reform policies initiated by Deng. The rigorous top-down political and economic model of the Maoist era has been replaced by the current semi-reformed and negotiated system.[1] While market forces have become an important factor, political elites at whatever level still have a determining role. Nevertheless, new forces leading to increasing diversity have been generated in the society. Lieberthal characterizes well what has happened within the last two decades.

> On the surface, Chinese life has changed greatly during the reform period. Even cities like Beijing, Shanghai, or Guangzhou in Mao's last years presented images of dull conformity—millions of people dressed in similar blue "Mao jackets," uniform hair styles among women, no advertising, and no sense of liveliness or entrepreneurship. In 1994, varied clothing, huge traffic jams, vibrant consumer culture, karoake bars, and other entertainment centers, and the seemingly unending construction of modern buildings are the norm. The near total isolationism of the late Maoist era has been cast aside; calling cards of important Chinese now boast both telephone and fax numbers, and few urban families lack a television set.[2]

Of course these transformations have affected the rural areas much less than the urban centers. Even in the most developed of the provinces, Guangdong, one needs only to make a trip from the provincial capital northward to the municipality of Qingyuan, and then on to the county seat of Yingde and finally to the rural town of Dawan. In this journey, especially if coming directly from Hong Kong, one will witness a progressive decline in affluence and diversity.

The Christian community in China lives within this vast and changing environment, and directly reflects many of the dynamics at work in the current political, economic, and social realms. We shall see how this fundamentally shapes the church and inquire as to the implications this might have for how Christians in North America relate to their sisters and brothers in China.

Religious Policy and Political Structure

Political Structure

The one over-riding factor that will decisively shape any relationship of overseas Christians with those on the China Mainland is the state policy and practice with respect to religion. This factor is unavoidable. Diverse responses are possible.

Perhaps every political system has both an overt and a hidden structure. The goal in a democratic society, though never fully achieved, is the overcoming of this divide in full political transparency. An authoritarian, one party state such as China does not labor under such a constraint. To ignore either aspect, the overt or hidden, is to misread the situation. Lieberthal's study, *Governing China,* has given a masterful account of this in the Chinese political system.

It is not our intent to expound on these relationships here, or to analyze the political structure. Nevertheless, a few comments should be made. First, the structure is hierarchically ordered. Second, from top to bottom the party and the state form parallel structures, but in such a way that the party always retains the initiative. Third, power is distributed both vertically and horizontally, the so-called line *(tiao)* and block *(kuai)* arrangement, the lowest units being the *danwei* (urban "units") and the *jiti* (rural "collectives" and later "communes").

The line and block system has become particularly problematic as China modernizes. Different blocks (e.g. work unity, village community) are linked not horizontally but through vertical chains of command. As can be imagined, coordination of the vertical lines with the horizontal blocks can become problematic if not a nightmare; yet the vertical line of authority must be maintained.

All this leads to what political scientists call the "matrix" problem. "Since China," Lieberthal observes, "has developed the largest bureaucracy in the history of the world, its matrix muddle is of unprecedented scale."[3] He describes the result as "fragmented authoritarianism," in which any given official may have several bosses to whom one is accountable. In such a situation to discern which particular boss has priority becomes a problem.

This of course often leads to endless referral, delayed action, and inaction. Anecdotal evidence is abundant. During the 80s, the writer visited various cities, when his wife, who is a nationally and internationally well-known professor of nursing, would ask a medical institution to be referred to a nursing school in the same city, it was almost always not possible. The formal structures could not respond without being channeled through block; to line upwards, to line downwards, to another block; and so back once again. It might take days. The alternative was to find a personal connection with someone who happened to have a direct or indirect personal connection with someone in the nursing school and so connect informally, or simply go directly there and act the role of a dumb outsider.

If the formal structure is already complex enough, the hidden structure, especially of the limited number wielding the ultimate power, makes it almost impossibly complex. Lieberthal analyzes it in terms of the several *xitongs* (systems) that are dominated by one or another highly placed official, and that interact with but exactly correspond to none of the formal structures. For our purposes it is sufficient to say that these *xitongs,* or domains of power are highly personalized and embedded in their own matrices, and that negotiation amongst these systems, or domains of *guanxi,* becomes a supreme art.

To sum up, three of the above factors are particularly important to keep in mind as one considers the church in China. First, the parallel structures of party and state from top to bottom; second, a command structure with absolute authority vested in the party and distributed along lines and blocks with the attendant matrix muddle; third, the highly personalized nature of decision making at virtually all levels. At many points one could say, "As in the government so in the church."

The Deng reforms, of course, have generated considerable new instabilities into the system. Lieberthal identifies an interesting dimension of this when he writes:

> [T]he Deng-era reforms have witnessed a conscious reduction in the state's tight control of social and economic activity. The decline of ideology, development of nonstate sectors of the urban economy, conversion to family farming in the countryside, greater use of market forces rather than official orders to determine the allocation of goods and services, emergence of relatively well-off people, increased exposure to the international arena, and purposeful policies of political relaxation have created a situation in which one must ask whether the society is beginning to gel in a fashion that will permit social groups on a regular basis to put pressure on the state itself.[4]

Whether that be so or not, it is clear that the space within which *guanxi* (personalized relations of reciprocity) can work has increased immeasurably.

Religious Policy

Basic Policy

All non-communist and non-governmental organizations must be related to the command structure in some way. This is achieved through the united front policy. Wickeri argues that "the united front is the key to understanding religious policy in contemporary China."[5] This is correct. The primary purpose of the united front is "to enlist the support of non-Communists" for the purposes of the party. In the case of religion, the united front seeks to elicit the goodwill and support of the religious communities for the building up of socialism. If this is the short-term practical goal, ideologically understood, this includes the long-term goal of the demise of religion. For all practical purposes however, it is the short-term goal that is our interest here.

The principal institutional expression of the united front policy is The Chinese People's Political Consultative Conference. It functions as a national advisory body that represents the voices of many, if not all, of the legitimated non-governmental sectors of society and that is in turn instructed in party policy.[6] Related institutional expressions of the united front policy, with somewhat more specific functions, are the United Front Work Department (UFWD) and the Religious Affairs Bureau (RAB). The former is a party office, and the latter a state office. The former serves to carry out political policy while the latter deals with the practical day-to-day matters relating to religious groups. As a party organization, the UFWD also supervises the RAB. The RAB in turn both assists religious groups in their relationships with the government and supervises them.

As for religious policy itself, one point will be worth emphasizing. The 1982 constitution states in Article 36 that "Citizens of the People's Republic of China enjoy the freedom of religious belief." This, of course, is not the same as a bill of rights, since the constitution is always subject to the will of the party, and has indeed been revised several times over the years to reflect current party policy.[7] It is, moreover, not a guarantee of religious freedom as understood in western democracies. The critical issue in religious liberty is not the right of belief but the guarantee of the right of association. The constitution provides only a privatized understanding of religion, whatever further understandings one may wish to attach to it.[8]

A Legal Framework?

Laws implement public order. To this end there have been serious discussions about the place of law with respect to religion. For instance, one discussion has centered around the need for a basic religious law to supplement and make specific what is implied in the constitution.

Ma Ninghong comments on this. At least three viewpoints are expressed on the issue of defining a basic religious law (jibenfa). One group says a vigorous "yes." Religious groups have been fairly vociferous in calling for this, since they believe this will more fully spell out their rights as religious people. Administrative measures then flow out of this and are accountable to it. Another group would rather see any basic law, if one ever does come about, as the outcome of a process of administrative measures. The law will then sum up the learning through this process. A concern here is that giving too much legal status to religion might encourage overmuch religious growth. A more moderate third group would have development of a basic law and administrative measures proceed hand in hand. In fact, by default the administrative approach of the second group is the current way of proceeding.[9]

The sum of these regulations is the effort to bring all religious activity into a clearly defined legal framework; to distinguish legitimate from illegitimate religious activity so as to suppress the latter while protecting the former, and to ward off all uncontrolled religious contact, viewed as infiltration, from the outside.

A Brief Look at the Church

The Church Formally Defined

The main outline of the story of the church in China since the Liberation of 1949 is well known and need not be repeated here.[10] What may be worth restating is that the church more or less replicates the parallel party/state structure on the political side—as in the government; so in the church. The TSPM and the CCC (the *lianghui*) give institutional expression to both the patriotic and ecclesiastical aspects of the church. The TSPM and its committees at national, provincial, and local levels provide vertically a two-way communication between itself and the party/state, guaranteeing the patriotic character of the Christian community on the one hand, and keeping the government informed of church activities on the other, accepting political supervision as necessary. Horizontally, the TSPM in turn communicates with and supervises the CCC in these matters. The CCC, also with national, provincial, and local committees, in its turn, is concerned for unifying and servicing the internal needs of the churches, to build up a well run self-governing, self-supporting, and self-propagating church.

It must be recognized that all key leadership posts in all non-governmental organizations organized under the united front are not sanctioned on the basis of the popular will. This, of course, is not the case politically either. Lieberthal comments in some detail on what he terms, after Soviet usage, the nomenklatura, that is, a "list of positions subject to party appointment"[11] On this he comments:

> Through its nomenklatura system, the CCP exercises control over who attains leading positions not only in the party, but also in the government, judicial system, schools and universities, enterprises, research establishments, religious organizations, museums, libraries, hospitals, and so forth. *All* positions of real importance in China fall under the CCP's nomenklatura.[12]

No one outside the Party is privy to these lists, or to the rules governing their use. In this respect, ultimate authority, even in religious affairs, derives from the party.

The Church Sociologically Understood

The church as a sociological reality is very different from the church as defined structurally and institutionally. One possible way to begin a description is to suggest three broad segments and articulate them as below:

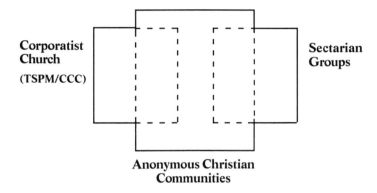

Corporatist Church

(TSPM/CCC)

Sectarian Groups

Anonymous Christian Communities

We suggest three segments, with the lines separating each segment from the other being often very unclear. These are the corporatist church (as described above), the autonomous christian communities, and the sectarian groups. By the corporatist church we mean that body of churches and institutions directly under the control of the TSPM/CCC. These churches as we have seen in the previous section are organized at the behest of the state, represent state interests to the church and church interests to the state, enjoy a state guaranteed monopoly in this area, and are officially recognized as such. It is a specific instance of a much wider phenomenon within state and society relations in China.[13]

Of course the social reality of the church in China is much more complex than the tidy arrangement a corporatist church might suggest. It is common knowledge that the Cultural Revolution brought the corporatist church to a complete standstill. During this time, and continuing into the present; there took place the unprecedented growth of spontaneous and unstructured home-centered worshiping groups. This phenomenon has become a dominant characteristic of the church in China. These groups became the basis for the reconstituted corporatist church, but was a phenomenon that was much bigger than the corporatist church itself. We represent this phenomenon, following Hunter and Chan, by the term Autonomous Christian Communities (ACC). They describe the phenomenon thus:

The ecclesial phenomenon known as the 'house church' movement is the other major institutional element of Chinese Protestantism. China has a long tradition of Christian home meetings, especially in rural areas. The religion was usually introduced to a village by one or two families, and it might take several generations before sufficient persons and funds were available to build a church. Also in cities, it was common for convert families to hold prayer meetings for themselves, and perhaps their extended family, in the privacy of their own homes. . . . During the years of repression, the faith survived in this organizational form, and the home meetings indeed appear to have spread their influence during the 1960s and 1970s. In the 1980s, home meetings and house churches expanded far beyond their original scope. Some of them developed extensive national and international networks, with thousands of members, and even publishing and training facilities. To reflect this change, in our 1993 publication we proposed the adoption of the term 'autonomous Christian communities' (ACCs) as now more appropriate than 'house churches' to describe these groups.[14]

Finally, we utilize the term sectarian groups to describe those segments of the ACC's that are in principle opposed to the corporatist church and refuse cooperation with it in any form, or indeed with any Christian group other than their own. These groups fade off into unorthodox or supposed heretical groups.

The diagram is not intended to reflect the respective size of these segments. Neither does the diagram intend to reflect rigid separations amongst the segments. The broken lines indicate that the lines of demarcation are fluid.

Civil Society and the State

Current Dynamics

We have already touched on the question of the Church as a non-governmental organization that falls under the jurisdiction of the Religious Affairs Bureau and ultimately the United Front Work Department and the party. It will be helpful to place the church within the larger discussion of the question of civil society in China, for the relationship of church to state in China is hardly unique. It is a relationship that is shared by any number of social groups/ interests that flourish apart from party or government. It is one of the weaknesses of scholarship on Christianity in China today that the question of the church is normally treated in isolation from the larger societal picture. This gives the impression that the matters relating to church and state are more unique than they in fact are.

White, Howell, and Shang provide a helpful study in this regard. This book asks the question about the nature of civil society in China. Its focus is on the economic ramifications of this question. Often the question of civil society has been raised in a political context. The issues to the fore then become the question of citizenship, civil rights, representation, and the rule of law, and the concern has to do with the potential there might be for the coming about of a liberal democracy in China. White, Howell, and Shang propose a more politically neutral understanding of civil society, a sociological definition. In this sense it is "an intermediate associational realm situated between the state on the one side and the basic building blocks of society on the other (individuals, families, and firms), populated by social organizations which are separate, and enjoy some degree of autonomy from, the state and are formed voluntarily by members of society to protect or extend their interests or values."[15] In short, they are concerned with forms of association which are neither family nor state, and which share the features of voluntary participation, self-regulation in their activities, and autonomy with respect to and separateness from the state.

Such associations—characterized by voluntarism, self-regulation, autonomy, separateness—they acknowledge are extremely diverse, partial, and fragmentary. Nonetheless, it is helpful to have some such ideal type in mind.[16] They consider this understanding politically neutral, since there is no guarantee that liberal democracy is the natural outcome of the existence of such kinds of social groups. The presence of these characteristics is always a matter of degree and the existence of such groups can lead to many different outcomes.[17] This is not to deny that civil society can have both a political dynamic as well as a market dynamic, and that these dynamics can interact and even reinforce each other. However, the interest of the authors is primarily in the market dynamic.[18] That fits more closely our interests in this paper as well.[19]

The policies of the current reform era have had a profound effect upon society as indicated earlier. The changes "have created a social soil which is potentially fertile for the growth of new forms of social association." This soil is seen in new attitudes towards self, society, and state. There is greater diversity of social groups and interests. Groups may even experience a greater sense of autonomy and may be more assertive towards the party and state. As individuals gain greater control over resources and their use of them, the state declines in its capacity to control. And so space is created for new kinds of interest groups to form.[20]

The state relates to this increasingly differentiated social space in a variety of ways. One may conceive of it as a continuum, from full incorporation into the state to full rejection by the state. White, et al. suggest these terms to characterize the way the state relates to the social space: "the caged sector: the mass organizations," "the incorporated sector: the new social organizations," "the interstitial, 'limbo' world of civil society," and "the suppressed sector: underground civil society."[21] It is clear that the last three categories fit well the way in which the church, as described above, fits within this social space. The "caged sector" need not draw our attention. It simply refers to the old-style mass organizations *(qunzhong zuzhi)* such as The Communist Youth League, All-China Women's Federation, All-China Trade Unions, and the like. These are organizations thoroughly subordinated to the party.

Paul Varo Martinson   *85*

However, the incorporated, interstitial, and suppressed are quite relevant. What is left wanting in this situation is genuinely free standing social groups characterized by voluntarism, self-regulation, autonomy, and separation from the state. As they rightly say, "What has been lacking—and this is important if one is seeking 'civil society' in any fully developed sense—is a decisive move on the part of the party/state authorities to recognize the freedom and autonomy of social organizations as an institutionalized principle of the political order."[22] This, however, as we saw with respect to religious organizations, is not a guaranteed freedom in the constitution.

The "incorporated sector" concerns a whole host of newly arisen social organizations (shehui tuanti)[23] that receive official recognition. Whether at the national or local level, these include business and trade associations, professional groups, academic societies, friendship circles, sports, recreational, and cultural clubs, and the like. Required to register, they are never fully free of state control. The "interstitial" world refers to groups that for one reason or another have not gained official recognition, or are allowed space by sympathetic agencies or individuals. They may include such things as "salons" of intellectuals, women's groups, trade organizations, religious groupings, lineage or clan groups, and the like. The "suppressed sector" consists of groups subject to active repression and surveillance. Obviously secret societies and criminal organizations are included. But any spontaneous mass organization that calls large groups of people together and can be deemed to pose a potential threat to the government can be included, such as Qigong groups, alliances of demobilized servicemen, groups for urban unemployed, household associations, not to mention, of course, spontaneous religious groups or efforts to establish an opposition democratic party. White et al. sum up this discussion as follows:

> There is a kind of "core-periphery" arrangement with a relatively well-integrated, but increasingly restless core of caged and incorporated associations, and a large and rapidly growing periphery of associations which are relatively fragmented and are kept so by non-recognition, surveillance, and repression. To this extent, there is no simple or single way of characterizing relations between the state and social organizations.[24]

Implications for a Dynamic Understanding of the Church

The writer has traveled widely in China as have many other of the readers of this paper. It is striking how well the description of an emergent civil society in China written from the viewpoint of political economy fits the situation with respect to the church. The only difference is that we use the term "corporatist" for the church since it is not a new social form but was "incorporated" as an accomplished fact in the early years of the 1950s.

What is clear from the analysis of White, et al. is that the social situation is very fluid. Reform has created a much less manageable social space. Since the state is unable to grant the right of association as a constitutional or legal guarantee, it is left with the single option of some kind of management. This became a compelling concern to the state after the incident of June 4, 1989. Registration of social organizations has been a central concern across the board since then.

In a recent conversation with a provincial leader in the Three-self Church the point was made to the writer that there are four kinds of situations that pertain to the current registration issue. These four reflect the diversity of situations within China today. In one kind of situation, the local government simply refuses to acknowledge any Christian group legitimate status, arguing that it is by definition a foreign entity and not a Chinese entity such as Buddhist groups. In these situations the churches, of whatever kind, become by definition illegal entities. The point is not that this situation is widespread, but that it is a fact. In a second kind of situation, a Christian group itself might refuse to register under any circumstances. In such situations the Christian community becomes illegal by choice. In a third kind of situation, either the Christian community or the local government might prefer that registration proceed independently of the Three-self Church. The Christian group does not desire to be formally linked to a national hierarchy, and the local government might consider that it has the right and the power to decide on legitimate organizations without the need to be subject to higher authorities on such matters. In a fourth kind of situation, which is generally taken to be the norm, registration implies a Three-self affiliation.[25] Indeed, in both government and church hierarchies, there is room for great diversity. In the case of the church, for instance, it is almost to be taken for granted that provincial and municipal *lianghui* (the two committees, i.e., the TSPM and CCC) have a sense of a certain independence from the national *lianghui*. Similarly, one can anticipate in any given area that the municipal and provincial *lianghui* are at odds with each other in significant ways. This last is often related to the fact that municipal committees enjoy control over fairly extensive properties and are therefore financially more independent, while provincial committees are less affluent. This tendency towards fragmentation proceeds down to the lowest level, even to individual Christian groups.

Intermixed with all of these things are the hidden connections that underlie many of the things that happen both within church and state. We identified that matter earlier with respect to the government, as an inherent aspect of a very complex matrix muddle. Personal connections, or *guanxi,* enable persons and groups to achieve goals that are otherwise unattainable, or nearly so, in the complications of line and block bureaucratic relations. Thus, for instance, in addition to the four situations identified above, one might also speak of hidden and often illegal arrangements. For instance, personal connections between a religious leader and a local authority, whether direct or indirect, may lead to the conduct of activities that are manifestly illegal under law, such as the printing of promotional Christian literature outside the regularly acknowledged channel of the Three-self, and the distribution of promotional religious literature through government or military channels.

Finally, over and above all of this, there are groups in China with a special interest in matters having to do with religion. A major area here is the academic world. Numerous programs in colleges, universities, and government run academies across the country include religious subject material; numerous publishing ventures of an academic nature deal with religious subjects; numerous organizations such as The Reformation Society, organized in December of 1989, deal with Christianity. Amongst the Chinese intellectual class there are also many who are well-disposed towards Christians or Christian ideas, whether they agree with them or not. Sometimes these persons have been referred to as "culture Christians," a perhaps not overly felicitous phrase. This brings the discussion of matters relating to Christianity into many fields of discourse, from literature, to journalism, to sociology, economics, and politics.

The sum of all these things is that the social situation with respect to Christianity is currently extremely fluid. With respect to the church one conclusion seems obvious. No single institution in China today exercises a *de facto* monopoly with respect to the church. The corporatist model, the one preferred by the state, and which indeed claims a *de jure* monopoly, is as such in the long term less and less viable. It has often been said that the Protestant church in China is post-denominational. This is clearly the perspective of the corporatist church. In many ways, however, it may be more correct to say that the Protestant church in China today is actually pre-denominational. The current fissures and fragmentations that are evident in the church nation wide suggest that when, some day, state authority no longer or less compellingly lies behind the religious monopolies now exercised by the recognized "patriotic" religious institutions, that the Christian community in China will define itself in its own way in a multiplicity of groups on the basis of locale, language, practice, belief, personalities, and history.

Where to the Future?

At the beginning we suggested China was in transition. The obvious question is from what to what? The "from what" is, of course, well known. The "to what" is anybody's guess. For our concerns, however, it might be helpful to try to get some sense of what some of the directions are for the near future.

There are inherent instabilities in the present because of the contrasting dynamics of political control and market forces. The former aims for a certain kind of homogeneity and predictability; the latter leads to diversity and change. The events surrounding Tiananmen marked a kind of turning point. Before Tiananmen it seemed that the market and societal forces were on the verge of gaining a political prominence. After Tiananmen the government has put great effort into regularization of all social forces and repression where regularization was not feasible. With renewed commitment to reform, especially after

1992, the market and societal dynamic seems to be gaining strength. The recent decision that state enterprises conform to market forces is a major modification in the treatment of the "caged sector," towards a greater openness, at least in this one area.

White, et al. suggest a tectonic plates imagery. The caged sector increasingly has to choose between autonomy and dependence; the incorporated sector is increasingly shifting towards the societal rather than governmental pole; the interstitial and illegal sectors nibble away at the capacity of the state to control and coerce. Are these tectonic shifts a preamble to a major tremor?[26] Should there be such a tremor, and the CCP was to lose power, it is clear that the present corporatist solutions would suddenly collapse. What would be left, as far as civil society is concerned, would probably be a chaotic mass of social groupings striving for influence and power.[27]

But perhaps it is premature to think primarily in terms of a possible cataclysm. It may be sufficient, for the near term at least, to think in terms of more gradual changes. Continued commitment to market forces would seem to guarantee the continuing diversification of the social space. Assuming that this commitment will require some measure of political adjustment,[28] it would seem that there will be a gradual weakening of corporatist solutions and a greater willingness to give due recognition to a much wider range of social groups. Furthermore, it is a question to what degree the building up of the hitherto rather primitive information and communications infrastructure (computer, roads, railroads, phone, etc.) will contribute to integration and diversity. It seems that social groups have at least as much to gain from these market driven efforts as does the state.

While this gradual, somewhat managed process of change seems both the most desirable and most likely, in either case it is clear that civil society will have an increasingly important role to play. Indeed, the organizations of civil society may even have an important constitutive role to play in defining the future. This assumption underlies the final section of this paper.

Theological Convictions

We began with the hope that a vision might be an interpretation, not an illusion. That is to say, the vision must be accountable to a context. We have now defined that context and clarified some of our major assumptions.

We need also, however, to make clear our basic theological assumptions. For the purposes of this paper we will identify five.

First, we have very deliberately focused upon the question of civil society in the preceding discussion. This is based on the prior theological conviction that one of the most important contributions the Christian faith has to bring wherever it is proclaimed and believed is a new texture in social relations. The proper consequence of faith in the gospel is trustworthiness in human relationships. Where such trust is not generated either the gospel has not been rightly preached or it has not been rightly believed, or both.

Since we have discussed this in some detail elsewhere, particularly with respect to China, we will not repeat that discussion here. Suffice it to say that one of the most disastrous consequences of Communist rule based on Leninist principles and exacerbated by Mao and the Cultural Revolution is the pervasive lack of trust in human relationships in China. If the Christian community is to make any contribution to China in the long term it will be in this area— providing one foundation for the development of a social capital based not simply on kinship relations, or locale, or reciprocity (e.g. *guanxi)* but a principled commitment to a public trust. The parable of the Good Samaritan is one of the most profound biblical images of the kind of social capital of which we speak.

Second, the earlier parts of this paper have spent considerable time in describing the ins and outs of church and state relations. We defined the church in China formally conceived as corporatist. This focus was also intentional, growing out of the conviction that a corporatist definition—which is essentially one way of defining the church in terms of church order—is not an adequate definition. In agreement with the Reformation definition, present in both Luther and Calvin, the church is defined by what happens rather than by structure and hierarchy. The church happens whenever and wherever the gospel is preached and the sacraments rightly administered.

This definition, of course, is clearly in tension with a corporatist definition. It is a definition that fosters genuine civil society. It is a definition, nonetheless, that does not require an antagonistic relation to a corporatist understanding of the church. Rather, it is an understanding that will seek to foster healthy mutual relations that contribute even here to the social capital (trust in relationships) of a people.

Third, that this paper concerns a community of people on the other side of the world is itself a reflection of yet another conviction. This is the conviction that the love of Christ obligates all believers to find their place in the sharing of the gospel with all peoples. This means, for instance, that North American Christians cannot abdicate their obligation to be in relationship with the Chinese people to businessmen and women, politicians, and entertainers. These do not represent our concerns. For very different reasons, Christians need to be at least as vigorously related to this large and dynamic human community as anyone else.

Fourth, integral to all of this is Jesus' call to discipleship, "take up the cross and follow me."[29] The three prior theological convictions—trust in relationships as integral to the gospel, the locus of the church limited only by proclamation and sacrament, obligation that the gospel be available to all without distinction—are held together by discipleship under the sign of the cross. These convictions only hold when the cruciform message is borne in a cruciform existence.

This leads then, finally, to the conviction that sharing the gospel in a life of faith is an organic process that partakes of the inter-relatedness characteristic of all of God's creation. This means that mutuality, whatever form it might take, is integral to the sharing. No person and no community has a monopoly on goodness and truth. Giving and receiving is at the heart of both a right understanding of creation, a right understanding of God's redemptive work, and a right understanding of God's own self-relatedness. What either party will gain in the exchange that any genuine relationship involves cannot be predicted ahead of time. It can only be experienced. Sharing, by definition then involves openness to receiving. It is certain, however, that much is to be gained from the experience of the Chinese people and of the Chinese Christian community in particular.

An Unsettled and Unsettling Question

Most North American Christians are profoundly uninformed about the situation of Christians in China. When they do begin to be informed it is often, perhaps mostly, the case that the more dramatic understandings come to the fore. For those inclined towards "evangelicalism," huge numbers of Christians and pervasive oppression are the keynotes. For those inclined towards "ecumenicalism," the high rhetoric of dissonance is replaced by the reasoned and dulling rhetoric of bureaucracy and institution. Key themes become post-denominationalism and political autonomy. The one side becomes the defender of oppressed "house churches," and the other the defender of a heroic, even if corporatist, church.

It seems that Christians in North America are faced with an either/or situation. Over the years, however, it has become increasingly clear to "evangelicalism" that this neat divide is not realistic. In fact genuine evangelicals are present in both corporatist and autonomous settings. There is, then, the desire to relate to both. This is then sometimes resolved by developing a dual track approach—an open and overt track that deals with the corporatist church, a hidden and covert track that deals with the interstitial and repressed elements of the church. Recently this dual track approach has led to a pointed statement by Han Wenzao, well articulating the corporatist stance.

Three major points are made. First, all church activity in China must be based on the principles of openness, honesty, and legality. This is biblical and has, in practice, made it possible for Christians to have a relationship of mutual confidence with the Chinese people as a whole. Second, the objection is to covert activity on the part of the Southern Baptist Convention even while pursuing partnership relations with the Three-self. Covertly they send workers to China to do "evangelistic work" and do not disclose their real intent and status either to the CCC or the government. This is behavior unbecoming to Christians. Third, the CCC will no longer have partner relations with those engaged on a double track system or who infiltrate in this way. This statement is dated November 4, 1997.[30]

Of course, this controversy does not arise in a vacuum. The extreme sensitivity to any unauthorized religious effort from the West goes back to the century of Christian entry into China under the protection of the Unequal Treaty System. It is an existential question of profound importance to many, especially within the educated classes. The Three-self or corporatist church, of course, reflects this sensitivity. For the government attitude to that history one need only read the disturbing account of western religious intrusion into China as presented in the recent White Paper defending Chinese religious policy.[31]

This then becomes the question. The reality of the church as presented in this paper and the interpretation given by the corporatist church are at times at odds with each other. How can one be both honest about the reality of the church, and act accordingly, yet remain in genuine friendship with the corporatist church at the same time?

Many groups, not only the Southern Baptists, have answered this question with a dual track response. Others have chosen to take one or the other horn of the dilemma. Some limit their relations to the CCC and Amity. Others quietly go about their own work, whether in the public sphere or "underground," keeping out of the way of the CCC and out of the public eye.

If the issue is posed in this way it seems that there is no way out of the dilemma, and choices will have to be made. Only those who take an ideological stance one way or the other will be ready to condemn those who make a choice different from their own. Yet, it seems, that putting the matter as we have above has its problems. The objection of Han seems to lie in two directions. One is the manner of the activity-covert activity, dissimulation, and what you see is not what you get. Han's charges, of course, neglect to take account of the severe lack of transparency within the TSPM/CCC itself. The other has to do with the substance of the activity—evangelism. As for this latter, it hardly seems fair to suggest that Han is, in principal, against the sharing of the gospel with other people. It seems rather directed against an unauthorized (by CCC) and organized activity of evangelism that will lead to independent worshiping communities not affiliated with the Three-self.

Is there a way of viewing the situation in China that does not simply accept a state guaranteed religious monopoly as exemplified in the corporatist church, yet is not covert and unauthorized?

Perhaps there is. It is the suggestion of this paper that a primary contribution that the gospel has to make for China is the fostering of a new social capital. This means fostering trustworthiness in relationships. This means, in turn, that Christians from the outside, when in China, will be honest about their identity. This ought not to mean, however, that the only way Christians can be in China is by a formal approval and sponsorship by the CCC. It is doubtful that the CCC would even be interested in taking on such a role. In fact, the range of opportunity for neighborly contact with the Chinese people is almost infinite.

Neighborly Contact

The Christian community in Hong Kong has already struggled with questions of this kind. The reasons are obvious. They had to face questions posed by the 1997 reunification. What would be the relationship of the Christian community in Hong Kong with that in China?[32] The parameters established by China were the three principles of non-subordination *(hubu lishu),* non-interference *(hubu ganshe),* and mutual respect *(huxiang zunzhong).* In practice this has left open a wide range of mutually beneficial activity. For instance, the Hong Kong Christian Council funded the building of over 30 churches in poor rural areas in China in 1997 alone. They plan even more for 1998. They, as well as numerous church and church-related organizations, are participating extensively in activities from disaster relief to Christian education.

Generally speaking there are three spheres of activity that churches and Christian related organizations in Hong Kong and Overseas engage in China. These are secular activities, institutional cooperation in specific projects with the CCC, and ministries related to the Autonomous Christian Communities. The opportunities for neighborly contact and service in these areas are vast. One should also keep in mind the Christian resources amongst the perhaps 50 or more million Chinese in what some call "greater China" or "the Chinese commonwealth" in SE Asia, North America, Australia, and elsewhere.

One could begin a list. Let us only start it:

- lecturing and teaching in Chinese universities;
- providing relief at times of disaster through any number of channels in a way that is not hidden about Christian identity;
- helping to build schools and churches, especially in economically deprived areas;
- training graduate students from North America in Chinese institutions so as to be best equipped for making future contribution to life and society in China;
- engaging in joint research projects with institutions and persons in China in areas of mutual interest;
- translate and publish works in China of academic value in the area of Christianity;
- providing study opportunities for Chinese students and scholars at Christian institutions;
- respond to requests by churches and church groups in specific areas for funding for provision of needed literature, for teaching, and preaching;
- establishing congregations in major centers throughout China to minister to the needs of the expatriate community;

- entering into joint ventures of many different kinds, from jointly sponsored conferences to jointly sponsored health care ventures;

- seeking a variety of means to reach Chinese scholars and their families in North America, and providing Christian training for those who so desire it.

This list could become almost endless. It might be more helpful to identify broad *action loci* and then identify fruitful ways of co-operating and interacting. Some of the principal action loci would be the following:

- *The Christian community in China.* There could be cooperation:

  - with the national offices of the CCC and Amity in specified areas such as publishing, media ministry, social welfare, health care, theological education;

  - with the Christian community as it exists at regional, municipal, and rural levels in similar types of projects and personnel sharing.

- *Secular entities in China whether governmental or non-governmental.* One should take note that there are increasing numbers of registered non-governmental organizations arising with which Christians will have common cause for the welfare of the Chinese people and society. More specifically, there could be cooperation:

  - in areas of mutual interest such as basic education, social service projects, health care and prevention, agriculture, and other infrastructure projects, perhaps even mutually beneficial economic ventures. In this last case, the church would obviously not be directly involved but could conceivably provide appropriate introductions between interested parties in China and North America as opportunity arises;

  - in highly specialized areas such as cooperation with the UFWD and the RAB in the study of policy and practice as these concern church, state, and society. The recent presidential delegation of three U.S. religious leaders to China in February 1998 helps to set the stage for this.[33]

  - in the area of university and graduate education moving both ways. This could include making it possible for secular scholars in China interested in studying theology, such as scholars belonging to the Reformation Society in China, to do so.

  - in joint research, symposia/conferences, and publication in areas of mutual interest in cooperation with counterparts in China (e.g., the Institute of Religion in the Academy of Social Sciences, departments and institutes associated with the various universities, and the like). See the Miller report of 1991[34] for examples of how this might be done in relation to the Muslim community in China.

- **The expatriate community in China.** This could involve direct ministry via word and sacrament as well as service in the area of education and in other ways. Besides the intrinsic evangelical value of such a ministry, it would also enable the growing community of business, diplomatic and educational personnel to understand and express their Christian witness in appropriate, meaningful, and effective ways.
- **The Chinese population in North America, particularly the Mainland scholarly community.** This could include such activities as:
  - outreach through hospitality and word and sacrament ministries. This would be properly and directly evangelistic;
  - providing for theological education to interested persons from this Chinese scholarly community with a view to their eventual return to and service in China;
  - provision of and, if necessary, development of Chinese language literature and media materials suitable for scholars in North America.

Organizational Considerations

This listing could be greatly expanded and concrete illustrations can be provided in a number of these areas. However, besides having a will to do something, which has already been addressed, it is also necessary to have a way. We will conclude, then, with a few reflections upon institutional initiatives that may be worthy of consideration.

- Give a mandate to the person in the relevant mission organization (e.g., DGM of the ELCA)[35] who is responsible for the China area that it is a high priority in the next five years to develop and initiate some such program as is envisioned here. After five years there will be a full review.
- Continuity of imagination and purpose is essential. Some kind of hands on, active advisory council of key persons would seem well advised for any Church body concerned with China.
- Initially there should be at least one person in China that will function as a hub of a network of information, ideas, connections. This can over time as opportunity arises become several networking hubs in Hong Kong and different regions within China.
- Develop a small core of western Christian scholars/theologians who will enter into study/research/service projects in China with a view to a commitment to long term involvement.
- It would seem wise to diversify the initiating agent. With a broad outline in place, encouragement could be given to individuals, groups, churches, and institutions, beyond simply the larger church body it-

self (e.g. DGM for the ELCA), but including it, to come forward with concrete ideas and proposals. Those with merit could be handled in a variety of ways.

- In some cases the larger church body might incorporate a proposal into its own program for direct supervision.

- In other cases encouragement could be given to churches or groups of churches or a group of persons to take on either short term or long term programs, remaining in consultation with the larger body.

The larger church body should be seen not only as a program agency in and of itself, and certainly not as primarily a fund-granting agency, but also as an enabling, consulting, and networking agency.

- Hong Kong has a particular relevance in relating to the Chinese community. It would be important to foster joint ventures with appropriate entities in Hong Kong. This possibility should not be limited to Hong Kong, of course.

Without question, a key feature of any viable strategy will be the presence, initially, of one long-term personnel living and working in China. This has been well articulated in a proposal made by John LeMond and Steven Ray. It reads in part:

> The next step involves assignment of long-term personnel to live and work on the mainland of China. In Chinese culture it is axiomatic to say that "relationship is everything." Cooperative ventures in China are founded, for the most part, on the basis of personal relationships with people who have proven their friendship and trust over an extended period of time, through regular and meaningful contact. On the one hand, this is a time-consuming process; on the other hand it is a time-honored tradition. Taking time to make regular visits to individual church and government leaders, engaging in conversations over tea or a meal, and being available at a moment's notice to discuss important concerns, requires that a person be in close proximity to the centers of influence, and open to developing these important relationships.[36]

Implementing measures of the kind indicated in the above paragraphs in a substantive way would bring a significant difference to the way matters with respect to China are handled today. This would foster, moreover, flexibility, openness to new initiatives, multi-lateral networking, and coordination as well as appropriate loci for assessment, direction, and accountability. The model envisioned would not be highly centralized, hierarchical, and remote from the area of activity but multi-layered, interactive, dynamic, and integrated. Accountability would be located at a diversity of points, depending upon each specific situation.

Conclusion

This paper has attempted to present a fresh paradigm for interpreting our relationship to the Chinese people and the Christian community in China. We believe the vision offered is accountable to a real context. We believe that a fundamental contribution that the Christian faith has to bring to all of China, not just believers, is that of a new basis for the social capital that can best contribute to China's future well-being. We believe that the North American Christian community has a special obligation to contribute in every way it can to the fostering of such a social capital. Christians ought not abdicate their God-given relationship with the Chinese people and Chinese Christian community to secular and business initiatives. We believe that contemporary social and political conditions in China argue for a multi-layered relationship with the Chinese people and the worldwide Christian community. We believe that basic theological convictions undergird these considerations. We believe that if all these things are taken together important new structural adaptations will need to be made by the North American Christian community.

The attention given to China in this presentation is well taken. China represents one-fifth of the world's people—one-fifth of the neighbors that we have. The Christian community in North American can no longer treat this community as a distant and irrelevant curiosity, consigned to the realm of tourist interest, business exploitation, and global politics. The fact of China's importance for the Christian community is reinforced with the realization that fully one-third of the people in the world who have not heard the gospel are in China. Most of Asia, of which China is the single largest entity, cannot be treated in the same manner as other parts of the world that have a high level Christian presence, whether it is Europe, North America, Latin America, or Africa. Each of these others have their own peculiar challenges for the Christian community. But the distinctive factors that make China a compelling reality for the Christian community today cannot be ignored. Never in history has there been the opportunity for the kind of multi-layered interaction with the Chinese people by the Christian community, the openness to the gospel, and the readiness for the social capital this gospel calls forth, than is present today. Historic events happen only once. We face an historic event.

Notes

[1] By "semi-reformed system" is meant "one that is no longer subject to disciplined planning but one in which state officials continue to drive almost all significant decisions." "Negotiated economy" refers to one in which, because many state officials have been turned into *de facto* business people, "economic outcomes are determined through negotiations involving local officials, who act without instruction from the Center," or again, "key economic outcomes are determined more through negotiations involving local officials than by purely market forces." See Lieberthal 1995 #140:259, 263.

[2] Ibid.:297-298.

3   Ibid.:169.

4   Ibid.:182.

5   (Wickeri 1988), 46. For a detailed discussion of the united front see especially chapters 3 and 4.

6   The 1954 constitution states well the role and function of the CPPCC: "The Chinese People's Democratic Dictatorship is the state power of the people's democratic united front of the Chinese working class, peasantry, petty bourgeoisie, national bourgeoisie, and patriotic elements based on the alliance of workers and peasants led by the working class. The Chinese People's Political Consultative Conference, composed of the representatives of the Communist Party of China, all democratic parties and groups, people's organizations, all areas of the People's Liberation Army, all national minorities, overseas Chinese and patriotic democratic elements, is the form of organization of the people's democratic united front." Religious groups, as one form of mass or people's organizations, also fall within this framework, and have representatives at national, provincial, and county level congresses. Selden 1979: 187. Cited from Wickeri (1988), 66. For a more detailed description of its functions see p. 67f.

7   1954, 1975, 1978, 1982.

8   These words also occur in Article 36 of the Constitution: "The state protects legitimate religious activities." This, of course, is not a guarantee of the right of association. The state defines what kind of association is legitimate. Thus, the "designated place of worship" is a requirement of the regulations. MacInnis (1989), 36. Philip Wickeri dismisses the call of groups such as Human Rights Watch/Asia for amending the constitution to allow right to "manifest" one's religion. He says "many other state constitutions subsume this under the right to the freedom of belief, and Chinese religious believers assume that they already have this right." While "manifest" seems a funny way to speak of right to association, this dismissal of the right of association that has implications far beyond religion seems less than candid. It is a matter of record that association has not in the past been so easily assumed and in fact in many situations in China still is not so assumed. See Wickeri (1997),11. The fact that the principal of the right of association is not accepted by the party in China is well known. White, Howell, and Shang Xiaoyuan (1996), 29, for example, say in passing: "Within the official realm, however, the principle of a fully autonomous social organization has not been formally recognized."

9   Ma Ninghong outlines the long process of attempting to formulate a basic law with, however, no positive result up to the present. Nevertheless, not a few administrative measures have been put forth which set the framework for the current religious policy and practice. Fundamental to all subsequent administrative measures is Document 19, a CPC directive of 1982. (1954, 1975, 1978, 1982.) Wickeri characterizes this as "the most important statement on religious policy since the founding of the People's Republic," as "realistic," and as reflecting a "flexible . . . understanding of the needs and aspirations of religious believers." Subsequently, in 1991, the State Council issued Document 6. For the first time, a document from the Center directly spoke of "control according to law," and expounded this theme. It pointed out that "to control religious affairs is so as to enable religious activities to enter into the scope of law, regulations, and government policy. It is not to interfere with normal religious activity or the internal affairs of a religious group." It has become a determined policy of the state to achieve this goal. Also issued in April of this year was the "Registration procedures for places of religious activity." In 1994 two crucial administrative decrees were issued by the State Council, documents 144 and 145. In July of 1996 the RAB distributed the "Annual review procedures for places of religious activity." Ma Ninghong (1996), 211f. Document 6 of 1991 specified that "Each province, autonomous region and municipality under direct central rule may also, on the basis of the

laws and regulations of the nation, sum up the concrete conditions of the locale and draw up administrative regulations of a local nature concerning religious affairs." Leung and Young (1993),186-309. As a result, many localities have set up their own regulations for governing religious bodies to amplify the regulations issuing from the Center.

[10] At the Third National Christian Conference (NCC), held in Nanjing from October 6-13, 1980, and the first such conference after the Cultural Revolution, important organizational decisions were made. Hitherto, the body that governed the Christian community and called the NCC together was the standing committee of the Three-self Movement (TSPM). Included in this meeting were adoption of a new constitution for the TSPM, election of a new standing committee and, most important, the creation of the China Christian Council (CCC). Wickeri (1988), 188f.

[11] Lieberthal (1995):197.

[12] Lieberthal (1995):209.

[13] We follow the definition of "corporatism" as offered by Schmitter (1974), 93-94: "Corporatism can be defined as a system of interest representation in which the constituent units are organized into a limited number of singular, compulsory, non-competitive, hierarchically ordered and functionally differentiated categories, recognized or licensed (if not created) by the state and granted a deliberate monopoly within their respective categories in exchange for observing certain controls on their selection of leaders and articulation of demands and supports." Cited in White, et al., (1996), 28. This defines well the procedure of bringing all non-governmental organizations under State control as done through the united front. White, et al., note four elements in the definition: 1) state organizes social groups/interests in such a way that state plays the dominant defining role; 2) it allows "interest intermediation" between state and that social group/interest; 3) the groups concerned are licensed and enjoy a monopoly in their specific area of interest; 4) they are given a guaranteed autonomy in their area of interest with certain special privileges.

[14] Hunter and Chan (1996):46f.

[15] White, Howell, et al. (1996), 3. See also p. 4.

[16] White, Howell, et al. (1996), 208.

[17] White, Howell, et al. (1996), 5f.

[18] White, Howell, et al. (1996), 7-9.

[19] We agree with Philip Wickeri that "churches are not human rights organizations." Wickeri (1997), 1

[20] White, Howell, et al. (1996), 25f.

[21] White, Howell, et al. (1996), 30-35.

[22] White, Howell, et al. (1996), 29.

[23] They come in many forms. Some are *minjian tuanti* (popular organizations), *qunzhong tuanti* (mass organizations), *lianyihui* (friendship societies), *xuehui* (learned societies), *xiehui* (associations), and *jijinhui* (foundations). White, Howell, et al. (1996), 98.

[24] White, Howell, et al. (1996), 38. They also later outline state interests and social group interests as they relate to registration. State interests include: building an ideological channel, consultation in policy-making, coordinating sectoral policy. Social groups take on certain government functions, regulating the market. Social group interests include: facilitating access to and extracting resources from the state, defending members' interests, protecting members against the anarchy of the market (for churches this would read, protection from religious chaos and heresies). See pp. 115-126.

[25] In regard to this last a comment can be made. Apparently, in registration regulations of 1989, in contrast to those of 1950, with respect to social organizations generally, it was required that each social organization affiliate to a supervisory body (*guakao danwei*) which acted as sponsor. White, et al. write: "The requirement to affiliate to a superordinate body is a form of state screening and licensing; a corporatist device which seeks to distinguish acceptable from unacceptable organization. . . . This requirement has made it very difficult for more independent social organizations." White, Howell, et al. (1996), 103f. For the church, of course, from the beginning only direct affiliation with the Three-self legitimated a group. It appears that with respect to the church there is considerable lack of clarity on this question as of the procedures settled upon after 1989.

[26] White, Howell, et al. (1996), 211.

[27] As White, Howell, et al.(1996) put it: "In the event of a collapse of the CCP regime, the mass organizations and many associations in the incorporated sector would be likely to collapse with it and their intermediary roles would be occupied by currently submerged or repressed organizations which would rush in to fill the vacuum," p. 216.

[28] Again, White, Howell, et al. suggest that "a stable and peaceful political transition— involving liberalization or democratization—can most effectively be achieved through a process of political bargaining and accommodation between key elites in state and civil society."

[29] Matthew 10:38.

[30] See *Tien Feng* 180 (12.1997):8. Were one to measure the corporatist church by these standards, it too would be found wanting. Transparency is not one of its noteworthy traits; it has often failed to defend Christians who have been suppressed, deferring to government definitions of what is "political," and the like.

[31] See *Freedom of Religious Belief in China* (1997).

[32] A sample of the many articles written to address the question is Chan Kim-Kwong (1995).

[33] Argue, McCarrick, and Schneier (1998).

[34] Miller (1991):117-126, "Proposal for ELCA Ministry Among Muslims in China."

[35] A recent draft document of the DGM/ELCA, "ELCA China Program Associate" drawn up by Tom Schaeffer has already developed a number of fresh ideas similar to some of those in this and the previous section. See Schaeffer (1998).

[36] LeMond and Ray (1997), 1.

References

Chan Kim-Kwong. "Cong xuanjiao shiming kan zhongguo jiaohui de fazhan (Considering the Development of the Chinese Church on the Basis of the Mission Mandate). *Tequ jiaohui toushi (Perspectives on the Church of the SAR)*. Hong Kong. Xianggang shijie xuanming hui (1995), pp. 2944.

Freedom of Religious Belief in China (Beijing: Information Office of the State Council of the People's Republic of China, 1997 Oct.).

Hunter, Alan and Chan, Kim-Kwong. "Growth Stress: Protestant Churches in China in the Mid-1990s," *New Zealand Journal of East Asian Studies* (1996 Dec) IV(2):42-63.

LeMond, John and Ray, Steven. "The ELCA China Program: An ELCA Presence in China: Living and Working in Shanghai" (1997 Dec. 33pp., Computer printout).

Leung, Beatrice and Young, John D., eds. *Christianity in China: Foundations for Dialogue* (Hong Kong: Centre of Asian Studies, The University of Hong Kong), 1993.

Ma Ninghong. "Jiqiang jiuwu' qijian zongjiao fazhi jianshedi sikao (Thoughts on strengthening the establishment of laws on religion during the ninth five-year plan)". The Office of Policy Regulation of the Religious Affairs Bureau of the State Council, ed. *1996 quanguo shengji zongjiaojuzhang peixunban jiangzuo huibian (A Collection of the 1996 Lectures at the Training Session for All Provincial Religious Affairs Bureau Chiefs)* (Beijing: Religious Affairs Bureau of the State Council, 1996), pp. 209-229.

Miller, Roland. "Planning Proposal for A Focus on Islam. Submitted to the Division for Global Mission of the Evangelical Lutheran Church in America" (January 1991).

Scheaffer, Thomas. "ELCA China Program Associate" (9 March 1998, revised).

Schmitter, P. C. "Still the Century of Corporatism?" in *Review of Politics* (1974 Jan), 36(1):85-131.

Selden, Mark. *The People's Republic of China: A Documentary History of Revolutionary Change* (New York: Monthly Review Press, 1979).

Tien Feng. (Shanghai: TSPM).

White, Gordon; Howell, Jude, and Shang Xiaoyuan. *In Search of Civil Society: Market Reform and Social Change in Contemporary China* (Oxford: Clarendon Press, 1996).

Wickeri, Philip L. "Human Rights Watch/Asia on Religious Freedom in China: A Response" (1997 Nov. 24; Typed Mss.).

Wickeri, Philip L. *Seeking the Common Ground: Protestant Christianity the Three-Self Movement, and China's United Front* (Maryknoll, NY: Orbis Books, 1988).

The Former Soviet Union:
Some Mission Realities

Allan R. Buckman

Introduction

In this status of Christianity report, attention will be given to factors that have shaped, and continue to shape, the formation of the Christian community. For the purpose of this study the former Soviet Union includes Armenia, Azerbaijan, Belarus, Estonia, Georgia, Kazakstan, Kyrgyzstan, Latvia, Lithuania, Moldova, Russia, Tajikistan, Turkmenistan, Ukraine, and Uzbekistan.

Historical Realities

Christianity. In Russia, Christianity and the Russian Orthodox Church trace their origins to 988 A.D. with the baptism of Grand Prince Vladimir of Kiev. In other parts of the former Soviet Union, however, churches were established much earlier. Between 300 and 350 A.D., Christianity was proclaimed the official religion in what are now the countries of Armenia and Georgia. Protestant churches were established in parts of the former Soviet Union soon after the launching of the Protestant Reformation. The year 1524 is recorded as the date for the establishment of the Evangelical Lutheran Church in Latvia. Approximately the same date is accepted for the establishment of the Estonian Evangelical Lutheran Church.[1] In Russia the first Protestant church, a Lutheran congregation, was established in Moscow in 1576, and a Reformed congregation was also established there a few years later. By the late 1600s and early 1700s, Protestant congregations had been established in Siberia (Tomsk) as well as the seaport settlements of Archangelisk and Astrakhan.[2] The Roman Catholic Church has been present in Poland and some of the western countries of the former Soviet Union since the 1400s, or perhaps earlier. In Russia however, the establishment of the Roman Catholic congregations was not permitted until the early 1700s.[3]

To put this another way, Christianity in all of its major forms—Orthodox, Roman Catholic, and Protestant—has been established in the former Soviet Union for centuries. By the beginning of the twentieth century, Christians made up 84 percent of the entire population.[4]

Primacy of the Russian Orthodox Church. During the years of the Russian Empire, the Russian Orthodox Church served as the state church and

Orthodoxy served as the state religion. By the time of Catherine the Great, during the mid-1700s "All members of the clergy, inclusive of monks and nuns, were paid benefits as decreed by the Emperatrice."[5]

Orthodoxy also served as the official state ideology. Regarded as inferior and of second class status, the activities of non-Orthodox communities were restricted. All attempts at conversion by members of non- Orthodox communities were forbidden, as only Orthodox priests were allowed to engage in missionary activity.[6]

The purpose of Russian law it seemed, was to induce the entire population to become Orthodox. By the end of the nineteenth century among the Slavic populations, to be Christian was to be Orthodox. By the beginning of the twentieth century over 80 percent of the entire Christian community was of the Orthodox faith.[7]

Persecution. The church that had for centuries occupied a position of preeminence in Russian society became, within just a few short years, a prime target for persecution. The wave of harsh repressions, begun shortly after the conclusion of the Bolshevik Revolution, continued through the 1930s and thereafter. One historian provides the following grim account:

> At one time as many as 150 bishops were in prison at the same moment (before 1917 the total number of diocesan and assistant bishops in the Russian Empire was less than 130). In 1918 and 1919 alone, about 28 bishops were killed; between 1923 and 1926 some 50 more were murdered by the Bolsheviks. Parish clergy and monks also suffered severely; by 1926, according to information supplied by a bishop living in Russia at the time, some 2,700 priests, 2,000 monks, and 3,400 nuns and other ordained persons had been killed, while (other) writers (who left Russia) today calculate that since 1917, among priests alone, at least 12,000, and possibly far more, have been executed or have died through ill treatment.[8]

For the Soviet government, the Russian Orthodox Church was a prime enemy. Of the many factors that might account for this, two seemingly predominate:

(1) the perception that Orthodoxy symbolized old, patriarchal, monarchist Russia, and (2) that religious ideology was viewed as one of the "chief obstacles to the path of the socialist reconstruction of the country."[9]

Overlooked at first, by the late 1920s Evangelical churches were subjected to the same brutally harsh repressions. Indeed, the Law on Religious Associations, passed in 1929, legalized all of the repressions Stalin had directed at the Orthodox community, and served to focus equally harsh measures against members of the Evangelical churches. The result of this vicious assault was that for the Evangelicals, "official religious life had virtually ceased to exist by 1938."[10] By 1940 the entire Christian community of the former Soviet

Union consisted of approximately 56 million members, down from 105 million in 1900.

After a Stalin instituted thaw during World War II, "this law again served as the basis for another wave of severe repressions, launched by Krushchev in 1959" when an estimated 10 to 12,000 Orthodox churches were closed.[11] With the departure of Krushchev the severe repressions gradually eased, though the 1929 Law was still very much in effect. In 1990 however, the Russian Parliament adopted a new law on religion that provided unprecedented toleration, thereby marking the beginning of a new era for the religious communities of the former Soviet Union.

New Realities

Freedom of Religion. The 1990 Law, together with a revision of the Russian constitution, did provide religious freedom. Almost all that the 1929 Law prohibited, the 1990 Law permitted. Among other things, it provided for the right to freedom of conscience, the equality of rights and freedoms regardless of attitude toward religion, the production of Christian literature, the development of charitable activities, loosening of restrictions on religious education, and accorded religious associations the right of juridical personality, thereby providing for the ownership of property.[12]

The impact of this dramatic change was both immediate and overwhelming. Among other things, the borders of the former Soviet Union were now open to religious workers of all denominations and persuasions. Missionaries, primarily from the western nations, never before seen in the Soviet Union or even imagined, began arriving in substantial numbers, growing from just a few dozen to a community of several thousand. Indigenous mission societies suddenly appeared, and varieties of ministries, long prohibited, began to emerge. Christian denominations suddenly experienced rapid growth, even as they struggled to reopen monasteries, seminaries, and Bible schools as well as reclaim and renovate long neglected church buildings.

Growth of the Religious Communities. With the exception of Judaism, all of the major religions of the former Soviet Union now claim more members than they did in 1900. Islam and Christianity are making the most rapid strides, at the expense of those who formerly regarded themselves as either atheist or nonreligious. Some 1900/1995 comparisons—in millions—include: Russian Orthodox 85.0/121.0; Roman Catholic 10.0/11.7; Protestant 2.0/4.2; Muslim 14.1/54.2 and Jewish 5.2/1.4.[13]

Moreover, surveys conducted between 1991 and 1995 reveal that people hold a favorable attitude of the Church as an institution. In Russia, Ukraine, Belarus, Estonia, and Latvia respondents, for the most part, placed a higher level of confidence in the Church than in other institutions such as the presidency, parliament, judiciary, or the military.[14]

Viewed in terms of church attendance however, it is clear the active Christian community remains relatively small. According to a recent survey, 60 percent indicated they do not attend church, 16 percent attend less than once a year, 17 percent between one and several times a year, and just 7 percent attend once a month or more.[15] The image given is one of flocks very loosely gathered, if they are gathered at all. One can only imagine this to be especially true of the Russian Orthodox community, given their huge numbers and the great losses they endured during the persecutions of the Soviet era. Interestingly, the distribution of some of the religious communities changed considerably during that time. The Buddhist, Jewish, and Roman Catholic communities have, for the most part, re-emerged in those areas where they were previously established. The Russian Orthodox parishes are probably distributed in a slightly more restricted pattern than before, in that the main concentrations of Orthodoxy are to be found somewhat to the west of the northern and central areas of European Russia which they previously occupied.[16]

The most significant change has to do with the distribution of the Protestant communities in Russia. From concentrations found almost entirely in European Russia at the turn of the century, significant numbers of Protestant congregations are now established in almost all parts of Russia, including Siberia and the central Asian republics. Reasons for this greatly altered distribution include:

1.   Forced migrations during World War II, from European Russia to Siberia and the Central Asia Republics. This was especially true of the German population.

2.   Massive migrations during the post war period from European Russia to correct the labor shortage produced by the industrial and agricultural development in Siberia, Kazakstan, and the Far East.

3.   Flexibility and resilience as demonstrated by the fact that the Evangelical communities were autonomous and "did not need fundamental houses of worship that the Orthodox, Catholic, and Lutheran churches require."[17]

Interestingly, the relatively small Protestant community is much more ethnically diverse than the other religious communities of the former Soviet Union.[18]

Missionaries. With the absence of freedom coupled with severe religious persecution, there was, of course, little or no discernable missionary activity in the former Soviet Union. As has been noted, that changed dramatically in 1990. "From 150 ministries working in the Soviet Union and Eastern Europe in 1982, the number rose to 311 in 1989, then to 691 in 1993, and to nearly 1,000 in 1997, with approximately 561 of the groups actively working in the former Soviet Union in multifaceted ministries."[19]

The number of Protestant missionaries increased correspondingly from a reported 1,113 foreign missionaries in 1993 to 5,617 in 1996, with an estimated 35 percent serving as career workers.[20] The presence and the efforts of these missionaries has evoked both praise and criticism from those among whom they labored, as well as from members of their sending communities. In an attempt to deal with this, some sponsoring agencies now offer guidelines as to how these workers might serve more effectively.[21]

Even more significant has been the rapid growth of indigenous Christian mission initiatives. In her *Directory of Christian Mission Organizations,* Dr. Sharon Linzey identifies 3,124 indigenous mission organizations. This total almost certainly understates the actual number, as some were no doubt reluctant to identify themselves. Nevertheless, it is clear indigenous Christian mission initiatives have been established in all the countries of the former Soviet Union, with the majority based in Russia and the Ukraine. [22] (See Table 1)

Bible Translation. The Holy Scriptures have been available in some of the languages of the former Soviet Union for a very long time. A few examples include: Slavonic, 1491 (Ukraine), Byelorussian, 1517 (Belarus), Armenian, 1565 (Armenia), Latvian, 1637 (Latvia), and Estonian, 1686 (Estonia).[23] The absence of religious freedom, however, produced a climate in which little translation work could be accomplished. During the Stalin and Krushchev repressions, it was forbidden to distribute or even read the Scriptures publicly, much less translate them into other languages.

This has changed. Thanks to the efforts of the Institute for Bible Translation and others, the Scriptures are now available in 52 languages with first translations underway in an additional 35 languages. It would be difficult to imagine any single missionary activity having a greater potential impact on the future evangelization of the peoples of the former Soviet Union. [24] (See Table 1).

Emerging Realities
Ambiguous Church/State Relations. Though the 1990 Law on Freedom of Conscience and Religion did provide religious freedom, the 1997 law passed by the Russian Parliament withdraws some of these provisions. Limitations focus especially on registration requirements for religious organizations as well as the status of "foreign religions" and religious workers. Moreover, during the past four or five years more than one third of the 89 political subdivisions of the Russian Federation have enacted laws attempting to restrict the activities of religious workers and organizations yet further.[27]

Though Russian federal law preempts laws enacted by provincial governments, little has been done to clarify the many current ambiguities. As matters stand now, on any given day, rulings handed down by Russian legal authorities may either help or hinder the efforts of emerging Christian communities. A May 1 release from the Keaton News Service reports for example, that the "Russian Union of Christians of the Evangelical Faith (Pentecostal)" was granted registration under the new law. Roman Catholic priests on the other hand, were finding it increasingly difficult to obtain visas.[28]

TABLE 1

Number of Indigenous Missions, Languages, Scriptures, "First" Translations and Least Reached Peoples in the Former Soviet Union

State	Population (1)	Indigenous Christian Missions (2)	"Living" Languages (3)	Languages With Scriptures (4)	"First" Translations (5)	Least Reached Peoples (6)
Armenia	3,800,000	5	6	2	0	2
Azerbijan	7,600,000	6	13	3	0	10
Belarus	10,300,000	130	1	1	0	2
Estonia	1,500,000	36	1	3	0	0
Georgia	5,400,000	19	10	4	1	4
Kazakhstan	16,400,000	99	6	1	1	13
Kyrgyzstan	4,600,000	18	2	1	1	11
Latvia	2,500,000	87	5	5	0	1
Lithuania	3,700,000	31	3	2	0	1
Moldova	4,300,000	239	5	1	1	2
Russia	147,300,000	1305	99	22	27	42
Tajikistan	6,000,000	7	10	1	0	8
Turkmenistan	4,600,000	3	3	1	1	7
Ukraine	50,700,000	1115	9	3	1	7
Uzbekistan	23,700,000	24	7	2	2	15
Eurasia Missionaries						
Totals	292,400,000	3124	180	52	35	125

Sources:

1. *World Population Data Sheet*: 1997
2. *Directory of Indigenous Christian Organizations of the Former Soviet Union and East Central Europe*, Dr. Sharon Linzey, 1966
3. *Ethologue*, Barbara F. Grimes, ed. 1996
4. *Scriptures of the World*, United Bible Societies, 1996
5. *World Translations Progress Report*, United Bible societies, 1996
6. *Global Guide to Unreached Peoples*, AD2000 and Beyond Movement, 1997

Another dimension of this problem is observed in the preferred status accorded the Russian Orthodox Church. Though it has often disavowed state church status, it is nevertheless perceived to act as though it is the state church of Russia. Clearly, it benefits from this ambiguity, as Jane Ellis has noted.

> In fact, the (Russian Orthodox) Church appears to have the best of both worlds, maintaining position in national life well to the fore of any other religious body. For the past few years it as been reaping all the advantages of the state church, while still claiming not to be one.[29]

It is probably safe to say the above referenced ambiguities, and others like it, will not be clarified anytime soon.

Emergence of Ethnic Identities. The 1989 Soviet census identifies 135 "nationalities" in the former Soviet Union.[25] Historically, they were always present, but were seldom acknowledged. The highly centralized Soviet bureaucracy provided little opportunity for diversity, let alone the recognition of ethnic identities.

It was little different in the pre-Revolutionary era. Russia emerged as a nation state by continually expanding its frontiers. In the process, it acquired an empire consisting of a very large number of ethnic groups. During the time of the Russian Empire as well as the Soviet era, these ethnic groups were deliberately ignored, thereby leaving Russians remarkably insensitive to ethnic problems.

> Characteristically, even liberal and social democratic groups in pre-Revolutionary Russia were inclined to ignore ethnic problems, and to treat demands of nationalities for a greater role in self-government as reactionary and enemy inspired.[26]

With the break up of the Soviet Union however, these nationalities have emerged as never before, adding yet another dimension to the missionary challenge. Any attempt to responsibly evangelize this region must give serious consideration to ethnic diversity. A total of 125 "Least Reached" people groups (less than 2 percent Evangelical or 5 percent Christian adherents) are to be found in this area. (See Table 1)

Effective Partnerships. Freedom of religion has meant almost unlimited ministry opportunities for the indigenous Christian communities. To pursue even a limited number of these, substantial resources are required, and they are available. A complicating factor however, has to do with the fact that the largest part of these substantial resources are only available from agencies based outside the former Soviet Union.

In the wake of the 1990 law, foreign based religious workers were allowed to minister in Russia with very few legal restrictions. The trend is now clearly in the opposite direction, more, rather than fewer, restrictions, especially as regards the expatriate workers. In other words, the days of "lone ranger" mission initiatives in Russia may be drawing to a close. In the future, new mission initiatives will likely require some type of partnership arrangement, if only to obtain the much needed approval of Russian government authorities. As has been rightly noted, effective partnerships require serious commitment; to the message to be proclaimed, to prayer, patience, and obedience to God, to the members of the partnership and to the people to be reached. Also, partnerships are best facilitated by attitudes that focus on learning and service. [30]

Commitment alone however, will not absolve missionaries and mission agencies from serious decision making in the future. Questions regarding dependency will persist as long as there are resources to be shared, and these questions will definitely test partnerships. Normally, whenever the availability of resources rather than opportunities for ministry drive church and mission agendas, relationships sooner or later tend to become dysfunctional.

The Rise of Islam. With 54.2 million members comprising 18.5% of the population in 1995, Islam is the second largest religion in the former Soviet Union. Since 1900 it has more than tripled in size from 14.1 million members. With the exception of Armenia, Islam is experiencing an increase of membership in every country of the former USSR. Countries with the highest annual rate of growth include Belarus (3.15%), Uzbekistan (2.96%), Kyrgyzstan (2.68%), Turkmenistan (2.63%), and Tajikistan (2.58%). Countries with the highest concentrations include Turkmenistan (85%), Tajikistan (83%), Azerbaijan (83%), and Uzbekistan (76%). Significantly, Islam gains almost a million new members every year, an astonishing 93 percent of whom are converts from other faiths.

Not surprisingly, in some of the central Asian countries, Christianity is currently experiencing a substantial annual loss of membership. Highest on this list: Uzbekistan (-8.9%), and Kyrgyzstan (-3.1%). Reasons for these shrinking Christian numbers have to do with defections, as well as the out-migration of large numbers of Russians and Germans, the latter probably accounting for the largest part of this reduction. Unless something is done soon, however, Christianity is destined to become a very small minority in several of these central Asian republics.[31]

In addition to a rapidly growing number of adherents, the geographical distribution of Islam has also expanded considerably. Significant numbers of Muslims may now be found in Siberia as well as the western countries of the former Soviet Empire; countries such as Belarus, Ukraine, Latvia and Estonia. Forced migrations and labor shortages during the Soviet era no doubt contributed in a significant way to this new trend.

Nor are these Muslims strangers to religious persecution. For them, persecution came in two forms, both emanating from Moscow: (1) blatant intolerances, accompanied by forced conversions during the establishment of the Russian Empire over a period of approximately 350 years, beginning in the mid 1500s, and (2) government sponsored attempts to drive Islam (and all religions) out of existence during the Soviet era. It has been noted that as a result, the Muslims of the former Soviet Union have likely developed an abiding distrust of any ideology associated with the West.[32]

The Need For Reconciliation. During the harsh repressions of the Soviet era, Christian leaders were faced with one of two options: (1) accommodation with government authorities in an attempt to obtain the best possible terms for their people, or (2) resistance and the inevitable consequences. It has been noted that, as a result, two very contradictory principles governed the life of the church during that time; one was self-sacrifice, the other survival:

> Alongside self-sacrificing, fearless witnesses to Christ stood collaborators who rationalized their collaboration as the only way for the church to survive the Communist regime. After the fall of Communism, no church in a post-Communist nation has managed to avoid a period of complicated and internal struggles... These conflicts were exacerbated by people who had lived through the Communist years and wanted swift, moral compensation for their sufferings.[33]

In 1989 the Latvian Lutheran Church took a radical step and elected an entirely new set of church leaders, including the archbishop. With but few exceptions, these leaders are still in office today. In most denominations however, those who accommodated and those who sacrificed now hold positions of responsibility in church structures, and attempt to work side-by-side on a day-to-day basis. Unless reconciliation has been accomplished however, this tends to be very destabilizing. It also serves as a mine field for missionaries and mission societies. Without intending to, the uninformed might easily further polarize a church body already torn by internal controversy.

What is happening in the church is also happening in post-Soviet society. It might therefore be appropriate to ask, to what extent is the church prepared to serve as an agent of reconciliation among the people of the former Soviet Union?

Conclusion

Between 1950 and 1995 the Christian community of the former USSR nearly tripled in size, from approximately 58 million to a little less than 155 million adherents, the sharpest growth spurt occurring between 1990 and 1995.[34] The Russian Orthodox, Protestant, and Roman Catholic communities grew in a comparable manner. Since 1995, however, growth seems to have leveled off. If momentum is to be regained, serious attention must be given to the following:

1) Church Planting. Mass evangelism techniques have succeeded in bringing the Gospel message to large numbers of people. These methods however, have not resulted in the planting of new churches.[35] Needed now are bold new plans and effective models that will provide for the planting of churches, not just in the large urban areas, but also in the countless rural villages where no churches are to be found.

Careful attention must also be given to the planting of churches among the various ethnic populations of Central Asia, a formidable task given their growing adherence to Islam.

2) Leadership Formation. As of May, 1996, a total of 99 Protestant seminaries and Bible Institutes had been established in the countries of the former Soviet Union.[36] Corresponding numbers of Russian Orthodox and Roman Catholic seminaries have no doubt been established as well, all of which is good news.

If the evangelization of the former Soviet Union is to be taken to the next level, however, additional steps must be taken to facilitate the identification and formation of indigenous leaders required for the re-emerging and newly established congregations. Qualified non-indigenous leaders can multiply their efforts many times over simply by serving as mentors for this new class of leadership. It is difficult to see how non-indigenous workers will accomplish very much by serving as pastors and leaders of parishes now being established in the former Soviet Union.

3) Publication of Christian Literature. As is well known, the population of the former USSR is, for the most part, highly literate. Thankfully there exist today hundreds, and perhaps thousands, of Christian titles in the Russian language. Those best informed however, suggest that up to 80 percent of these titles are translations.[37] If the huge gains in Christian membership realized over the past few years are to be consolidated, indigenous leaders must be skilled in the creation of Christian literature. This need will become even more urgent as the new Scripture translations are completed, and new communities of believers search for spiritual nurture materials not now available.

Limitations of this study. Due to lack of space, several topics were not included in this report including interchurch relations, human care issues, media ministry, Christian education, martyrdom, and cults. All of these are truly significant, but must be treated elsewhere.

A Word from Scripture. In the book of Revelation we are told that in the day of our Lord there will be gathered before Him, "from every nation, tribe, people and language, standing before the throne and in front of the lamb." (7:9) By the grace of God, much has been done to gather the great multitude from among the peoples and nations of the former Soviet Union—and much remains to be accomplished.

Notes

1   Bailey, J. Martin. *One Thousand Years: Stories from the History of Christianity in the USSR.* (New York. Friendship Press. 1987), p. 4.

2   Krindatch, Alexei D. *Geography of Religions in Russia* (Decatur, GA. Glenmary Research Center, 1996), p. 4.

3   Ibid., p. 5. Soviet and Orthodox animosity toward Roman Catholics is historical and deep seated, and helps explain why Roman Catholicism is not widely established among the Slavic population in Russia, even though it is established as the "state church" in other Slavic countries such as Poland. It also explains the fact that when foreign specialists and farmers were invited to Russia during the later part of the eighteenth and the early part of the ninteenth centuries, preference was given to Protestants.

4   Information from the World Evangelization Resource Center.

5   Krindatch, Alexei, op. cit. p. 3.

6   Ibid., p.3. During the days of the Russian Empire, atheism was also forbidden.

7   Information from the World Evangelization Resource Center.

8   Ware, Timothy. *The Orthodox Church* (Baltimore. Penguin Books, 1963). As quoted in *Christianity in Russia: The Past and the Future* by Wallace Schulz, pp. 29, 30.

9   Sawatsky, Walter. *Soviet Evangelicals Since World War II* (Kitchener, Ontario. Harold Press, 1981), p. 28.

10 Ibid., p. 29. In *Russian Resurrection,* Michael Rowe provides the following information as regards the Lutheran community. "By 1933 only 41 of the 90 Lutheran pastors who had been in office in 1929 were still at liberty, and most of them were unable to conduct any meaningful parish life. Some of the elderly pastors managed to immigrate to Germany. In 1934 the number fell further to 24 and in 1935 to eight. The last pastor in western Siberia was sentenced to prison in 1935, the pastor in Valdivostok disappeared in 1936 and the last pastor in Moscow was arrested in 1937," p. 100.

11 Ellis, Jane. *The Russian Orthodox Church: Triumphalism and Defensiveness* (New York. St. Martin's Press, 1996), p. 5.

12 Ibid., p. 29, pp. 163-165.

13 Information from the World Evangelization Resource Center.

14 Gibson, David G. "High Public Confidence in the Church" in *East-West Church and Ministry Report,* Vol. 4, No. 3, p. 9.

15 Bacon, Edwin. "The Church and Politics in Russia: A Case Study of the 1996 Presidential Election" in *Religion, State and Society,* Vol. 25, No. 3, p. 255.

16 Krindatch, Alexei D. op. cit. p. 6.

17 Ibid., p. 25. This author ascribes to the Protestants a staggering 25 percent of all religious communities in the former USSR as of 1995, and places them into three groups: (1) "Ethic Protestants"—Lutherans and Mennonites—with membership drawn primarily from the German, Latvian, Estonian, and Finnish ethnic groups. (2) "Slavic Protestants"— Baptists, Pentecostals, and Adventists—with membership from the Slavic populations all over Russia, and (3) "Non-Traditional Protestants"—the New Apostolic, Methodist, and Presbyterian churches.

    In Russia at the turn of the century to be Protestant was to be Lutheran, as Lutherans comprised 95 percent of the entire Protestant community. Today the Lutheran segment is less than 15 percent. The "Slavic Protestants" are by far the largest, and are growing the most rapidly (pp. 16-26).

18   The Roman Catholic Church, well established among the Ukrainian and Lithuanian populations, has yet to make significant inroads among the Slavic peoples of Russian origin. The Russian Orthodox Church, though established in all the countries of the former Soviet Union, is to be found almost entirely among the Slavic peoples.

19   Information by Mark Elliott as quoted by Peter and Anita Deyneka in "Evangelical Foreign Missionaries in Russia," *International Bulletin of Missionary Research* (April, 1998), p. 56.

20   Elliott, Mark and Sharyl Corrado. "The Protestant Missionary Presence in the Former Soviet Union" in *Religion, State and Society,* Vol. 25, No. 4, p.335.

21   Deyneka, Peter and Anita. op. cit. pp. 57-60. Guidelines rightly place heavy emphasis on language acquisition as well as highly developed cross-cultural capabilities for all missionaries.

22   Linzey, Sharon. *Directory of Indigenous Christian Organizations of the Former Soviet Union and East Central Europe* (Evanston. Berry Publishing Services, 1996).

23   Lupes, Liana and Erroll F. Rhodes. *Scriptures of the World* (Reading, England: United Bible Societies. 1996), pp. 77-78.

24   The Institute for Bible Translation works closely with the Summer Institute of Linguistics and the United Bible Societies.

25   *1989 USSR Population Census* (Eastview Publications: Minneapolis, 1996).

26   Katz, Zev. *Handbook of Major Soviet Nationalities* (New York:The Free Press, 1975).

27   Homer, Lauren and Lawrence A. Uzell. "Federal and Provincial Religious Freedom Laws in Russia: A Struggle for and Against Federalism and the Rule of Law" (Draft version) to be published in *Emory International Law Review*.

28   Titova, Tatyana, "Ministry of Justice Grants Registration to Pentecostal" and "Roman Catholic Priest Face Continuing Visa Difficulties," Keaton News Services, April 30, 1998 release.

29   Ellis, Jane. op. cit. p. 156.

30   Reimer, Johannes. "Mission in Post-Peristroika Russia" in *East-West Church and Ministry Report,* Vol. 4. No. 4, pp. 8, 9. A clear presentation of what effective partnerships require today.

31   Information from the World Evangelization Research Center.

32   Fairbairn, Don. "Islam in the Soviet Era" in *East-West Church and Ministry Report,* Vol. 2, No. 4, pp. 10-12.

33   Rubenis, Juris. "Rebirth and Renewal in the Latvian Evangelical Lutheran Church" in *East-West Church and Ministry Report,* Vol. 5, No. 4, p. 9.

34   Information from the World Evangelization Resource Center.

35   Akimoff, Al. "Post-Soviet Soil: Harvesting or Sowing?" *East-West Church and Ministry Report,* Vol. 5, No. 2, pp. 4, 5.

36   Information provided by Anita Deyneka.

37   Information provided by Anita Deyneka.

The Former Soviet Union and Central Asia:
Mission in the 21st Century

James J. Stamoolis

The Ultimate Aim of Mission

The premise of this vision paper is that the ultimate end of mission is to be in partnership with the Triune God in the fulfillment of the purposes of the Godhead for humankind. The work of God, the *missio Dei*, is the only correct mission. The church must continually evaluate its aims, motives, priorities, and methods to determine if these are indeed furthering the *missio Dei* or hindering the purposes of God. It is possible, and indeed demonstrable in history, that Christians have promoted concepts of mission not only inimical to but actually counter productive to the work of God.

The church's main task is the proclamation of the liberating and healing gospel of the Lord Jesus Christ which transforms the individual and through the community of transformed people challenges, renews and recreates society through the life giving power of the Holy Spirit.

The danger is that the proclamation of the message and the recreation of society will owe less to the liberation found in Christ and mediated through the working of the Holy Spirit than to a cultural or ideological construct that is not based on the revelation of God but on human tradition or intellect. Therefore, one could mistakenly promote a free market economy as the most important feature of a message of liberation. Equally, one could promote a vision of a pluralistic and accepting society as the highest form of human interaction in which all religious options are equally valid as an expression of healing. Any materialistic construct of society in which material prosperity is seen as the ultimate good must be condemned for not fully recognizing the supreme value of the spiritual nature of humankind. Perhaps the dual nature of Christ and the gospel narratives that indicate His human needs as well as His spiritual nature serve as more of a model than is often considered.

In following the example of the Lord Jesus, we need to minister to both physical and spiritual human needs, never forgetting that to overemphasize one may lead to the death of the person to whom we are attempting to communicate Christ's message.

Christ's community has significance to the task before us since there are immense physical needs that could occupy all our personnel and resources. At the same time, if we do not meet the physical need, we may not have the opportunity to present the gospel that can answer the inner questions that a person who is not starving to death or scrambling for existence will have. Furthermore, considerate and non-patronizing aid will provide opportunities for the one who has met a physical need to share a solution to the person with spiritual hunger.

None of this is new. It has been the stock and trade of mission from the example of the church in Jerusalem following Pentecost (Acts 2:44-45) through the missionary collection for the poor saints in Jerusalem (1 Cor. 16:1-4) to today's relief and development agencies.

What is critical is the same question the Apostle Paul faced with his converts, the pressure to conform to the customs of the older established church. Could the Gentiles remain Gentile Christians or did they first have to become Jewish Gentiles so that they could become Jewish Christians? I have used this awkward construction to illustrate the levels of transformation an adherence to the older Jewish Christian traditions would have entailed. We generally don't think of these Jewish Christian traditions since, for the most part, it was Paul's converts who wrote the majority of church history and the older tradition passed into oblivion. The church became a Gentile church and for several centuries in the West tolerated no dissent from the one Gentile tradition. It is arguable that the Reformation only corrected some abuses of the one tradition, but did not radically reform it. This Anabaptist criticism is echoed by the Eastern Orthodox who would also consign the Anabaptists to the same tradition.

The First Task of Mission: Theological Understanding

In light of the preceding discussion, the first task of mission is theological. The worldview of the indigenous populations of this vast area has been formed by a different history or more pointedly, histories. Any churches in the region, Orthodox, Catholic, or Protestant, have a different theological framework. Mission work that assumes that this framework needs to be totally swept away before mission will proceed will have only marginal success. These missionaries are akin to the Judaizers who were sincere in their desire to bring the message of salvation but who believed only their experiential channel to faith in Christ could be the authentic representation of the Christian faith. Mark Elliot has a telling quotation that highlights this myopia on the part of westerners.

> Orthodox and Catholics have been on hand for more than a millennium, and even indigenous Protestants have had a presence here for more than a century. More than once Fr. Leonid Kishkovsky, ecumenical officer of the Orthodox Church in America, has publicly deplored a 1991 ministry advertisement in *Christianity Today*, which under a reproduction of an icon, appealed for help in

its campaign to take the real Christ to Russia. The implication that without this initiative the real Christ would remain absent from Russia is clearly offensive to Orthodox Christians. Slavic Evangelicals, who managed to survive over 100 years of tsarist and Soviet attacks on their existence, might justifiably take offense as well. Guidelines for ministry in the East published by the British Evangelical Missionary Alliance second Fr. Kishkovsky: "Mission teams that say 'We are taking Jesus to Russia,' show that they don't understand the situation at all. Nobody is taking Jesus to Russia. He has been there all the time! His Holy Spirit was moving behind the Iron Curtain before Christians from the West could go there. Remember that many Christians you meet have lived under persecution, whilst you have lived with religious freedom."[1]

Those of us who have been asked to brief missionaries going to the former Soviet Union are amazed at how little instruction in the history, religion, and culture even short term workers are exposed to. I personally have conducted briefings on Orthodoxy with the knowledge that my presentation of an hour or two was all that these candidates would receive. The gap between the Gentiles and Jewish Christians could hardly have been wider.

Since theology in general seems to have fallen on hard times and may be regarded in some circles as irrelevant, the task of teaching how Orthodox theology differs from the western theological constructs is made doubly difficult.[2] However, this is the first task of mission if we are to faithfully and accurately proclaim a gospel of transformation that is based in Christ rather than the missionary's home culture.

We need to see how God has gone before us in His mission and to find the points of Biblical contact with the people among whom we seek to minister. To say this is not to baptize the whole of the target people's theological position, nor is it to condemn the tradition of the sending group. However, it is to ask the Holy Spirit to assist us in discerning the truth of the Gospel revealed in the Christian tradition that is present.

Mark Elliot, in the same article quoted above, deplores the lack of theological understanding of Orthodoxy that even some career missionaries evidence.[3] The first task must be a thorough understanding of the life and experience of the people the missionary seeks to serve. This is true even if the anticipated audience is the secular individual since even this type of person is a product of the general religious and cultural environment.

By the same token, we should not suppose that the people we are witnessing to have the same view of their tradition and heritage that we have learned. Even if we have been taught by Russian Orthodox experts resident in the West, the reality of those who lived under the shadow of Communism will be different. There is a limit to what we can learn without interviewing those to whom

Mission at the Dawn of the 21st Century

our evangelistic activity is directed. The purpose of theological preparation is two-fold. In the first place, to understand, as much as possible, how our theological framework has been impacted by our cultural understanding. We will not be able to see this completely until we are able to see ourselves as others outside our cultural framework see us. To do this requires considerable theological analysis. Not all who are called to minister in the former Soviet Union would be qualified to undertake such an examination. However, every Christian can be taught to see how her/his view on salvation is conditioned by the church situation that he/she experienced. Furthermore, western Christians, of whatever denomination, can be taught that the expression of the faith once delivered is not only encapsulated in their own tradition (even if they are convinced that theirs is the truest essence of the Christian faith), but is present in some form, however embryonically, in all Christian traditions that acknowledge the Triune God who has been revealed in Jesus Christ.

Theological seminaries should include in their curriculum some elementary introduction to Eastern Orthodoxy that is taught from a sympathetic standpoint. Ignorance of the traditional Christian expression of the faith in the Orthodox countries will make inter church cooperation, as described below, very difficult. The same type of education is needed to understand the other Christian traditions encountered in the former Soviet Union, Catholicism, and Protestantism in their Slavic formulations. We need to understand how the historical and cultural framework has shaped the expression of the faith if we are to work with national believers in evangelizing their country.

The Second Task of Mission: Active Listening

We need to listen to what the expressed needs of the people we would work with are. Too often, the approach is that the outsider knows what the target people need. The plan is formulated (most often an adaptation of a successful North American model) and transported to the host country. This paradigm is true whether we are talking about evangelistic work or development work. The outsider has all the answers before ever hearing the questions.

How do we accomplish active listening? In some situations the needs are obvious. If a person is starving or dying of thirst, we don't need to wait until they ask for food or drink, indeed they may be too weak to do so. But even where the need is obvious, the problem that created the need and the best solution may not be. A friend of mine who spent a dozen years in development work in an African country channeling money into projects conceived in Europe said that for all the good the millions of dollars did he might as well have dug a hole and just buried the cash. Solutions that do not take into account the local factors are not solutions at all.

The same may be true of spiritual needs. Our answers to spiritual questions that are common in the West may not be sufficient for the heart needs of the people we find ourselves among. Their fears that must be answered by the life-changing gospel may not be the fears that rule our lives. It is rare that an outsider will hear those deep fears. It is a matter of trust for me to express to you my deepest fear because I do not know what you will do with that knowledge. You may use it to control or manipulate me.[4]

To expect honesty in the expression of need requires an attitude not just of service, but of humility and willingness to make ourselves vulnerable. Humility and vulnerability are not necessarily qualities that rate high on the list of missionary qualifications. Especially for Protestants, the perfect missionary is the self-sufficient (trusting in God's grace, of course) self-starter who knows how to present his/her missionary call to the supporting churches and who knows just what to do when she/he arrives on the field. It is the rare individual and even more rare mission society that sets up operation and then asks the nationals, Christian or non-Christian what they should do. The mission is set up with a specific goal, sometimes determined with input from the "field" but often with an inspiration for a valid ministry. Many times these inspirations turn out to be from God and actually do bring blessing. But even in these cases, we could wonder if more benefit would have been obtained by having had the vision shared by nationals before the organization was set up.

Therefore perhaps I should stop my vision paper. For me to go further would risk violating what I have just said about listening. Entering where angels fear to tread, I would like to point out some areas where we could prepare to be of assistance. This is not as risky of an undertaking as it might seem since there have already been expressions of need for assistance in some of these areas. What may be a new departure will be the model of partnership that I hope to clearly advocate based on what I believe our goal of self-sufficiency and interdependence should be.

The Third Task of Mission: Biblical Partnership

What does it mean to do something in partnership? At the minimal level it is a sharing of resources. However, not all sharing of resources is partnership. In fact some sharing of resources works against partnership because of the resentment based on how the allocation of resources is made. For the most part, this is because the partner who pays the bills often exerts control over the operation. It is the golden rule of development work: he who has the gold makes the rules.

We have moved, in principle at least, to the idea of mission on six continents. That means that the whole world, not just the underdeveloped or the former colonial countries, is the locale where mission must be undertaken. This concept sets the stage for partnership because it is an explicit confession that the task of evangelization and discipleship is not completed in the former "sending" countries. It is an implicit recognition of how the church needs all its members to carry on God's task of mission. While in theory, there is mutuality, this is more difficult to achieve in practice.

To have partnership in mission there must be a mutuality in which each partner benefits from the resources of the other. When the apparent benefit is only one way, e.g. financial sponsorship of a project, then it can be questioned if indeed partnership, let alone biblical partnership exists. How can Christians in the territories of the former Soviet Union benefit western Christians with their resources? This is the question of mission for the twenty-first century.

The temptation is to answer this question in a facile fashion, talking about visits to the USA from national Christians to share in our churches or perhaps training our missionaries in cultural understanding. While these might be worthwhile activities, are they the best or only examples of partnership?

The first lesson of partnership is a frank analysis and evaluation of what our fellow believers can contribute. We need to do an analysis of the gifts and talents that our potential partners bring to the discussion. They might not realize themselves what they have to offer. Part of the purpose of this exercise is to develop their self-esteem. But a big part is to enable the westerners to honestly see the value of what our fellow believers can contribute. Some examples of the skills they might bring would be an understanding of how society functions in post-Soviet society, organizational talents appropriate to their settings, leadership gifts, and a willingness to adapt traditional forms to the post communist era. They can also testify to the sufficiency of God to meet the tribulations of life under an oppressive regime.

They also have one thing that western agencies desperately need in light of the 1997 Russian restrictive legislation on religious groups: longevity of registration.[5] The temptation is that this would be a commodity that western groups might bid for. One would hope, albeit perhaps naively, that none of this would go on. However no doubt a futures commodity market will develop in partnership agreements to circumvent the restrictions in the law. It would seem to this observer that any mercenary approaches to partnership would be seen as unbiblical means to what appeared to be a worthwhile end.

What does the West have to offer? Obviously money, personnel, and expertise would be at the top of any list. But an understanding of biblical ethics should also be listed. This is not ethics as traditionally applied in the West, where for the most part our moral dilemmas are more in keeping with what are loosely termed Judeo-Christian values. What we can contribute is a solid biblical base of ethics that is cognizant of both the biblical worldview and our own society. We need to be able to critique our own ethical blind spots before we undertake to critique our sisters and brothers ethical problems in post-communist society. Here is where a real partnership could occur as they look and in the light of biblical standards analyze our practices. We wrongly assume that those who have lived under the shadow of the Hammer and Sickle have little or nothing to offer us in certain areas. To do so is to reveal two things: our cultural arrogance and our lack of trust in the Holy Spirit working in our fellow believers.

Here we come to the real hub of partnership. We can partner because we recognize that they are equal members of the same family and share with us the same gift from the Father,[6] the indwelling of the Holy Spirit. Therefore, while we focus on the external things we bring to the partnership: money, technical skills, and even experience in material concerns, the real issue is do we both come to the table with an appreciation for the eternal dimension which is the basis for our partnership?

The missionary statesman and prophet of mission, Roland Allen put it succinctly when he showed the contrast between St. Paul and the missionaries of his day:

> St. Paul's churches were indigenous churches in the proper sense of the word; . . . his profound belief and trust in the Holy Spirit indwelling his converts and the churches of which they were members, which enabled him to establish them at once with full authority. It is not easy for us today so to trust the Holy Ghost. We more easily believe in His work in us and through us, than we can believe in His work in and through our converts: we cannot trust our converts to Him.[7]

While Allen was concerned with the planting of missionary churches, his lessons on handling finances and dealing with the church as a body apply to working with existing church bodies. His words on mission-church relationships are relevant to what passes for partnership in some settings today. "We have done everything for them except acknowledge any equality. We have done everything for them, but very little with them. . . . We have treated them as 'dear children,' but not as 'brethren.'"[8]

Real partnership starts when both partners ask what is God telling us to do to fulfill His mission.

The Fourth Task of Mission: Preparation for Service

After having outlined our need to become culturally sensitive, the imperative to listen to what our sisters and brothers are saying, and finally the real basis for any joint action, can any vision be cast for missionary service or should we remain silent and passive until we are asked to respond to what our sisters and brothers ask for?

We should not sit by quietly lest we become like the priest and Levite (Luke 10:31-32) who saw a need and passed by on the other side. We need to be prepared to offer the type of assistance that is appropriate.

What is appropriate? I refer back to our second task, that of listening, but I also offer the following suggestions.

Education for moral training is always in season. Education only for education's sake may meet some needs, especially for literacy, but ultimately education must be focused on producing moral, i.e. godly, individuals who will order society in a just and equitable fashion. This may be a challenge to those who would come from the West to teach, since we need to be honest with ourselves as to whether our societies are just and equitable. Our capitalist societies have not solved our own social problems. Notwithstanding our shortcomings, we can, with the appropriate humility and sensitivity point out biblical principles and work toward collaborative solutions.

A subset of education is education in English. Teaching English as a Foreign Language (TOEFL) will continue to be a growth industry for some time as English becomes the new lingua franca. Tent makers who teach English, especially subsets that are directed to business and industry, will be welcome.

I think that appropriate entrepreneurship training, backed by a small loan program, may also be a way of assisting the redevelopment of post communist society. This approach is fraught with dangers. To close a connection between economic advancement and the gospel may make "rice Christians" out of some people. This is where partnership with indigenous people is critical since discernment at this level is best left in their hands. A second danger is the prevalence of the Russian Mafia and the possible pressure and entanglement that this would bring. However, the presence of obstacles is not a reason not to do good. The Samaritan of Jesus' story could have thought about the problems his act of mercy would cause and be tempted not to act, but he acted regardless of the cost and personal consequences. So must we.

Notes

[1] Mark Elliott and Sharyl Corrado, "The Protestant Missionary Presence in the Former Soviet Union," *Religion, State & Society,* Vol. 25, No. 4 (1997): pp. 339-340.

[2] It reminds me of my early days as a Bible College lecturer attempting to teach Greek grammatical structure to students who had never learned English grammatical structure.

[3] Elliot: p. 338.

[4] As is done to the main character in the novel *1984*, when his tormentors play on his fear of rats.

[5] I realize that this is not true of all groups, especially those that chose not to register under the former regime.

[6] I am avoiding here the *filoque* issue which our sisters and brothers in the Eastern Orthodox Church still dispute with our western versions of the ecumenical creeds.

[7] Roland Allen, *Missionary Methods: St. Paul's or Ours?* (Grand Rapids: Eerdmans, reprint ed. 1989), p. vii.

[8] Ibid., p. 143.

Glimpses of India Today:
A Mission Approach for One Billion People

Roger E. Hedlund

Introduction

According to information received from the Congress organizers, "This Colloquium will consider India, the largest religiously free country in the world, and its challenge in the light of current developments in religion and society, including inter-religious tensions. It will seek creative responses to these developments." A large order. It is further pointed out that there are about three billion more non- Christians in the world today than in 1900, and that India and China together hold more than half of the world's non-Christians. Challenging. Ours is a new missiological age. But, the document continues, "mainstream Protestant churches have exhibited some dilution of resolve, fragmentation in response, and a certain bewilderment as to the nature of the continued Northern American involvement in the global spread of the Gospel." This Colloquium seeks to address these two interrelated issues as they impinge upon the mission task in India.

Mission today is a global affair. Decline and retrenchment in the West is offset by a vigorous and growing missionary engagement by churches in the South with Indian Christians in the lead. What, then, should be our response? Scherer's paper[1] provides a quick overview of the recent past and earmarks a number of issues to inform our quest for a meaningful definition of contemporary partnership in mission. Colloquium Two will seek to set forth the present situation in India.

Post-Missionary Asia

The foreign missionary era has ended! While not true in many regions of the world, it is certainly true in much of Asia where the world's least evangelized peoples dwell. In post-colonial India and Sri Lanka, for example, foreign missionaries are a vanishing species. This fact is cause for concern, reflection, and appropriate response. Consider the following realities.

The three billion! More than half of the world live in Asia! Out of a 1998 world population of 6 billion (5.1 2 billion in 1988), three billion are in Asia.[2] A third of this Asian population is found in China. Another third is in India. India alone has a population greater than all of Africa (650 million) and South America (290 million) combined!

Complexity. A vast sub-continent, India presents the most complex society on earth speaking a medley of 312 languages and living in 4,635 communities, according to the Anthropological Survey of India.[3] Given India's sociological and cultural diversity, "whole country" thinking is cumbersome and less productive than regional concentration, which is more manageable. People are separated not only by geography but by language, culture, and social structure. The context is further complicated by economics, politics, and religion. The present volatile situation, accentuated by bombs and Hindutva, has something of all of these factors.

Regional Diversity

Least evangelized Hindu and Muslim population groups abound in North India. States such as Gujarat and Rajasthan, geographically North, are distinct cultural regions each with its own colorful minority populations. Rajasthan is the home not only of proud Rajputs but of Bhil and Meena tribals. The Rajasthanis are mainly Hindus of numerous sub-castes and clans with a minority of syncretistic Muslims but very few Christians. Gujarat which has seen considerable conversion among its tribal populations, remains predominantly Hindu. Engagement here must take into consideration the varying receptivity of the tribes, the volatile Hindu-Muslim tensions, and the vitality of a vibrant minority Church in a state where Christian population is less than one percent.

On the opposite side of India, is an ongoing Christian conversion movement among the tribes accompanied by a militant Hindu re-conversion effort as well as legislation against conversion. West Bengal with few Christians, a large Muslim minority, and a majority of Hindus, has large numbers of needy tribals and impoverished "scheduled caste" untouchables. Bihar, classed along with Orissa as a "most backward" state, has a very substantial Christian "island" at Ranchi. Lutheran, Roman Catholic, and Anglican (Church of North India), the Ranchi Christian community is almost exclusively tribal. The Hindu Bihari population remains largely unevangelized, but in North Bihar a recent conversion movement has brought 20,000 oppressed Maltos into the Church.

The Himalayan region, stretching across several states, has its own peoples and characteristics. The same must be said regarding Jammu-Kashmir which has Hindu as well as Muslim districts and sub-regions. Central India cannot be understood apart from the immense tribal population of Madhya Pradesh overlaid by Hinduism in several forms, schools and sects. The huge area comprising Maharashtra can best be analyzed district by district each with its own tribes and majority segments and minority Christian denominations.

North East India has a complexity all its own. Primarily tribal, the region today has Hindi and Bengali non-tribal immigrant minorities as well as its native Assamese. North East India, next to South India, comprises the other "Christian India" (described as the most evangelical place on earth)! Mizoram and Nagaland are almost entirely Christian. Manipur and Meghalaya have major Christian populations. Arunachal is rapidly converting. Assam and Tripura have growing tribal Christian communities. North East India is an outreach base for missionizing other areas of South Asia.

Tribal India

Tribal India comprises one of the concentrations of Christianity in India. Tribal NEI is the only region where a majority population is Christian in four (out of seven) states! South India has a major share of India's Christians, but they remain a minority even in Kerala (about 20%) as well as in Tamil Nadu, Andhra, and Karnataka. The second concentration of Christians is in tribal India in NEI and Jharkand (Chotanagpur). Christian tribals are also found among other tribes in other areas, e.g. the Kui-speaking people in the Khond Hills of Orissa, in lesser numbers among Korkus and Gonds and other tribes of Madhya Pradesh, in the Bhil tribes of Rajasthan, more recently among the Maltos in North Bihar, also among several tribes in South Bihar including the Santals who spread into Assam and Bengal. Examples are numerous throughout the region.

India's scheduled tribes probably comprise the least known and least understood minority population in India, substantially cut off from progress by a dominant, traditional Hindu society.[4] Therefore the tribals suffer severe handicaps as they enter the mainstream in Indian life. Here is a major sociological problem. The Christian mission must respond to this pressing need and address the related issues. Isolation of India's tribes from the national mainstream fosters a natural tendency toward separation. A transition from tribe to caste is postulated by advocates of Sanskritization as a means of assimilation. Satisfactory to Hindus, Sanskritization produces contradictions and tensions destructive of the tribal entity. Hardly a solution. Assimilation means that tribals become new low castes whereas ideally they should become first class Indian citizens. Christianization is to be viewed as a viable alternative which preserves tribal culture and identity.[5]

Various social movements among the tribes should be considered including religious fringe activities, political agitations, and social protests.[6] Such movements were found among the Munda and Oraon in Chotanagpur and among the Gond in Madhya Pradesh, as well as others. Social mobility movements, aimed at solidarity of the tribe, actually resulted in vivisection. These and other dynamics are part of the force behind the Jharkhand movement and other developments.[7] Such developments are of keen missiological interest and are the stuff from which a truly Indian tribal missiology is to be constructed. It may be time for a missiological re-examination of the church's history, ecclesiology, and contemporary expression throughout tribal India.

Despite a significant on-going indigenous Indian missionary outreach, a majority of India's tribals remain unevangelized. The task is urgent. The tribes are in transition. They cannot remain in isolation forever. The church must respond.

Years ago McGavran designated the "people movement from tribe" as a distinct type of church growth. The designation remains valid. India has a large, diversified tribal population. Wherever tribals have become Christian, it has been primarily by group decision, often family by family, within the tribe. This pattern is clearly discernible at the present time in areas of conversion growth such as among the Gamits and Kuknas and other tribes in Gujarat and bordering Maharashtra and Madhya Pradesh. This is the pattern among the Bhils in Rajasthan, the Maltos in North Bihar, and also among the Kolami-speaking people in Yavatmal District in Maharashtra. The Tribal People Movement remains a valid church growth model in India today.

Caste Stratification

Volumes have been published about India's caste system. Numbers of castes have been described by anthropologists and sociologists. This paper need not replicate except to note that caste is an important and on-going aspect of the complex diversity of this ancient-modern society. Individual castes are described state-by-state in the People of India project of the Anthropological Survey of India. Caste dynamics impinge upon other social, political, religious, and economic issues.

The Poor

Economic reform and the poor. Poverty and its related concerns must stand foremost among burning missiological topics in India. In a recent CSI Jubilee publication,[8] S. Manickam states that the real wealth of the church are the Poor who constitute 60-70 percent of its membership, oppressed and marginalized by society, denied access to power and responsibility in the church. In the same volume Mohan Larbeer pleads for the church to abandon its elitist wealth and power preoccupations and respond to needs of remote rural areas neglected by government. The Amirthams' "Kerala Magnificat" tells the moving story of thousands of broken lives touched by acts of solidarity and empowerment of abused and suffering women. More seriously, K.C. Abraham's "Criteria for Development" laments the folly of development without justice which resulted in a poverty set back for 20 million people in the first year of India's economic reform. But C.T. Kurien indicates that "Globalization" policies, which benefit the rich, have made 40 percent of the population more oppressed and vulnerable. If so, this should serve to mobilize the church for mission to the Poor who daily increase in number while their socio-economic strength deteriorates.

This disturbing trend calls for more effective international partnership in mission to respond to the massive human needs. The New Economic Policy is accompanied by liberalized NRI and other policies making cooperative projects a more viable option. CSI which began as a Church of the Poor has become a Rich Church. CSI is challenged to devote this wealth to mission among suffering humanity, a pointed reminder to us all.

The Dalits. Movements of protest are a prominent feature in India today. Politics and economics, theology and missiology reflect the struggles of India's "broken" people for human dignity, security, and advance. Sushil Aaron[9] laments "the denial of affirmative action benefits for the Christians Dalits, i.e. those who have their origin in the lower castes of Hindu society."

Christian Dalits, who comprise 60 percent of the Christian population, are not entitled to "reservations" in education and in jobs as per an order passed by President Rajendra Prasad in 1950. The order said "no person who professes a religion different from Hinduism shall be deemed to be a member of Scheduled Caste." The order was later rectified to exempt the Sikhs and Buddhists who can be categorized as Scheduled Castes but left out Christian Dalits.

Dalit Christians thus are twice alienated, by discriminatory legislation as much as by the prejudicial caste system. Political assertion has not gotten them their rights. An added disability is their too-frequent assignment to second-class status within the church. As Santishree Pandit[10] states, despite an egalitarian Christian theology, caste practices have been replicated "and fossilized" in the church. Christian mission cannot ignore this aberration.

One response has been a Christian Dalit theology with A.P. Nirmal, M.E. Prabhakar, Abraham Ayrookuzhiel, James Massey, and Samuel Rayan as leading exponents. Objection has been raised that theirs is an articulation by "elite" Dalits rather than the heart cry of the downtrodden. Vinod John[11] suggests a more adequate reaction in the form of a Dalit theology of mission that will actively seek the full liberation of all the oppressed. James Massey [12] challenges the churches to become facilitators for the Dalits to regain their human dignity. Abraham Ayrookuzhiel laments that the church as a whole "does not see it as part of its mission to join the struggle of the broken Dalit people.[13] He urges dialogue and community building with Hindu "Protestant" reform movements which share a "spiritual affinity with the Christian worldview as regards sacred human dignity."[14] This proposal appears similar to the ministry of evangelical activist theologian Vinay Kumar Samuel in the Bangalore slums.[15]

The CNI Synod in 1992 called for solidarity with the demand of Christian Dalits for equal rights from the Government. The Catholic Church appears to have gone further in its efforts for justice for Dalits. Mission in India cannot ignore the cry of the oppressed. Our faithfulness to the Gospel requires deliberative action as well as veritable proclamation of the Gospel to all humans.

Urbanization

Urban context. India today has more than 300 cities. Many cities have little Christian presence. Rapid urbanization is accompanied by exploitation and oppression. More than 65% are slum dwellers. Great cities of India include Mumbai (Laksmi; wealth, business, capitalism); Calcutta (Kali; City of the Poor, City of Joy, of Hope, City of Mother Teresa & Mark Buntain); Delhi (power; religious & ethnic tensions); Chennai (cinema! politicians and film stars; bishops; great church growth; religious corruption). Hyderabad, Bangalore, Ahmedabad, Allahabad, Varanasi, Sri Nagar. . . . The life of Christ somehow must become incarnate in each urban setting.

Indian population is undergoing a massive urban redistribution, a fact which has great strategic significance. Missions in the past rightly concentrated on rural populations. In much of Asia today, however, strategizing might very properly begin with the cities. Even in largely non-Christian regions, Christian enclaves may be found in urban centers as, for example, in Muslim Sri Nagar (Kashmir) and in Hindu Varanasi (Uttar Pradesh). Christians have migrated from the rural villages to the cities where they are an important component for any thrust towards the region. The missionary movement of the past two centuries was largely rural. Strategy was dominated by regional and provincial comity considerations. Churches and leaders with a rural mind-set generally did not see far beyond the local community and district. Today's cities are an essential key for a larger strategy.

India's cities are characterized by poverty and empowerment. Cities represent a massive demographic shift and social upheaval. Urbanization provides an arena for mission.

Urban church multiplication. Mission today increasingly is an urban affair, and rightly so. The multiplication of new congregations is a distinct possibility in any of India's 300 cities where the Gospel is already planted and vibrant. Chennai (Madras) provides the most obvious example where the Christian population is steadily increasing and new churches are found throughout the city—the story is told elsewhere and need not be repeated here.[16]

Much more should be said on this important subject. The mission of the Church in India today has shifted from a predominantly rural bias that characterized the colonial era to urban centers of influence. Relatively easy to begin new churches in centers of Christian population such as Madras, it is a challenging task to do so in more hostile cities in the North where Christians are a rare commodity and the Christian message largely unknown. Today's mission frontiers are increasingly urban and among the major Hindu-Muslim population blocks which comprise numbers of the least-evangelized.

Religious Diversity

Not infrequently India is interpreted in terms of religion. Religiously, India is not to be viewed merely as Hindu. In addition to Hindu India, one must also consider Muslim India, Tribal India, and Christian India. The latter is an essential starting point for Christian evangelical strategizing toward all of the other Indias. There is also the India of lesser minorities, e.g. Jains, Sikhs, and Buddhists. Religious fundamentalism, Hindu and Muslim, has created an explosive situation with tragic repercussions in Coimbatore, Mumbai, and other cities.

It is necessary to take a closer look at the context which is the matrix for mission today. A prominent feature is the religiosity of the Indian populace. Politicization of religion has become a hazardous contemporary reality. The recent 1998 election has produced uncertainty, inter-religious tensions, and fears of communal violence. "The communal agenda of the BJP and its ideological project of Hindu Rashtra stand directly opposed to the foundations of a modern Indian state. Without safeguarding these foundations, the unity and integrity of this vast country cannot be maintained," writes Sitaram Yechury (*The Hindu,* March 11 1998).

Hindutva is a recent phenomenon resting upon a flawed interpretation of history. As Mallampalli[17] demonstrates, the perception of Hinduism as an ancient, monolithic world religion is a modern construction largely based upon the imaginings of western Orientalists. Hindu tolerance historically meant an aggregation of diverse cults, different religious sects, contrasting philosophical schools and ideologies in sharp contrast to the monolithic Hindutva proposed by religious fundamentalists.

Of the world's 988 million Muslims, most are in Asia: India with the second largest Muslim population in the world, exceeded only by Indonesia, has more Muslims than Pakistan, Bangladesh, or the Arab world. The Hindu world of 736 million consists mainly of India and Nepal—with minorities in Fiji, Singapore and Malaysia, South Africa, Nairobi and London. . . . The world's 20 million Sikhs are located mainly in India (Punjab and Delhi), but also in Vancouver. . . . Probably half of the world's 100 million tribal religionists are found in India, centered in Madhya Pradesh! India's tribals are off-limits to foreign missionary activity, yet they are a primary focus of more than 200 Indian mission agencies and several thousand Indian missionaries.[18]

Christianity

India has 2000 years of Christian history! Christianity is an important and integral part of the religious context of India which has a most ancient, apostolic tradition. Historically Christianity is one of the ancient religions of India. India today has an estimated 22,460 Catholic and 97,796 Protestant congregations.[19]

Christian distribution. With 2,000 years of Christian tradition, Christianity is firmly established and respected in the South (Christian India). A favorable attitude from this 2000 year presence is one of the factors creating a climate of response in the South. Great Roman Catholic and Protestant missionary evangelists and scholars of the past were well received and laid a foundation upon which the church continues to build in South India. In Madras, where the congregations increased from 525 to 700 in five years (1981-1986), the Christian population grew from 7% to more than 8%, and is now estimated at 12% of the population.[20] Most of India's Christians are found in the coastal areas of 4 southern states and in 4 tribal states in North East India.

The other Christian India consists of Tribal Christian majorities in NEI & Ranchi. Christianity is only beginning to take root in North India. Christianity in North India to a large extent began with the coming of William Carey and the Serampore missionaries only 200 years ago.[21] The contrast is sharp. Christianity, which is well known in the South, is scarcely known at all in much of the North. In many regions the Gospel has not begun to scratch the surface. Nevertheless Christian influence is far-reaching, especially in education and social concerns. The great growth of the Church is yet to come in most regions of North India.

It may be helpful to take a closer look at certain contemporary expressions of Christianity.

The mega-church. India today has several mega-churches, congregations of worshipers numbering several thousand. Most (with the exception of NEI) are found in key urban centers such as Mumbai, Hyderabad, Chennai, Shillong. Mega-churches are a recent phenomenon. Such churches were not part of the missionary landscape of the past. Mega-churches are a testimonial to the impact of capable Indian leadership. They are an indigenous product!

Known mega-churches in India include churches with traditional Baptist, Presbyterian, and Pentecostal denominational identities as well as Independent charismatic fellowships.

One striking example is the New Life Assembly of God at Saidapet in Madras. With a brief 20 year history, this dynamic congregation under Indian leadership grew to 2,000 attendees in 1993, then 5,000, now 7,000 Sunday worshipers through a program of evangelistic preaching, systematic teaching, and leadership multiplication-training.

In Hyderabad, Pastor G. Samuel has led the Baptist Church Hyderabad in a steady expansion beyond 2,000 members. A feature of this church is its training and induction of lay elders who in turn oversee an extensive outreach program of church planting in a 50-mile radius of the city.

A multiple use of church facilities by several ethnic groups is common among these churches. On Sunday it is not uncommon to share facilities. Separate language congregations, each with its own pastors, meet at stated times throughout the day. Thus a Telugu congregation may be followed by a Marathi group, an English congregation preceded by a Hindi service, Tamils share with Kannada worshipers, etc., according to need. Multi-use is an emerging urban pattern in India among many types of churches. Methodists in Bombay, for instance, follow this pattern.

Cell-group churches. Cell-groups, called by various names, may be found in various forms in a number of churches. Frequently this may mean a small fellowship or nurture group within a larger church. This is the case with the weekly "house church" of St. Andrew's Church in Madras that meets in the homes of members.

A cell-group church is a distinct model. In Bombay the large and rapidly growing charismatic New Life Fellowship centers its entire ministry in more than 1500 cell-groups which function as "mini-churches" engaging in worship, Bible study, and outreach throughout the city. A "congregation" of more than 12,000, in terms of numbers, New Life Fellowship would qualify as a "mega" church! But it owns no central edifice. There is no large celebration function, nor the possibility of such a gathering on a regular Sunday basis except through rented "celebration centers." The church is found dispersed throughout the city and is engaged in missionary outreach in every state of India. The cell-church deserves closer attention and study as an urban church model.

Indigenous "small church" models. Glimpses of a uniquely Indian model may be seen in remote places, in the villages, and in urban slums and housing colonies, away from the trappings of western (missionary) Christianity. This is not to disparage the monumental contributions of the foreign missionaries—a story that is outside the purview of this paper. But for the most part Christianity in India is viewed as something foreign and exotic. Hence the considerable discussion about contextualization, indigenization, Indianization of the Church. Whatever the language, the process implies a search for something that is lacking: an authentic Indian model both biblical and rooted in the soil. Christianity with a 2000 year history in India, still is perceived as less than Indian!

The hypothesis that a more uniquely Indian model is to be found among some of the lesser known fringe groups, sects, and movements is the basis for a Pew-funded "Churches of Indigenous Origins" project.[22] Of significance is the fact that the entire Church in nearby Nepal is an indigenous Church having emerged within the past 50 years through Nepali initiative despite persecution and repression. The Nepali Church is completely indigenous in origin, until recently with no foreign missionary connections. Hundreds, yes, thousands, of Independent Churches of Indigenous origins are found in several regions of India.

Diaspora Mission in Reverse

Dramatic emergence of new forces for evangelization that God has raised up in South India and in the north east must be part of any consideration as to the continued role of North American involvement in global mission. The indigenous Indian missionary movement proceeds largely from these two regions. Another significant development is the involvement of nonresident Indians in mission to their motherland. Diaspora, says Tom Houston, is a neglected biblical and theological theme for mission. Diaspora mission is a reality in India today as NRIs create new models of response.

Missionary work as traditionally understood is not possible in many parts of the world. A majority of the world's least evangelized peoples are not accessible to western missions. Creative new models are needed.

Street children, the homeless, women, the handicapped, the substance addicted and AIDS afflicted, prostitutes and their children—these are some of the human needs addressed by Indian Christians in mission today. Christian apologetics in Hindu contexts and other categories are pioneered by Indian Churches in mission.

Conclusion

India has much to teach the world from her perception of Christ.

According to some scholars, all religions are syncretic to some degree, and all missions lead to syncretism.[23] If so, this applies to us all! Christianity has proven to be culturally translatable in India. Therefore there is great hope, and the possibility of big surprises, as the Kingdom spreads and the community of faith takes shape in every region among the diverse peoples, tribes and tongues of India's cities, towns and villages.

Notes

[1] "Key Issues to be Considered in Global Mission Today" by James A. Scherer.

[2] Population statistics are approximate, based on world population data of the Population Reference Bureau and other sources. Religious statistics for the most part are from David Barrett's annual statistical tables.

[3] This information was released by the Anthropological Survey of India, said to be the longest and most extensive social science project ever carried out in India. Completed in 1992, but not yet published, the data fills 120 volumes. The Survey produced a definitive list of communities including castes, tribes, minorities, and scheduled castes.

[4] R. A. Schermerhorn, *Ethnic Plurality in India* (Tucson: University of Arizona Press, 1978).

[5] See *Religion and Modernization* by Augustine Kanjamala and other studies.

[6] Stephen Fuchs' survey of *Rebellious Prophets: A Study of Messianic Movements in Indian Religions* (Bombay, 1965), is of value and should be consulted.

[7] L. K. Mahapatra, "Social Movements Among Tribes of India"(1972).

[8] *Greater Peace Closer Fellowship Fuller Life,* edited by Lily & Sam Amirtham (Chennai: Church of South India, 1997).

[9] Sushil J. Aaron, "Christians need to create niche in the public square" (1998).

[10] Santishree D.N.B. Pandit, "Dilemmas of Dual Identity of Dalit Christians in India," *Dharma Deepika* (December 1997):39-48.

[11] Vinod John, "Towards a Dalit Theology of Mission" (1994).

[12] James Massey, *Dalits in India: Religion* as a *Source of Bondage or Liberation with Social Reference to Christians* (New Delhi:Manohar, 1995).

[13] Ayrookuzhiel, "The Church's Mission to the Dalits," p.294.

[14] Ibid., p.304.

[15] Vinay Samuel's philosophy and ministry are portrayed by Chris Sugden in his published thesis, *Seeking the Asian Face of 1997.*

[16] Hedlund, *Evangelization and Church Growth Issues in the Indian Context* (1992).

17 Chandra Mallampalli, "The Construction of Modern Hinduism: Contributing Factors" *Dharma Deepika* (December 1997):49-54.

18 Various statistics have been published with estimates at 11,000 to 20,000 Indian missionaries. One leader recently estimated publicly that 90% of the mission effort is devoted to the tribals who comprise 11% of the population.

19 S. Aaron, "Christians need to create niche in the public square," 1998.

20 S. Subramaniam, *Strategy to Reach Greater Madras* (1996), p.18.

21 There were prior missions including those of the Roman Catholics, the Anglicans and others. However these earlier missions generally were colonialist and for the most part did not direct the Gospel to the Indians. The brilliant Henry Martyn was a most notable exception as were certain other evangelical chaplains of the East India Company.

22 Research is just beginning. A one-year academic research project, "Churches of Indigenous Origins, The 'Little Tradition' In Indian Christianity," began in August 1997, and is expected to yield considerable information. This is a team project supported by the Pew Charitable Trusts, administered through the Overseas Ministries Study Centre directed by Roger E. Hedlund at Chennai with research in North East India guided by Dr. O. L. Snaitang at Shillong.

23 Andre Droogers, "Syncretism: The Problem of Definition, the Definition of the Problem," 1998.

References

Aaron, Sushil J. "Christians need to create niche in the public square," Unpublished manuscript (Chennai: Deepika Educational Trust. 1998).

Amirtham, Lily & Sam, eds. *Greater Peace Closer Fellowship Fuller Life* (Chennai: Church of South India. 1997).

Ayrookuzhiel, Abraham. "The Church's Mission to the Dalits: A Dalit Perspective." *Mission Studies* Vol. XIII, 1&2, 25/26 (1996):291-305.

Barrett, David. *World Christian Encyclopaedia* (Nairobi: Oxford University Press, 1981).

Bentley, David. "Islam and Human Rights-Protocols for Christian Understanding," *Dharma Deepika* (June 1996):29-41.

Caplan, Lionel. "Popular Christianity in Urban South India," *Religion and Society* XXX, 2 (June 1983):28-44.

Conn, Harvie M. and Samuel F. Rowen, eds. *Missions and Theological Education in World Perspective.* (Farnington, Michigan: Associates of Urbanus, 1984).

David, George. *Communicating Christ Among Hindu Peoples* (Chennai, 1998).

Droogers, Andre. "Syncretism: The Problem of Definition, the Definition of the Problem" in *Dialogue and Syncretism, An Interdisciplinary Approach,* edited by Gerald Gort, Hendrik Vroom, Rein Fernhout & Anton Wessels, 7-25 (Grand Rapids: Eerdmans; Amsterdam: Editions Rodopi, 1989).

Fuchs, Stephen. *Rebellious Prophets: A Study of Messianic Movements in Indian Religions.* (Bombay: Asia Publishing House, 1965).

Garrison, David. *The Nonresidential Missionary Strategy* (Monrovia, CA: MARC, 1991).

Hedlund, Roger E. "Subaltern Movements and Indian Churches of Indigenous Origins," Prepublication draft article for *Journal of Dharma* (January 1998).

International Bulletin of Missionary Research. Various issues, especially David Barrett's statistical tables every January.

John, Vinod. "Towards a Dalit Theology of Mission," Unpublished manuscript. (Chennai: Deepika Educational Trust, 1994).

Johnstone, Patrick. *Operation World,* Revision in process, 1993.

Mahapatra, L.K. "Social Movements Among Tribes of India"(1972).

Mallampalli, Chandra. "The Construction of Modern Hinduism: Contributing Factors," *Dharma Deepika* (December 1997):49-54.

Massey, James. *Dalits in India: Religion as a Source of Bondage or Liberation with Special Reference to Christians* (New Delhi: Manohar, 1995).

Newbigin, Lesslie. "Theological Education in a World Perspective" in Conn and Rowan (1984):3-18.

_____"Can the West Be Converted?" *International Bulletin of Missionary Research* Vol.11, No.1 (January 1987):2-7.

Pandit, Santishree D.N.B. "Dilemmas of Dual Identity of Dalit Christians in India," *Dharma Deepika* (December 1997):39-48.

Population Reference Bureau. "World Population Data Sheet," Washington, D.C., 1988.

Schermerhorn, R.A. *Ethnic Plurality in India* (Tucson: University of Arizona Press, 1978).

Subramaniam, S. *Strategy to Reach Greater Madras* (1996)

Ward, Ted. "Servants, Leaders and Tyrants" in Conn and Rowan (1984):19-40.

Webster, John C.B. "Christians, Sikhs and the Conversion of the Dalits" in *Dharma Deepika* (June 1998):25-32.

Younger, Paul. "Hindu-Christian Worship Settings in South India" in *Hindu-Christian Dialogue: Perspectives and Encounters,* edited by Harold Coward (Maryknoll: Orbis, 1990),191-197.

India Colloquium:
Vision Paper

Roland E. Miller

Introduction

A question arises as to what distinguishes a mission vision paper from futurology. Futurology, at its best, is intended to be an intelligent appraisal of what lies ahead in the light of the past and present. Perhaps there is no difference, other than a verbal one. On the other hand, futurology as it is ordinarily used, has a personalist and speculative flavor. It may not have direct application in terms of idea shaping and planning. Whether that is true or not probably a mission paper should have a concern for operational possibilities. It is not merely to be imaginative and stimulating, but it can also be readily debated and challenged. The difference may therefore be a simple one of time frame. A vision paper cannot leap into the future as far as futurology might.

Against this background we will conservatively set a time frame of about 30 years to look ahead missionally, a period often described as a "generation." The period of 25-30 years is now fairly commonly used for long-term planning in the business world. We may therefore ask, what should Christians—in the first instance, Indian Christians, but in the final analysis surely all Christians—desire and endeavor to see accomplished in India over the next three decades? Others might prefer to push the time frame to 2047, thereby moving to the date when India celebrates its centenary as a free nation. What a great moment that will be, and because of that, it is hard to resist the symbolism of "the next fifty years." In this paper, however, I will draw the circle in to a three-decade period for which it is easier to find an empirical base.

It seems to me that there is an unchanging element in the task of mission. The unchanging element has to do with God's salvific will as it has been classically understood by the church; with Christ's mission command, and with our determination to be faithful to both. Within that unchanging reality we must reckon earnestly with the factor of change. If to live is to change, then to be alive missionally is to change missionally. In an essay on "Missions Tomorrow" that I prepared twenty years ago I tried to express the factor of change in mission:[1]

> Becoming what we are, present or future, is a risky business. To become what we are, the lovers of the world, as we travel on that journey into the unknown called missions tomorrow, will involve

us in a great variety of hazards; but perhaps the greatest risk of all in ministering to the future will be the risk of change. The world is changing, conditions are changing, people are changing, and no anticipatory analyses or well-laid plans will suffice either to control the change or to manage the future to our satisfaction. In fact, the church in mission to a changing world will itself undergo change with all the peril and opportunity that implies. Perhaps the proper attitudinal response to the call of God into the far country of missions tomorrow may therefore be that suggested by Eugen Rosenstock-Heussy's phrase: *respondeo etsi mutabor*. "I will respond, even though I shall be changed." That resolve is sufficient material for the Spirit of the future, who has always enabled and will always enable His people to speak His Word to every age, and to do so in faithful obedience.

Despite the changeless elements, therefore, Christian mission in India, if it is alive, will both have to respond to change and create change. To respond to change requires a reasonably accurate assessment of the major factors involved in the state of India and the condition of the church. To create change in order to move forward requires a responsible estimate of the achievable goals and appropriate planning possibilities. The latter, it seems to me, is the task of the Colloquium. I would like to suggest some groundwork for that discussion by touching on the future condition of society and church.

India: The Next Generation

Any consideration of mission in India must attempt to answer the question: What is the probable profile of Indian society in the medium future? This discussion will be restricted to five components of that profile, recognizing that there are many other factors.

The Socio-Political Condition

India's democratic approach and population growth will be treated under this head.

Arguably the major and most promising social experiment in the world has taken place in India in the period 1947-1997. What amounts to 15 per cent of the global population within one country, a country renowned for its legendary disparities, has decided to combine its varieties into a modern functioning democratic society. The potential promise of the experiment for the world is undeniable. If it is "successful," it may also become possible for the world as a whole, with its wider disparities, to fashion itself into a working global community. The question is: will the experiment continue? I suggest that when the year 2028 arrives, it will still be alive and reasonably well.

The basis for the assertion rests on three points. The first relates to the fact that the Indian system is not throwing up strong leaders who might take society into a new direction. This lack of dominant leaders is a reality in many societies in the world today. It can bring weakness and even chaos, but it can also result in the continuation of the tradition. The second factor is that the currently upward mobile economic development in India precludes the perceived need for and undermines a possible basis for the emergence of demagogic leadership. Finally, the coalition format of contemporary politics has been at least subconsciously accepted by the populace as a balance-of-power methodology appropriate for a multicultural and multi-religious political reality.

Conclusion: It may be assumed that as one element in the democratic experiment a measure of religious freedom will continue to be politically necessary and supported by the public. With it the freedom for gospel work will continue, although its modalities may be affected by some restraints.

Planning Implication: Mission planners are not driven to frenetic forms of activity forced by emergency conditions, but rather responsible three-decade planning is possible and desirable.

The population of India is a highly significant factor in the sociopolitical condition of India, and has great implications for mission planning. By 2028 that population will be about 1.523 billion people, exceeding China's population of 1.517 billion. Thus India will have become the largest nation in the world. By the end of the new century (2999) the estimated population will be two billion.[2]

This development will not be the result of failed population control efforts in the present, but rather it will represent permutated growth carried forward from the past. By the year 2000 the annual growth rate in India will have been reduced to 1.5 per cent, and by 2028 the 3.4 per cent fertility rate will have been reduced to 2.1, or replacement level.[3] These figures represent tremendous efforts and achievement. However, in absolute numbers the population will continue to grow throughout our planning period, with the current annual increase of 14 million rising to about 18 million.

From a social point of view one cannot view this situation with equanimity. The same must be true for a missiological perspective.

Conclusion: The fact that by 2028 India will be verging on the largest population in the world, combined with the probable fact of a continued freedom for the proclamation of the gospel, will constitute the most important contemporary mission reality. It will require all those aware of the reality to have a willingness of mind and spirit to deal with it freshly.

Planning Implication: Mission planning must include a way to make India's situation come alive in global Christian consciousness, and even more importantly awareness—creation must be assured among Indian Christians with respect to their unique role, as well as real encouragement for the formidable task.

The Economic Condition

There are varying estimates of the future of India's economy. They range from rather flowery assessments from government sources to rather critical evaluations from national and foreign economists. The former point to the drastic changes in economic management that took place between 1991 and 1993, which have irretrievably altered the course of India's economic development and have produced the current upsurge in the national economy. The latter unfavorably compare the Indian GDP growth rate of 4 per cent between 1960 and 1990 with the high rates of the "Asian tigers."[4] To those who have observed the change from 1947 to 1997, however, it is clearly evident that the Indian economy is on the march. Moreover, since 1994 the growth rate has been 6 per cent, which means a doubling of the national income. The impact of the improvement is visible in the standard of living, the growth of consumerism, and the increase in the size of the middle class. It also, unfortunately, is visible in a further distancing between the rich and the poor, especially in cities.

Will the development continue? India's economy is now less isolated than it was during the first 40 years of its existence when it was protected within the entanglement of government regulation and it is not much more susceptible to the vagaries, as well as to the benefits, of Asian and global economic development. In view of recent events in Asia, prophets of doom suggest that Asian economies are beginning a long recession period. The opposite, however, may be closer to the truth. Optimists estimate that rapid growth will begin again soon, and by 2025 "Asia will likely resume its place at the center of world economies," accounting for 50-60 per cent of world income, a share it is said to have had in 1820 before the industrial revolution. Relative to the U.S.A., per capita income will grow from 9.2 per cent to 21.3 per cent.[5] While India is always placed at the low end of the scale of development, it will continue to participate in the improvement.

Indian economic development must also be placed within the context of global reality. Two related factors, in particular, must be noted: the rate of foreign investment in India, and the increase of new global monopolies. In regard to the former it may be noted that almost all the household savings (83 per cent) are utilized for public sector activities, leaving private development heavily dependent on foreign capital. However, only 3.8 per cent of direct foreign investment is channeled into India, contrasting with 25 per cent in China.[6] It is maintained, therefore, that there is need for a second wave of economic liberalization. This position, held by many economists, is a problematic one for the government. It conflicts with the continued commitment of the India body politic to socialist realism in relation to the poor, which a large majority of Indians support. It is also received cautiously because of concern about the multiplication of global monopolies that place national destinies into distant hands.

The new monopolies include: a) technological ones, requiring huge expenditures that only a wealthy state can envisage; b) control of worldwide financial markets; c) access to the planet's resources, especially oil; d) media and communication monopolies; and e) armaments.[7] Remembering the past, the nation's leaders will remain wary of the onset of a new economic colonialization, and this resistance will counteract the liberating aspects of economic globalization.

Conclusions: The Indian economy will continue to grow modestly, guarded from wild fluctuation by its protective policies and social commitments. By 2028, the development of a core middle class, already about 160 million in number, will be virtually complete. Along with that will come some negative values, including materialistic emphases on possessions and self-centeredness. Secularization and its accompanying phenomena will be visible at all levels, and the poor will become poorer.

The Cultural Condition

The cultural transition that is visible in 1998 will be accelerated by various forces of change and, by 2028, society in India will be even more sociologically complex than it already is. The change is remarkable: it seems to be qualitative as well as quantitative.

In Malabar, in December (1997), I noted that a carpenter now receives Rs.150 plus Rs.15 food daily. But I am more taken by what appears to be a qualitative rather than a merely quantitative change. Admittedly that judgment is partly intuition. However, everywhere one looks there is some sort of change. The change has its symbols but runs much deeper than the symbols. For example, the citizens of the southern city of Calicut used to joke that their town had not visibly altered since Vasco da Gama arrived (whose 500th anniversary is being very reluctantly commemorated). The presence of a new five-star Taj Residency Hotel, however, seems to signal something new. The transformation is bordering on the radical. Something very new is being born—it is not at all yet clear as to what its final stage will be—and in that process the old is dying. The transformation seems to be bringing India close to the analysis of Paul Tillich that the birth of the new always implies the death of the old.

That, to some, may appear to be an over-stated opinion requiring more evidence and contrary to the ethos of India. Indian history, after all, is not normally described in those terms. It has always absorbed, comprehended, added the new while retaining the old. Is it possible, however, that something more profound is going on, an actual metamorphosis? In a huge and very youthful society, with the remembering generation almost gone, an ersatzian new is in the process of formation that words like modernization, materialism, secularization, and so on, only partially cover. It may be suggested that a genuinely new Indian culture is being born involving most aspects of life, and the fact that some of its phenomena seem unattractive in comparison to the old is hardly the point.

In that regard two cultural phenomena, in particular, will have strong impact on mission planning. The first I will call the superficialization of Indian culture. The second I will refer to as the "youthification" of India.

A kind of surface mono-culturalism, over laid on India's diversity, will become more and more evident within our three-decade time frame. We may refer to it as a superficializing effect that in turn has an apparent but shallow universalizing influence. It will issue from a powerful combination of TV/high speed technology/new communications media/global advertising. It will generate a kind of deceptive "airport sameness." When combined with the increase of common consumerism, it will have a major impact on mores. The inherent depth, gentleness, sense of time, live and let live philosophy, and other aspects of the traditional culture will be challenged though not entirely replaced. The movement to change will be accelerated by Indian society's inherent adaptability. On the other hand, it will be resisted by the proponents of the traditional culture and by representatives of religion, but even though the resistance at times will take on revivalist and chauvinist forms, it will be generally ineffective. This is powerful change.

Conclusions: The superficialization will undermine commitment to traditional values that have yielded stability and a unitive ethos, at the same time being too trivial itself to produce a new bonding effect. It will reduce the sense of importance that religious truth has held. Reactive forces will develop, some of which will be marked by an emphasis on formal identity, a probable loss of spiritual content, and at their worst, psychologies of resentment and anger. On the other hand, "lovers of God" may recognize each other more clearly, and may wish to work together in cooperative action to deal with societal problems.

Planning Implications:

a. The term indigenization will have to take on different content.

b. Indian Christians will have to seek learning from western Christians as to why the latter have *failed* to deal effectively with secularization.

c. It will become apparent that only the figure of Jesus Christ will be powerful enough to stand up against the new forces, as contrasted with Christian institutional forms.

d. Mission planning will have to be tuned in and innovative, even as it remains faithful to the hallowed core of the kerugma.

e. The possibility of united religious efforts to deal with common moral issues will have to be addressed.

By 2028 the youthfulness of India, in terms of its population, will be even more visible than it is today. It is true that the percentage of senior citizens will increase, but that factor will not be so obvious in our time-frame as the "youthification" of the nation. Current statistics suggest that about 35 per cent of the population is under the age 15, while 45 per cent may be under 18.

These percentages will not decline as the current increase in the population works its way through to 2028.

As this large body of young people comes into positions of leadership and brings with it its new technological learning, great energy will be released and formidable achievements can be expected. The loss of cultural memory alluded to above will be offset by a strong sense of possibility. The industrial revolution set in motion by Nehru, the agricultural revolution started by Shastri, and the technological revolution initiated by Rajiv Gandhi will be harmonized or at least combined in some way by an imaginative youth. The new form will perhaps come down heavily on material culture, blended in a unique Indian paradigm that will include traditional elements, modern technological components, and post-modern fragmented pieces. The development will take the society closer to western forms, to which youth are open through the media, and to the issues of secularism.

Since the western effort to deal with those issues has not been marked by success, one cannot look upon the Indian development with equanimity. It may be argued that India's traditional spirituality will carry it through. That would be to place one's head in the sands and not to reckon with the magnitude of the issue. Or is it possible, since India is at the beginning of the process, to contemplate the development of an accompanying spiritual revolution, or at least a renewal of the spirit, to prevent the plague of materialism? It is evident that something must happen rather quickly to avoid the same path that others have taken. To call for spiritual revolution, however, is to call for Christian vocation. Indian youth desperately need models and heroes. Does it fall within mission planning to examine how to present Jesus as an authentic model for the new age?

Planning Implications:

a. There must be awareness-creation regarding the gravity of the situation and its potential for stress and loss.

b. It is crucial to involve Christian youth in the awareness-creation and in the content and work of the gospel.

c. Mission planning must include an invitation to the youth of India to meet the 30 year old Christ, model and hero.

The Religious Condition

The formal statistical profile of religious India will not change dramatically in the next 30 years. A secular source reflects the general demographic analysis. It suggests 80 per cent Hindus, 11.1 per cent Muslims, 2.4 per cent Christians, 0.8 per cent Buddhists, 0.5 per cent Jains, 1.9 per cent Sikhs, and 3.2 per cent others. Christian sources differentiate the figures, and tend to suggest a considerably higher percentage of Christians (from 3 to 4.7 per cent).[8] Factors that may produce some change by 2028 include the Muslim birth-rate, Hindu re-conversion activities, and Christian outreach. Barrett's attempt to distinguish believers and secularists will have increasing merit, but its confident application will remain difficult.

Hindus will be increasingly affected by the reactionary influence of their political wing, as the latter unhesitatingly plays the religious card. The traditional recognition of *ishta-devata* and *adhikara* theory will be down-played as forms of neo-Hinduism urge the greater development of a common Hindu consciousness and as some portray the faith as a "membership" religion rather than as a way of life or as a family of religions comprehending and delighting in various views.

Muslims will strengthen their already highly developed minority psychology, resulting in less flexibility and openness to religious change. The vibrant Indian Muslim intellectual life of the past will continue to suffer from a utilitarian approach and a preoccupation with salvation by politics. Paradoxically, Muslims will become the most outspoken defenders of the secular state.

Minorities in general will become more conscious of each other's common problems. Christians will feel more targeted than they have felt in the foregoing half-century. The slaying of four Indian missionaries in northeast India since 1992 is already viewed as an alerting trend.[9] Christians will be compelled to emerge from a kind of protective state of wary caution to forthright responses and new relationships.

The lack of commending religious leadership will be felt particularly by minorities. It will result in youth seeking their models from the field of arts, politics, or business, rather than from religion. Religious leaders in Christianity, already under criticism, will be more and more consigned by laity to the same "dustbin" that Muslims have already relegated their ulama. Even the current resurrection of charismatic leaders in right-wing Hinduism will be short-lived, and by 2028 will have been effectively destroyed by the political disease. The vacuum of religious leadership will be a startling phenomenon in the India of the next generation.

This will make it extremely difficult for the religions to deal with the internal cancer of superficialization and secularization. The latter will present a similar challenge to all religions, producing in them a concern for survival. Survival strategies and the resulting psychological defensiveness may—unless jolted in some way—become a series of fortress mentalities rather than the dialogical openness and mutual conversation that the situation will require.

Conclusion: The evangel-sharing task of the Christian church will be more difficult as it sails between the Scylla of hardened religious identity and the Charybdis of nominal belief, as it simultaneously strives to keep the faith and to communicate it, as it seeks not only to maintain the light of the Gospel in static lighthouse fashion, but to carry it high, confidently, and energetically forward as an Olympian runner with the sacred flame.

Roland E. Miller   *141*

Planning Implication:

a. The task of evangel-sharing will have to be made the primary discussion issue among Christian communities in the near future, and the discussions will of necessity have to be rigorously honest, in touch with the real world, aware of the restraints, and controlled by Christian hope.

b. A new contextually alert theology of mission must be formulated that applies evangelical insight to the situation, and that is controlled by Christian hope; in such a theology of mission the task of Christian mission will be seen as equally crucial for the church's condition as it will be for Indian society.

c. Both up-front ministries of reconciliation and an out-spoken defense of the oppressed will become necessary.

d. A high quality of leadership will be required, and must be assured.

The Church: Condition and Task

The task of the church—to make Christ visible, to proclaim the good news, and to serve in Christ's pattern, all within the context of a changing society—is a wondrous and demanding vocation. It raises the question of the church's own condition and the things it must do. In dealing with the condition of Indian society above we have already entered into the questions. The vision of where the church in India will be in 2028 divides into two possible questions: where will it be, extended out a generation along the lines of its current development, and where could it be with renewed determination and planning? Indian Christians are the ones to assess these questions and their possible answers, and what follows can only be described as an observation by a participant friend.

The Church and its Mission: Mere Extension or Determination?

Statistically, some have projected that the Christian population of India will experience an annual increase of 4 per cent by 2028, up from the present 3 per cent. Over the 30-year period from 1960-1990 the Christian population increased by 250 per cent, as compared to the general growth rate of 190 per cent. Following the same pattern, by 2028 the Christian population will increase from the present 35 million (cf. Johnstone) to 52 million. This growth will represent an encouraging, albeit modest, increase along present lines, and will reveal that the church in India is evangelistically active. By 2028 the Christian population in India will exceed that of many nations. On the other hand, some may regard this projection as one that could be readily enlarged, given the inherent potential of the church and the staggering need. For example, BIMARU alone (i.e., the four states of Bihar, Madhya Pradesh, Rajasthan, and Uttar Pradesh) by 2028 will hold over half of the massive Indian population, with only a relatively small Christian presence.

Contextually, the church will have entered a threatening period of intermittent persecution, a factor already noted above. This will not be an entirely new experience for the church, but it will contrast sharply with the caricatured image delineated by its critics. That image points to the church's inherited position reflecting a government-favored, land-owning, foreign-financed, superior-educated, and relatively successful religious conglomerate. While this is a caricature, there is enough truth in it to attract negative attention. That negative attention will come in the future more forcefully, and the church as a body will re-experience what Christian converts have regularly encountered in the past. The church will lack appreciation, will not attract through dominance, and in some areas it will become a struggling and oppressed minority. As the church experiences these early church realities, and as it conducts mission under the cross, its theology and its spiritual life may well be strengthened. It is not, however, clear that the church is spiritually or psychologically prepared for the almost inevitable change.

Ecclesiastically, the Protestant church has moved from its rather unified character that it had in 1947, affected by both conceptual and ecclesial drift. The conceptual drift involves a double movement into what are sometimes described as the ecumenical and evangelical streams, descriptives apparently imported from abroad. The former is superficially characterized as social justice oriented, dialogical, learned, structure-related; the latter is viewed as evangelism-oriented, conservative activist and spontaneous. Unintervened with, these lines will harden and the drift may result in a two-track church by 2028, having little to do with the denominations as such.

The ecclesial drift refers to the development of an ecclesiocentric mentality, as described by J. Hoekendijk, with primary interest in structure and organization, in contrast to dynamic missional engagement with society. Many have observed that the ecclesial drift is accompanied by forms of moral drift including the phenomena of dissension, litigation, corruption, clerical manipulation, and declining growth. Continued to 2028 this condition would end up in an exhausting gridlock in the official church, already partly immobilized, and Christian energy would seek other outlets. At the same time, with some confidence one can also predict that by 2028 there will have been a series of lay reform movements, along the lines of similar phenomena in other religions, the lay revolution expressing the Protestant reality of *ecclesia semper reformandum est*.

More significant for the task we are discussing is the surging grassroots activism within the organized church and the dramatic missional activity outside the mainstream, through a proliferation of mission societies. These are producing the growth of the church, symbolized by the baptism of 2231 people in Chennai on January 17th, 1998.[10] Contrasting with the *incurvatus* of hierarchical oligarchies, they point to the actualization of the fundamental mission spirit of the people of God, and the possibility of a measured program of nationwide evangelization. It is possible that an outcome of the current dichotomy between the official church and the its preoccupations with the less visible but active effort of ordinary Christians in congregations and societies will be the development of a house church configuration that will in a small way parallel developments in China. One of the tasks of mission planning will be to decide whom to plan with, in an approach that is both respectful and practical.

Spiritually, the Protestant church in India is full of powerful resources. Few churches are endowed with such riches. These include commitment to the idea of evangelism and service, a practical ecumenism, a profound practice of prayer, and a faithful Biblical centrism. These are resources that must be recognized, drawn upon and maximized for a determined missional engagement. Built on them the engagement will go on with positive results despite the battering that the church will receive from secularizing and superficializing forces on the one hand and oppressive religio-political forces on the other hand, and despite the phenomena of ecclesial formalization and decay. The question is, to what extent will it go on? What determination will there be, what energy expended? There is a huge resource of faith and piety, joy and hope in the mass of Indian Christians, and these appropriately built upon will mean that the church's best days are yet to come.

Conclusion: The church, ever both saint and sinner, is an imperfect instrument of God's peace. In the Spirit's hands, however, it is an adequate instrument for the accomplishment of God's saving will. What is required is a renewal of vision, a revival of the spirit, and mission planning that makes sense. The Christians of India, with possibly some collaborative help, will be able to shoulder the greatest single missional task in the world today. Thus the church will move from a mere extension of the present during the next three decades, to a vital gospel-centered engagement with the people of India and with people beyond its borders. Given that mega response to a mega reality the profile of the church will be a startling one by 2028.

Planning Implications:

a. In mission planning, it is crucial to build upon and to maximize strengths rather than to dwell on weaknesses and insolubilities.

b. As part of mission planning a new call must be issued to mission and unity in view of the formidable task and the need for common action. In a meeting on mission and evangelism at Calcutta, February, 1997, it was suggested that "Evangelicals and Ecumenicals have to come together, transcend barriers of bias and prejudice, see new vision, and together work for God's mission."[11] They must be brought together to consider the reality that "Kerugma, koinonia, and diakonia belong together."[12]

c. A more effective presentation of Jesus must be made, one that liberates Him from institutional and personal Christian failure (cf. the Muslim affirmation: "We Muslims are bad, but Islam is beautiful!"). Certainly Jesus must be lifted up to draw people to Himself.

d. Given the relatively straightforward possibilities of an "Each two, reach one" mission effort, the statistical goal for the task of evangelization should not be less than a 5 per cent share of the population by 2028. This is an achievable goal for a church that desires to move forward from an approach of present extension to a determined effort. With a church alerted and with its mission well planned the number of believers in India may reach 72 million by the close of the three-decade period, and 90 million by 2047.

e. The church must raise up a symbol or a set of symbols that signals its new determination and that excites the imagination. Perhaps such a symbol may be related to Protestant history. The year 2006 serves that purpose as the 300th anniversary of B. Ziegenbalg's arrival in Tranquebar. It may be possible for a Cross-centered celebration, involving a million Christians, to take place at the geographical center of India.

The Task of a Determined Church

It is not the intention of this vision paper to enter into the details of idea packages that the colloquium will produce. The ideas will take into account both the condition of India and the condition of the church, and their implications. Drawing upon the record of what the church in mission is already doing, however, the range of possible activities, becomes clear.

The range is so broad that focusing and prioritizing become essential. The church must distinguish between what it has been sent to do, and that to which it sends. Some of the things that the church has programmatically done in the past fall into the area of the civic responsibility of Christian citizens, and can be carried on in that role. What the church has been sent to do, however, must be agreed upon and then focused upon. Otherwise prioritization will become impossible, and the church's efforts will be gravely diluted. The proclamation of the Gospel will only be one of the many things the church does, and a focused concentration on the church's ministry of invitation to India's mega population will become virtually impossible. This is an old dilemma, but it must be faced again.

A Missiological Note

The concern of the congress and this colloquium is that all the people of India may hear the gospel in such a way that they may make a decision about its inviting call to consider the love of God in Christ. This does not mean, however, that the number of conversions becomes the criterion for outreach planning. The use of the number of adherents to validate Christian activity must be scrutinized for its biblical rationale. Followed to its conclusion it would mean that the world church should abandon concern for India and concentrate its attention on Africa and China. In that connection it is well to remember Kenneth Cragg's trenchant phrase: "The mission is not a calculus of success, but an obligation in love."[13]

There are other missiological themes that need consideration. Our well-established commitment to wholistic theology must also be re-examined for its bland assumptions and in the interest of maintaining core content for the task of mission. The term mission cannot disappear into a fog of generalization. We must return to the concreteness of Jesus' language: "Preach the gospel and heal the sick." Mission, too, is essentially a concrete idea, and means sending.

The latter implies that the missionary character of the church must be re-stated in the context of the new India. The term "missionary" implies the crossing of boundaries. That significance must be lifted up even as the importance of kinship relationships is recognized. It is essential to recognize that with a new determination to engage the whole of Indian society with the gospel, the profile of the church will change by 2028. This also means—and this is the final point—that the tendency to do mission planning solely in terms of anthropological and ethnic realities must be counter-balanced by the recognition of the supra-ethnic self-identity of religious adherents. The fact of religion must be given much greater prominence in contemporary missiological thinking, alongside the fact of secularism. We must missionally recognize that Muslims, Sikhs, Buddhists, Jains, and discrete segments of Hinduism represent unit concerns. Muslims, as the largest minority in India, require special attention. Far more Muslims in India have chosen to follow Christ in the last decade than in the previous four decades, and determined efforts are needed to deal with the developing spheres of opportunity. No major religious group, and no major group within Hinduism, may be neglected in mission planning, either on the basis of inhibition or felt difficulty or prior claim.

Current "Mission" Activities

The reason for listing current activities in a vision paper is simply to highlight once again the difficult task of moving toward a united or concentrated vision of what must be done in the next 30 years. The following list includes things that Christians are doing now, that still need to be done, and that need to be addressed on the basis of appropriate criteria for achieving some sense of priorities:

Mission Issues:
- the identification of people who have not heard or fully heard the Gospel, especially large untouched populations;
- the recognition of both religious groups and people groups;
- the encouragement of appropriate research for mission;
- the commending of the need for fresh mission planning to church leaders;
- the training of missional leaders; the role of theological education;

- the manner of presenting Jesus in a freshly relevant manner;
- the organizing for mission, and the management of mission;
- the relation of organized church and mission societies in evangelization;
- the financing of mission;
- dealing with the urban-rural distinction, in terms of mission;
- the task of getting people who are not Christians into the Bible;
- the production of new and relevant literature;
- the more effective use of the mass media;
- modules for networking among churches and societies;
- criteria for recognizing prime opportunities in mission;
- understanding new and old partnership theories;
- the possibility of collaboration and joint ventures with world Christians;
- the task of Indian Christian sponsored and developed mission abroad.

Ministry Issues:

- service to the following:
    - the sick
    - the poor and hungry
    - the oppressed children
    - oppressed women
    - oppressed dalits
    - the refugees
    - leprosy and AIDS sufferers
    - drug-users
    - the homeless and uncared for
    - the illiterates
- the overcoming of violence and conflict; reconciliation and peace-making;
- the response to the oppression of minorities;
- the spiritual preparation for marturia;
- the ministry of healing;
- the ministry of education;
- the ministry of prayer;
- the ministry to youth;
- the overcoming of Christian dissension;
- theologies of inter-religious cooperation and Christian citizenship.

The Vision

What, then, is the vision around which we can rally and which can refocus our energies, unite us, and send us on a 30 year mission in India. Perhaps we can state it in the following way:

By the year 2028, under the blessing of the Spirit of God, we shall see

(1) Christians in India more consciously and unitedly related to the task of outreach within and beyond India;

(2) Jesus Christ and the love of God more visible in India in the year 2028 than in 1998 and at least five per cent of its people following the Master;

(3) Christians in the wider global community including North America, understandingly and appropriately engaged with Indian Christians in creative forms of collaboration; and

(4) Christians rejoicing to bear Christ's Name and energized to do His will, and reflecting the spirit of Sadhu Sundar Singh, ready to say: "It is better to burn quickly and melt many souls than to burn slowly and not melt any."[14]

Notes

[1] Roland E. Miller, *The Sending of God* (Calgary: Concord Canada, 1980), p.143. Rosenstock-Heussy is quoted from *The Future of Christianity* (New York: Harper 1966), p.xvi.

[2] "India's Economy, Work in Progress," *The Economist* (February 22, 1997): p. 41.

[3] Ibid.

[4] "A Survey of India, Time to Let Go," *The Economist* (February 22, 1997): pp.3f.

[5] Steven Radelet and Jeffrey Sachs, *Foreign Affairs*, 76:6 (Nov-Dec 1997), 44-49, quoted in *Future Survey*, edited by Michael Marian, Vol.20, No.4 (April 1998): p.12.

[6] S. P. Gupta, quoted in "High Growth Not Sustainable," *Indian Express* (December 6, 1997): p.16.

[7] Samir Amin. *Capitalism in the Age of Globalization: The Management of Contemporary Society* (London: Zed Books, 1997), quoted in *Future Survey*, op.cit.: p.7.

[8] Cf. David Barrett, ed. *World Christian Encyclopedia* (Nairobi: Oxford, 1982), who estimates 4.7 per cent Christian population in 2000, and Patrick Johnstone, *World Churches Handbook*, ed. by Peter Brierly (London: Christian Research, 1997), p. 414, who suggests 4 per cent. *Encyclopedia Britannica* provides the standard census report.

[9] Samudra Gupta Kashyap, "Christian Missionaries to Carry On," *Indian Express* (November 27, 1997): p.11. The subhead is: "Despite repeated attacks on its institutions and members."

[10] Indian Missions Association, E-Mail release, April 24, 1998.

[11] *National Christian Council Review* (June-July, 1997): p. 416.

[12] Ibid.

[13] Kenneth Cragg. *The Call of the Minaret*, 2nd ed. (Maryknoll: Orbis, 1985), p.305.

[14] The young 40-year old Sadhu Sundar Singh also said this as he headed into the Tibetan unknown:

"I must do my best to do my duty. I set no value on my own life as compared with the joy of finishing my course and fulfilling the commission I received from the Lord Jesus to attest the Gospel of the grace of God." A. J. Appasamy, *Sundar Singh* (London: Lutterworth, 1958), p.239.

Re-encounter and Reconciliation:
The Task for Latin America Today

Rafael Malpica-Padilla

In the midst of the repression during the 1980s, Ruben Blades, a salsa singer and composer, wrote a song to America; the poor, oppressed and marginalized America.

> I am searching for America and I fear I won't find it.
> Its traces have become lost amongst the darkness.
> I am calling for America, but it can't answer me.
> Those afraid of truth have made it disappear.
>
> Surrounded by shadows we deny the certain
> (While we live) without justice there will never be peace.
> Living under dictatorships, I search but I can't find you;
> No one knows where your tortured body is.
>
> You have been kidnapped America; you have been gagged,
> and it is up to us to free you.
> I am calling for you America. Our future awaits;
> before it dies, help me to search.

The decade of the 1980s is considered by many as the "lost decade" for Latin America. The debt crisis, along with the civil unrest sweeping through the region created a hostile and adverse socio-economic environment for the countries in the region. The International Financial Institutions reacted to the crisis by asking the countries in the region to accept a package of neo-liberal measures aimed at controlling the situation. These measures predicated upon the assumption that a free market will produce a more efficient and productive society, have not proven to be as effective as it was anticipated. Although the hyperinflation that characterized this period has been controlled, and in many cases substantially reduced, a result of these "structural adjustments" has been an increase in the unemployment rate, a widening of the gap between those who have and the have nots, degradation of the environment, social violence, and a chronic economic crisis.

This is the *Sitz in Leben* of the Latin American churches. Today they are trying to assess their roles as good news agents in a society where hope is dwindling. The churches continue to search for America, calling out her name, trying to rescue the tortured body and to heal her wounds. The church continues its march toward the utopia: the Kingdom of God that is at hand (Mark 1:14). God's people in Latin America insist that this Kingdom demands a praxis that leads to partial realizations through historical mediations. God's promise of life and God's victory over the dehumanizing power of evil is the source of hope, the dynamic force that drives the community of faith forward, seeking, building, and planting glimpses of the Kingdom that broke into history in Jesus, the Christ.

Let us briefly examine, in *"largas pincelaldas"* (broad strokes) three moments of the Latin American mosaic: the economic moment, the religious moment, and the socio-political moment.

The Economic Moment

A recent report published by Witness for Peace[1] describes the hard reality in which the people of Nicaragua live after the implementation of the Structural Adjustment Program (SAP) designed to foster economic growth and economic development in the country:

Don Arsenio Tellez is a farmer in San Jose del Bocay in Nicaragua. Don Arsenio has given up on farming. From the small store he and his wife now run to make ends meet, he gazes sadly at the empty buildings that surround the village square. The coffee and grain marketing warehouses, the Ministry of Agriculture office, the bank, the farm supply store, all stand desolate. The services that once helped farmers survive in this community are gone.

Last year Don Arsenio grew corn, but by the time he paid to transport his crop to the market, he could not meet his production costs. This year he is growing only enough corn and beans to feed his family. His pastures lie empty. The bank will not lend him money to buy a few cows or to improve his land:

> What is sad is that farmers like me are selling our land and going
> to work for the new owners for $1.50 (dollars) a day.

The story of Don Arsenio is not particular to Nicaragua. It is the experience of thousands of people that do not have access to a free-market economic system that systematically excludes them from participation.

After more than two decades of trade liberalization, cuts in government spending, opening of "Free Trade Zones," and a movement to integrate the market by regional and hemispheric agreements, 200 million Latin Americans live in poverty, with monthly incomes of $60 dollars or less. There are more people unemployed today than a decade ago. Parents cannot afford to send their children to school because of its high costs. Health care is another commodity that is sold in the market to those who can afford it. The support systems that existed in previous times for the small producers are gone. The World Bank and the Inter-American Development Bank fear that this widespread misery is a "dynamite stick waiting for a match."[2] The social unrest created by this crisis could have disastrous consequences for the "political stability" needed to attract foreign investors in order to keep the economy "growing." The unrest in Mexico, Argentina, Peru, and Ecuador are but a few examples. Even Chile, praised as a neo-liberal success story, is showing signs of economic erosion, and now has the fifth worst income distribution in the region.[3]

Under the neo-liberal economic model the social/person oriented state has been forced to relinquish its responsibilities for the well-being of all its citizens, especially those living at the fringe of the formal economic activity. Required cuts in government spending have severely reduced funds for public health services and primary education. Maternal mortality, hunger, malnutrition, cholera, and other preventable diseases are on the rise. Women have been particularly hard hit by SAP's because their access to resources has been diminished while their responsibilities for caring and providing for themselves and their families has increased due to cuts in jobs, wages, and social services. As the job market becomes more competitive and specialized, women are being forced (by the need to feed, clothe and educate their children) to work a double shift both at home and in the formal or informal sector of the economy. Eighty-five percent of all workers in the "maquiladoras" are women, especially younger women who work in an unsafe and exploitative environment. Poverty in Latin America increasingly has a female face.

The free-market economic system with its neo-liberal policy declares itself not responsible for the fate of the excluded and marginalized. These are the social costs that the vast majority of people have to endure, and have to offer as sacrifices to the market idol. The only alternative left to people is to believe undoubtedly in the "invisible hand" of the market; this market that, according to one of its theologians, Michael Novak, is the "incarnation of God's presence in this world."[4] When questioned about the inconsistencies of the system that has not delivered the "land of milk and honey" for the vast majorities, this prophet of the court explains the social differences as natural:

> Nature made human beings equal in dignity before God and among themselves, but it did not make them equal among themselves in talent, personal energy, fortune, motivation, and practical abilities.[5]

The Brazilian economist and theologian Jung Mo Sung established some parallels between market economy foundations and Christian theology. At a missiological consultation in San Jose, Costa Rica[6] he asked:

> Why does someone buy an expensive Ferrari, when there are so many other cheap and useful cars? There is something behind this sacramental act that can not be seen. It is like in the Eucharist, where behind the bread is the body of Jesus Christ.

The market has its religious sense: the necessity of sacrifices, such as starving children, marginalized women, and exploited people, but it also has a clear concept of salvation, where the efficient ones, those who are strong enough to survive (social Darwinism) will be rich and will continue to have access to the "free" market and the inefficient ones, the by-product and discarded residue of the system, will be poor. In other words, the faithful to the market and its laws will be saved, and the sinners, those who challenge the market and its laws, will be condemned and sent to hell (here and now). The "free-market" economy constantly reminds us that "extra mercadus nulla sallus est" ("outside the market there is no salvation").

The collapse of historical socialism has created the impression that we are "at the end of history." This expression is an ideological cover-up for the affirmation that there are no possible alternatives and that this historical crisis marks the end of all utopias. As Elsa Tamez has pointed out:

> The capitalistic system is the hope of everyone. To create other hopes is to be against the only feasible hope. We must have no other expectations, then, but must live the expectation (with readjustments, from time to time) of the promised hope.[7]

Life under these circumstances is "absurd, a huge void, a mess, a 'piece of crap'."[8]

This is not a call to resignation or to passivity. In times of crisis and confusion, the church must draw on the spiritual reserves that reflect clearly the vital center of its proclamation; the newness of life, plentiful, and abundant, offered by God in and through Jesus. All of life exists within the sphere of God's care and judgement. Individuals, corporations, multinational enterprises, governments, and the international financial institutions are objects of God's concern and subject to moral accountability. The church is called to denounce the evil that is brought upon God's people by systems that deny the right to live and to announce the "acceptable year of the Lord." The task of the Christian community, according to Jung Mo Sung, is to unmask the claim of the market as the sole provider of "life and salvation" and to expose its idolatrous demands :

> We must unmask the sin of idolatry. We must veil the spirit of idol worship—the worship of work, of human and social actions and relationships undertaken solely for the accumulation of wealth and for the purpose of unlimited consumption.[9]

We must remember the challenge that Luther presented to the economic system of his time,[10] based in a profound experience of God. This is an experience of a God that is not concerned with the merits of people, but rather a God that in Jesus identified with those who had no merits at all. With his death, Jesus assumed the place of those without merits, to free us from the power of the world[11] and to restore us to the dignity with which we were created.

If we say that the source of all human value is not our merit but God's free and unconditional love, then the way in which we use the market and its products need to change, because we do not seek to value ourselves by the acquisition of its goods; neither do we value the other by what he or she has, or by their usefulness for our "making it in this world," but by what he or she is, a child of God, where God finds us, even in the midst of suffering. (Matthew 25)

The Religious Moment

The major force shaping the religious landscape of Latin America is the rapid growth of Pentecostal Christianity. Many scholars have predicted that early in the twenty-first century Latin America will have an evangelical majority. Even now, in terms of church participation, "practicing" Evangelicals (92 million) may already outnumber "observant" Catholics (40 million).[12]

The question that every church leader is pondering, from the Roman Catholic camp to the trenches of historical Protestantism, is how and why this growth. There are many explanations for this growth[13]: The sociological explanation sees Pentecostalism emerging and developing in a society that was in transition, a transition toward modernity (the studies of Emilio Willems and particularly of Christian Lalive d'Espinay, who studied the Pentecostal movement in Chile from 1965-1966); the psychosocial explanation that places Pentecostalism as a movement searching for and providing a sense of community in a society characterized by anonymity, anomie, and superficial and pragmatic relationships (the study of Pentecostalism in the Puerto Rican community in New York by Renato Poblete), and the pastoral explanation, as developed by Ignacio Vergara, that simply states the "thirst for God" as the basis for the emergence of this movement.

Without trying to oversimplify this important issue, and by acknowledging my limitation in the formal study of Pentecostalism, the "secret" for the growth of Pentecostalism is that this movement has been able to make the church and the God-experience relevant for the popular masses. For many years people lived a peripheral Christianity. The experience of God was *mediatizada* (mediated) by the church and interpreted for them. What Pentecostalism has offered to the people is a new and "direct" experience of God and a community in which the person who sits at the pew has the same participation in the life of the church as does its leader (priesthood of all believers or the ministry of the baptized). This is the "thirst of God" that people had experienced for many years, the desire to participate actively and meaningfully in the life of the community of faith. This movement has been able to rescue the "relevancy" of the Christian faith (a relevancy that has been sacrificed for the sake of logic in both Roman Catholicism and in historical Protestantism), and to present itself as an element of inclusion and participation in an exclusive and self-centered society. The familiarity with which they treat each other astounds us. Every one is an *hermano* (brother) or a *hermana* (sister). The "Pentecost paradigm"[14] offers a community where the people are valued as they are. Here we find the reason for its growth. It has been able to reach people where they are, in the midst of their suffering, poverty, marginalization, and alienation. Once they have been reached, people do not have to become in order to belong.

Allow me to give an example from my own denomination (Lutheran). I remember the days when the rail at the altar was more than a "spot" where you knelt to receive the Eucharist. It separated those who were authorized to "offer" God to the people and the people themselves. Before someone could pass beyond its clearly defined limits (for preaching or serving as a liturgist, a reader, etc.) the person had to spend a lot of time sitting in the pew (earning your way up). Not only did we have to wait a long time to assume a leadership role in the cultic experience, but, even if you were a participant in the worship experience, you had to do it with someone else's categories; you had to become in church something you were not in the streets. As Lutherans in Puerto Rico we had to celebrate God's fiesta as it was defined by others and not *a la Puertorican* (the Puerto Rican way).

A person that comes today to a Pentecostal church—or for that matter to an Ecclesial Base Community—could be sharing a testimony a week from now, or could be asked by the community leader to lead the worship experience, or participate in a communal reading of scripture to address a community problem. The community welcomes them and asks them to participate as they are. They are valued, they are affirmed, they are restored to the humanity and dignity that has been taken away by the system. In a society of *salvese quien pueda* (every person for oneself) (Tamez), in which the constant crisis and chaos is the principal way in which the poor experience life, the Pentecostal experience is a "homeopathic cure"[15] that ". . . invites people to plunge into the chaos in order to overcome it by the power of the Holy Spirit."[16]

However, we need to be mindful also about the criticisms that have been raised against Pentecostalism; its escapist theology which makes it insensitive to social problems, its dualistic conception of life in which the world is totally evil, the legalism and fundamentalism that denies its members the evangelical freedom, the retributionalist emphasis—that creates a certain classism based on some elements of the market ideology—of the Theology of Prosperity, and the puerile attempts to engage in political activism.[17] All these issues, and their implication for life in the community, lead to the proverbial revolving door that has prevented the movement from being an even stronger force in the Latin American societies.

This criticism comes not only from outside the Pentecostal movement, but also from within, particularly from the *pentecostalismo criollo* (native Pentecostalism), which could be described as the "progressive" wing of the Latin American Pentecostal movement.[18] For the *pentecostalismo criollo* the challenge that the movement has is to overcome the ideological, theological and cultural heritage that it has received from western Protestantism, and to be immersed in the socio-political reality of the people it serves.

Bishop Gamaliel Lugo, of the Union Evangelica Pentecostal Venezolana, urges the Pentecostal movement in Latin America to reach back to its original roots in the Black Pentecostal movement originated by William Seymour, a movement that had a strong social and political conscience.[19] This influence is pivotal in developing a Pentecostal social ethics that is shaped by a strong creation theology ("The earth is the Lord's and all that is in it, the world, and those who live in it . . ." Psalm 24:1) that overcomes its dualistic cosmovision ("I am not asking you to take them out of the world, but I ask you to protect them from the evil one." John17:15) and leads to a "*santidad comprometida*"[20] (involved holiness), which for Lugo is the *sine qua non* of following Christ.[21]

I believe that this kind of Pentecostalism, *un pentecostalismo criollo mas aterrizado* (a more earthly native Pentecostalism), presents itself as a great challenge to Roman Catholicism and to Historical Protestantism. It is an explosive and subversive combination; the power of the Spirit articulated in a Theology of the Cross and rooted in God's grace. This experience could lead to what Walter Altmann calls "the revolutionary force implicit in Luther's ecclesiology"[22] with its:

> . . . drive toward liberation from institutional tutelage, its conviction that ecclesiastical structure is both reformable and meant for service, its preference for the mark of the cross (and the weakness manifested there), and the primacy of the Word of God.

Along with the Pentecostal movement, there are two other important elements in the Latin American religious experience: a) the ecumenical moment and b) the relation between gospel and cultures.

The Ecumenical Moment

It is evident that the ecumenical movement in Latin America, like all the other ecumenical movements and expressions in the world, is going through a difficult and uncertain transition. Some of these difficulties are perceived in the changes in the church's leadership in the region, the monopolization of the ecumenical arena by some denominational leaders, and the distancing of the ecumenical movement and its leaders from the church's base.

The movement, as it was articulated in the 1970s and 1980s, had a highly centralized structure that created an *ecumenismo de cupula* (ivory tower ecumenism), and an ecumenical caste that attempted to *masificarlo* (make it public). Julio de Santa Ana and Juan Luis Segundo constantly reminded us that ecumenism is never a mass movement, it is always a "minority" project.

The religious climate that emerged in Latin America after the Second Vatican Council has drastically changed. The progressiveness that characterized CELAM has significantly diminished. Today it is hard to identify the position of the Roman Catholic Church on ecumenism. On the one hand the Vatican is pursuing some dialogue with Protestant churches (e.g. the Joint

Declaration on Justification between the Vatican and the LWF), on the other hand, statements made in the CELAM IV meeting in Santo Domingo are not encouraging:

> We should not underestimate a particular strategy aimed at weakening the bonds that unite Latin American countries and so to undermine the kind of strength provided by unity. To that end, significant amounts of money are offered to subsidize proselytizing campaigns that try to shatter such Catholic unity.[23]

The present ecumenical movent is one that tries to search for a new model, for a new vision, for an alternative project. As such it is not concerned with grandiose ecumenical endeavors, but rather small-scale relationships that strengthen the movement toward unity and undergird the search for concrete possibilities for expressing that unity. Ecumenism is not a formula to be applied, but rather a road to be traveled.

Gospel and Cultures

Eduardo Galeano in his book *The Open Veins of Latin America*, summarizes how the western world has perceived the people of the Americas and those who were brought to work in this continent as slaves:

> The dominant culture accepts the Indians as objects of study, but it does not recognize them as subjects of history: they have folklore, not culture; they practice superstitions, not religions; they speak dialects, not languages; they make crafts, not art. [24]

From the beginning of colonization the religiosity of indigenous communities was described as barbaric, superstitious, and evil. This attitude provided the theological justification for the destruction, pillage, and exploitation to which these peoples and their communities were submitted. The colonial enterprise closed itself to recognize the presence of God in the cultures and lives of the people of the Americas. Whether for political and economic advantages or for theological myopism, "the Christian vision of the Spanish empire embodied in this continent, could not tolerate the existence of another faith experience, even though this experience showed traits similar to the gospel."[25]

Even today the same attitude prevails. The long history of the "mission enterprise" among indigenous people in the Americas tells us that these communities had to leave behind the "old ways" and accept not only the gospel, but many of the elements of the culture that brought the gospel to their lands. This attitude, seen particularly among fundamentalists groups and sects (Jehovah Witnesses and Mormons), has created serious divisions amongst the people. The crisis in Chiapas is more than a political struggle, it also has strong religious connotations.

A consideration of the relationship between Gospel and cultures must lead inevitably to the discussion of various essential points:

1.   There is recognition of the need to reclaim the nurturing roots of Latin America's indigenous cultures in spite of the effects of many centuries of colonialism and oppression. This will include the recognition of the fundamental role that slavery and racism played in the domination and destruction not only of indigenous societies, but also of Afro-Caribbean and Afro-Latin American groups.

2.   There is acceptance of diversity and difference as positive and necessary in the process of recognizing and affirming cultural and ethnic identities. These are the voices of the persons who have been silenced and excluded during these five centuries. That principle of plurality implies the need to understand and enter into ecumenical dialogue with the indigenous and Afro-Caribbean/Latin religions and their diverse ritual expressions, within a framework of cultural and religious solidarity.

3.   The Latin American indigenous cultures have been co-existing for centuries. Despite their specific characteristics and differences, there is a unifying element among all: Abya Yala, the god-mother earth that nurtures her children and who is the focal point of her children's action.

4.   The church has to promote a spirituality that is rooted in the experience and symbolism of the indigenous peoples. If not, it will be denying the people a fundamental dimension of their identity.

It is helpful to keep in mind the words of the Indigenous communities as they reflected on their experience of the Christian faith:

> We, the Indians from the Andes and of the Americas, decided to take this opportunity to return to you your Bible. For the last five centuries this Bible has given neither love, peace nor justice. Please, take your Bible back and return it to our oppressors, because they need its teachings more than us, From the arrival of Columbus, there was imposed on us, by force, a culture, a language, and a religion with European characteristics. The Bible came to us as a part of the imposed cultural change. It was the ideological weapon of this colonial assault. The Spanish sword that attacked and killed the Indians during the day, became at night the cross that killed the Indian soul.[26]

The Socio-Political Moment

During the 1970s and 1980s, repressive governments (mostly military) maintained power by the deliberate and premeditated injury of their peoples. State terrorism fostered the systematic violation of human rights. Individual and social dignity was terribly defiled and profoundly altered. Entire communities were terrorized, tortured, and massacred.

What changes has "democracy" (free and fair elections and integration into the free market economy) brought to the region? How much have we changed from the last two decades? In spite of the cease-fire in many countries and the halt of widespread state terrorism (although the economic violence against the masses and the government insensitivity toward their needs could be labeled as such), nothing seems to have changed that much. Just a couple of months ago Augusto Pinochet, whose military government is responsible for the lives of thousands *desaparecidos* (missing ones), assumed his seat as senator for life in Chile, and Bishop Juan Gerardi, Auxiliary Bishop of Guatemala City, was killed after presenting a report on human rights violations during the 36 years of Guatemalan civil war. These actions, as well as thousands of many other violations of human rights and crimes against humanity, have been forgotten by the Latin American governments who have condoned them by passing amnesty laws that prevent the truth from being known. These laws are efforts at self-forgiveness to avoid responsibility and to "lend legitimacy to state terrorism."[27]

Impunity is the single most pressing human rights question in Latin America today. It is the moral (and political) test of democracy's capacity to heal deeply injured nations and to establish just political order. The desire to "forget" what happened is the main obstacle for reconciliation in Latin America. People need to know the truth of what happened; the women in the Plaza de Mayo need to know where are their children and grandchildren. To know the truth implies the unmasking of the "narrative of the lie" and to embrace the "redeeming narrative"[28] that opens the door to the *reencuentro y reconciliacion* (re-encounter and reconciliation) of Latin America.

This re-encounter and reconciliation seem to elude our present reality. Crime is on the rise in Latin America. The increase in the crime rate is intimately linked to the worsening economic situation for the great majority of people which has created a culture of survival, a daily struggle to live. The social tissue continues to deteriorate. The region's "new democracies" have failed to maintain public order and guarantee the rule of law for all citizens. The abundance of lynchings (Guatemala) reflects the widespread ineffectiveness of state institutions charged with controlling violence and crime.

The political climate is also deteriorating. The extreme situation in Columbia[29] concerning violence and human rights violations can also be extended to other countries in the region, where paramilitary forces still continue to be active, in spite of the recent signing of the Peace Agreements. During a recent visit to Guatemala members of a community in Huehuetenago told me "La paz no se firma. La paz se construye." (Peace is not signed. Peace is built.)

Those who today are building this peace are the poor. The "irruption of the poor" (Gustavo Gutierrez) or the "crucified people" (Ignacio Ellacuria) is the "sign of the times" (Jon Sobrino). God becomes present in them. Through them (all the excluded), God intervenes in our history.

Among those who are the "signs of the times," there are two groups that deserve our attention; the indigenous communities and women.

Before 1980, indigenous organizing was largely confined to local communities. Organizations that united different indigenous groups were not common. Indigenous people who became involved in politics usually did so under the banner of the traditional left, which considered the indigenous struggle to be subordinate to the larger class struggle. The emergence of the Zapatista Army of National Liberation in 1994 has changed the picture.

Indigenous people are forging strong national movements that are bringing together local groups to form regional and national organizations. They have also built alliances with other progressive sectors both at home and internationally. As the groups have developed into regional and national networks, the agenda for the organization has also changed. Constitutional rights have become another focal point of indigenous organizing. A principal demand of the communities in Guatemala and Ecuador has been the revision of the constitution to recognize those countries as plurinational states. Indigenous organizations have also tried their hand at electoral politics. In Guatemala the New Guatemala Democratic Front (FDNG) elected six of their candidates to the Congress, including two Mayan women, Rosalina Tuyuc (a leader of CONAVIGUA) and Manuela Alverado.

Women have also assumed a greater role in the society. But they continue to be the invisible victims in Latin America. Women are the poorest of the poor, making up the majority of refugee and displaced peoples, and because of their gender, continue to suffer from economic, social, and political discrimination.

For women to be taken into account as political, social, and religious actors they must fight a permanent battle—both within themselves and their organizations—to change the role that society assigns to them. Women need to live a double process: winning demands in the social, political, economic, and cultural spheres, as well as transforming themselves, and eradicating their internal submission. Women must educate their sons not to be *macho* and teach their girls to have self-esteem. While this means a struggle at the heart of the family to change the perception of the roles of men and women, it also includes working at the level of society to ensure the enforcement of laws protecting women against domestic violence.

Women face two major issues in their struggle: a) how to reverse the cycle of violence against them and b) how to assume power (*asumir el poder*) without reproducing the patriarchal model. This second issue presents a great challenge to the women's movement in Latin America.

Patriarchal ideas are ingrained in the minds of men and women from their earliest days and it will be no easy task changing preconceived notions of gender roles as they pertain to the socioeconomic relationship between women and men. "The main role for women should be in the home with their families" was a statement made by Martha Chavez, the head of Peru's Congress and a member of President Fujimori's ruling *Cambio 90—Nueva Mayoria* (Change

1990—New Majority) coalition. During the government of Nicaragua's President Victoria Chamorro, Latin America's only female president, the rights of women were not increased. Nicaragua was one of a handful of Latin American countries protesting the inclusion of reproductive rights at the Beijing conference.

Conclusion: A Time for Hope

> Because He entered the world and history;
> because He broke the silence and the agony;
> because He filled the earth with His glory;
> because He was light in our cold night . . .
> therefore we have hope,
> therefore we struggle with persistence,
> therefore we look toward the future with confidence.

As reflected in this hymn by Bishop Federico Pagura, written during the years of the "Dirty War" in Argentina, we live in a favorable *kairos*. We must discern this decisive moment correctly within the call that God extends us to participate in the *missio Dei*. Discerning the signs of the times is already a wise and appropriate way of accompanying the Latin American people in their long struggle toward its *reencuentro y reconciliacion*. The praxis of our faith and the theological reflection that springs from it ought to form a substantive part of our daily effort to live out the faith.

In the historical development of Latin America, the churches have learned the urgency and relevance of hope. There is a formative accumulated experience that comes from the hope lived in the midst of suffering, oppression and persecution. It is a hope refined by the certainty of what is not yet seen (Hebrews 11:1)

Often, the ideologies that promote "the end of history and all utopias" have tried to stop the people's ability and desire to dream and to cherish the new horizon of justice and dignity. However, throughout all Latin America the will to fight and to struggle for the dawn of this new day continues to be felt heavily in people's hearts and minds.

As people of God, called, empowered and sent to proclaim God's creating, redeeming and sanctifying activity to the people of Latin America, let us continue to affirm this ". . . new birth into a living hope through the resurrection of Jesus Christ. . . ." (1 Peter 1:3)

Notes

1   Hostetler, Sharon. *Bitter Medicine: Structural Adjustments in Nicaragua* (New York: Witness for Peace, 1996).

2   *Rhetoric and Reality*, published by NACLA, Volume XXIX No. 6 (May/June 1996).

3   In Chile in 1970 only 17% of the households were poor; in 1989, poor households represented 38.1%.

    In 1995, the richest 20% of Chilean households earned 18 times the income of the poorest 20%. The 1998 report of the United Nations Programs for Human Development (PNUD) describes the harsh reality that many Chilean families face today. The title of the report is "El Jaguar esta Triste." (The Jaguar is Sad).

4   "For many years one of my favorite texts of scripture was Isaiah 57:2-3: 'and they enter into peace; those who walk uprightly will rest on their couches. But as for you, come here, you children of a sorceress, you offspring of an adulterer and a whore.' I would like to apply these words to the modern business corporation, an extremely disdained incarnation of the presence of God in the world." Quoted by Jung Mo Sung, *La Idolatria del Capital y la Muerte de los Pobres* (The Idolatry of Capital and the Death of the Poor), (San Jose: Editorial DEI, 1991), p 105.

5   Ibid., p. 105. La naturaleza hizo los seres humanos iguales en dignidad frente a Dios y entre si, pero no los hizo iguales entre si en talento, energia personal, suerte, motivacion y habilidades practicas.

6   A consultation sponsored by the NCCCUSA. See Oscar Bolioli, *Hope and Justice for All in the Americas: Discerning God's Mission* (New York: Friendship Press, 1998).

7   Elsa Tamez, "When Horizons Close: A Reflection on the Utopian Ratio of Qohelet." Presentation at the ELCA/DGM Central American Consultation in San Jose, Costa Rica.

8   Ibid., p.1.

9   Jung Mo Sung, "Hunger for God, Hunger for Bread, Hunger for Humanity: A Southern Perspective," in Oscar Bolioli, ed., *Hope and Justice for All in the Americas: Discerning God's Mission*, op. Cit., p. 35.

10 For a discussion on Luther's contribution to the discussion of economic issues see Altmann, Walter, *Luther and Liberation* (Minneapolis: Fortress Press, 1992): "Luther's economic writings reveal a deep compassion for the poor. His denunciation of economic abuses reveal a strong concern and commitment to justice. His economic views are radically centered in the basic needs of the people, not in profit making," p.111.

11 Based on his studies of the New Testament language, Walter Wink suggests that the word "world" should be translated as "the domination system" that he defines as "the human sociological [and I will also include the spiritual] realm that exist in estrangement from God." See Walter Wink, *Engaging the Powers: Discernment and Resistance in a World of Domination* (Minneapolis: Augsburg Fortress, 1992) p.51.

12 Escobar, Samuel. "The Training of Missiologists for a Latin American Context" in *Missiological Education for the Twenty-First Century*, Woodberry, John Dudley., Elliston, Edgar J., Engen, Charles Edward, eds. (Orbis Books, 1996); See also by Samuel Escobar, "The Church in Latin America" in *New Face of the Church in Latin America*, edited by Guillermo Cook.

13 For a summary and critique of these explanations see two articles by Juan Sepulveda, "The Pentecostal Movement in Latin America" in *New Face of the Church in Latin America*, edited by Guillermo Cook and "El crecimiento del movivmiento pentecostal en America Latina" in *Pentecostalismo y Liberacion* (The Growth of the Pentecostal Movement in Latin America), edited by Carmelo Alvarez (Editorial Dei, San Jose, Costa Rica, 1992).

14   Here I make a distinction between the institutionalization of the Pentecostal movement and the movement itself that can be found in the charismatic renewal experience in the Catholic Church and in the historical Protestant Churches. This "paradigm" includes: 1) a direct and intense experience of God ("mediatizada" (mediated) by the Holy Spirit), which is articulated in the language of the people, 2) baptism of the Holy Spirit, 3) a strong affirmation of the priesthood of all believers, and 4) a call to all believers to share this God experience (the new life found in Christ, the life of sanctification) with others (every member is a missionary).

15   Cox, Harvey, "Mission in the Americas in the Twenty-First Century: A Northern Perspective" in Oscar Bolioli, *Hope and Justice for All in the Americas*, op.cit., p. 90 "Part of the reason for Pentecostalism's appeal is that it permits people to hold on to something of the traditional symbolic world while at the same time coping with the new world. Today, many former practitioners of folk healing are Pentecostal preachers and healers, still practicing a healing art that stands both in continuity and in conflict with what they did before."

16   Ibid., p. 91.

17   Jose Miguez Bonino is very critical about the naivete of many Pentecostals involved in political activity: . . . there is still no conscious linkage of the faith that they profess and the political activity that they have assumed, except in the very general affirmation of "do good" or "seek help" and the possibilities of evangelization (e.g., carry the Bible and prayer to the center of political life or better the work conditions of the church and also protect religious liberty). Not that those motivations lack genuineness and, as far as they go, legitimacy. But the lack of mediation of a structure of ethical-social thought and of a analytical-critical comprehension of the political field can easily betray the honesty of the persons that take part (when they choose ideological positions with *social* consequences that they do not perceive) or give place to a "theocratic" arrangement of power—usually very limited—of that participation. Miguez Bonino, Jose, *Rostros del Protestantismo Latinoamericano* (Faces of Latin American Protestanism) (Buenos Aires: Nueva Creacion, 1995), p. 70.

18   Here I follow the commonly agreed typology of Latin American Pentecostalism: Missionary Pentecostalism very dependent on the Mission Boards from the USA, the Pentecostalismo Criollo (native Pentecostalism) a more independent movement with a "nationalistic" character. Carmelo Alvarez. "Los Pentecostal es en America Latina: ecumenicos o evangelicos" (The Pentecostals in Latin America: Ecumenics or Evangelicals) in: *Revista Pasos*. San Jose: DEI,\\I, No. 18 (1988), p.4 and Neo-Pentecostalism.

19   "Finally, an important datum for understanding the Pentecostal movement in Latin America, is the revolt that this ethical-prophetic attitude of the Negro Pentecostals caused in the United States. The North American press catalogued that activity of the Negros as an invasion of the African culture in the Yankee civilization. This occasioned that the white Pentecostals, in 1908, began to separate themselves from the Negroes. They affirmed that the Christ of the Negro Pentecostals was a Negro Christ, a liberator of the Negro race. With that separation, the white Pentecostals disassociated themselves from the social and political struggles in which the Negro Pentecostals were engaged. Unlike the whites, the Negro Pentecostals maintain that experience until today.

It is lamentable that the Pentecostalism of the whites came to Latin America. However, there exist Pentecostal experiences that keep alive the ethical-prophetic flame of the origins of the movement." Lugo, Gamaliel, "Etica social Pentecostal: Santidad Comprometida" (Pentecostal Social Ethics: Involved Holiness), in Alvarez, Carmelo, *Pentecostalismo y Liberacion: una experiencia latinoamericana* (Pentecostalism and Liberation: A Latin American Experience) op.cit., p.107

20   Ibid., p. 121.

21   "Holiness separates us from this kind of world, but places us in the very center of the world in order that, without conforming us to it, we may transform it to a new and liberated world. . . . To be holy and radical people, is an inescapable condition of following Christ. The contrary would easily lead to mediocracy and lukewarmness." Ibid., pp. 120-121.

22   Altmann, Walter. *Luther and Liberation*, op.cit., p. 66.

23   B. Peerman, Dean. "CELAM IV: Maneuvering and Making Time in Santo Domingo" in *Christian Century* (February 17, 1993), p. 180-185.

24   Galeano, Eduardo. *Las Venas abiertas de America Latina* (The Open Veins of Latin America) (Colombia: Siglo Veintiuno Editores, 1979). La cultura dominante admite a los indigenas como objetos de estudio, pero no los reconoce como sujetos de la historia: tienen folklore, no clutura; practican supersticiones, no religiones; hablan dialecto, no idiomas; hacen artesania, no arte.

25   Tamez, Elsa. "Queztzalcoatl y el Dios Cristian" (Queztzalcoatl and the Christian God) in *Pasos*, No. 35, p. 12.

26   My own translation from the Spanish text in Pablo Richard, *Teologia India yBiblia Cristiano* (Indian Theology and Christian Bible) (II Encuentro de Teologia India de la region Mayense, 1992).

27   Norris, Robert E. "Las leyes de impunidad y los derechos humanos en lasAmericas: una respuesta legal" (The Laws of Impunity and Human Rights in the Americas: A Legal Response) in *Revista* IIDH (January-June 1992), p.48.

28   Schreiter, Robert. *Reconciliation, Mission and Ministry in a Changing Social Order,* The Boston Theological Institute Series, Volume 3 (Maryknoll and Cambridge: Orbis Books and Boston Theological Institute, 1992), pp. 34-39.

29   The report to the 1997 53rd Session of the UNCHR states that last year "Colombia has been exposed to a widespread internal armed conflict and rampant killings continued. The preser.ce of paramilitary, guerilla, and drug trafficking organizations, and the armed confrontations among them, as well as with the armed forces, have displaced 750,000 persons. Violence against women and children is a serious problem. Unofficial, but extensive discrimination against women, minorities, and the indigenous continues. Child labor is a widespread problem. Vigilante groups engaged in social cleansing (the killing of street children, prostitutes, homosexuals, and others deemed socially undesirable) continues to be a serious problem."

The Future of Christianity in Latin America:
Missiological Perspectives and Challenges

C. Rene Padilla

The so-called "acceleration of history" places us in a precarious position when we attempt to discern the future of Christianity in Latin America. The rapid changes taking place in the world, many of them on a global scale, make it extremely risky to venture any forecast for the future. In spite of this, we cannot—and we may not—elude our responsibility to reflect on the path we are to take in order to attain the goals inherent in our commitment to the kingdom of God, and this necessarily implies making the effort to discern the future. We must, then, undertake the task with appropriate humility, being very careful as we seek to interpret the "signs of the times."

The present paper attempts to do just this. In the first section we will make a brief analysis of the religious revival-taking place at present in the countries of Latin America. In the second and the third sections we will consider the dreams and hopes that this revival has caused in Catholic and Protestant circles respectively. With this in mind in the fourth part we will attempt to project a vision of the future, desirable from our own (Protestant) perspective, and of the challenges that this vision presents to us today. The basic concern that motivates this study could be summarized in this key question: What is the vision that should determine the mission of the Church of Jesus Christ in the midst of the dramatic socio-economic, political, cultural and religious changes taking place in Latin America? What should be the role of the Church as she looks toward the future of a world that today is in a period of transition, under the spell of the empire of the mass media?

The Explosion of Popular Religiosity in Latin America

It is evident that on the periphery of the West, of which Latin America is part, the predictions of those who in the past held that the scientific and technological progress of these nations would render religion obsolete have simply not been fulfilled. Although it is true that today non-religious people are quite free to express their position, it also is true that Latin Americans in general consider themselves "believers" and many are faithful adherents of one form or another of religion or cult, organized or not. What does this situation imply for the church's mission at present and as she looks to the future?

Religion in the post-modern world

A thoughtful reading of the current religious situation in Latin America demands an understanding of the changes that have taken place throughout this century in people's perception of the place of religion in personal and social life, partially as a result of modern scientific and technological development, with special emphasis on the mass media.

This leads us to the thesis proposed by Arend Th. van Leeuwen, at the beginning of the 1960s, on the impact of western technology on the modern world. This Dutch theologian holds that the technological revolution is achieving that which Christian missions were unable achieve—the unification of the world. This took place initially in the West, in the heart of Christian civilization, as the result of a unique process in which "clearly discernible spiritual motives and a particular view of God, man and the world have played a decisive part" (1964:401). In recent centuries, little by little, it has expanded to "all nations" and has penetrated even the most remote corners of the planet. It has thus become one of the factors that have opened up centuries-old, traditional societies to modern influences, with the resulting integration of these societies into "a planetary world." For the first time in human history, van Leeuwen states, "ontocratic" societies—"religious, closed, and traditional"—, in which it was very difficult for the values of other cultures and even the gospel itself to enter, have been replaced by "technocratic" societies, characterized by openness to change. "Whether they like it or not," says our author, the non-western civilizations are confronted now with a full-scale invasion by technocracy; and it is not possible for them— even should they wish to do so— to dodge the impact of that intrusion or the relentless transformation that it involves (1964:409).

Although van Leeuwen refers to Asian societies, not directly to Latin America, there can be no doubt that his analysis fits the ontocratic societies of Latin America, "religious, closed, and traditional," including the Roman Catholic society developed since colonial times. Today, even more than when the distinguished missionologist cited above was writing, it is evident that we are entering a new period of history, a period dominated by technocracy, especially by the mass media, and open to change in every dimension of life.

It is not surprising that the transition to the technocratic period should have profound religious repercussions. In the past, in the rich countries of the West, the Industrial Revolution slowly displaced Christianity from the dominant place it had held in society, in order to put science and technology in its place. This same process of "secularization" is taking place at present in Latin America, but with one great difference: in this continent secularization generally does not lead to atheism, but to a noticeable withdrawal of the faithful from the Roman Catholic church, which is identified with the authoritarian, traditional society of the past.[1] Thus the way is cleared for a search for other religious alternatives, other "gospels" which will better respond to felt needs and which are more in consonance with the spirit of the day.

Someone has said that "the existential void is the mass neurosis of our time." It may well be that the present common religious search, even in the industrialized areas of this continent, is no more than an expression of the desire to fill that void. Today it is not rare for business tycoons to hold spiritual retreats. "Transcendental meditation" attracts the attention of a growing number of people. The "New Age" champions a position characterized by an openness to all that is spiritual as well as by the negation of the uniqueness of the revelation of God in Christ Jesus. Bookstores display and sell numerous titles, many of them best sellers, on topics related to what Beatriz Sarlo, the author of *Escenas de la vida moderna* (Scenes of Post-modern Life), has called "friendly spirituality," by authors such as William Proctor, Brian Inglis, Louise Hay, and H. Benson. It is safe to say that in Latin America there are not many people willing to accept the "death of God" and still less to sign a death warrant or to attend his funeral.

At the same time, there are fewer and fewer Latin Americans who think that the religion inherited from their ancestors since the colonial period has the title deed to their conscience. Latin America has become a shopping mall of religious options. As Peter Berger has pointed out, "secularization brings about a demonopolization of religious traditions and thus, *ipso facto,* leads to a pluralistic situation" (1973:139). And religious pluralism creates a "market situation" in which "the religious tradition, which previously could be authoritatively imposed, now has to be *marketed"* (:142).

Christianity has no future in Latin America if it does not take seriously this aspect of the world today. The end of the Constantinan era, marked by "the death of christendoms" (Richard: 1987), is the essential starting point for understanding the role of the churches at the outset of the third millennium.

Pentecostal and Neo-pentecostal Growth

As we have already mentioned, not all the religious fervor that characterizes our peoples today is taking place in terms of adherence to Christianity, even less to the type of Christianity identified with the closed society of the past. Nevertheless, it is a fact that much of this fervor results in unusual growth of Evangelical churches, especially the Pentecostal and Neo-charismatic churches. Indeed, the growth of these churches in the last three decades has attracted the attention of many throughout the continent. It may be exaggerated to predict that in the foreseeable future the majority of Latin Americans will be Evangelical. There seems to be, however, good reason to affirm that "if the growth of the last few decades continues, Latin Americans claiming to be *evangelicos* could still become a quarter to a third of the population early in the twenty-first century" (Stoll 1993:2). For traditional Roman Catholic leaders, including Pope John Paul II, we are in the presence of a real "avalanche" or "invasion of sects" which threatens "the religious unity" of our nations. For a growing number of social scientists we are witnessing an unprecedented phenomenon deserving careful analysis because of its social consequences. For a few astute politicians we have before us a new popular force that can be used to serve their respective ideologies.[2]

This is not the place to discuss the manifold, and sometimes contradictory, attempts that have been made to explain the growth of these churches.[3] Whatever the explanation, the fact remains that Latin American Protestantism is a growing force and is changing not only the religious but also the social and political landscape of the continent.

Undoubtedly, one especially important element which, in the last few years, has contributed and continues to contribute to the growth of the "megachurches," many of them Neo-charismatic, is their adoption of the culture of the *Mass Empire*.[4] In a paper presented recently in a congress of the *Federacien Latinoamericana de Facultades de Communicacion Social* (Latin American Federation of Schools of Social Communication), Gina Gogin and Rolando Perez, research scholars at the University of Lima, have analyzed the interaction between the so-called "culture of the mass communication media" and the Latin American religious scene. The study shows that today the mass media increasingly determine religious conduct, and that religious organizations in turn are increasingly making use of the resources of mass communication. The paper points out that "mass" culture finds expression in the religious field in areas such as changes in the decoration of church buildings, the "theatralization" of the preachers, the use of religious talk show hosts on radio and television, and the presentation of concerts of religious music on "secular" stages such as stadiums. At the same time, traditional styles of presentation of the religious message in the mass media have changed, especially on radio and television. Even in traditional churches, the traditional discourse in the form of a sermon has given way to marketing techniques and audiovisual systems, with the professional presentation of "electronic preachers," "spiritual counselors," religious rock concerts, talk shows, and spectacular scenography in church buildings. Even the physical appearance of church buildings demonstrates the influence of the esthetic structure of the world of television on the churches, especially on those where middle- and upper-class believers congregate. In the churches of the lower social classes, sound systems and sophisticated musical instruments are considered indispensable, while their leaders experiment with new ways of relating to the public with mannerisms like those of business executives. Solemn leaders and ceremonious preachers—according to the researchers—have been replaced today by personality-pastors, while Biblical exposition has been replaced by strident shouting, applause, choruses sung with modern rhythms and, in some churches, with the participation of folkloric or rock bands, not necessarily religious.

The use of the mass media in Charismatic churches, which are generally those that grow the most, is part of a whole combination of elements with which they have tuned in to the spirit of the times: the business approach, the use of marketing techniques to achieve numerical goals, the offer of material prosperity, help so that people will "feel good," and the emphasis on entertainment. All this goes accompanied by a reduction of the content of the message to its minimum expression and an apathetic attitude toward the formation of disciples who live out their faith in every dimension of life.

In fact, we are facing a phenomenon that we might call *Evangelical popular religiosity,* unprecedented in these countries. In the Catholic camp, there is extensive bibliography that covers the topic of popular religiosity. In contrast, this socio-religious category is not even part of the Protestant vocabulary, probably because it is considered an exclusively Roman Catholic phenomenon. There is a need for field studies to detect the similarities as well as the differences in the manifestations of popular religiosity in both the Evangelical and the Catholic contexts. Our personal perception is that one of the principal characteristics of popular religiosity in both contexts is a combination of a privatized faith, having little ethical content, with an outstanding sense of emotional celebration in the religious meetings. Segundo Galilea (1979:28) has pointed out that the sectors of the population that have sprung up as the result of the industrialization of our cities—laborers, underemployed, and unemployed—tend to reserve their participation in public manifestations for political rallies, popular sporting events, and artistic festivals. Nevertheless, the significance of the religious meetings should not be minimized, especially in the case of Pentecostal and Neo-charismatics.

It would appear that the inevitable conclusion is that the extension of this type of Protestantism is intimately related to the *light* culture of post-modern times. Although the probability is that it continue for some time yet, in spite of various attempts by the Catholic hierarchy to detain its advance, it does not fulfill the necessary conditions to sustain the hopes of those who wish to see in Latin America a continent deeply affected by the message of the kingdom of God and his justice.

The New Evangelization

Pablo Richard has defined Christendom as "a particular class of relationship between the *church* and *civil society,* a relationship in which the *state* is the primary mediation" (1987:1). This relationship, which has characterized Latin America throughout its history, "since 1492 until our days" (ibid.), has been definitively broken. Today, on the threshold of the third millennium, it is no longer possible to ignore this rupture which has been progressively deepened during the twentieth century. An important sector of the Roman Catholic Church (RCC) recognizes the urgent need to overcome Roman Catholic integralism in the interest of the authentic evangelism of Latin America. The project of "the new evangelization" sponsored at present by the Vatican, however, basically represents an effort to recuperate lost ground and to reaffirm "the medieval synthesis of the two swords"—one belonging to the emperor and the other to the pope—which is "the essence of Christendom" (cf. Hanson, 1987:53).

The Crisis of Christendom

If there is anything especially difficult for the RCC hierarchy in general to accept, it is that the unity of colonial Christendom, imposed in Latin America by the force of arms, is past history and that this continent is no longer, if it ever was, *a Roman Catholic continent.* There are many reasons to believe that the majority of Latin American bishops and archbishops would agreed with Galindo, that "Catholicism in Latin America is not insured against *the risk of being reduced to become just one among many religious options* and having no other recourse to be taken into account than its own power of conviction" (1992:22, my emphasis).

The problem is that for several centuries, in order "to be taken into account" in Latin America, Roman Catholicism relied on resources that had little or nothing to do with "its power of conviction." It is not necessary to demonstrate that the Spanish conquest, since the end of the fifteenth century, was a political-religious project inspired by the ideal of establishing in the New World a Christian kingdom under the power of the Catholic sovereigns and the power of the pope. This was the conquerors' dream, and in order to realize it they relied on the military support of the Spanish empire and the participation of several religious orders.

The Other Spanish Christ (1992), the classic work by John A. Mackay, published originally in English in 1933, carefully demonstrates the decisive importance of this fact for the understanding of "the spiritual history of Spain and Hispanic America." For Mackay, the RCC that accompanied the Spanish conquerors in the sixteenth century was the Church of the Crusades, with a mission intimately related to military conquest and coherent with the "Islamic soul" (:63) of these conquerors, forged during the eight centuries of defensive fighting that followed the Moorish invasion of Spain. The conquest was "the last of the Crusades," in which "the sword and the cross formed an offensive alliance in order to take Christianity, or what was considered Christianity, to foreign lands" (:85). Thus evangelization was carried forward at an incalculable ethical cost, and the *corpus Christianum,* the colonial Christendom, was established by means of

> the tremendous power of the Crusades, which imposed on the indigenous races, by good means or bad, their edicts and decrees [so that] religion was rapidly degraded until it became only a magic method to obtain what could not be attained by ordinary means (:109).

In his study of the history of Christendom and of the RCC in Latin America, Pablo Richard (1987) has proposed a periodization of this history in three large circles: the first, from 1492 to 1808; the second, from 1808 to 1960, and the third, from 1960 to our day. According to him, colonial Christendom entered a period of crisis following 1808, as the result of the revolutions that culminated in the independence of the Latin American countries from the Spanish crown. It was not easy for the RCC to accept that the republican state should replace the monarchical order that had served as her royal protector for three centuries. The crisis was not resolved, and, with time, following 1930, the RCC was forced to find a way to redefine its relationship to the state, with the purpose of restructuring a "new Christendom" that could be called "populist, nationalist, Latin American, culturalist, and developmentalist" (:77). This attempt, Richard states, resulted in the strengthening of the presence and the power of the Church in civil society, but it caused a new crisis: the clash between two models of Christendom, the colonial and the new, during the period from 1930 to 1960. The cycle that begins in 1960, according to our author, faces the RCC with two alternatives: a revised model of the new Christendom, at the service of the capitalist economic model, or a process of dissolution of this new Christendom in order to make way for "a church that is either beyond the New Christendom model or has clearly broken away from it" (:79). For the first time in the history of the Church in Latin America "there is a direct contradiction between Christendom and church: one will be able to survive only if the other disappears" (ibid.). The future of Christianity in this continent depends to a large extent on the resolution of this crisis, comparable to that of colonial Christendom at the beginning of the nineteenth century.

A Contemporary Version of the New Christendom

Richard wrote his analysis of the Christendoms—the colonial and the new —prior to the destruction of the Berlin Wall. On the horizon there still was no indication of the dissolution of the Soviet empire or "the end of history" of Fukuyama. In these circumstances, our author still believed he had a basis to predict that the crisis of Christendom would lead "irreversibly to its complete breakdown," although he admitted the possibility that Christendom should be "radically and totally" restructured (:160).

Everything seems to indicate, however, that the ecclesiastical institution with its headquarters in Rome has not rejected, to say the least, the historical legacy of medieval Catholicism. On the contrary, the RCC in general continues to conceive of herself as the agent of a new civilization in which, in order to relate to civil society, she will continue to rely on political power and the institutions of the established order.

The second General Assembly of the *Consejo Episcopal Latinoamericano* (CELAM II), held in Medellin in 1968, was a watershed for the RCC. The purpose of this conference was to consider the practical significance of Vatican II for Latin America. Instead of this, Medellin '68 turned out to be, so to say, the "official inauguration" of the most significant *aggiornamento* in the history of the RCC in Latin America since its initiation in the fifteenth century, for it introduced a change of direction that affected every aspect of the life and mission of the RCC. In a way, it was a legitimization of the progressive sector of the church. In effect, from the perspective of several observers, what gave transcendence to the event was the encouragement given there to the theology of liberation in terms of the "preferential option for the poor" and the support for the *comunidades eclesiales de base* (grassroots ecclesial communities).

Unfortunately, it must be observed that the three decades that followed Medellin '68 have proved beyond doubt that, with some outstanding exceptions, the hierarchy of the RCC has not abandoned its dream of a Roman Catholic Latin America and that the traditional integralist position has the ardent support of the Vatican. In this regard, Jose Miguez Bonino, a well-known ecumenical theologian, stated in the third General Assembly of the Latin American Council of Churches:

> It seems to me that the principal project of the RCC today returns, with variations, to the traditional line. . . . To be sure, this turn has not been accompanied equally by all the church, not even by all the clergy or the Episcopal leadership. But I believe that it is not unwarranted to think that it will be the dominant line in the RCC in the more or less immediate future (1995b:33).

Already in Puebla, at the third General Assembly of the CELAM, it was obvious that there was an effort to promote the integralist position of the ecclesiastical establishment and to neutralize the influence of the advocates of change. Although the conservative wing did not achieve its objective, it is evident that since Puebla little by little this sector of the Church, with the support of the Vatican, has significantly gained ground. The hierarchy in general has continued to be closely associated with conservative political forces.[5] Although it would be correct to state that within the Latin American RCC there are competing ideological positions that are as diverse as that of the military national security regime and that of liberation theology, time and again Pope John Paul II has shown his preferential option for the bishops committed to the status quo. Add to this all the measures that leave no doubt with regard to the ideological position of the RCC: the official support to orders or movements such as *Opus Dei,* erected by the Pope in 1982 as "a personal prelature" for urgent missions (Hanson 1987:87); the inclination to demand from the states special privileges in exchange for ecclesiastical political support; the undisguised effort to control government welfare programs and the system of public education, to the extent of attaining the reinstitution of religious teaching; the struggle to obtain the approval of laws defining the religious activities which are officially allowed; the relentless publicity campaign against the "fundamentalist sects,"[6] and the acceptance of the so-called neo-liberal economic program, however conditioned to the need to minimize, through the application of the "social teaching" of the Church, its damaging impact on the poor. It is inevitable to conclude that, in contrast to what Richard could foresee in the 1980s, the RCC has chosen to resolve the crisis of the new Christendom in Latin America by making an effort to insure the preservation of her political power. Evidently, all too many of the bishops believe that, now that "Christianity is no longer being transmitted from one generation to the next by any closed milieus," (Segundo 1978:32), political power is still quite useful as a way "to create or simply maintain consumer majorities who are artificially bound to Christianity" (:34).

The CELAM document, *Jesucristo, vida plena para todos: Plan global del CELAM en la aurora del III Milenio—1995-1999* (Jesus Christ, Abundant Life for All: Global Plan of CELAM at the Dawn of the Third Millennium—1995-1999), points in the same direction. Written in light of the conclusions of the 1992 CELAM conference in Santo Domingo, this is the official plan for the *new evangelization* of Latin America. Although the document repeatedly states that the roots of this plan are already found in Vatican II, in actual fact it responds to Pope John Paul II's call for an inculturated evangelization which will affect every aspect of social life on the continent. One of the reasons that this document gives to explain the crisis through which the RCC is going at present is religious pluralism. In the same section it emphasizes that the "new era" merits "peculiar attention" because "it produces a deep transformation in the perception of transcendence and it is manifested in a vague spiritualism, which is individualistic and without a permanent commitment." Other factors are added, such as the chronic scarcity of priests—the RCC never had enough priests to attend to her people—and secularization.

Without denying the validity of these factors, we would suggest that the notable desertion of members which so deeply concerns the Roman Catholic hierarchy is due primarily to the centralism and the authoritarianism that have marked the RCC for centuries.[7] As Bastian has pointed out, during the colonial period the Roman Catholic religion was "the means to legitimize unequal and pyramidal social relations" which were artistically represented in certain pictures of the eighteenth century (1997:31). It is not necessary to prove that in today's religious market, where one can find food for every palate, that role of a hegemonic power has become obsolete: despite Galindo and many of those who share his religious views, Roman Catholicism is "just one among many religious options," and whether it will be taken into account or not will depend on "its power of conviction." Not an anti-Catholic prejudice but an analysis of the facts and certain premises derived from the Gospel move us to affirm with Jose Miguez Bonino that, "What we Protestants reject is not that there has been established, or may be reestablished, a 'Roman Catholic Christendom,' but that a 'Christendom' be established at all" (1997:111).

The New Utopia: A Protestant Latin America

As Peter Berger has argued, "religion has been the historically most widespread and effective instrumentality of legitimization . . . because it relates the precarious reality constructions of empirical societies with ultimate reality" (1973:41). A fact that need not be proven is that in Latin America Roman Catholicism served in the past, and sometimes continues to serve in the present, to legitimize the established socio-economic and political order. Now that Protestantism is gaining weight not only in the religious camp but also in the political field, the question is whether there is a basis to think that a sort of

Protestant Christendom will replace the Roman Catholic one. Evidently, not all Protestants reject the idea of establishing a Christendom!

A Concerted Global Plan?

History shows that one of the favorite weapons that the Roman Catholic hierarchy has used to fight against the inroads of Protestantism in Latin America has been the argument that in Latin America Protestantism is a "foreign religion," that it came "from outside." In face of such an argument one may ask if in this continent there is a church that, in the final analysis, does not have a foreign origin. The accusation, however, gains strength when it is combined with the "conspiration theory," according to which Protestantism is the "spearhead of American imperialism."

A contemporary variation of this theory is one that links Protestant growth to "the apogee of militant fundamentalism starting from the United States" (Galindo 1992:78) and a supposed "global plan, with well defined priorities and tactics" (:294), for a *religious as well as political conquest* of the Latin American countries. For anyone to accept that Protestantism, which is "divisive, divided, and fissiparous" (Miguez 1969:57), could be aligned with a "global plan" of such magnitude, a high dosage of credulity is required. The idea seems believable, however, when it is developed in a doctoral thesis which has been accepted by the Faculty of Theology of the Jesuit Fathers in Frankfurt, Germany, even though the author, Florencio Galindo, builds his whole case on one single document—one produced by *Amanecer,* a rather unknown group, one of the many Charismatic groups to be found in Latin America (:294-312). The fact that such a document has been reprinted by the CELAM "for information" (:295) shows the extent to which this topic is a matter of deep concern to the Roman Catholic hierarchy.

It cannot be proved that there is a religious-political "global plan" to which a significant number of Latin American Protestants would adhere. If such a plan existed, however, it is highly doubtful that in the present circumstances it could be carried out, since the determining factor for the life of these countries is a capitalism dependant on international political, socio-economic, and cultural "macrostructures" over which we have no control.[8]

The Constantinian Temptation

Having said that, it would not be difficult to prove that the Constantinianism that for centuries has characterized the Roman Catholic Church has made amazing progress among Evangelicals in Latin America in the last few years. In other words, the ambition for power has slowly gained ground in Evangelical ranks.

Traditionally, Evangelicals in Latin America have abstained from politics; at least in theory, they have been "apolitical." In the last twenty years or so, however, they have experienced a political awakening to such an extent that today participation in political parties plays an important role in the lives of many pastors and churches, especially in countries were the percentage of Evangelicals has reached a significant figure. This is not the place to describe in detail this phenomenon or to attempt to evaluate its possibilities and limitations.[9] We will limit ourselves to the following observations.

In the first place, Evangelicals in Latin America have a long history of presence and service in civil society, even though all too often this has not been documented nor has it been publicized. Especially in the last few years Evangelical churches have experienced notable growth in what is called "holistic mission," which focuses on the totality of life. From this perspective there has been and there is an active participation in nonpartisan politics, "from below," in response to a wide variety of social and economic needs.

More recently, the surprising numerical growth of Evangelicals, their social ascension, their educational level and professional improvement, and their greater importance in society have made the question of their participation in party politics, especially in some countries, an inevitable question. While they were an insignificant minority they could remain unnoticed; under the present circumstances it has become unavoidable that they not only be noticed but also compelled to define themselves politically.

It must be said, however, that with a few exceptions, Evangelicals are simply unprepared to face, on the basis of their faith, the challenges that the new situation poses to them. Their inheritance of the Anglo- American "awakenings," with a "double reduction, Christological and soteriological" (Miguez 1997:111), places them in a position of disadvantage in relation to the task of providing a solid theological and ethical basis for political action which is faithful to the Gospel and relevant to society. In this sense, they have a long way to go.

On the other hand, the exercise of political power requires much more than willingness to serve; it requires a program with an appropriate theological and ideological basis, political ability, and technical knowledge. The last few years of active participation in politics on the part of many Evangelicals have demonstrated that, generally speaking, they did not meet these requirements. They entered the political arena by virtue of their popularity, without the necessary tools. As a result, their role has been far from exemplary.

Furthermore, it must be taken into account that the political career is fraught with dangers. At least in Latin American, an outstanding danger is corruption. Without taking this factor into account, nor the need for a political ethics coherent with the gospel, several Evangelical politicians have fallen into the typical vices of Latin American politics: opportunism, nepotism, and authoritarianism.

Supposedly in order to prevent these evils and to articulate a political program and practice in line with Christian ideals, in the last few years political parties have been formed in several Latin American countries. The problem is that the assumption is made that there is *one* "social doctrine" that all Evangelical Christians should accept and *one* political party for which all Evangelicals should vote, with the result of creating a new basis for division within the churches,the political one, as has in fact already happened in many an occasion already. Those promoting these confessional parties need to see that there is no such thing as *Christian politics:* there can only be *Christians serving God and neighbor in the political field.*

In the last analysis, the creation of Evangelical political parties is an expression of the Constantinian mentality, the mentality that engenders the proposal "that the church should seek the mediation of *political society* in order to ensure its ecclesial and pastoral presence in *civil society*," which is "the quintessence of the Christendom model" (Richard 1987:133). Nevertheless this is apparently the model that has been adopted by a minority, but influential, sector of Latin American Protestantism aspiring to replace the RCC in her privileged relation to the state in order to play her traditional role of defining ethics and regulating moral conduct for the whole of society. David Stoll (1990) focuses on this topic and warns Evangelicals, at this moment of great numerical expansion, about "the danger of allowing their missions to be harnessed to U. S. militarism by the religious right" (1990:xv). If that happens, says Stoll, it will frustrate a religious transformation from which "a social vision with the potential to alter Latin America's cultural, moral, and political landscape" could emerge (1990:10).[10] His warning is realistic in light of episodes such as the support that the "Consejo de Pastores" (Pastoral Council) gave to Pinochet's dictatorial military government in Chile in the 1970s (cf. Lagos 1988), and the financial support that Pat Robertson provided for the "freedom fighters" in Nicaragua in the 1980s (cf. Stoll 1990:250-253), to mention two cases.

One of the worst possible scenarios for the future in Latin America would be an open confrontation between two types of Christendom—one Roman Catholic and the other Evangelical-Protestant—fighting to gain adherents not only in order to maintain hegemony in the religious field but also to control the political and economic power. The "confessonalization" of politics resulting from the "catholicizing" of Evangelical (especially Charismatic) churches would be as damaging to the cause of the gospel as the politicization of faith in the past.

Beyond Christendom:
Toward an Ecclesiology for the Third Millennium

All that has been said so far makes evident the urgent need for an ecclesiology rooted in the Gospel—an ecclesiology that will totally discard the premises of Christendom. Among both Roman Catholics and Protestants the alternative is still the one clearly described by Richard in the eighties: *either* Christendom *or* the church. Despite the theological and other differences that exist between the RCC and the Evangelical churches, on the threshold of the third millennium history places them before the very same alternative to define their identity either on the basis of the powers of this world and the love of power, or on the basis of the Kingdom of God and the power of love.

The two options may also be expressed, following Juan Luis Segundo (1973), in terms of *masses and minorities*. For him, at the root of the *corpus Christianum* is the premise that "society is coextensive with the community of adherents" (:12), and this premise leads the clergy to use *any means* so as to attain "a numerical universality of adherents to the doctrine of Christ" (:14). Thus, the determining factor is the law of the least effort, even at the cost of denying the essence of the gospel.

The Christological Basis

The reference to the essence of the gospel leads us to consider the basis of ecclesiology, which is Christology. In Roman Catholicism, it was the desire to include the large majority of people in the church that opened the door to popular religiosity, in which "ethics is absent and ritualistic magic takes its place" (Mackay 1991:152) and Christ "has lost prestige as someone who is able to help with regard to daily affairs" (:162, my translation) because he has lost his humanity and "in relation to his earthly life he appears almost exclusively in two dramatic roles—that of a child in his mother's arms and that of a suffering and bleeding victim" (:160).

In Evangelical Protestantism, on the other hand, the obsession with numerical growth is leading many leaders to assimilate many elements of the *light* culture that dominates society, to emphasize the individualism and subjectivism that mark the christological and soteriological reductionism inherited from the past, and to minimize the ethical demands of the gospel.

Placed at the service of Christendom, both Roman Catholicism and Evangelical Protestantism take the shape of popular religiosity. In this way they turn Christianity into a *popular religion* which appeals to the masses, but fail with regard to the purpose of the church derived from the gospel—that of contributing *from below* toward the formation of a community of disciples of Christ who are "the salt of the earth" and "the light of the world," to use two of Jesus' metaphors, full of meaning. Richard is right in saying that "Evangelization is inherently incompatible with a Christendom model. [Roman Catholic] Christendom 'produces' unevangelized Catholics" (1987:114); Protestant Christendom—we would add—"produces" unevangelized Evangelicals.

The alternative, of course, is not an *elitist* Christianity designed for a thinking minority, but a Christianity that seeks to be faithful to Jesus Christ and to the gospel as "good news to the poor," at whatever cost. That kind of faithfulness is possible only if there is a Christology which looks at Jesus Christ from a trinitarian perspective, recovers all events of redemption in him, including his life, death, resurrection, and ascension, and places him at the very center of the life and mission of the church as the Lord of the totality of human life and history.[11]

The "Grassroots Ecclesial Communities"

It is not an exaggeration to say that in the whole of the history of the RCC in Latin America there has never been another moment as full of promise for the life and mission of the Church as the decades of the 1960s, the 1970s, and the 1980s, when the famous *comunidades eclesiales de base* (CEBs, the *grassroots ecclesial communities*) flourished in several Latin American countries. There was a good reason for many theologians to see in these *comunidades* a real "ecclesiogenesis," "the emergence of a different way of being the church, based on the axis of the Word and the lay people" (Boff 1984:10, my translation), "one of the most significant ecclesial movements and social forces in the twentieth century" (Cook 1985:251)

As a matter of fact, the CEBs meant a return to an ecclesiology which conceived of the church as a faith community built "from below;" a community *with* the poor and *from* the poor, where people reflect on the faith and celebrate it, but also where "human situations are judged from an ethical perspective in God's light" (Boff:1982:25, my translation). In the CEBs all the members are carriers of *charisms* through which the Spirit of God acts for the common good, to such an extent that these *charisms* become the "organizational principle," "the structure of the community" (:234-249).

In this ecclesiology, bishops, archbishops, cardinals, and popes have an important role as those who have the "gift of help, direction, and government" and the "charism of unity" (Boff 1982:247-249; 1984:43). But "their specialty does not consist in accumulating or absorbing, but in integrating and coordinating. It is a gift located not outside but inside the community, not above the community but for the good of the community" (1984:43).

This ecclesiology, therefore, overcomes not only the Constantinian model, which brings ecclesiastical and political power together, but also the clerical model of the church, which reduces her to a "hierarchiology," to use Boff's term. The people of God are viewed as "a vast network of communities that include Christians, religious, priests, and bishops, without class distinction" (1982:249).

From the perspective of an Evangelical theologian it is quite impossible to go beyond this *vision of the church in her internal relations and her relationship to the world.* The ecclesiology of the CEBs has its roots in the New Testament and projects a church model which is quite coherent with its teaching regarding what God wants of the church as the first fruits of the new humanity, the sign and agent of the Kingdom, the community in which God's purpose to unite all things under the lordship of Jesus Christ is made visible.

The future of Roman Catholic Christianity in Latin America depends to a large extent on the historical realization of this vision of the church. Already in the sixteenth century the RCC opted for a hierarchical model of the church, thus blocking the possibility of radical renewal through an ecclesiology based on the universal priesthood of believers. According to Leonardo Boff, "the exclusion of Protestantism was a great error because it excluded not only Luther but also the possibility of true criticism and a controversial attitude with regard to the system, in the name of the Gospel" (1982:141). The greatest crisis of Catholicism in our continent today is the crisis posed by the alternative between accepting the CEBs as the means through which God wants to renew the church or expelling them as counterproductive to its ecclesiastical project.

"The Protestant Principle"

The dilemma is no less radical for Evangelical churches. They are the direct or indirect descendants of the sixteenth century Reformation and, as Samuel Escobar argues, in the Latin American context they have retained an "Anabaptist character" (1975:131). Nevertheless, they are changing in the direction of "massification," allowing numerical success to make them victims of political power plays. As a result, they are losing what Tillich has called "the Protestant principle," that is, "the divine and human protest against every historical absolutization," which Segundo considers "an essential dimension of Christianity. . . although. . . totally opposed to the pastoral endeavor to make the task of gaining converts universal" (1973:14).

The theological agenda, in general, and the ecclesiastical agenda, in particular, of these churches has been clearly defined by Jose Miguez Bonino in *Faces of Latin American Protestantism* (1995). Basically, it concerns making mission the "material principle" of theology, that is

a theological orientation which, as the best expression of the life and dynamic of the religious community, will give coherence and consistency to the understanding of the Gospel and become a point of reference for the theological building of the community (1997:131).

Space does not allow us to summarize the whole significance of this for Miguez, but we can emphasize the importance for him that mission not be conceived of as conquest—the "I conquer" as the "nucleus of the missionary consciousness"—but rather in terms of *sending*, a sending that "is not an accidental or limited act in a given moment" but rather an act that "finds it source in an eternal 'mission' that corresponds to the very trinitarian reality" (:140) and that is "the invitation to participate in faith in the very life of the triune God and hence in the totality of what God has done, is doing, and will do to fulfill God's purpose of being 'all in all'" (:140).

When the validity of this view expounded by Miguez—a view in which mission is inseparable from the work of the triune God—is not acknowledged, the totality of mission is reduced to evangelism "narrowly conceived as announcing the so-called plan of salvation and inviting people to conversion," and "we have failed to participate in the fullness of the work of the triune God" (:142-143). The consequence of this approach to evangelism, which has been common practice in Latin American Protestantism, is churches for which *how to win more converts* is the key question, often sadly forgetting people and their concrete human needs. Evangelism becomes a question of marketing, and falls into the absolutization of the means provided by the consumer society. With this we return to the topic of the church's adaptation to the Constantinianism that for several centuries has characterized it in its Roman Catholic model, and that today would seem to be powerfully penetrating Protestant churches. In this situation the recovery of the "Protestant principle" is urgent, in order that these churches recognize their role in society, to which Miguez refers in the following terms:

> Our conception of the church based on the community of faith, empowered by a personal vital commitment to Jesus Christ as Lord and Savior, our understanding of Christian freedom and of the priesthood of all believers, the rejection of a non-reformable doctrinal and ethical *magisterium* definitively close the way for us to attempt to become the religious actor of an old or a new Christendom. Socially and theologically, our missionary, social, and ecumenical commitment must begin "from below," from the sectors of society with the least power, from the believing community, from the life of the believers, from open and equal social dialogue. (1995a:34, my translation)

These words synthesize the vision of the church that the gospel calls on us to build, by the power of the Spirit, in faithfulness to the Son of Man who came not to be served but to serve and to give his life in ransom for many. The future of Christianity in Latin America depends on the fulfillment of this vision modeled on the politics of the crucified Messiah.

Notes

[1] On this issue, we must take into account David Martin's thesis (1990) on the numerical growth of Protestants, especially Pentecostal and neo-Pentecostals or Charismatics, and the loss of members who leave the RCC. According to Martin, what is happening in Latin America is similar to what happened in England in the eighteenth century, at the time of the great revivals under Wesley and Whitefield. Many people, tired of a static and authoritarian ecclesiastical organization—the Anglican church—turned to a popular religious movement. As a result, the Anglican church was practically emptied and the Methodist church came into being. Wesley had no intention of creating a new denomination. Nevertheless, the revival originated Methodism, a movement that emphasized voluntarism and became a powerful counter-culture in a society in which the Anglican church was a part of the establishment. The results were unpredictable. As time went on, Methodism became a decisive factor in the cultural shaping of the Puritan colonies, for it impressed on them quite definitely its emphasis on individual freedom and personal responsibility, and with this emphasis it exercised a great influence in the United States, even on the political level. What we now have, says Martin, is a Latin American version of Anglo-American Methodism which, as its predecessor, may be interpreted as an anticipation of a freedom which is initially experienced in the religious sphere but has the potential to be extended to all of society. It is not Methodism itself, but it is a spiritualist revival movement. While the RCC decreases, Protestantism grows in the space of freedom resulting from the rupture of the

old socio- religious and cultural system, by attracting millions of persons who are searching for religious options which are more open to everybody's participation and less dominated by hierarchical power.

2   It would probably be quite correct to say that the greatest concern on the part of the Roman Catholic hierarchy with regard to Protestant growth is closely related to political interests. On the growing social and political significance of Evangelical Christians in Latin America, see my chapter in Cook (1994).

3   For a summary of some of these conflicting attempts, see Escobar (1994):112-134. Sadly, as we shall see further on in this paper, this author is probably correct in suggesting that "the Protestant upsurge and the Catholic reaction could be sparks that ignite a religious war of catastrophic proportions" (112).

4   I am taking this expression from Nathan Gardels (1995), editor of the magazine NPQ, with Costa-Gavras, Michael Eisner, Jack Lang, and Benjamin Barber. It should be noted that the RC church as well is decidedly entering the world of the mass media, with the consequent "risk of transforming religious rites into senseless shows, and of rupturing the communities of the faithful" Zizola (1997):11.

5   One paradigmatic case is that of Argentina, where the bishops who opposed the military dictatorship (1976-1983) could be counted on the fingers: Angelelli, Hesayne, De Nevares, Novak. . . . For a detailed analysis of the "new right" social and political project of the Roman Catholic hierarchy, based on the social teaching of the church, for the Latin American countries, with emphasis on Argentina, see Ezcurra (1988).

6   Samuel Escobar (1994:17-29) has documented this campaign and, on the basis of documents issued by the Roman Catholic hierarchy, has shown the progressive hardening of the official attitude toward the Protestant "sects" from the first General Assembly of CELAM (1955) to the fourth (1992). At this last gathering the pope, in his opening speech, described them as "rapacious wolves" (:20). According to Escobar, it is not surprising that "some North American Catholic commentators have publicly expressed their disappointment at the intransigent posture of certain sectors of the hierarchy at Santo Domingo and at the return to attitudes that seemed to have been overcome" (:21).

7   With this conclusion agrees Stoll, who states that, "What has flung open Latin America to evangelical Protestantism . . . is the Catholic Church's inability to decentralize its system of authority" (1990):xvii. In the second chapter of his detailed study of the politics of Evangelical growth, "Reformation and Counter-Reformation in the Catholic Church," Stoll (1990:24- 41) shows how counter-productive it is for the RCC to affirm its centralism precisely at this time of "disintegration of Latin America's paternalistic social order, a society of mutual obligations between upper and lower classes in which the church served as spiritual guarantor" (:25). In the same vein Bastian relates the Protestant expansion to the effort on the part of the RCC to safeguard her hegemony "by instrumentalizing the religious demands of the masses through a corporate model of religious management" (1977):95.

8   The following anecdote, written by Chuang-Tzu (fourth century, B.C.) and translated by Octavio Paz, may be quoted here: "Penumbra said to Shadow: 'Sometimes you move, sometimes you are still. One time you lie down, another time you get up. Why are you so changeable?' 'I depend,' said Shade, 'on something that carries me here and there. And that something in turn depends on something else that compels it to move or to remain still. I am like the rings of a serpent or the wings of a bird, which do not slide or fly by their own will. How am I to answer your question?'"

9   There is a growing number of books and articles dealing with this topic. See, for instance, the papers edited by Padilla (1991) and Garrard-Burnett and David Stoll (1993), and the doctoral thesis by Freston on the Brazilian case (1993).

10 For Stoll it is clear that the same danger threatens the RCC. As an example he refers to the case of the Belgian Jesuit Roger Vekemans, in Chile, who "became a conduit for millions of dollars from the CIA, which also subsidized Catholic radio broadcasts to peasants in Colombia" (1990):14.

11 "The limitation of space does not permit us to elaborate this topic. The guidelines of this "Trinitarian Christology" and its practical implications for the Church have been outlined in general terms by Jose Miguez Bonino (1997):117-127.

References

Berger, Peter L.

1973 *The Social Reality of Religion* (Harmonsworth, Middlesex: Penguin Books Ltd.).

Boff, Leonardo

1982 *Igreja: carisma e poder: ensaios de eclesiologia militante* (Vozes, Petropolis).

1984 *Eclesiogenesis: las comunidades de base reinventan la Iglesia* (Editorial San Terrae, Santander).

CELAM

1995 *Jesucristo, vida plena para todos: Plan global del en la aurora del III milenio* (CELAM, Bogota).

Cook, Guillermo

1985 *The Expectation of the Poor: Latin American Basic Ecclesial Communities* (Maryknoll: Orbis Books).

Cook, Guillermo, ed.

1994 *New Face of the Church in Latin America: Between Tradition and Change* (Maryknoll: Orbis Books).

Escobar, Samuel

1975 «El Reino de Dios, la escatologia y la etica social y politica en America Latina», *El Reino de Dios y America Latina,* ed. C. Rene Padilla, Casa Bautista dePublicaciones, El Paso, Texas.

1994 «La presencia protestante en America Latina: conflicto mision revision y deinterpretaciones», *Historia y perspectivas,* Ediciones Presencia, Lima.

Ezcurra, Ana Maria

1988 *Iglesia y transicion democratica: ofensiva del neoconser-vadurismo catolico en America Latina, Puntosur, Buenos Aires/Montevideo.*

Freston, Paul

1993 *Protestantes e politica no Brasil: da Constituinte ao impeachment.* Universidade Estadual de Campinas, Campinas.

Galilea, Segundo

1979 *Religiosidad popular y pastoral.* Ediciones Cristiandad, Madrid Galindo, Florencio.

1992 *El Protestantismo fundamentalista: una experiencia ambigua para America Latina.* Editorial Verbo Divino, Estella, Navarra, Espana.

Garrard-Burnett, Virginia, and David Stoll, eds.

1993 *Rethinking Protestantism in Latin America* (Philadelphia: Temple University Press).

Hanson, Eric O.

    1987 *The Catholic Church in World Politics* (Princeton: Princeton University Press).

Lagos Schuffeneger, Humberto

    1988 *Crisis de la esperanza: Religion y autoritarismo en Chile,* Presor y Lar, Santiago de Chile.

Mackay, Juan A.

    1992 (1952) *El otro Cristo espafiol: un estudio de la historia espiritual de Espafia e Hispanoamerica.* Colegio San Andres, Lima. Only the Spanish translation was available to the author.

Martin, David

    1990 *Tongues of Fire: The Explosion of Protestantism in Latin America.* (Oxford: Blackwells).

Miguez Bonino, Jose

    1969 *Integracion humana y unidad cristiana.* Seminario Evangelico de Puerto Rico, Rio Piedras, 1969.

    1997 *Faces of Latin American Protestantism* (Grand Rapids: Wm. B. Eerdmans Publishing Co.).

    1995 «Hacia un ecumenismo del Espiritu», *Rena cer a la esperanza: Ponencias presentadas en la Tercera Asamblea General del CLAI.* CLAI, Quito.

Richard, Pablo

    1987 *Death of Christendoms, Birth of the Church: Historical Analysis and Theolog'cal Interpretation of the Church in Latin America* (Orbis Books, Maryknoll, N. Y.).

Segundo, Juan Luis

    1973 *Masas y minorias en la dialectica divina de la liberacien* (Buenos Aires: Editorial La Aurora).

    1978 *The Hidden Motives of Pastoral Action* (Maryknoll: Orbis Books).

Stoll, David

    1990 *Is Latin America Turning Protestant? The Politics of Evangelical Growth* (Berkeley & Los Angeles: University of California Press).

van Leeuwen, Arend Th.

    1964 *Christianity in World History: The Meaning of the Faiths of East and West.* (London: Edinburgh House Press).

Zizola, Giancarlo

    1997 "From the New On-Line Pulpits, *Electronic Christianity* Preaches to the Whole World," *Idoc internazionale* (julio-septiembre) : 11-18.

Interaction of Global and Local:
A New Look at Mission Responsibility and Planning for Churches in the U.S.A. and Canada

Wayne C. Stumme

This Colloquium has been asked to assess North American mission responsibility and planning in terms of what currently is happening and what our developing situation may require in the future. The task set before us is both necessary and daunting. Most would agree that the contemporary social and missional reality is multifaceted with respect to causes and expressions, and few commentators have been able to give us an adequate grasp of the whole. The author of this paper makes no claim to remedy that deficiency.

It is important, therefore, to note the limitations that apply to this essay. Clearly, what is said about the United States differs in many respects from what others would say in describing Canadian society and mission: The particular Lutheran perspective, experience, and knowledge of the essayist requires supplementation and, perhaps, correction by other members of the Colloquium. The selection of relevant data and the value judgments offered in this paper will differ from those made by persons representing alternative perspectives. Finally, the limitations of time and space have an obvious bearing on what can be presented for our initial consideration.

This paper will begin with an impressionistic overview of where we are with respect to North American society and the mission responses of the churches. It will be followed by a preliminary but partial critique of mission efforts, failures, and opportunities. Concern for the interrelation of the global mission experience and our own self-understanding and practice will be expressed in both sections of the essay.

An Impressionistic Overview

Impressionistic? How else can one attempt a description of the social context of North American mission activity? The efforts of cultural historians, sociologists, political analysts, economic pundits, and religious scholars have illuminated significant aspects of this society, but few are able to offer a coherent and convincing picture of our total social reality. That is not surprising, of course. Ours is a time when older certainties seem to be fading and new assurances are not forthcoming. The global hostilities that shaped our thinking and acting for half a century now are replaced by diminished but still disturbing threats to our well being. We are uncertain about the future direction of our society and our individual lives but, at the same time, we cannot suppress feelings of cautious optimism. These broader currents of our time sweep us in the churches along with others, and we frequently react in ways not far different from those not sharing our Christian convictions.

What characterizes our North American culture today? A helpful survey is provided by our Colloquium colleague, James Engel, in his study, *A Clouded Future? Advancing North American Missions.*[1] Describing the dominant "baby boomer" generation, he identifies the following as differing from more traditional assumptions: individualism, pluralism: skepticism, holism, activism, and isolationism. Each of these presents urgent challenges to current mission consciousness and practice. The fascination with technology and growing sophistication in its use is to some extent offset by widespread uncertainty about the direction and personal implications of a rapidly changing society. Anxieties about the meaning of one's life, one's children's education and future, one's work and wider social relationships are endemic to North American people. I sense a greater generational separation, even hostility, than we have known before, and all age groups exhibit hedonistic preferences. To a greater extent than many have wanted to admit, our unifying social vision has steadily eroded and no new national self-understanding has emerged to take its place. Popular culture—as articulated in music, movies, entertainment, print media —reflects these changes, confusion, and self-doubt. Neither is intellectual life immune from these influences. Academic work, particularly in the social sciences and the humanities (including theology), often exhibits more interest in the "deconstruction" of existing beliefs, practices, and institutions than in advancing those proposals for the "common good," which take into account both necessary continuity and promising innovation. Cultural historian Christopher Lasch, in his final book *The Revolt of the Elites and the Betrayal of Democracy,*[2] gives impassioned expression to this charge. At the same time, some observers have noted more positive aspects of contemporary culture. We enjoy a greater toleration of diversity; we have less patience with racial and ethnic and gender discrimination; we are capable of remarkable acts of communal and individual generosity; we agonize over ethical decisions even when our corresponding practice falls short of our best insights. We mourn the loss of earlier certainties while we question the contending alternatives urged upon us. What does this mean for us in the churches? At the very least, North American culture impacts the understanding and performance of Christian mission in ways we sometimes recognize but frequently overlook.

What we have described as "culture" also reflects underlying political and economic currents that carry our common life in uncharted directions. Impacting all of our society from rural village to megalopolis is the rapidly emerging global market economy. This phenomenon, of course, extends beyond our borders to the developing countries where its consequences in terms of exploitation of workers, depletion of natural resources, distortion of national priorities, and the corruption of national elites already are far advanced. The "ideology" of this form of market capitalism permeates nearly every aspect of global society, and its controlling values constitute a direct threat to Christian understandings of a just, free, egalitarian, and participatory social order. Those values, unfortunately, receive little effective criticism from North American church leaders or theologians.

Politically viewed, the United States is still coming to terms with its leading role in international affairs. The recent trip of President Clinton to Africa has highlighted this country's past neglect of the continent's problems and potential. Africa's rapidly growing Christian population makes this neglect a matter of urgent concern to all who affirm the interdependence required by the Christian mission. National politics in the United States, often driven by single-issue movements, seems unable to reach consensus on needed social legislation. Christians themselves are deeply divided politically, particularly with respect to those issues related to sexuality and the role of religion in this society.

For many of our citizens this is a time of economic promise and well being. Unemployment is at a twenty-year low, the stock market continues to soar, and inflation is apparently under control. The other side of the economic picture is more grim. More than thirty-four million persons in the United States live below the poverty line, and the majority of those are women and children. Nearly one in four children is found in the ranks of the poor. A growing number of children from all socio-economic levels are being raised in single- parent or nontraditional families. Even the jobs newly created are largely in the low-paying service sector, and the number of the working poor remains shamefully high. Many of the persons at the bottom of the economic ladder are immigrants, poor whites, and persons of color. Corporate opposition to a genuine living wage has blocked necessary political remedies to this situation. Many other workers face the threat of job loss through employers' decisions to move production facilities to overseas locations where lower pay scales and lack of worker protection offer higher profit margins. Goaded by the ruthless "union-busting" efforts of the last two decades, American workers are responding with new militancy and a growing sense of solidarity. Finally, the growing disparity in income and wealth between a small number of the fiscal elite and the majority of Americans has reached alarming proportions. Already this gross imbalance has negatively affected the working of our democratic system. There is justifiable fear that this situation of persistent inequality of opportunity and reward could lead to future social unrest on a vast scale.

What is the role of religion in this entrepreneurial, troubled, and yet strangely optimistic society? No longer is it possible, if it ever was, to speak of a "Christian America." The growth of Islam, the vitality of various marginal religious movements, the popular fascination with every variety of "spirituality," and the more limited appeal of eastern religions attest, however, to the continuing "religious" character of our populace. For many evangelicals and some ecumenical Christians, the insights and practices of the church growth movement have seemed to offer new evangelistic possibilities. Most Christian bodies have renewed their efforts to attract unchurched persons and establish congregations in promising locations. There is, unfortunately, a clear avoidance of outreach to the working poor and the poor except for efforts of some of the black churches, fundamentalist groups, and pentecostal Christians. Here Christian practice tends to mimic the class preferences of the dominant society. Aside from issues of sexuality, school prayer, individual morality, and the relation of church and state, North American Christians devote comparatively little thought, time, or energy to urgent matters of social justice.

While there is some evidence of cautious rapprochement between conservative evangelicals and ecumenical Christians, genuine cooperation in mission occurs only rarely. Whatever we may make of the claim that ours is a post-Enlightenment age (and many would consider that claim greatly exaggerated), theological work in many of our churches has not demonstrated its adequacy for the present demands of mission in this society. Some claim that the education of ordained leaders by North American seminaries generally fails to prepare men and women for cross-cultural outreach and ministry or to instill a commitment to evangelistic outreach. Here, as elsewhere among both evangelical and ecumenical denominations, cultural accommodation saps the vitality of the essential mission impulse.

This impressionistic overview makes no claim to comprehensiveness but seeks to highlight specific factors in our social setting which influence the churches' faithfulness and effectiveness in mission. More than ever before in our common history, the attitudes and practices of North American Christians impact the lives of our brothers and sisters in the churches and nations of the two-thirds world. We are just beginning to recognize how their own insights and experiences can positively affect our self-understanding and missional activity.

A Preliminary Critique

Scholars of Christian mission have addressed the inadequacies of much of our current theory and practice and have identified the challenges awaiting the churches in this "post-colonial global era." James Scherer, in a paper prepared for this conference, identifies "major elements of a biblically based and theologically sound mission practice," and his reflections are helpful for western Christians as they view their local responsibilities in the light of global mission.[3]

What follows are observations which apply directly to the North American scene but which are informed by the insights of Scherer and others.

Who needs to hear the Gospel of Jesus Christ in this society? Obviously, the answer is "all persons." Specifically, however, we need to turn to those most frequently overlooked and neglected by the churches. Here I would point to working people, the working poor, and the poor, as these are represented in all racial, ethnic, linguistic, and cultural groups. As noted above, this lack of concern may reveal profound class and racial biases within our congregations and, perhaps, among our clerical and lay leadership. Many of these people suffer serious and continuing disadvantage within American society, and some are victims of what can only be called economic and political injustice. This is demonstrably true with respect to more recent immigrant populations. Evangelistic outreach to all of these people lacks credibility when our churches show little awareness of and concern for their legitimate life needs. That unwillingness to understand is attested, for instance, by the widespread hostility within our churches to the American labor movement, a movement which directly and indirectly embodies the uphill struggle to achieve economic justice for workers and destitute Americans, and which shares significant ethical commonalities with Christian communities. How seriously can working people and the poor take our professions of concern for their spiritual well-being when we callously ignore those attitudes, policies, and practices that demean, exploit, and marginalize them? Can they believe what we say when our actions, even in church-related institutions, deny their rights to fundamental economic justice? Is not this situation a further indication of the cultural captivity of North American churches, a captivity all the more threatening because we do not recognize our subservience to the controlling values of a market-dominated society? Our mission failure here not only threatens the integrity of our congregations but also undermines the effectiveness of our global missional partnerships and efforts. We cannot ignore the fact that the vast majority of our fellow Christians in the Two Thirds World are themselves working people and the poor.

Already this suggests that the necessary renewal of mission consciousness and practice in North American churches calls for something like the emergence of a "counter-cultural" awareness on the part of ministers and people in our congregations. That awareness includes a profound sense of our failures and a summons to repentance; it builds upon humble attentiveness to the divine gift and the call announced by the scriptural writers; it invites us to a recovery of the missional implications of the foundational Trinitarian and Christological dogmas; it directs us once more to those in our society who have been ignored by the powerful, wealthy and influential . . . and also by us; it warns us against the uncritical acceptance of techniques and methods which may subvert the truth of the Gospel itself; it summons us to the difficult task of determining authentic expression of Christian discipleship within a complex, challenging, and often corrupt society; it encourages an informed, sensitive, and faithful encounter with the religious and non-religious alternatives to Christian faith whose adherents are our neighbors, friends, and fellow citizens; it compels us to take our stand with those whose basic human rights are denied, whose suffering and hopelessness are treated with contempt by too many of our contemporaries, whose cries for justice are ignored by those who profit from their misery. All of this, and even more, is part of the urgently needed renewal of Christian congregations for mission in this society. Few have seen the costly implications of this renewal with greater clarity than the great missionary theologian, Lesslie Newbigin. He writes:

> Christians can never seek refuge in a ghetto where their faith is not proclaimed as public truth for all. They can never agree that there is one law for themselves and another for the world. They can never admit that there are areas of human life where the writ of Christ does not run. . . . The church can never accept the thesis that the central shrine of public life is empty, in other words, that there has been no public revelation before the eyes of all the world of the purpose for which all things and all peoples have been created and which all governments must serve. It can never accept an ultimate pluralism as a creed even if it must—as of course it must—acknowledge plurality as a fact.[4]

We have yet to discover what these implications might mean for those churches—whether they term themselves ecumenical, evangelical, confessional, catholic or other—whose representatives will gather for this Congress on the World Mission of the Church. There are inescapable questions we must put to each other. In the light of our eschatological unity and in view of the urgency of the missionary imperative, *what can we do together in this society and at this time?* Will the approaching millennium see us reassessing our existing divisions—whether theological, ecclesiological, ethical, or other—within the emerging context of mission needs and opportunities? Will renewed congregations lead to renewed churches? And are we prepared for the possibility that the approaching century may again be a time in which Christians will hear the summons to "take up the cross" as we follow our crucified and risen Lord?

We do not yet know the answers to these questions, but we are confident that the Christ who has called us and who goes before us into every new tomorrow will open for us undreamed of mission opportunities. God grant that we are ready to respond in faith and obedience.

Notes

[1] Engel, James F. *A Clouded Future? Advancing North American World Missions* (Milwaukee, Wisconsin: Christian Stewardship Association, 1996), Pages 12,13.

[2] Lasch, Christopher. *The Revolt of the Elites and the Betrayal of Democracy* (New York: W.W. Norton, 1995).

[3] Scherer, James A. "Key Issues to be Considered in Global Mission Today: Crucial Questions about Mission Theology, Context, and Expectations." A paper prepared for the Congress on World Mission of the Church, 1998.

[4] Newbigin, Lesslie. *Foolishness to the Greeks: The Gospel and Western Culture* (Geneva, Switzerland: World Council of Churches, 1986).

North American Global Mission:
A Clouded Future

James F. Engel

Much that is said in this paper is drawn from two publications that ana-lyzed the dilemma facing North American global missions. The first entitled The Peril of Outmoded Paradigms for World Mission *focuses on theological issues and is subtitled "An overdue call for biblical fidelity and common sense." The second entitled* A Clouded Future *reports on a Lilly Endowment study of the practices of more than 100 mission agencies and is a critical analysis from the perspective of both local churches and agencies. For details see the citations in the References at the end.*

As James Scherer aptly summarized in his position paper for this Congress (Scherer, 1998, 1), North American Protestant mission enterprises established the foundation for a growing worldwide Christian community. But what a change in the last couple of decades:

- The North American church, broadly speaking, is listing in the spiritual waters and is losing its message to the world.

- The historic philanthropic commitment of North American churches and individual Christians to international ministry is declining precipitously.

- The momentum and leadership in world mission has shifted to the Two Thirds World to the extent that North America is rapidly becoming a secondary force on the scene.

- Large numbers of mission agencies have plateaued in growth and are facing stringent realities of financial crisis.

It was a kairos moment when Dr. Paul Cedar stood before an audience of more than 4000 leaders from over 200 countries. This was the historic GCOWE '95 gathering of the AD2000 & Beyond Movement in Seoul, Korea. These were his sobering words on a radically changed North American missiological role:

> We, the United States delegation, in sincere humility, and in the spirit of reconciliation, like Daniel and Nehemiah, acknowledge and confess our sins of omission and commission, knowingly, and unknowingly, by us or by others, including the following:
> - Our arrogance expressed in exaggerated national pride,
> - Our unjust treatment of minority groups within our own nation,

- Our insensitivity to other nations and cultures,
- Our undue dependence on our own plans and technology,
- Our unteachability,
- Our extravagant appropriation of God's resources for our own use,
- Our conspicuous consumption of global resources,
- Our fragmentation of the Body of Christ,
- Our imposition upon others of our own cultural forms as though they comprised the gospel itself.

This message was ended with the statement, "now it is our turn to learn from you in humility." Some of us, from the North American contingent, by no means a majority, rose to our feet to give Paul a standing ovation for his prophetic courage. We no longer have the luxury, if indeed we ever did, to ignore the root causes of what is becoming a genuine crisis in North American mission.

Two years ago I summarized the results of a Lilly Endowment survey of global mission agencies on this continent in these words:

> North American Christian commitment to world evangelization (mission) is in sharp retrenchment. Unless there is an intervention by God leading to across-the-board willingness in churches and agencies to cope with changing paradigms and realities, North America will become a secondary force in the world church (Engel, 1996, 4).

Nothing has happened to diminish this prognosis of a heavily clouded future.

I approach my topic as an Episcopalian with a centrist evangelical theology embracing the historic missionary role of the church as affirmed in the missiological conferences of the twentieth century (Motte, 1995). Furthermore, I speak from first hand experience. Much of my ministry in the last three decades has been in the Two Thirds World through service as a missions strategist, leadership developer, and consultant with hundreds of churches and agencies.

While I agonize with the implications of this clouded future, there is no question that our Lord Jesus Christ *is* establishing and extending his kingdom worldwide. A changed but significant role, in my opinion, still exists for the North American church and its agencies if we are willing to come to grips with the necessity to change our paradigms of world mission in four significant ways: *(1) theological*—restoration of the kingdom of God to its rightful place at the center; *(2) missiological*—acceptance of a radically-changing mission role; *(3) ecclesiological*—acceptance of the necessity of church revitalization as the key to mission involvement; and *(4) strategic*—development of new wineskins.

Restoration of the Kingdom of God as Our Theological Center

I have long been of the conviction that the primary obstacle facing North American global mission over the last century is a defective theology which has led to distortions of Christ's mandate for his church (Engel, 1998). For all our protests to the contrary, we still are a divided body licking our wounds over longstanding theological controversy. It is not surprising that we embrace radically different and often outmoded paradigms of world mission.

To oversimplify a bit, much of the evangelical arm interprets Christ's historic words in Matthew 28:18- 20 to mean, "go into the world" and plant the maximum number of churches using the full arsenal of "managerial missiology" duly documenting numerical progress toward "finishing the task" (Escobar, 1991). All too seldom do we engage in prayerful consideration of whether these churches truly become the Bride of Christ and function as a winsome "hermeneutic of the gospel" (Newbigin, 1989).

The mainline church, on the other hand, lies exhausted from a well-meaning commitment for many decades to developing institutions to bring about social transformation. Unfortunately the outcome all too often is a meager yield of lasting fruit. As Scherer notes, there seems to be little energy or vision for new mission ventures because of self-recrimination over past failures, whether real or alleged (Sherer, 1998, 2).

None of us can ignore the lessons of Rwanda which many declared to be our greatest missiological success (Adeyemo, 1996). There now is broad agreement that:

- Christianity was little more than a veneer on a secular lifestyle in which tribalism and animistic values were largely untouched.

- A controlling, top-down style of leadership built large churches but fell tragically short in discipleship designed to unleash lay people to be the priesthood of the believers.

- The church did not speak with one prophetic voice on such critical life and death issues as the dignity and worth of each person made in the image of God.

- The church relied on outside financial resources, thereby creating a debilitating dependence.

Distinguished African leader Phineas Dube refers to the church in his home continent as "20 miles wide and one inch deep." There are large numbers of converts but the lifestyle is little more than a superficial veneer on a secularized worldview. If we are honest, this is an apt description across the world (with some notable exceptions), including the United States and Canada. There are many churches, but how can we justify widespread economic, social, and moral decline even in so-called "Christian countries" which makes Sodom and Gomorrah seem mild by comparison? This makes a mockery of claims by Barrett and others that we are approaching the point where we can declare the task of reaching the unreached as a *fait accompli* (Barrett and Johnson, 1998).

Something has gone radically wrong with the harvest. In a virtual frenzy to "reach the unreached" we have all but forgotten that the mandate of Jesus is to make disciples in all nations through an intentional process of spiritual formation. I will never forget the words of a prophetic leader in Francophone Africa who said, "The missionaries brought us the gospel, but they never taught us how to live."

Dallas Willard describes much of contemporary mission practice as exemplifying "the great omission in the Great Commission" (Willard, 1988, 15). By his life and words, Jesus called us to make disciples who then individually and collectively join him in the process of extending the *present realities of the kingdom of God, his lordship over all phases of life, throughout the world.*

This divine purpose requires ongoing initiatives to establish faith communities which proclaim the good news, model the narrow way of personal holiness (Matthew 7:13-14) and death to self-seeking (John 12:15) and to infiltrate all segments of society with the salt and light of authentic Christianity. God's expected outcomes are economic lift among the poor, social and political justice, and Christian living characterized by integrity and holiness. In short, the church should present a model that stands in sharp contrast to the ways of the world. When this is not the case the message of the church lacks the power and validity which are necessary if it is to earn a hearing.

Surely everyone would agree with this obvious conclusion. But if that is the case, why are we still planting churches with well-meaning but ill-trained pastors who perpetuate the sterile institutional model which characterizes so much of the western world? I have asked this question of pastors in more than 75 countries: "What percentage of those attending your church are actively engaged in a truly Christian lifestyle which moves beyond passive Sunday attendance? The response: *five to ten percent!* The church all-too-often simply exists as just another cultural entity that is indrawn and largely oblivious to what the kingdom of God is all about.

In short, now is the time to embrace once again the totality of Christ's mission to the world expressed in the mandate to *make disciples in all nations* and to affirm these foundational truths expressed in scripture and validated through the history of Christian witness:

- God is a missionary God whose plan since the beginning calls for establishing his kingdom through his son, Jesus Christ, who came to earth as Lord over all of creation, reconciling all things unto himself (Col. 1:15-20).

- World mission is undertaken by ongoing initiatives to plant and build churches which model and proclaim the Good News through their words

(I Peter 3:15) and a lifestyle of personal holiness exemplified by Jesus (Mat 7:13-14).

- Extension of the kingdom occurs through initiatives which infiltrate all segments of society, starting with the poor, in which there is no dichotomy between evangelism, spiritual formation, and social transformation (Luke 4:18-19).

- Biblical mission is manifested as alleviation of the burdens of ignorance, poverty, hunger, racism, the struggle for cultural identity, and other forms of oppression (Amos 5:21; Luke 3:10-14, 4:18-21).

Acceptance of a Radically Changed Missiological Role

It is easy to lose sight of the fact that North American agencies originally came into existence to send missionaries who were pioneers in every sense as they took the message of Christ to a largely unreached world. These pioneers, in turn, were forced to play a dominant role in all that was done at least until national leaders were reached and discipled. Sending churches, on the other hand, assumed the important but largely passive role of serving as the primary source for personnel and funds.

In other words, we adopted the paradigm that embraced *missionary sending and financial support* as our primary mandate and, in so doing, have often lost the broader implications of *world mission* as a cause. The agenda setting, directive missionary role of an earlier period is no longer appropriate once indigenous initiative has emerged through the AD2000 & Beyond movement and other cooperative alliances. Furthermore, its continuation builds an unhappy dependence on the West which all too often destroys indigenous incentive. Indeed, the primary guiding premise of sending missionary personnel and financial and logistical support always should be to "work ourselves out of a job."

Few today would question the fact that there has been a radical shift of missiological power and initiative to the Two Thirds World, but our structures, systems, and practices have been slow to change. This shift has some serious implications:

- Churches and qualified nationals in the Two Thirds logically are taking both leadership and initiative in the primary task of extending the kingdom of Jesus Christ. Therefore, missionary sending in the traditional sense now becomes just one option rather than the normative strategy for both churches and agencies.

- The old dichotomy of "sending" vs. "receiving" nations makes little sense, because we are part of the same process of proclaiming and manifesting the lordship of Christ.

- Independent, non-coordinated efforts to reach the unreached are giving way to formulation of strategic, holistic ministry alliances and partnerships that transcend organizational, denominational, ethnic, or geopolitical boundaries.

In other words, world mission is a vastly different enterprise than it was not many years ago. An open door to North America will close rapidly unless expatriates are motivated and equipped to use their talents and gifts in a non-directive enabling role through contributions of vision, wisdom, empowerment, facilitation, cooperation, and specialized skills.

Now more than ever missionaries must be able to cope in a team environment in which they contribute an entrepreneurial spirit and specialized skills and abilities. This requires a mature spirit of servanthood based on mutuality, accountability, and submission. The primary objective is to contribute to the building of capabilities of others as a necessary stepping-stone toward establishing a vibrant, multiplying indigenous church.

Moreover, this changed context no longer tolerates the outmoded remnant from an unfortunate period of North American and European church history in which evangelism and social transformation were dichotomized often in hostile and polarizing ways. All of us have been tarred and wounded by the fundamentalism/liberal controversy which still lives on in many quarters, even though there has been welcome movement to a more centrist, holistic position.

An enabling or empowering missionary role expressed in the form of alliances and partnerships is, of course, not new in missions history. But it is all the more important now, because North American presence tends to signify power, money, and influence regardless of our motivation and commitment. I question whether it even is possible unless we adopt the suggestion of the late Orlando Costas (Costas, 1974) and be willing to come as *Galileans.* By this he meant a shedding of all trappings of power through our lifestyle and demeanor in order to establish necessary common ground. Perhaps it is time to restore the examples of such stalwarts from the past as Taylor, Moffat, and Carey in recognition of their sacrificial spirit of servanthood.

Church Revitalization as the Key to North American World Mission Vitality

Mission agencies, across the board, are discovering that the provision of funds, candidates, and other resources from local churches, with few exceptions, is falling significantly short of meeting their needs (Engel, 1996). This is even true among the staunch evangelical churches that historically have been the most globally minded. Furthermore, financial giving in response to individual direct marketing also is stagnating (Engel, 1996).

The main problem, quite frankly, is a pervasive slump in spiritual vitality. One of the most corrosive factors is a pervasive pluralism in all sectors, especially among those under 50. Growing evidence verifies the existence of widespread skepticism that the words of Jesus are universally valid and relevant. It is small wonder that interest in world mission is crumbling—the trumpet is giving forth an uncertain sound. This leads to just one conclusion, in my opinion: *there is no need for a global mission outreach if we do not accept that Jesus is the way, the truth and the life!*

The corrosion of pluralism is compounded by the idols of materialism and self-actualization that have crept insidiously into the heart of Christianity. A quest for holiness is being supplanted by a spiritual consumerism and isolationism that dulls a sense of concern for the poor and the lost. This is underscored by the fact that giving for global ministry is among the leading items to be cut in the church budget when funds get tight. This virulent cancer, if continued, would result in a virtual elimination of benevolent Christian giving by the year 2050 (Ronsvalle and Ronsvalle, 1994, 40).

There are no obvious strategic or programmatic answers to a dilemma of this nature other than a return to the historic and validated practice of corporate and individual prayer and fasting. Revival and renewal always have been the predecessors of authentic, spiritually motivated missions outreach. Why else would thousands have responded to the call of John R. Mott for sacrificial commitment to "completion of the Great Commission in this Generation"?

The obvious starting point is to obliterate our complacency with a recognition that something indeed has gone wrong with the harvest—a superficial Christianity which, with notable exceptions, is little more than a veneer on a secularized world view. It is time to ask: what has happened to the narrow way?

Perhaps some within the seeker-sensitive church movement have overemphasized the attracting power of a self-actualizing life style in spiritual wrappings. But other churches within this movement have not compromised and manifest a genuine and vital spirituality that extends far beyond the walls of the church.

The problem as I see it is a reluctance to recognize that the message of Christ to die to self and to seek the narrow way is decidedly counter culture. Those who respond always will be a minority, a numerical down-sizing if you will, which never sets well in upwardly mobile ecclesiastical communities and denominations. But this is a price that must be paid by those who follow the way of Jesus. Repentance, prayer, and fasting—a wholehearted search for the motivation and empowerment to become a Christian community which indeed functions with salt and light as the hermeneutic of the gospel. Have we any choice?

There are two cardinal components of ecclesiastical renewal which are essential if the resources of the body of Christ are to be released as Christ intends. The first is rediscovery of community—motivated interdependence—whereby Christian life moves out of the pews into vital relationships that strengthen and encourage discipleship and accountability. The second is a leadership style focusing on empowerment of the individual. When this is evident, church life moves far beyond the programmatic to motivating and equipping individuals for kingdom living. Church history verifies the principle that missions interest flourishes most naturally when genuine revitalization takes place.

One of the significant byproducts of AD2000 & Beyond and other grass roots movements is a profound commitment to pray for church revitalization and renewal. I have been impressed time and time again by the deeply held conviction that a revitalized church is the indispensable key to mission and outreach. Millions are praying daily. Are we in North America numbered in their ranks? If we are not serious about prayer and fasting this Congress will be quickly forgotten and overlooked!

New Wineskins

With the new wine of changing paradigms that I am calling for here, old wineskins will never do. It is time for both local churches and mission agencies to subject their practices to critical scrutiny.

The Local Church

It can be argued that local churches fall into three broad categories or outlooks with respect to their commitment to world missions (Camp, 1994):

- Supporting: a form of church/agency relationship in which the church depends upon agencies, in effect, to become their mission arm. The church plays the passive role of providing financial support, personnel, and prayer. This, of course has been the traditional bedrock of North American missions.

- Sending: a shift from agency dependence to a more active role in selecting, motivating, and sending missionaries. Much of the time, candidates still are funneled through existing agencies but only if there is a proper match between candidate profile and the board itself.

- Proactive: the church begins with world need and moves from there to exploration of ways in which the congregation can utilize its resources to make a strategic impact. Some, in effect, establish their own agency, whereas others enter into strategic alliances with other congregations or with agencies themselves.

The traditional passive, supporting role today usually represents little more than nominal involvement. Missions is just one minor interest. Frankly very little is asked of the congregation other than to pledge funds from a poorly understood overall budget. But it is not a priority of the church, and there is little done, apart from outright spiritual revitalization, to jolt such a congregation out of its lethargy. It is here that missions giving may disappear altogether.

There has been some movement away from the passive, supporting role in the last two decades, especially in churches that have taken steps toward becoming seeker sensitive. The usual distinguishing characteristic is a growing short-term program, which, if properly done, can generate some lay interest. Only a relatively small handful has become totally proactive, however, because few have the resources to support such an endeavor.

Recently five mission agencies cooperated in a survey of supporting churches with the goal of isolating those factors that seem to differentiate a mission active congregation from one that is passive or inactive. While the results have not yet been published, here are some of the major conclusions:

- The passive supporting style is gradually disappearing as younger leadership emerges with a broader international worldview.

- To the extent that congregational interest moves beyond financial support, there is growing tension with boards and agencies that are accustomed to viewing the church as a "customer." There is reluctance to continue longstanding relationships unless there are greater benefits of mutuality and partnership on both sides.

- The pastor is the gatekeeper for mission interest and involvement. If this cause is not championed from the pulpit, missions quickly will fall to the rear of other congregational interests and priorities.

- To the extent that evangelism, holistic ministry, and other outreach efforts are vital and healthy, missions has the best environment in which to flourish. A missions effort without this climate, however, is destined to failure.

- Another strong catalyst for mission interest is short or long-term mission service by respected members of the congregation. Support now moves beyond the abstract and takes the form of stronger interpersonal interest.

- An informed decision-making group is a necessity. Training in missions proves to be a real asset.

- Missions committees on the whole are discouraged with the uphill struggle to maintain missions interest within congregational life today. Those who are breaking free from this dilemma are doing so with short-term programs and other means of encouraging world travel and involvement.

- Mission boards themselves still are viewed favorably on the whole, but there is a clear trend away from unquestioning support and relationship. Agencies now are viewed more in the sense as partners and are expected to become involved in designing and facilitating congregational strategy.

The more proactive a local congregation becomes, the greater the need for training, partnering, and motivation. Agencies no longer will be welcomed unless there is a mutually beneficial relationship. In effect, agencies are expected to become consultants and friends, not promoters. Furthermore, an "old paradigm" agency that is not on the world cutting edge will find a disappearing welcome mat.

I cannot over emphasize the critical role of the pastor. If he or she is not championing the cause, it will be an uphill struggle. This will mean, without exception, that seminary training for the pastorate will need a drastic revamping. World mission can only be learned and sensed by meaningful, continuing field involvement and relationships. This is not an easy challenge to meet, but there is no way to avoid it.

Can we break through once again at the congregational level? Frankly I am not sure that this can or will happen in the more ecumenically minded denominations which have assigned missions to a pretty low overall priority. Any leader or pastor who bucks this trend is not likely to experience the usual perks of advancement.

Once again, I come back to theological foundations. Is God a missionary God or not? Are we going to sacrifice the essence of what Jesus taught and did on the altar of pluralism? The mission-active church, by definition, will go against the grain of culture and take Jesus seriously.

Mission Agencies

Agencies probably face the greatest challenge, because they are unmistakably caught in between changing paradigms. First, as we have stressed, the role of the North American missionary is radically different today. As if that is not enough of a dilemma, churches are changing to the point that missions is a dying cause in many quarters. And to make matters even worse, missions-revitalized congregations no longer are eager to provide the necessary resources unless there is much greater mutuality.

In many ways, this paradigm shift is of the magnitude of the earlier industrial revolution in North America and the more recent upheavals caused by information technology. Change simply is not an option! But few agencies have the level of financial support to permit aggressive experimentation and overhaul. Also, most of the remaining creative energy is devoted simply to keeping the enterprise alive.

Now is the time for all agencies to ask themselves this searching question: what would happen if we closed our doors? Unless compelling justification can be given based on solid empirical evidence, the handwriting may be on the wall. Now is not the time to throw resources at programs and agencies that have outlived their time. The need is for adaptation and change.

Here are some of the possible outcomes that I see on the horizon, all of which are presently evident in one form or another:

- *A number of agencies or boards will cease to exist because of financial realities.* Some already have fallen by the way because of unwillingness or inability to shift from a "business as usual" mentality. Others are in the last stage of death and decay. This is especially likely with denominational agencies for two reasons: (1) a theological stance which yields to pluralism and pulls away from mission encounter; and (2) the continued existence of "planting our brand" on the field as a motive for mission.

- *There will be a growth in mergers* to provide a smaller number of large mission conglomerates that have the financial and technical resources to meet world needs with greater impact.

- *It is entirely possible that local churches and agencies will work alongside each other in unprecedented initiatives.* Only limited examples of successful alliances can be found at this point, but the potential for growth seems high.

- *There will be a growth of small "niche" ministries* launched to meet specific needs and opportunities through offering tailored, specialized services. These enterprises will be specialists in providing the enabling and specialized services that are needed to help empower local churches and agencies in the Two Thirds World to meet their challenge.

- *Ministry will be carried out through international alliances* that assume their own identity and are funded and staffed from diverse sources worldwide. New wineskins will generate new funding.

Agencies which are unwilling to cope with these issues are doomed, I predict, to lingering death. Some leaders and boards will hesitate to innovate and will, instead, embrace a "play it safe" mentality. Yet, many will continue to exist indefinitely on the dwindling support of fewer and fewer donors, but their vitality will inevitably fade. To me, this is the most tragic outcome of all, because well-meaning, innocent donors will unknowingly prop up an institution that probably should be allowed to die. Strong words? You bet, because it is time to face reality.

Having said this, however, let me state my wholehearted belief that death is not inevitable, no matter how great the crisis. Those who undergo transformation and creatively adapt to changing paradigms not only will survive but may emerge even stronger (for some suggestions on the steps in organizational transformation, see Engel, 1996, Chapter 10). To take this step demands an unshakable faith in God who prunes, restores, and renews to his glory.

Some Concluding Words

Yes, the future of world mission outreach from North America is clouded, but I am unwavering in my belief that we may be at the threshold of the greatest mission thrust in the history of the entire church. Our challenge now is to join hands with our colleagues in the Two Thirds World, forsaking our past practices of independent initiative and full control of what happens. I am encouraged that restoration of the kingdom of God as our theological driving conviction will have the same impact today as was true at other times in the long, often tortured history of the church.

What can North America contribute? First of all, we must continue to offer the availability of Christians, long-term or short-term, lay or clergy, with the gifts, motivation, and specialized skills required in today's environment. While pioneering church-planting missionaries may be less needed than in the past, we are in an especially significant position to help develop and empower others with new technology, strategic thinking, and resource development skills.

Furthermore, we still are in a position to contribute financial resources, but this must be done with caution and discretion. The leadership in the Two Thirds World is increasingly reluctant to seek funds from us because of a fear of dependency. They feel, and I agree, that our financial support base must be worldwide. North America's unique contribution will be seed funds that are given without strings attached to those who covenant together in field alliances.

Are we willing to respond in a creative and entrepreneurial way to this period of turmoil resulting from shifting paradigms? The choice is ours.

References

Adeyemo, Tokunboh (1996), "The Lessons of Rwanda for the Church in Africa," *World Pulse* (December 20):5.

Barrett, David B. & Johnson, Todd M. (1998), *International Bulletin of Missionary Research*, 22 (January): 26-27.

Bosch, David J. (1991), *Transforming Mission* (Maryknoll, NY: Orbis).

Camp, Bruce (1994), "Paradigm Shifts in World Evangelization," *Mobilizer* (Winter): 1-16.

Costas, Orlando E. (1974), *The Church: A Shattering Critique from the Third World* (Wheaton, IL: Tyndale).

Engel, James F. (1998), *The Peril of Outmoded Paradigms for World Mission: An Overdue Call for Biblical Fidelity and Common Sense* (St. Davids, PA: Development Associates International).

Engel, James F. (1996), *A Clouded Future* (Milwaukee, WI: Christian Stewardship Association).

Escobar, Samuel (1991), "A Movement Divided," *Transformation* (October): 7-12.

Motte, Mary (1995), "World Mission Conferences in the Twentieth Century," *International Review of Mission* (July): 211-222.

Newbigin, Lesslie B. (1989), *The Gospel in a Pluralistic Society* (Grand Rapids, MI: Eerdmans).

Ronsvalle, J. and Ronsvalle, S. (1994), *The State of Church Giving Through 1992* (Champaign, IL: Empty Tomb).

Scherer, James A. (1998), "Key Issues to be Considered in Global Mission Today" (Paper distributed to this congress.)

Willard, Dallas (1988), *The Spirit of the Disciplines* (San Francisco, CA: Harper).

Towards an Evangelical Theology for a Pluralist Age

Israel Selvanayagam

The Greatest Challenge

Understanding and developing an approach to religious pluralism is one of the gravest concerns of the Church and will continue to be so as long as Christians believe in one God with a special reference to Jesus Christ and feel it is their bounded duty to communicate the gospel to all people whilst, at the same time, meeting people of other faiths with different experiences and perceptions of God. The problem has been approached and analyzed from different perspectives ranging from a crude exclusivism which consigns all non-Christians to eternal condemnation to an absolute pluralism according to which all religions are essentially the same. My approach has its own bias characterized by the combination I carry within myself namely—a grandson of a new convert to Christianity, a minister of a minority Church (The Church of South India), a student of religions, and a scholar of Hinduism, someone specialized in the ministry of inter-faith dialogue and committed to mission and evangelism. Whilst this combination may look very strange, I believe that one can be both evangelical and dialogical at the same time in the truest sense of the terms. This means that being evangelical is not the same as being fundamentalist and likewise, being dialogical does not require me to hold to a fixed or particular model with regard to the traditional divisions of exclusivism, inclusivism, or pluralism.

For obvious reasons I present the "dialogue on dialogue" which has been going on in India, the so-called "Mother of religions" (John Jones) and "laboratory for dialogue" (Paul Knitter). I hasten to add that this "mother" is a perplexing one not only because she produced many visions and traditions often contradicting each other but also because, despite her acclaimed spirituality from antiquity, nearly 50% of her 950 million children today are illiterate and live below the poverty line. However, India has been a constant referent in ecumenical discussions on the theology of religions. It is not insignificant that the third World Missionary Conference (Tambaram, Madras, 1938) and the third General Assembly of the World Council of Churches (New Delhi, 1961) were held in India. One of the hottest debates on the theology of religions took place in the WMC 1938 when Hendrik Kraemer presented his preparatory volume entitled *The Christian Message in a Non-Christian World.* Rejecting pervasive and omnipresent "relativism and pseudo-absolutes," Kraemer called for a recognition of the *sui generis* nature of God's revelation in Christ with an emphasis on biblical realism. Other religions, he believed, should be viewed as representing human attempts to apprehend God using the extraordinary capacity of creating *gods*. While the "Rethinking Group of Christians" in Madras argued for the universal presence of God and points of contact with Hinduism Kraemer refuted their claims. For him, "Religions are no series of separate dogmas and practices but indivisible unities. In the light of Christian revelation, all apparent similarities are dissimilarities. Points of contact are only to be found by antithesis. The only real point of contact is the disposition and the attitude of the missionary."

At New Delhi in 1961 the International Missionary Council merged with the WCC. In his keynote address for the assembly, P.D. Devanandan, the founder director of the Christian Institute for the Study of Religion and Society, called for an effective Christians witness in a multi-faith context. This witness included recognition of God's work in the renaissant and resurgent movement within Hinduism as well as Christian co-operation in the building of the nation. Christians should live as a community transformed and transforming, in accord with the new creation wrought by Jesus Christ.

There is one more reason for using the situation in India as a basis for a discussion on "an evangelical theology of religions." No other situation is more challenging for mission today. After nearly two thousand years of Christian presence, five hundred years of Catholic mission, three hundred years of Protestant mission and the establishment of considerable institutions, India still has only a tiny minority of 2.5% Christians, and I maintain that an authentic evangelical theology can only emerge in a context where Christians are in a minority. This discussion, however, is very relevant for the Church worldwide and hence related and parallel trends around the world will be highlighted as appropriate.

Carriers of the Light Encountering New Lights

It is erroneous to think that more positive approaches to other religions represent a modern aberration of a specialized group of Christian thinkers contributing to a loss of confidence in the gospel and strengthening the complex ambiguities of the "new age movement." The theological consideration of other religions started when the Christian missionaries first encountered them. Those who thought that they were carrying the Christian light into the heathen darkness were surprised by different forms of light already present in their new field and they reacted and responded in a variety of ways. Kenneth Cracknell has made a significant contribution to our knowledge of the history of the Christian encounter with people of other faiths by his classic of *Theologians and Missionaries Encountering World Religions (1846-1914)*.[1] Of the eight missionaries detailed in his book, six worked in India and recognized the positive values of Hinduism, some even claiming that they saw in Hindus the "broken lights" of God. But I want to mention two missionaries who are perhaps outside the scope of this book.

Barthalomaeus Ziegenbalg, the first Protestant missionary to India, a member of the then Pietist Movement, sent by the Halle Mission in Germany, landed on the eastern coast of Tamilnadu in 1706. Even before bringing out his first Tamil translation of the New Testament in 1714, he studied the beliefs and practices of the Hindus around. He had to work hard visiting shrines and employing interpreters. A manuscript was ready for publication. In his preface he wrote, "Wise people will not make an ill use of this our work of 'hay and stubble,' nor be induced to do evil, but on the contrary learn from it, how much more the grace of God has bestowed on them in spiritual matters than on these heathens, and thereby be moved to have compassion on them and when opportunity offers, try by every means in their power to bring them out of their idolatry."[2] Ziegenbalg sent the manuscript to Halle with the opening word that it aimed to "rejoice the patrons" but the response was on the contrary. The director of the Halle Mission wrote back saying that the printing of it was "not to be thought of, in as much as the missionaries were sent out to extricate heathenism, and not to spread heathenish nonsense in Europe".[3] The manuscript was shelved for 154 years before it was printed in German. Subsequently it was translated into English in 1868. The translator, who shared the fundamental position of the missionary movement of his day, after affirming the Bible as the true revelation of God, the absolutely perfect personal Being, and Christ as the true revelation of God and the only mediator between God and humankind, noted that "this little work may, by its faithful exposure of the religious errors of the Hindus, be subservient to the spreading of the saving knowledge of the truth."[4]

Those who read carefully Ziegenbalg's book would realize that the patron of his mission and the translator of his book failed to take note of some significant observations he had made in his study. It is true that he calls the religion of the Hindus he encountered as not only heathenism in general but at time he uses words like "foolish heathenism," "heathenish darkness," and "blind heathens." Nevertheless, with reference to the belief in one Supreme God Almighty found among them he wondered "how much further they have in his knowledge, by the light of nature, than the heathens of Rome." But "the light of nature," he continues, "has been quite obscured by their ancient poets and Brahmins, who have written many fabulous stories, and introduced a confused idol worship, out of which they cannot easily extricate themselves, though they feel much opposition to it in their conscience and can speak very reasonably of the Supreme Being."[5] In his own assessment of varying and shifting theories of God amongst Indians Ziegenbalg could not go beyond speaking in terms of "God as the object of Christian faith and the subject of Hindu speculation."[6] It is interesting to note that such disparaging remarks as the above about certain aspects of Hinduism have been made not only by Christians but also by some radical thinkers of modern India, both religious and secular.

The other was G.U. Pope (1820-1907) who as a SPG missionary went to an Anglican mission field in South Tamilnadu. In the course of his language study he came across a Hindu devotional text of the Tamil Saiva tradition. The devotional appeal of the text moved him so greatly that he translated it into English.[7] This experience not only won him great respect among the Tamil Hindu scholars but also equipped him to teach his fellow missionaries in India, as well as around the world, as to their attitude to people of other faiths. In his preface to this book he mentions that "in regard to all religious systems thorough rational investigation, searching historical criticism, and a careful candid consideration of the meaning of the symbols by which doctrines are supposed to be expressed, are quite necessary everywhere." Recognizing "an evolution of religion," Pope was confident that the result of his "searching, yet reverent analysis" was "of the utmost value in the West" and "TRUE DIVINE FAITH lives on, and grows more vigorously for the conflicts in which it is ever, of necessity, engaged." He advocated that his fellow missionaries "should take pains to know accurately the feelings and convictions of those for whom, and in the midst of whom, they work."

Pope was not simply proposing a missionary strategy but a new theological outlook in the context of religious pluralism. In the same preface he states: "In matters of religion the greatest hindrance—and the most truly religious thing—is the spirit of ignorant, unreasoning, unsympathetic antagonism. Every system has its truths and profounder thoughts; and these lie deeper than 'full fathoms five' in man's nature; and must be fundamentally and essentially in large measure the same for all men, and for all time. It is only by recognising these *common truths,* and making them the basis of enquiry, as to further alleged Divine communications, that it is possible to gain a true religious development."[8] Pope makes more specific observations in reference to the legendary history of Manikkavacakar, the poet and sage, the author of the text who had a conversion experience. This popular poet's historical character appeared to the missionary "a mixture of that of St. Paul and of St. Francis of Assisi." "Under other circumstances," he states, "what an apostle of the East might have become! This is his conversion, as South India believes it; and in almost every poem he alludes to it, pouring forth his gratitude in ecstasies of thanksgiving, and again and again repeating the words 'I am Thine, save me!' His poetry lives in all Tamil hearts, and in the main and true essence of it deserves so to live!"[9] Further, he compares the poem to the Psalms and concepts like grace and supreme power to the New Testament teaching on grace and Holy Spirit respectively. But he made no attempt to compare the fundamentals of the Christian faith with that of Hinduism in general or Tamil Saivism in particular.

While Pope's concern with removing ignorance of and understanding other religions was shared by many of his colleagues and scholars of religions, in due course, the comparative study of religion itself developed in such a way that the implications of such study for the mission and theology of the Church were no longer considered by most of those involved in it. Today that study has found a respectable place in universities and research centers with a high degree of specialization with just a few scholars having drawn insights from it to formulate a new Christian approach to other religions. The first World Missionary Conference (Edinburgh, 1910), the watershed of the modern ecumenical movement, devoted one full commission (no.4) to find out and clarify the "Missionary Message in Relation to Non-Christian Religions." The commission prepared a questionnaire containing eleven questions—nine addressed to missionaries in general, one to foreign missionaries and the other to new converts to Christianity. The response was overwhelming. A careful analysis of the replies to the above questions revealed that, barring some negative notes, the overall position "was characterized by sympathy and respect in the Christian approach to other religions."[10] The general conclusion of the commission on the "Missionary message" emphasized (a) proper attitude towards other religions undergirded by sympathy, appreciation and love, (b) training for a different approach to this effect, (c) renewal and reformulation of the Church's theology in the light of many theologies found among the people of other faiths, (d) the urgent need for the study of religion in theological education, and (e) an incipient theology of inter-faith dialogue.

The "Missionary Message" is still worth considering. However, although several arrangements have been made for the study of other religions and sympathetic approach to their adherents, there is no ground to claim that an adequate reformulation of the Churches' theology in the light of religious pluralism and a satisfactory theology of other religions and inter-faith dialogue has so far emerged. There are many reasons for this. First, while agreeing on the necessity for a loving approach, no evangelical Christian has been ready to seem to dilute the newness, relevance and the universal significance of the Christian message. Second, blanket views on religions, without taking each in its own merit to determine the relevance of the Christian message to it, have confused the matter. Third, the presentation of the message in single formulas such as "Jesus IS the gospel" or "reconciliation IS the gospel," etc. failed to communicate the Judeo-Christian vision as whole. Fourth, theologies of other religions have been mostly Christian monologues with imaginary partners of dialogue. Thinkers of other religions have hardly made any serious efforts to correct these monologues by studying the Christian vision, traditions and interpretations with empathy and comparing them with their own. Fifth, the missionary competition and confusion created by denominational titles and sectarian labels have obscured the core vision of the gospel.

Different Types of "One and Many"
The age long position of the Holy Roman Church was that of "no salvation outside the Church." The Council of Florence in 1442 reaffirmed this explaining further that "no one outside the Catholic Church, neither heathen nor Jew nor unbeliever, nor anyone separated from the unity, will partake of eternal

life, but that he will rather fall victim to the everlasting fire prepared for the devil and his angels if he does not adhere to it before he dies." Roman Catholic missionaries who went to India before the arrival of Ziegenbalg worked with this position. Although a few of them like Robert de Nobilie who went there in 1605 worked out new strategies of adapting the life style of the Brahmin priests and incorporating elements from their traditions into their literature, their hidden agenda was marked by the same view. This was amended only in the Second Vatican Council during 1962-65 in which it was stated that all people of good will could achieve salvation. However, the Council's categorization of ordinary and extraordinary ways of salvation with a strong emphasis on the unique and sacramental nature of the Church left many questions unanswered.

While for the Roman Catholics "Church" continues to be the central focus, some Protestant theologians in this century made revelation the central point. Karl Barth, Hendrik Kraemer, and Emil Brunner are the chief advocates of this position. Although they base their work wholly on the bible, they insist that Christ is the only revelation of God. All other religions represent the supreme *human* possibility of trying to apprehend God. They would not have regarded the scriptures of other religious traditions as being "revealed." Their presumptuous claim for the gospel hindered them from having any regard for those who come up with similar claims and experiences of God.

Lesslie Newbigin's *The Finality of Christ* popularized the term "finality" in relation to inter-faith relations. The word is used in two senses—chronology and quality. Originally this was made with regard to Judaism which was relegated to the position of simply promising Christ and preparing the way for him. When other religions are considered they are taken to be either inferior or imperfect. But Islam, which emerged after five-centuries of Christianity, claimed finality suggesting correction for some of the biblical records, proclaiming Mohammed as the seal of all the earlier prophets and declaring the Holy Qur'an as the "Last Testament." But Sikhism emerged after nearly ten centuries of the birth of Islam, synthesizing within it aspects of Hinduism and Islam. Later traditions like Bahaism also demand due recognition today as world religions. Any claim of finality in a qualitative sense is therefore judged as immature just like someone saying "my wife is the most beautiful woman" or "my daddy is the best of all men." This could be most upsetting to those involved in mission as they may be surprised to learn that, in the matter of their "unique" vision or message, their wife or daddy belongs to others, too.

J. N. Farquhar's *The Crown of Hinduism* was a popular book in the area of Hindu-Christian dialogue in the early part of the twentieth century. As a Scottish missionary in India, Farquhar studied the Indian religions using scientific methods and was caught up by "a feeling of deep surprise at the riches of the heritage of some of the great religions, especially in philosophy and in art." At the same time he could not appreciate people being carried away by curiosity and romantic thoughts. He notes that "Men and women who have lost hold of their religion, and miss the warm glow of faith in their lives, are caught up by a fancy for some curious or attractive element in another faith; and, without waiting to consider what its practical worth may be, snatch at it and sing its praise."[11] Taking insights from the theory of evolution and Jesus' insistence that he came "not to destroy but to fulfil," Farquhar declared that "Christ is already breathing life into the Hindu people. He does not come to destroy. To him all that is great and good is dear, the noble art of India, the power and spirituality of its best literature, the beauty and simplicity of Hindu village life, the love and tenderness of the Hindu home, the devotion and endurance of the ascetic schools."[12] He denounced any form of arrogance and partisanship and claimed to be "with wide open eyes and with full consciousness of the stupendous character of the missionary claim about the Christian message." He expressed his agreement with the NT teaching of the universal and internal witness of God but appealed to every individual to respond to Jesus' invitation to follow him, which would imply for many giving up their old religion. For him "Hinduism must die in order to live. It must die into Christianity." Although the term "crown" could be misleading in the context of the British crown ruling in India, Farquhar was passionate in his call for a new approach for the missionary. In his words, "The missionary's life must be a daily death to self in every aspect of his behaviour, if he is to exercise his full influence for Christ. No words are sufficient to tell how meek and lowly in heart the winner of souls must be, what humility of speech, what quietness of manner, what superlative self-effacement are necessary, in order that the light of Christ may shine through him into Hindu eyes."[13] In fact, Farquhar realized that "India [being] under Britain complicates matters for the Christian rather seriously."

Despite good intentions on his part, Farquhar's position was not fully appreciated by his own missionary colleagues and Hindu thinkers. The situation has not improved since then. The primary problem perceived was the claim that Christ fulfilled all the aspirations and fulfilled all the questions of Hindus. It was not difficult to point out that either the Hindus have their own answers for their questions or the questions that Jesus answered had never been asked by the Hindus. Therefore, for people like A.G. Hogg it was truer and more right to say that Hindus needed Christ rather than claiming that he fulfilled their aspirations. Further, there was the popular notion that all the world religions, from the foulest to their finest manifestations, occupied rungs on one long ladder of development. Farquhar assigned a lower rung to Hinduism and claimed the highest one for Christianity or Christ. But Hindu thinkers like Vivekananda and Radhakrishnan claimed that although every religion had its place on the ladder, the experience of oneness with the Supreme Reality or *Brahman* was the highest. Hence one crown countered with another crown and indeed, many more crowns could be identified if we had the space to refer to the different crowns claimed in Hinduism itself.

Experience, rather, mystical experience, is often presented as the core of religious life transcending different religious traditions. As it is said to be ineffable, very often any sensible talk about it is discouraged and silence advocated. However, studies of the "varieties of religious experience" show that different religious traditions do matter in understanding them. Sometimes sweeping generalizations in this regard have contributed to a kind of religious indifference that has no interest in understanding other peoples' experiences. Dr. Radhakrishnan claims that all mystics speak the same language. But the phenomenological studies on different mystical traditions clearly show that particular religious traditions contribute to interior journeys, perceptions, and post-experience expressions. One can see in Radhakrishnan a position of a staunch *advaitin (non-dualist)* for whom all the phenomenal varieties are ultimately unreal and this can be realized in the intuitive leap of getting oneness with the absolute *reality (Brahman)*. The belief is that what is reached in this experience is *the* reality, not an improbable entity as psychoanalysis may suggest.

Mystery is another overarching category used to explain the one and many. Stanley Samartha holds that different religions are different responses to the Mystery. But he also talks about the mystery of Christ and mystery of God. Hence his division between what is revealed and what is deeply hidden in God. What Paul claimed for Christ when he said that the eternal mystery was revealed in Christ, the Muslims claim about the Qur'an, the Buddhists about the enlightenment of Gautama Buddha which revealed the non-existence of a supreme God, and the Hindus claim about the incarnations and appearances of God in different forms and names. Thus as far as the religious traditions are concerned there is no mystery without some glimpses into it and these glimpses can contradict one another. The question then is where to set the boundary of what is knowable and known, and what is unknowable about reality or God. Unless there is a clear indication of the need to know more and that what is known is not fully comprehended and the ethical demand not yet exhausted, setting such boundaries may be construed as an exercise of arrogance and pride.

The term "Truth" is very popular in inter-faith discussions. Book titles like *Truth and Dialogue* (John Hick) and *Truth is Two-Eyed* (J.A.T. Robinson) serve to illustrate this. Many Christians continue to do mission with watchwords like "Jesus is the only Truth" whilst holding the position of "one Truth and many errors." There is no consistency however in understanding or explaining the "Truth." This is as true of street preachers as philosophers of religion. Truth remains either abstract or narrowly defined. At this juncture it may be worthwhile mentioning the Hindu view that "Truth is one and the wise call it differently." The popular analogies like one tree and many branches, one hilltop and many pathways, one sea and many streams, and one sun and many photographs are based on this view. Elsewhere I have done a study of the above verse, which is mentioned in the RgVeda, the most ancient text of Brahmanic Hinduism.[14] Let me make a few observations and their implications. The Truth here was not an undefined reality. It is said in the context of describing sacrifice and its many forms. It was a necessity when the Vedic ritual was developing as a grand mechanism. The same thing could be said with reference to Krishna's saying in the *Bhagavad Gita* that "whichever way people approach they come to me." This was very significant at a time when the figure of Krishna was taken as the rallying center of many conflicting strands. But only when Hinduism was encountered and challenged by Islam and Christianity were the above verses popularized. As some scholars of Hinduism, including those adhering to it have observed, this view has contributed to the disinterest of Hindus in understanding other religions. It has led to a reductionist view of religious life, taking only the ethical notions like love and being other-centered, resulting in an indiscriminate view of religions. It has concealed the creative dialogue with its affirmations and refutations that have taken place between different traditions and schools of thought within the complex religious traditions called Hinduism. A related position is a kind of relativism propagated by using the Buddhist folklore of six blind men sensing different parts of an elephant each claiming what he saw was the real elephant. In this story the king who arranged for this action alone could see the whole and real elephant. Those who copy this story and point it out in support of their relativist theology of religions seem to place themselves beside the king or to stand on an Olympian height with a condescending view of religions. There is a tendency among scholars to push the arena of Truth beyond the realm of comprehension, equating Truth with Mystery. The Theosophists declared that Truth is higher than all religions and they have not taken the pain of defining the boundaries of and the relationship between what is knowable and tangible and what is not knowable but indispensable. One might wonder whether this has been a technique adopted by modern Hindu thinkers to upset any challenge coming from outside in the name of a religion.

Those who talk about a "Copernican Revolution in the Theology of Religions" in the West (e.g. J. Hick of Britain and W.C. Smith of America) actually repeat an old story as far the Indians are considered. This "revolution" puts God at the center and sees all religions as rotating around him. In order to accommodate religions like Buddhism in which belief in one God is not fundamental they alternate their use of the word "God" with "Reality." They seem to think that in a pluralist age this position is theologically generous and socially charitable, thereby challenging the traditional western attitudes of triumphalism combined with racial superiority. But they must realize that such an Amer-Eurocentric view can hardly help the members of the Third Church like the Indian Christians. To them they appear like the *Advaita Vedantins* and Theosophists who have in various ways made the search for inter-religious understanding redundant and unnecessary. Consequently, in the name of tolerance and communal harmony, interreligious ignorance is perpetuated in India. It is important to study the various senses in which terms like "Truth" and "Mystery" are used in inter-faith discussions.

An initiative taken nearly fifty years ago in India in this direction may be worth mentioning. D. G. Moses, in his *Religious Truth & The Relation Between Religions,*[15] analyses Truth from general, religious, philosophical, artistic, and scientific viewpoints. He then consults the positions of Radhakrishnan, Hocking, and Kraemer with reference to their different understandings of Truth. The findings should serve as a warning to any one speaking and writing on Truth without specifying the particular sense in which they use the term. Moses' concluding words are on Kraemer, which can be taken as his own points to initiate further discussion. He criticizes Kraemer for his untenable extreme anti-rational dogmatism in reaction to the other forms of extreme pragmatism and relativism. Without raising any question as to the possibility of "a final or unique faith," he says that, "If the claim of religion to truth is taken seriously, one cannot but admit that religions can at least be evaluated in terms of more true and less true. But it does not fit the facts of the case to say that the relation between religions is one of utter 'discontinuity.'"[16] Of course Kraemer would not have agreed with this conclusion. In his response to this book he does not touch upon Moses' conclusion but to his earlier note that "if a religious truth is to be judged it must be judged primarily in terms of the *satisfaction* it will render to those dominant religious needs." For Kraemer, Moses' "reasoning is alien to Biblical thinking, which unequivocally teaches that man has *not* the right knowledge of his religious needs, nor the right knowledge of their satisfaction."[17] Noting a change in Moses' position with reference to a later essay of his Kraemer hoped for "a new substantial contribution from Moses' pen." This debate needs to be pursued.

Before we leave this section it is important to acknowledge a new trend in thinking of the "one and many" in the Hindu revivalist camp. Moving away from the age long position of one Truth or God and many forms or names, "the revivalist traditions argue that belief in one God is an ideology connected with absolute imperialism and the only solution to this doubtful connection is going back to the Vedic pantheon of affirming many gods and choosing any one according to taste."[18] In this light alone can one understand some Hindus explaining to outsiders in their temples that the Hindu temple is a supermarket of gods and goddesses and the devotees approach particular ones according to their special taste and need! Before any serious discussion can take place, such Hindu pluralists will need to be convinced about the difference between plurality and contradiction and the consequential repercussions for the understanding of the socio-economic discrimination that mars people's life in India. Even if there is openness on both sides, it should be pointed out that the Hindu pantheon has encountered constant conflict between the various deities over supremacy. This is so despite the ecumenical attempt to bring together the major ones: Brahma, Vishnu, and Siva by assigning to them the works of creation, preservation, and destruction respectively. This attempt was short lived. This may occasion Christians to clarify the Trinity as a divine community of supreme love and humility, which maintains a harmony without destroying the differences. It may also provide a model for human community.

Christ Unknown and Acknowledged

St. Paul's speech in Areopagus, appreciating the religiosity of the Athens and affirming God's universal work, referred to an altar-inscription "To an Unknown God" and said, "What you worship but do not know I proclaim"(Acts 17:23). A few Christian theologians have made an attempt to create a theology of religions on this basis. Raimundo Panikkar's *The Unknown Christ of Hinduism*[19] is the most popular example. Panikkar, son of a South Indian Hindu father and Spanish mother, a Catholic priest, philosopher, and theologian, holds that Christ is the meeting point of Hinduism and Christianity. He takes the Vedantic category of *Brahman* who is the "total ultimate cause of the world" and *Isvara* (the Lord) who becomes the "link between the undifferentiated *Brahman* and the created world including humans." For him *Isvara,* the personal aspect and revelation of *Brahman* is none other than Christ who remains unknown yet worshiped in Hinduism. Christ has to unveil his whole face, completing his mission within Hinduism till he grows to be recognized. He still "has to be crucified there, dying with Hinduism as he died with Judaism and the Hellenistic religions in order to rise again, as the same Christ." "Jesus is the Christ, but Christ is not only Jesus but the *logos* that enlightens Hinduism, as the principle of life." Panikkar's use of words like Christ, God, *Logos, Brahman, Isvara,* Mystery, Truth, and Reality need very careful reading as he uses them both interchangeably and with subtle difference. However, what concerns us is that Panikkar's use of "unknown Christ" or "hidden Christ of Hinduism" in the place of Paul's "unknown God" raises a number of problems. Going to the original context in the Bible, Paul, after his theological preamble of acknowledging that all human beings subsist in God, goes on to call for men and women everywhere to repent because God has fixed a day in which he will judge the world "by a man whom he has designated"(Acts 17:30,31). Further, Panikkar does not recognize the fact that the name Christ comes from the Jewish tradition with a particular expectation attached to it and that cosmicizing him as a principle may result in removing him too far from his original context. Further, Panikkar, like others, has fallen into the trap of *advaita Vedanta,* not taking seriously the complex nature of the Hindu religious traditions and for that matter "the whole gamut of the human spirit, from the crude fetishism of the savage to the creative affirmations of the saint" to use Radhakrishnan's words. The same could be said of Karl Rahner, Panikkar's European colleague. On the basis of the transcendental common human experience oriented towards the infinite Mystery of God whose gracious self-communication is available to all and of Jesus Christ as the absolute fulfillment of human destiny in acceptance of this communication, Rahner has chosen to call all truth seekers without explicit faith in Christ as anonymous Christians. On the whole both Panikkar and Rahner are evangelical so far as they are passionate about the name Christ, not Krishna, Siva, or Buddha, and for the Church which for them is unparalleled by any other organisation. However, both of them are vague in isolating Christ and the Church from the

Judeo-Christian framework and not giving concrete examples of knowing the hidden operation of Christ.

M.M. Thomas, one of the most creative theologians of India, paralleling Panikkar's *Unknown Christ of Hinduism,* spoke of *The Acknowledged Christ of the Indian Renaissance*[20], "not of Traditional Hinduism but of Renascent Hinduism, seen as part of the total renaissance of India." He has consulted the major figures of modern India including Rammohan Roy and Gandhi who could not ignore Jesus Christ but draw insights from his life, teachings and death in their own way. Their perceptions of Jesus were, for Thomas, partial and inadequate but he saw in them, and in the thinking of some Indian Christian theologians a significant direction towards a missionary theology in India. Building upon the idea of "new creation in Christ" emphasized by Devanandan, his predecessor in CISRS Bangalore, Thomas saw a divine-humanity in Christ. He interpreted salvation as humanization combining the love of God that finds its goal in mystic union with love for humans and doing God's will on earth. For him the glorified divine humanity of Christ is to be realized within the historical process in the form of just and loving relations in communities in order to testify to the "happenedness" of Jesus' resurrection. And he was open to not only radical thinking in other religions but also to secular and humanist thoughts such as that of Karl Marx. It was in this light that, in response to Hick's *God and the Universe of Faiths* in which the "Copernican Revolution in theology of Religions" had been introduced, Thomas brought out his *Man and the Universe of Faiths*[21]. In this book, Thomas analyses various positions in modern thinking on the human person as individual and corporate and acknowledges his fascination for the idea of a "Christ-centered secular humanism" or "a secular fellowship in Christ." While lamenting all the tragedies in history in the name of religion, Thomas affirms the possibility of a true witness to the gospel. "In secular society the witness to the New Humanity in Christ and its redemptive power for politics, society and persons takes a different mode, namely the instrumentality of believers gathered in voluntary congregations and scattered in secular groups in civil society. Even so, it remains a witness to the Lordship of Christ over all creation and all human life."[22] He expects that in the process of the abolition or relativisation of all religions and quasi-religions, in so far as people are caught up in the New Humanity of Christ through implicit or explicit faith and being open to the judgement of God at the cross, they will "become increasingly receptive to the power of the Risen Christ and His humanity" and will enter into dialogue with other religions within the context of a concern for human fellowship. And today when Christians are confronted with a world-wide pluralism of religious and secular faiths and cultures and ideologies, Christocentricity, for Thomas, means, "a Christ-centred syncretic process which is to be welcomed." Even if there is a risk in this process, in fact, it is for him *Risking Christ for Christ's Sake.* M.M. Thomas is extraordinary in bringing together the insights of orthodox theologians like Kraemer and creative atheists like Marx. His Christ-centeredness would be acceptable for many of those involved in a theological debate on religious pluralism. However, while enjoying enormous freedom in criticizing the Church for its various pitfalls, Thomas and those who share his views have not shown concrete models of Christ-centered fellowships outside the Church which can demonstrate that of which they speak.

Commitment and Openness

This title comes from the title of a study of inter-faith dialogue and theology of religions in the work of Stanley Samartha by a European scholar.[23] Samartha, a minister of the CSI, scholar of Hinduism and creative writer, after his study of *The Hindu Response to the Unbound Christ,* teaching in India and working with a study project of other religions of the World Council of Churches, became the founder-director of the sub-unit on Dialogue in the WCC in 1971. Since then his *Courage for Dialogue,* his initiatives for bilateral and multi-lateral encounters and reflections on *One Christ and Many Religions* are considerable. He defines dialogue as "a mood, a spirit, an attitude of love and respect towards neighbours of other faiths" which "goes far beyond a sterile co-existence or uncritical friendliness. It does not avoid controversies; it recognises difficulties in relationship as well." "It is not a gathering of porcupines; neither is it a get-together of jellyfish. Sensitively understood, it helps people not to disfigure the image of the neighbours of other faith. In multi-religious societies dialogue cannot be just the activity of a few interested individuals. It can only be "dialogue in community" . . . communities of concerned people (must be) ready to take risk, to move beyond safe boundaries, to replace old particularities with new profiles."[24] For him, religion is "not like the smooth swallowing of jelly-ice-cream," but that which involves serious commitment to one's convictions and openness to the extent of being vulnerable. In other words, real dialogue can take place only between commitments. The test ground of Samartha's views was the fifth General Assembly of the WCC held in Nairobi, 1975. It was the first time that the topic of dialogue was taken for a discussion in the main assembly. And also it was the first time representatives of the World Religions were invited to the assembly as guests and observers. "Seeking Community" was the theme of the third of the six sections charted for the assembly. The preparatory document on this theme was characterized by "a constructive attitude which both recognizes the potentialities of dialogue which looks forward to a realisation of a World Community distinguished by a constructive interplay between different communities." The document was introduced in an introductory session that was followed by subsections. The reports of these sub-sections were presented and approved by the main section that presented a collective report with an introduction. The report had to be revised with the addition of a preamble recognizing the missionary obligation of the church because of negative reaction from north European theologians in the plenary, which attracted Asian rejoinders. The tension between 'commitment and openness' became very clear. The whole business of dialogue was questioned. The sub-unit on Dialogue was asked to provide clarification in particular of the relationship between the uniqueness of the Christian faith and openness to people of other faiths. Samartha organized a consultation in Chiang Mai, Thailand, 1977, the outcome of which was The *Guidelines on Dialogue* that was approved by the Central Committee of WCC.

One can easily notice the influence of Samantha's position on the *Guidelines*. It explains dialogue as a basic life-style characterized by both commitment and openness. It encourages Christians to see the diverse ways in which God has been dealing with humanity through the experience and traditions of different religious communities. It deliberately avoids the terms mission and evangelism because of the wrong notions attached to them in the past, but emphasizes Christian witness which might include sharing of the gospel in a dialogical encounter. Although there are many points which the fundamentalist or conservative wing can pick up for further debate, the *Guidelines* deserve to continue to be studied in churches. The scope of the ministry of dialogue in the WCC, despite some structural changes, has also been widened further. Samartha, since his return to Bangalore, through books, essays, sermons, Bible studies, and poems continues to elaborate and clarify the controversial issues involved in relating commitment to openness. On the one hand, as we mentioned earlier, he affirms the Mystery to which different religions have responded in their own ways. Further, he sees this Mystery not only in nature and history but also in the universal presence of Christ that cannot be exhausted by particular understandings of him. The remarks we have already made in this regard are applicable here. On the other hand he acknowledges the kerygmatic nature of Christian faith, the work of the Holy Spirit with a pivotal reference to Christ and the missionary obligation of the church which has to be carried out in innovative ways suitable to particular contexts. One important question one might raise here is that if real dialogue is between commitments, how to approach those nominally religious, including Christians?

Samartha's clarification of the uniqueness of the Christian faith in the context of religious pluralism is remarkable. For him "Jesus Christ is God's gift to the whole world" but he refuses to let it be "received, unwrapped and appreciated only in one particular way." For example, he points out how the ideas of the kingdom of God and the Lordship of Christ carry with them monarchical and imperial overtones. He suggests that we should recover the servanthood of Christ and the servant role of the Church. Samartha is not the only one to point this out. Most recently George Lindbeck in his insightful essay on the uniqueness of the gospel[25] draws attention to the "Israel-like aspect of the church" to be a blessing and witness through service. He emphasizes the fact that the church should follow the original model of servanthood for which it is called. It is "called to serve other religions for the sake of the neighbour, for the sake of humanity, for the sake of God's promise to Abraham that through his seed all nations will be blessed." Of course the idea of servanthood is very respectable and acceptable in today's world. However, those who try to develop an evangelical theology of religions may rightly point out an issue here. I am tempted to refer to the story of Naaman, a Syrian commander, who had a young Israelite servant girl. She had been brought to his home as a captive. She, through her mistress, dared to guide her master to "the prophet of Samaria" for a cure of his leprosy. The solution suggested by the prophet was to wash in the river of Jordan, which appeared to the furious Naaman so inferior compared to the Damascus rivers of Abana and Pharpar (2 Kings 5). Finally he had to dip in Jordan to become clean. Being in the servant role, can the church in all humility point to the "Jordan" or should it guide to the great rivers of Ganges and Brahmaputra if some Hindus find the "Jordan" a problem?

Samartha is fully aware that he lives in a country that is marred not only by poverty and corruption but also by "the politicisation of religion and comminalisation of politics." However, he would not allow Hinduism to bear all the blame. His suggestion is that all religious communities work with proximate goals leaving the question of ultimate goals for later discussion. In this respect his approach is much more comprehensive than "the liberation praxis" of Paul Knitter and the "global ethics" of Hans Küng. However, modesty requires the recognition of a supreme force or person who is both compassionate and compelling to work for the transformation of a country like India as well as the whole world. As a "Sovereign Socialist Secular Democratic Republic," India affirms repeatedly the popular slogans like justice, peace, and love. But in the midst of several gods and goddesses or several forms and names of one reality or God what image will stimulate people's conscience and urge them to work for transformation? What kind of ultimate goal has immediate impact on setting proximate goals? These are important questions in a multi-faith context.

Ingredients of an Evangelical Theology

Basically, as I have maintained elsewhere, fundamentalism in any form—literalist approach to the scripture, superiority complex, triumphalistic or militant attitude, indiscriminately anti-modern—is not an ally but an enemy of the gospel. Similarly, a conservative church unwilling to change any of its tradition and pattern of worship and ministry has no right to preach the gospel.[26] Any association with an uncritical praise of the history or monument of imperialism and exploitation is contrary to a genuine evangelical position. I have also maintained that evangelism and inter-faith dialogue are not contradictory but complementary to each other.[27] Here I point out very briefly some outlines for further development.

The Judeo-Christian tradition is unique and universally significant not because of its stories, proverbs, devotion, or moral teaching but because of its distinctive framework and character. It represents a particular dialogical process. Anti-Semitism in many ways has blinded Christians to take the whole biblical vision starting from the story of Israel. Jesus was not racialist nor ethno-centric when he told the Samaritan woman that "It is from the Jews that salvation comes"(John 4:22). He was a devout Jew, but with a universal outlook and he enjoyed full freedom in criticizing the excesses of his own tradition.

Whether he was aware of it or not, seen from the multi-faith perspective today, no other religious tradition has preserved the faith as centered around the past experience of slavery and liberation as Judaism. The Bible contains major experiences of a long process. The dialogical process started when God in the mysterious and enigmatic form and name of Yahweh chose to be an intimate partner of a people groaning in slavery and in their journey of freedom and in their attempt to establish such a model community as to be a blessing for the whole world. This choice was for them both a privilege and fearful responsibility. Initiatives and deviations, prophetic challenges, and new visions for the future were recurrent aspects of this process. The "Jesus event and the post-Jesus events" and new perceptions opened new horizons for embracing those who were away from the "commonwealth of Israel." The missionary movement helped many world communities, including Indian Christians, to feel themselves accepted into this commonwealth and be part of the process.

Gospel is neither a one-word formula nor a single concept. It signifies the core insights coming from the dialogical process of the Judeo-Christian tradition. They include primarily God's preferential option for the poor and the weak, his loving call for a new orientation in life, unconditional acceptance of the repentant sinners, socio-economic equality of all God's people, ongoing transformation of persons and communities, the twin commandment of loving God and loving our neighbor as ourselves, and ultimate hope for eternal life. Any denominational stubbornness and doctrinal rigidity can blind one's eyes to see these core insights of the gospel. With truthfulness and integrity we need to recognize the plurality of ways in which Jesus is perceived and confessed, his cross interpreted, and the revelation realized in the New Testament.[28]

There are many areas in which human life, history, nature, and an undeniable evolutionary process remain a perplexing wonder and mystery. But this fact need not make us wander around seeking after an undefinable abstract Truth without a clue. Again the Jewish tradition helps us to take a right perspective. "There are things hidden, and they belong to the Lord our God, but what is revealed belongs to us and our children for ever; it is for us to observe all that is prescribed in this law"(Deut. 29:29). One can add more dimensions of this "law," the scope of which was never restricted. We have more than sufficient inspiration and guidance to adore God in freedom and love and to work vigorously for a better society with justice, peace, and integrity of creation. The death and resurrection of Jesus is a historical attestation of the struggle for life and promise of a hopeful future. We don't claim that we know everything. "At present we see only puzzling reflections in a mirror, but one day we shall see face to face"(1 Cor. 13:12). We still need to "attain to the unity inherent in our faith and in our knowledge of the Son of God—to mature manhood, measured by nothing less than the full stature of Christ"(Ephesians 4:13). It should be the prayer of all churches and their ministers that God:

> may grant *us* inward strength and power through his spirit, that
> through faith Christ may dwell in *our* hearts in love. With deep

roots and firm foundations may *we,* in company with all God's people, be strong to grasp what is the breadth and the length and height and depth of Christ's love, and to know it, though it is beyond knowledge. So may *we* be filled with the very fullness of God (Ephesians 3:16-19).

At the risk of being labeled as narrow-minded and even cunning, let me dare to affirm that the dialogical process of the Judeo-Christian tradition is significant for all people irrespective of their religious adherence and ideological persuasion. This, in my opinion, is something all Christians should affirm. The God we believe in is immeasurably tolerant. He tolerates even those who deny his existence and those who misuse his name. However, we have to distinguish between "sceptical tolerance" and "productive tolerance" as Moltmann suggests. Sceptical tolerance makes dialogue sterile, dispassionate, and non-committal. Creative tolerance helps to take care not to bear false witness against our neighbors of other faiths, listen seriously what they have experienced, and share joyfully the gospel insights. Further, in the light of the dialogical process of the biblical tradition we may profitably view every religious tradition as representing a particular dialogical process. The complex development of different strands and traditions within Hinduism can be taken as the best example of such a process. It is not sufficient to state vaguely that God, Christ, Spirit, or the Word operates in every religion, culture, and human person. Wherever there is radical movement towards love, freedom, equality, openness, and transformation, there we see God's wrestling and success very clearly. Despite many defects and points of weakness the Judeo-Christian vision has inspired the world both directly and indirectly. It need not be a partisan view that all religions and cultures move towards the central spot and limelight movement of this tradition. Jesus, crucified and risen, representative of all victims of history as the Son of Man and the living image of the divine humanity as the Son of God, without exploiting any moment of weakness or confusion remains the rallying center of all goodness, love, and freedom. It is our hope that "the universe, everything in heaven and on earth *will* be brought into a unity in Christ"(Ephesians 1:10). In other words, he is the crucified center to which all powers are to be subjected until his penultimate role comes to an end and "God will be all in all" (l Cor. 15:28).

Authentic communication of the gospel insights requires a community or fellowship which is conscious of being caught up in the dialogical process of God within the Judeo-Christian tradition. Hit and run preaching, amplified proclamation through loud speakers, campaigns and rallies on a grand scale, and overlapping production of repetitive literature cannot be a substitute for constant efforts to establish a model community with corporate charisma. This community should be culturally indigenous, socially liberated, politically free, and economically independent. It is a servant community yet reserving the right of communicating the gospel insights with humility and humor, clarity and confidence, and honesty and hospitality. Ongoing reformation is the primary condition for a church to be such an evangelical community.

Notes

1   One of these missionaries advocated "Justice, Courtesy and Love" that Cracknell used as the title for his book. (London: Epworth Press 1995).

2   B. Ziegenbalg, *Genealogy of the South Indian Gods* (New Delhi: Unity Book Service, 1984), p. xix

3   Quoted by W. Germann in his foreword to the book, ibid., p.xv

4   Ibid., p. xiv.

5   Ibid., p.22.

6   Ibid., p.14.

7   G.U. Pope, *The Thiruvasagam or "Sacred Utterances" of the Tamil Poet, Saint and Sage Manikavasagakr* (Oxford: At the Clarendon Press, 1900).

8   Ibid., p.x.

9   Ibid., p.xxiii.

10   For such an analysis, see Cracknell, op.cit., pp. 196-286.

11   J. N. Farquhar, *The Crown of Hinduism* (Humphrey Milford: Oxford University Press, 1913), p. 13f.

12   Ibid., p.54.

13   Ibid., p.55.

14   I. Selvanayagam, *The Dynamics of Hindu Religious Traditions* (Bangalore: Asian Trading Corporation, 1996), pp.98f.

15   Madras: The Christian Literature Society for India, 1950.

16   p.159.

17   H. Kraemer, *Religion and the Christian Faith* (London: Lutterworth, 1956), p.230.

18   I. Selvanayagam, op.cit., p. 133; the representative book referred to here is *History of Hindu-Christian Encounters* by Sita Ram Goel (New Delhi: Voice of India, 1989).

19   Published first in London in 1964 and an enlarged and revised edition has been brought out by the Asian Trading Corporation, Bangalore in 1982.

20   First published in 1970 and then in 1976 and 1991 by the Christian Literature Society, Madras.

21   Madras: CLS for CISRS, 1975.

22   Ibid, p.143.

23   Eeuwout Klootwijk, *Commitment and Openness* (Zoetermeer: Uitgeverij Boekencentrum B.V., 1992).

24   Samartha, *Courage for Dialogue* (Geneva: WCC, 1981), p. 100.

25   Lindbeck, "The Gospel's Uniqueness: Election and Untranslatebility," *Modern Theology*, 13/4 (Oct., 1997): pp. 423-450.

26   See I. Selvanayagam, *A Dialogue on Dialogue* (Madras: CLS, 1996), pp.125f.

27   See I. Selvanayagam, *Evangelism and Inter-Faith Dialogue: Are they incompatible or complementary?* Occasional Paper no. 13, (Birmingham: Selly Oak Colleges, 1993).

28   For Biblical reflections on these themes, see I. Selvanayagam, ed. *Biblical Insights on Inter-Faith Dialogue* (Bangalore: BTESSC-BTTBPSA, 1995), pp. 72-80; 114-126; 255-258.

Theology Colloquium:
Vision Paper

Terry C. Muck

As a boy I was a featured soloist in my dad's evangelistic campaigns. My biggest number was "Bringing in the Sheaves," and it is easy for me to see in retrospect that the message of that song, more than anything else, shaped my understanding of Christian missions. Christian missions meant harvesting lost souls.[1]

Several things over the years, however, have been instrumental in changing the harvesting image as my most important metaphor for missions. For one thing, a voice change meant I could no longer hit high C, and I quit singing "Bringing in the Sheaves." More importantly, theological study convinced me that the missions impulse is wider and deeper than the idea of reaping lost souls, although I have not abandoned totally the idea of fields "white already to harvest."[2] It has also meant to many, for example, the almost militaristic engagement of another culture (as in "Onward Christian Soldiers") and the care of souls *and* bodies (as in "Lord, Whose Love Through Humble Service"). Missions has meant many things, both to the biblical cultures and modern cultures.

In some senses, metaphors are culture specific. They are only as effective as they relate to their cultural context, and our culture, a global, interdependent, technological, multicultural society, demands a new key metaphor, or metaphors, to communicate the world mission of the church. Of course it is debatable whether we have any freedom whatsoever in setting the metaphors of our time or whether the culture(s) determines that for us.[3]

Most effective metaphors relate to a universal cultural trait or identifier. The harvest metaphor, for example, is agricultural. It communicates to a society whose livelihood is based on the plowing, planting, watering, growing, harvesting, resting cycle dependent on annual seasons and the vicissitudes of the weather. It speaks to a monocultural society all involved in a similar agricultural endeavor. Our current culture is not totally dedicated to the agricultural model. It also has elements of the technological, the managerial, the therapeutic, and the industrial. At the very least the agricultural metaphor speaks directly to a declining portion of the world's population; the rest need different kinds of metaphor.

Given this complexity or, better yet, lack of cultural homogeneity, it is difficult to think of a metaphor that relates to the vocation of missions that can hope to inspire an entire culture. Perhaps the answer is to insist on a complex of metaphors. These are readily available in Scripture. Or perhaps there is a dominant, non-occupational experience that all human beings in the twenty first century can relate to. If so, a metaphor drawn from that experience would have the best chance of inspiring the church to missional activity.

Before we can discuss specific metaphors and before we can discover such metaphorical language that will be powerful today, we must look at the current cultural context in which the church does missions, the theological understandings of mission that must be brought to bear on that context, and a vision of missions that results from this interaction.

Trends

Two cultural trends seem especially crucial for our understanding of today's church mission.

Multiculturalism. Since multiculturalism has been multidefined, let me be clear about what I mean by multiculturalism. Perhaps the easiest way to do it is to distinguish it from another term, multiethnicity. Multiethnicity is a situation where groups of people distinguishable by language, national origin, race, religion, or other identifiable traits live in a situation of dominance by a majority group of people similarly distinguished by language, national origin, race, religion, or other identifiable traits. In contrast, I define multiculturalism as a situation where groups of people distinguishable by language, national origin, race, religion, or other identifiable traits coexist under conditions of relative equality of power and opportunity.[4]

Most cultures[5] today can be seen as poised somewhere on a spectrum between multiethnicity and multiculturalism. In the United States, for example, we should probably consider ourselves still tilted toward the multiethnic end of the spectrum as far as African-Americans, Hispanics, Native Americans, and some Asian-American groups are concerned. But we are tipped toward the multicultural pole as far as Quakers, Jews, Irish, and other Asian American groups are concerned.

Although the horrific abuses that can occur in situations of multiethnicity are by no means absent from the world, the trend is toward situations of multiculturalism.[6] Bitter ideological enemies agree on this one. Democrats *and* Republicans are trying to co-opt the issue for their political platforms. The United Nations *and* Amnesty International consider multiculturalism one of the prime indicators of human rights in a country. The People for the American Way *and* the Christian Coalition champion racial harmony. The National Organization of Women *and* Promise Keepers stress racial reconciliation. An unsuspecting bystander can get crushed in the stampede toward the higher moral ground of multiculturalism. Immigration, intermarriage, economic interdependence, and, yes, theological idealism all drive us inevitably toward multiculturalism.[7]

Primacy of economism. The days of religious idealism are long dead, the era of nationalism is dying, and economics rules the roost. A savvy reading of the morning newspaper is all it takes to see how world decisions are made today. Money talks. The most important force in the world today is money, if force is measured by the influence it has on major decisions. Economics tilts the balance on almost every issue facing the world community, turning an important aspect of human social structure into an ideology-"economism." Economism is not a passing fad; it is here to stay and if we are to think wisely about the future of the Church's mission, we must take economism into account.[8]

First, we must place economism in historical context. It has not always been the prime force. In fairly recent western history, for example, the church and religion occupied that primary place. As recently as the European Middle Ages, any important decisions made by individuals, group of individuals, or societies considered the church and its distinctive way of looking at the world the primary factor. Then, beginning with the Enlightenment and continuing with the Industrial Revolution, nations and their political interests became the driving force. This age of nationalism has lasted to the present day. In the twentieth century, however, a new sun has risen. Although neither religion nor nationalism are by any means dead as important forces in world events, they are being eased into positions of secondary importance when compared with the power of economism.

An illustration might help. Consider the major buildings constructed during these respective eras. In the Middle Ages, any city, town, or village in Europe boasted the cathedral as its major building. The local church reached high into the sky above all other buildings, proclaiming not just physical but ideological dominance. Later, during the era of nationalism, the prime buildings were (and are) city halls and public monuments. Palaces dominated the landscape. Today the prime buildings are business oriented: The World Trade Center in New York, the Sears Tower in Chicago, the Gedung BMI building in Jakarta, and on around the world.[9] This changing architectural fashion from cathedral to palace to skyscraper mirrors changing cultural fashion and force.

Take another recent example of economism's rising dominance. In 1990, Saddam Hussein had his Iraqi army invade Kuwait. Accompanied by a good deal of moralistic and nationalistic rhetoric to be sure, the United States put together a coalition to defeat this affront to church and nation. But what was the real reason? Why did we choose to defend human rights, democracy, and national honor in this case and not in the equally compelling cases of ten others around the world, including Bosnia, Rwanda, and Cambodia? Economism. The determinative reasons were business interests dependent on the Middle East oil industry.

Second, once we realize the relative strengths of the principalities and powers[10] in world affairs, we must consider to what extent the church's mission has been and is affected by this hierarchy of powers. It is arguable that in the past the church's mission has sometimes gone too far in accommodating its form (and in some cases quite a bit of its substance) to the prevailing power.[11] Early Roman Catholic missions often equated the planting of a huge church building as the *sine qua non* of the missions effort. Early Protestant missions could be faulted for riding the nationalism bandwagon too snugly. If economism is indeed the prevailing force in the world today, those of us interested in the missions effort of the church must both acknowledge the lay of the land without letting it determine the substance of our message, which has an "economy" to it quite different from the materialistic one dominant on our globe.[12]

Multiculturalism and economism are the two root forces that both drive and perplex our current world community. In the mission context, multiculturalism drives our perception of the world as a religious puzzle to be solved by the church, and at the same time it is what keeps us from agreeing on the content and form of the church's mission. Economism shapes the current penultimate goal of the world community, yet like all such penultimate goals (each age has one or more), it persistently threatens to take over as the ultimate goal of the church's mission. These two root forces are the deep trends out of which a plethora of facilitating trends (globalization, technological progress, etc.) and supporting rationales (ecology, scientism, etc.) grow.

Truths

In spite of concerted twentieth century assaults on both, two theological realities cannot be gain said.

The Great Commission.[13] The Great Commission has lost most of the cultural support it once enjoyed. As traditionally taught, the Great Commission runs afoul of a cultural anathema towards obedience and a common sense rejection of revelation. Since embrace and acceptance of both obedience and revelation are necessary in order to fully embrace the Great Commission to go and preach the gospel to all the nations, our anti-authoritarian, scientistic culture has a hard time listening.[14]

Consider obedience. One of the largest cohorts of our current cultures, babyboomers between the ages of 35 and 50, are primarily defined by their resistance to allegiance to any kind of authority. Being obedient to someone else is to reject our individual freedom and our sense of responsibility for shaping our own lives in such a way that will bring personal fulfillment.

Revelation, the idea that God speaks to us in definitive ways, is equally absurd to the modern mind set. It doesn't make sense when compared with the scientific worldview that demands empirical proof for everything; it subverts the existential mind set that experience is the final authority; and it seems like a copout from the rugged individualism and pragmatism that measures success by whether or not we have the personal initiative to succeed.

Ironically, there is a way of looking at obedience and revelation so they support one another and together become palatable to the modern and postmodern way of looking at things. The resistance to obedience is mainly a resistance to obeying other human beings; revelation claims that we are obeying God, not human beings.[15] The resistance to revelation lies in the implication that we are to accept the words of the Great Commission without analyzing them with our rational minds.[16] This is a misunderstanding of an overly rationalized understanding of God's revelation. It leads us to think that we can understand everything there is to know about God's revelation. Once this mistaken estimation of our human abilities is made, obedience to someone's rational understanding of the gospel becomes the test of orthodoxy. Given the extraordinarily wide range of rational opinions regarding gospel truth, it is no wonder that calls for obedience to diverse views of truth often end up in bloodshed and death. It is no wonder obedience to human representations of the gospel has taken on such negative connotations.

A correct understanding of revelation, however, recognizes that much of God's revelation remains clothed in mystery, and is God's to reveal as the divine purposes require. If this is our understanding of revelation then we can refocus the object of obedience to God. The Great Commission understood this way-as a call to seek God and God's unfolding plan by pursuing the witness of the gospel to the ends of the earth-is nonnegotiable.[17]

The spiritual nature and spiritual need of humankind.[18] One of the greatest temptations of a secular, scientistic age is a skewed vision of what it means to be a human being. The religions are our only hope in the face of this temptation. The religions all come together at this point. Human beings, they say, are more than the sum of their parts. There is an aspect, call it a spiritual nature, that distinguishes human beings from the animals and connects each one to some kind of transcendent principle, call it God. And then, as quickly as they come together on this point, the religions drift apart again, describing the details of that human nature and the transcendent principle in idiosyncratic ways.

Sometimes even different Christian groups divide on the details of our spiritual nature. Some emphasize the divine aspect as if it is a tangible reality. One such theologian called it the *logos spermatikos,* the seed of reason.[19] Some consider the divine aspect to be most visible in the human conscience where we innately become aware of our connection to God. This *sensus divinitatus,* the sense of the divine, infects us all.[20] Some emphasize the seemingly universal condition of human beings to want to be in relationship to each other and God. This relational predisposition, they say, is evidence of the *imago Dei,* the image of God imprinted in everyone.[21]

Given the complexity of human nature and the difficulty of talking about humanity's seemingly insatiable desire for a spiritual solution to human problems, a desire that seems to endure in spite of historical efforts to eradicate it, it is probably just as well to consider all three positions as describing one aspect of a complicated spiritual nature. At any rate, from almost any vantage point, humanity's spiritual nature seems one of the safer postulates about what makes us human.

Deconstructions

Given this unique combination of cultural trends and theological truth, three things have to change about the way we view mission:

Decouple politics and religion. It has become almost commonplace to recognize that in the history of the Christian church, we have taken a wrong turn whenever we have sought or been given the "advantage" of political and economic power.[22] The abuses have been drummed into our heads for years: the Crusades, the Inquisition, the established churches of European nations, and colonialism.[23] When the church has used political and economic power to attempt to further its aims of conversion and correct doctrine, evil has been the result. Political advantage tips the sensitive balance of power between love and justice in Christian theology too far in the direction of justice (or our sense of justice, at least), and, ironically, hatred and injustice result.

One exception to this is often cited-Constantine's original endorsement of Christianity which overnight (in historical terms) transformed a smallish Christian sect into the official religion of the Roman Empire.[24] If seen by itself as a single event of advantage for the church, then this may be a defensible argument. A more realistic view of it, however, is to see this endorsement as the one that led to the establishment of European Christendom when Rome fell, which in turn led to the abuses cited above. The Crusades, the Inquisition, established churches, and colonialism all had their roots in the social power given to Christianity by Constantine. The exception turns out to be not so exceptional after all when seen in light of its long-term effects.

The temptation of secular power is still with us. Those of us committed to the mission of the church will forever be looking for ways of telling the gospel story more effectively. In order to avoid giving into the temptation of improperly using secular power, we must be constantly reminded, by a reading of history, if nothing else, that giving into the temptation to use secular power to promote spiritual ends, turns those same spiritual ends into secular ones. The more political power becomes available to us for use in our mission, the less we should use it, the faster we should run away from it, the further we should distance ourselves from it.[25]

Disconnect the we/they construct with other religions. Despite our massive efforts at evangelism, efforts so successful that one-third of the people on our planet go by the name Christian, the other world religions are growing and spreading also, although at varying rates. Islam is probably growing faster than Christianity; Hinduism and Buddhism less fast. But all are alive and well, and they are coming to a neighborhood temple or mosque near you, if not this summer, then next.

The way mission-minded Christians should respond to the growth of non-Christian religions is counter-intuitive. We must stop thinking of people in other religions as enemies. They are not so much the competition as the context of mission. We simply must bring back into biblical focus our understanding of who the enemy really is. The enemy is sin, not people of other religions.[26]

Every summer I read the Bible in a different translation or paraphrase, and I read it each time with a different question foremost in my mind. Several summers ago I read it with this question in mind: Who did Jesus (and the other leaders of the early church) get most upset with? What I discovered is this: Jesus rarely got even a little angry with people who were wrong; he got furious with people who knew the right, but were acting on their right understanding in inappropriate ways. He upbraided sorcerers because they used their knowledge of religion and human nature to bilk people; he cursed the fig tree for not doing what it was created to do; and he went off the charts against a segment of his own religious clan, the Pharisees, because they were perverting the practical implications of their understanding of the law. Jesus lambasted incorrigible, unrepentant sinners but never flickered in his love and respect for people who were simply wrong.

What does this mean in practical terms about how we relate to people of other religious traditions? If we are not choosing a we/they approach, what is the nature of the approach? I'm afraid it means more work. It means that every position we articulate regarding our theology must be expanded to include not only what our religious tradition says about it, but how that might fit into the wider field of religious traditions.[27] Regarding Christian missions, for example, we must consider not only what God, through Jesus Christ, has said to us about missions, but then how that revelation fits in to the wider religious experience of humankind. We must be theologians first, but we also must become historians/phenomenologists of religion. We must develop a we/all-of-us mentality toward the world of religious ideas and experience.

Abandon an isolated rationality. One of the reasons we have developed such a destructive and confrontational view of other people is our truncated view of human rationality. We have rightly determined that the distinguishing feature of being human is rationality. We have wrongly defined rationality as something limited to logical syllogism, thereby emptying the richness of our rationality of emotion, will, and performance. In isolating our theological understanding of the gospel from these rich mines of human resources, we have made truth suspect in the eyes of all. By setting up what amounts to a caricature of truth, we have made it easy prey for the silliness of relativism and the description-run-wild of postmodernism.

The effects of this on the understanding of the mission of the church have been many, but three stand out. First, an isolated rationality can easily lead to the disparaging of peoples who don't similarly reduce rationality to logical syllogism.[28] In our mission to indigenous people groups, for example, we needlessly criticize their approach to rationality, an approach that often leans less on abstract, empirical thought and more on concrete, mythological thought. Both are rational approaches to religion, if rationality is understood as the attempt to explain the meaning of existence (rather than attempt to locate it purely in human feeling or social construct).[29] The hunger for concreteness (storytelling) and mythology (deep meaning) are palpable in our culture, and too often we needlessly cut ourselves off from utilizing these rational approaches because of a too narrow understanding of rationality. In fact, we cut ourselves off from some of the richest expressions of the gospel these days that are coming from cultures which recognize these richer views of what we call rationality.[30]

Second, an isolated rationality leads to the caricaturing of the gospel and our own understanding of it.[31] Ironically, we do include these other elements in our *practice* of Christianity, but impoverish our theology, ecclesiology, and missiology by not finding a place for them in it. It is, in the end, impossible to eliminate emotion and performance from our understandings of theology. But when we deny they exist we create an inadequate explanation of the meaning of the gospel. By becoming too "rational" we become less rational. We hurt the very cause to which we dedicate ourselves.

Third, an isolated rationality can create a very limited vision of what mission means. In particular, it leads to a heavy bias in missions toward a view of proclamation only. A heavy emphasis on rationality-lite tends to focus on verbal forms of mission. Verbal forms of mission are very important, of course. But from the beginning, even outsiders to the Christian tradition have seen the much broader implications and effects of mission. Eusebius, for example, intimately connected the work of evangelism with a prerequisite of "distributing all (one's) goods to the needy," and then a post-requisite of establishing and maintaining churches by "nurturing those that had already been brought in."[32]

Christian Missions

Given these cultural trends and core theological values, what should the Christian mission be in the twenty-first century? Christian missions should be a witness to the story of the gospel in a way that is sincere, faithful to my community's best understanding of itself and its theology, and fully respectful of individual human freedom and others' religious traditions (or lack thereof), and that contributes to overall human flourishing.[33]

1. Witness to the story of the gospel. The most basic form of witness is *identity witness*. When people know what you stand for, everything you do is a witness to that identity.[34] You don't need to attempt to persuade, proclaim, discuss-people associate what you do with the (religious) identity you carry. If

you are Buddhist then people interpret your actions, attitudes, and words as Buddhist. If you are atheist, people interpret your actions, attitudes, and words as atheistic. Identity is a powerful witness.

I do a lot of public lecturing on different world religions. One of the most common forms of post-lecture comments I receive goes something like this: *Thanks for your lecture on Islam. I worked with a Muslim once. He was a great guy. Islam must be a good religion.* Or the reverse form of the same comment: *Thanks for your lecture on Islam. I worked with a Muslim once. He got caught stealing from petty cash. Islam must not teach honesty.*

There are many other forms of witness besides simple identity witness, of course. Perhaps the most stereotypical of all these forms is *verbal witness.* People tend to hold to their religious tradition because they think it is true or good or both. It helps them cope with life's biggest questions: Who am I? What am I doing here? Where am I going? It usually makes them happy or at least satisfied. Because of this general satisfaction, they tell other people about it. It is something like finding a great restaurant-you spread the word (one beggar telling another beggar where to find food). There seems to be a twofold motivation for this kind of witness. One is a general desire to help people find the happiness you have found. The other is a certain pride of having learned about this great thing. That pride may have some negative overtones (triumphalism), but can also be relatively benign.

A third general form of witness is *helping witness.* Most religions have, as part of their teaching or ethos, a tradition of serving humanity. This service can take the form of providing food, shelter, and clothing for those less fortunate; or it can take the form of working for justice for the oppressed of the world; or it might mean working for reconciliation among alienated peoples. This kind of witness differs from identity witness in its intentionality.

There are other forms of witness, of course. The witness of prayer, of worship,[35] of public service. When one considers the extraordinary diversity of witness, in fact, one is tempted to draw the conclusion that witnessing to one's religious tradition, or lack thereof, is universal.[36] The minute another person knows the name of your religious commitments (or non-commitments or even lack of commitments) you are a witness to those commitments. The question, then, for the vast majority of the world's religions and their adherents is not whether or not they witness, but how.[37]

2. In a way. Some people object to the very idea of witness. Most often they base their arguments on negative consequences of the way religions have promoted themselves. In the case of Christianity, for example, they point to the use of military might during the Crusades to drive Muslims out of the Holy Land. Or they point to the use of economic and political leverage to further the conversion aims of the church during the times of the great western colonial empires.[38]

It should be said that many of these critics do not spare the same chastening rod in reference to other world religions. Some of the excesses of Islamic jihad receive the same critical approbation; or some of the early Hindu traders' forays into Micronesia; or early Buddhist monastic alliances with kings and kingdoms of Southeast Asia; or indigenous peoples' propensities to war on neighboring tribes. Indeed, the world's religions tend to fare badly across the board in these analyses.

On the other side of the ledger, when people favorable to a religious tradition's advocacy efforts write about them, there seems to be no end to the good that has resulted from these efforts. Christian medical missions raised the world's overall health quotient; benign Muslim rulers earned their non-Muslim people's respect through their just rule; the civilizing power of Buddhist rulers and monastics is evident wherever Buddhist culture has spread. From this point of view it seems evident that religious advocacy has been a good thing for the flourishing of humanity.

Any attempt at a clear and objective view of history would have to conclude that both of the above groups are correct, at least in the substance of their views. Religious advocacy has been both a force for good and a force for evil. History is witness. If, then, one is attempting to evaluate religious advocacy from a position outside of that advocacy (that is, by not using arguments for or against it that come from the teachings of a religious tradition or traditions), you would be forced to conclude that advocacy by itself can be called neither a good thing or a bad thing, but must be judged by considering how it is done and what effects it has on the group of people with whom it is done.

We have already noted that obedience to the commands of the Great Commission is a non-negotiable for Christians of any era. We have no alternative when it comes to considering whether or not we do religious advocacy. The only alternative we have is to consider *how* we do advocacy.[39] That makes advocacy an instrumental value. In considering advocacy for the twenty-first century, we must determine the best ways to do it, ways that satisfy both the command to do it and the ethical commands of Scripture that call us to love our neighbors as ourselves.

3. Sincere. It sounds like a cliche: Religious advocacy can only be done by a sincere advocate. Sincerity is one of those words that slides easily off the tongue, passes through the brain like a zephyr, and connects with the deepest level of consciousness possible. We all think we know what sincerity means, and this supposed familiarity often blocks us from articulating why it is so important to a task like advocacy.[40]

The dictionary definition of sincerity is clear: sincerity means honesty, truth, consistency. It is in the area of the relationship between sincerity and advocacy that some of the subtlety begins to emerge. And it becomes especially important. Of course it is good to be sincere at all times. But one can be an advocate for, say life insurance, and get away with a sort of half-hearted sincerity. It helps to really believe the sales pitch you make for a $250,000 whole-life policy, but you can have a considerable amount of skepticism about the product and still be a pretty successful sales person.

The same kind of tepid sincerity doesn't work quite so facilely with religious advocacy. [41] To get the full impact of why, we probably have to introduce the word closest to sincerity's opposite, hypocrisy. Nothing brings the wrath of Christ more in the New Testament than people who know what is right and do what is wrong. We are not talking about Paul's recognition of human fallenness here-we are talking about willful disregard for truth even in areas of apparent control. [42]

A religious advocate, a witness, will see the effectiveness of his or her testimony rise and fall, not on the basis of linguistic skill, mission methodology, or good timing, but on the level of one's sincerity. We must believe the message we proclaim.

4. Faithful to my religious community. Sincerity slips off the edge into self-centered arrogance when one's witness is not rooted in the larger religious tradition. Witness is personal insofar as the individual is the instrument of witness-but witness is also corporate in that the story witnessed to is larger than any individual (or even groups of individuals). The story is 2000 years old and 25,000 miles wide and stretches from the tip of consciousness to the archetypes of humanity-it covers all ages and most of the earth. An individual life is 70 years long and usually only one culture wide. Because of its limited perspective, individual witness must be cross-checked against the teachings of the tradition. [43]

Faithfulness to one's religious community has never been more important than in a technological age where various media enable an individual voice to be heard with power and scope formerly reserved for the thunder of the gods. Christianity, unfortunately, has not been immune to the demagoguery this individual power can create. Televangelists, cult leaders, and misguided institutional leaders have exploited the power of the media, the gullibility of the listening public, and the depths of human depravity. The thunderous power of the technology enhanced individual has proven to be a drug that tempts the most pious among us. [44] None of us, not one, is good enough to withstand the temptations of a witness unchecked by our traditions.

Faithfulness to one's religious community has never been more important than in a rational age where the complexity of religious belief *within* individual religious tradition approaches the comprehension threshold. There is no such thing as a Christian theology, only Christian theologies. [45] Who among us can argue with Calvin's reported and perhaps overly optimistic statement that no theology (including his own) can be more than 80 percent correct. [46] On the one hand, this complexity and diversity reflects the richness of the tradition and the breadth of cultures into which Christianity has spread. On the other hand, it tests the best of us in our attempt to speak the simple gospel truth to those who have not heard. We need the help of our tradition to ensure our "simple gospel" is not simplistic.

Faithfulness to one's religious community, in an age where advocacy methodologies proliferate, protects the community from the ultimate betrayal, methods of advocacy that prove inconsistent with the message being proclaimed. The gospel message is one of love, on that all the "theologies" agree. But can some of our methodologies be truly said to be loving? Copies of Madison Avenue marketing strategies too often don't stop to factor in the gospel-leavening agent. Notoriously cold numbers and sizzling images have to change when the subject is the self-effacing love of Jesus Christ.[47]

5. Respectful. Human beings shorn of the spiritual dimension, the human being of a secularized, scientistic society, do not need to be respected. Such a human being needs to be counted, analyzed, organized, pacified, and controlled. You can even reason with such a human being. But respect, the showing of honor and esteem, is replaced by calculation and craftiness, to the smartest and swiftest go the spoils.

Advocacy of one's religious tradition, when seen as dealing with human beings shorn of the spiritual dimension, follows course. It becomes indistinguishable from advocacy of a political cause, an economic endeavor, a personal whim. It can be couched in correct theology (as correct as our theologies can be), and even done with good intentions. But lacking a spiritual dimension, lacking a supernatural reason, it is little different from social engineering.[48]

Advocacy when seen as dealing with spiritual beings, however, is advocacy of a different kind. Recognition of the spiritual dimension of humanity is not just faithfulness to the scriptural witness, as if that were not enough! Recognition of our full-orbed humanity drastically altars the way we relate to other people.[49] It changes our ethics from materialistic power exchanges to give and take conversations with beings created in the image of God. The simple recognition that this person in front of me was made by God, to seek and glorify God, makes it impossible for me not to honor him or her.[50]

We live in a culture very short on honor. In our material, secular, everyday lives we fail and fail, and we become cynical beyond all measure. Without our spiritual dimension there is nothing to honor. We are simply not good enough to earn honor. All that changes when we see human beings as spiritual beings. We honor the individual, we respect him or her because God made, loves, and sustains each and every person we meet. That demands our respect, and changes everything we do in the way of mission.

6. Individual human freedom. It is not enough to give a general, universal respect for every human being we meet, important as that is. We must go one step further and recognize that each and every human being has God-given individual freedom to choose a religious path. No single general aspect of human nature, if operating correctly, insures a choosing of the God of Abraham, Isaac, and Jacob. If human nature is operating correctly, it is still up to each individual to listen for the voice of God crying out the divine creatorship of all that is. Everyone is free to choose whether or not they hear that voice.[51]

In many ways this very specific freedom seems counter to the general ontological status we all have as human beings created in the image of God.

Mission at the Dawn of the 21st Century

The latter is universal, the former specific. One calls for specific respect of what we are; the other recognition that we each make ourselves what we become (and are made by cultural and historical forces). In many ways it is the strictly theological version of the more general debate in our society between human rights and multiculturalism. As Charles Taylor has pointed out, "As against the notion of honor (which is intrinsically a matter of preferences) we have the modern notion of dignity, now used in a universalist and egalitarian sense where we talk of the inherent dignity of human beings."[52] The theological version has powerful implications for Christian missions and advocacy.

First, it means proclamation is okay, persuasion is usually okay, manipulation and coercion are out.[53] Proclamation is okay because if we allow everyone else the right to speak their religious mind, we have the right to speak also. Persuasion is usually okay because if these exchanges of viewpoints take place on a level playing field, then it is consistent with biblical anthropology to provide individuals with the information necessary to make good religious choices toward God's gracious initiating activity. Persuasion in that context is legitimate. Persuasion when we are in the power position, however, is problematic. Persuasion in such a situation too easily degenerates into manipulation, sometimes even coercion, neither of which is ever allowable.[54]

Second, it means that we can each have our views of what ultimate truth is. Another person's freedom is my freedom also. There is nothing wrong with being convinced I am right, as long as I allow that other people may think they are right. I do not have to agree with them that they are right, simply recognize and allow for their freedom to think what they are led to think. This, of course, is the tricky part. It means tolerance of other people and their right to hold views; but it does not mean agreement with all views.

Third, it means that our methods of advocacy, theoretically at least, must be as varied as the number of people to whom we advocate.[55] Since everyone is both made in the image of God and free to believe what they want, everyone is unique in the way they come at the ultimate questions of life. Their universal image means they all, in their own way, seek God, but it means that their answers are different. The implications for missions are that our witness cannot be a monologue but a dialogue of listening, understanding, and responding to what other people believe in light of what we ourselves believe.

7. Other's religious traditions. As we have seen above, the world's religious traditions are alive and well. Even the consciously taken position called secularism, which some call an a-religious religion, is growing.[56] Of course, if you accept the anthropology basic to all the major world religions, that human beings are made to be spiritual, then it should not be surprising that the world's religions are alive and well. Secularization, as a social theory predicting the decline of religious belief in the twentieth century, has been thoroughly disproven by the facts of the century just past.[57]

But if secularization has been shown to be bankrupt as a theory, so has the prediction made by the title of one of our best read Christian magazines, that the twentieth century would be the "Christian Century."[58] To be sure, Christianity has grown in the twentieth century. It has not, however, taken over the world by any means, and is growing slower than both Islam and conscious agnosticism among the peoples of the world. Hinduism and Buddhism are both thriving. Only religions that concentrate in the main on membership in a specific tribe, single culture (Shinto), or ethnic group are declining or remaining static.

In this general climate of religious growth, and in the changing sociological climate, multiculturalism, technological growth, the Christian response to the other religions of the world is undergoing a shift. On the one hand this shift is subtle. On the face of it, what we actually do regarding people who belong to other religions is the same, we tell them the gospel story as we understand it. We witness. We proclaim, hoping they will understand and be blessed by their understanding. What is changing perhaps, given the complex of cultures and religions in any given social grouping, is the conscious identification with people of other religions as neighbors, religious neighbors, spiritual friends. We are all sinners on the spiritual path to better understanding.[59] All people, Christian and non-Christian, are on that path and are thus the hearers of our witness. We hope they all, Christian and non-Christian, benefit from that witness.[60]

On the other hand, the change is more dramatic. It is dramatic not in terms of what we do, but how we do it. The change required is the attitude we hold toward people of other religions.[61] Non-Christians are not the enemy, but fellow human beings seeking God. Because of cultural conditions and changing demographics we can no longer allow ourselves the luxury of impersonal, anonymous missions. We must relate personally and corporately to people of other religions, recognizing their incipient divinity and our common humanity. We are called to make a change as dramatic as the one Martin Luther proclaimed at the time of the Reformation when he taught us the priesthood of all believers. We now are being called upon to recognize the missionhood of all believers.[62]

Although this change in attitude (and role) is in some ways more dramatic than the more subtle change of message, it is not a 180-degree about-face. Economists have a theory that bad market conditions almost never call for more than tiny changes in supply and demand. Tiny changes, by the time they are worked out on the enormity of the world's stage, have huge effects. I am convinced that a small change in attitude toward people of other religions on the part of Christian missionaries (all of us) will have major impact on the peaceful coexistence of the world's religious peoples.[63]

8. Human flourishing. The church's mission should make things better, even by earthly standards. When we witness, the effect should be not just the spreading of the gospel story, but an improvement in the well being of human

beings. That improvement can be measured by the psychological well being of those who hear and learn, the physical well being of the cultures in which the gospel gains a hearing, the justice of societies in which the gospel is planted and grows. If the gospel does not bear good fruit, then, like the fig tree, it might as well be uprooted and die.[64]

True, improvement may not be immediately evident in the case of some advocacy efforts. Short-term effects are often not reliable indicators of the truth of what is being proclaimed, but the escalating of the fever before true health comes. It is a commonplace of historical study that critical distance is required before the true effects of human actions can be clearly seen. Even then, the biases of the observers and evaluators play a huge role in how the vicissitudes of history are analyzed. Still, any advocacy effort of any religion should be willing to be measured by an objective look at whether human beings have become better for it.

Is this requirement an abandonment of the strictly theological rationales for doing advocacy work?[65] Shouldn't we be willing to preach the gospel to all the nations regardless of whether or not humanity flourishes as a result of it? In one way of looking at that question, the answer is yes. Those of us who believe the gospel story and for whom the Great Commission is a non-negotiable aspect of the church's mission must be willing to plunge ahead with witness in spite of the objections of the principalities and powers and the arguments thrown in our path by Christianity's cultured despisers. As we are actually doing the work, who of us can do other than rely on grace and trust in the will of God as communicated to us by Scriptures, as reason to forge ahead in the darkened waters of earthly existence?

In another way of looking at it, however, who of us could live with a gospel-proclaiming effort that seemed to be working against the very message we are proclaiming?[66] The good news proclaims love for all of God's creation, of peace among the creatures of God's creation, of growth in the glorifying of God's creation in everything we say and do. In our day and age, with the historical tools and knowledge we have available to us, it must be possible to see the overall historical effects of what we are doing that contributes to human flourishing and what we are doing that is not, and then do the one and stop doing the other. Can we do anything else?

Notes

[1] The agricultural image has probably been the most used mission metaphor in the history of the church.

Matteo Ricci, in his journal of his mission efforts to China in the sixteenth century, commended one of his coworkers, Father Cattaneo, by saying he "managed well and increased the harvest" by winning "many converts" from among the Chinese. One section of his journal is named "A Future Fruitful Harvest is Planted at Sciauguin." See *China in the Sixteenth Century: The Journals of Matthew Ricci: 1583-1610*. Louis J. Gallagher, ed. (New York: Random House, 1953), 200.

[2]   John 4:35.

[3]   Emile Durkheim would say the culture determines them, Karl Marx would say the prevailing ideology imposes them on the culture, and Max Weber would acknowledge a dialectical relationship between the two. I opt for Weber on this point.

[4]   Although the exact words of these definitions are mine, many have made similar distinctions. See, for example, *Ethnic Variations in Dying Death, and Grief: Diversity in Universality*, Donald P. Irish, Kathleen F. Lundquist, Vivian Jenkins Nelsen, eds. (Washington D. C.: Taylor and Frances, 1993), 2.

[5]   Let me define culture. According to Webster's Dictionary it is "the concepts, skills, arts, and institutions of a given people in a given period." *Concise Edition Webster's New World Dictionary of the American Language*, David B. Guralnik, ed. (New York: World Publishing Company, 1966). This usage corresponds most closely to the way the word is used when people discuss issues of "multiculturalism." I recognize that anthropologists, sociologists, and esthetes all have specialized definitions of culture, but because of the interdisciplinary nature of this article, this general definition serves best. A "complex culture" is one in which many cultures coexist.

[6]   Mission statements of recent years have tended to celebrate this diversity also. For example, "We are unanimous in celebrating the colorful mosaic of the human race that God has created. This rich variety should be preserved, not destroyed, by the gospel. The attempt to impose another culture on people who have their own is cultural imperialism . . . cultural diversity honors God, respects man, enriches life, and promotes evangelization." "The Pasadena Consultation," Lausanne Occasional Paper No. 1 (Wheaton, IL: LCWE, 1978), 4-5.

[7]   The drive toward multiculturalism is not indiscriminate, however. Even multiculturalism's most ardent advocates recognize limits: "While we affirm and celebrate cultures as expressing the plural wonder of God's creation, we recognize that not all aspects of every culture are necessarily good. There are aspects within each culture which deny life and oppress people. . . . There is an evolution of a new culture due in part to modernization and technology. There is a search for a culture that will preserve human values and build community. We need to reassess the role played by the relationship between this process and the demands of the Gospel and our witness to it." "Gathered for Life," Official Report, VI Assembly World Council of Churches, Vancouver, Canada, 1983 (Geneva: WCC, 1983), 32-34.

[8]   Of course, some missiologists have already done work in this area, particularly the funding of the missions effort. For a good discussion of the issues here see Jonathan Bonk, "Mission and Mamon: Six Theses," *International Bulletin of Missionary Research* (October, 1989), 174-181. Excerpted in *Ministry and Theology in Global Perspective: Contemporary Challenges for the Church*, Donald Pittman, Ruben Habito, Terry Muck, eds. (Grand Rapids, Michigan: Eerdmans, 1996), 309-314. Still, the broader implications of economism are still being drawn.

[9]   I'm indebted to Joseph Campbell's video series "The Power of Myth," for this illustration idea. Campbell drew the distinction between cathedral and skyscraper. I have augmented it by adding the city hall/palace.

[10] Colossians 1:16.

[11] Trying to ascertain the line between making the gospel relevant to the society in which it seeks expression and making the gospel captive to the thought forms of that society has been a key issue in the mission of the church from the beginning. One of the earliest expressions of the dilemma was made by Origin in his letter to Thaumaturgus: "You should devote all the strength of your natural good parts to Christianity for your end; and in order to do this, I wish to ask you to extract from the philosophy of the Greeks what may serve as a course of study or a preparation for Christianity, and from geometry and astronomy

what will serve to explain the sacred Scriptures." Excerpted in *Classics of Christian Missions*, Francis M. DuBose, ed. (Nashville: Broadman Press, 1979), 203.

[12] "While on the one hand people seem to be pursuing material prosperity and to be sinking ever deeper into consumerism and materialism, on the other hand we are witnessing a desperate search for meaning, the need for an inner life, and a desire to learn new forms and methods of meditation and prayer." "Redemptoris Missio, An Encyclical Letter on the Permanent Validity of the Church's Missionary Mandate," Pope John Paul II (Typis Polyglottis Vaticanis, 1990). Reprinted with commentary in *Redemption and Dialogue*, William Burrows, ed. (Maryknoll: Orbis Books, 1993), 26.

[13] Matthew 28:16-20. Actually it is not just today that the continuing applicability of the Great Commission has been challenged. Gustav Warneck, in his mission history, comments how "orthodoxy" of the eighteenth century opposed Great Commission missions because it was championed so strongly by the Pietists: "'Go into all the world,' the Lord of old did say: But now: 'Where God has placed thee, there He would have thee stay,'" was a ditty used to express this disdain. *Outline of a History of Protestant Missions from the Reformation to the Present Time* (Edinburgh: Oliphant, Anderson, Ferrier, 1906), 57.

[14] The dynamic is similar to many of the issues related to missions. For example: "'It is more blessed to give than receive.' A woman who accepts that statement of our Lord Jesus Christ as a fact and not as 'impractical idealism,' will make giving a principle of her life." "Letter from Lottie Moon to Southern Baptist Women," *Foreign Mission Journal* (December 1887), 2.

[15] The argument for participating in mission based on obedience is a powerful and pervasive one. Adoniram Judson, the Baptist missionary to Burma, put it this way in reference to the Great Commission: "The command can be obeyed by every believer and that no profession ought to be regarded as sincere, no love to the Savior genuine, unless it be attended with a sincere endeavor to obey (it)." Quoted in *Classic Texts in Mission and World Christianity*, Norman Thomas, ed. (Maryknoll: Orbis, 1995), 66.

[16] "*Missio Dei* . . . asserts that mission is God's, not ours." Phillip Potter, *Life in all its Fullness* (Geneva: WCC, 1981), 70.

[17] "The Great Commission is truly the most genuine utterance of the risen Jesus." Karl Barth, "An Exegetical Study of Matthew 28:16-20," in *The Theology of the Christian Mission*, Gerald Anderson, ed. (New York: McGraw-Hill, 1961), 67.

[18] See *Catechism of the Catholic Church* ("The desire for God is written on the human heart.") and *Veritatis Splendor* ("In this witness to the absoluteness of the moral good Christians are not alone: they are supported by the moral sense present in peoples and by the great religious and sapiential traditions of East and West, from which the interior and mysterious workings of God's Spirit are not absent.") Both of these official Catholic documents, approved by John Paul II in 1992 and 1993, are cited in *Interreligious Dialogue: The Official Teaching of the Catholic Church (1963-1995)*, Francesco Gioia (Boston: Pauline Books, 1997), 104, 107.

[19] The idea of *logos spermatikos* (seed of reason) was suggested by Justin Martyr, a second century Christian apologist. The primary arguments are found in the "First Apology of Justin" and the "Second Apology of Justin," *Anti-Nicene Fathers, Vol. 1* (Grand Rapids: Eerdmans, 1981), 159-194. "All men have some knowledge of God through his general revelation in nature." "The Lausanne Covenant, Article Three," *Let the Earth Hear His Voice*. J. D. Douglas, ed. (Minneapolis: World Wide Publications, 1975), 3.

[20] According to John Calvin, the *sensus divinitatus* is an immediate, intuitive sense we all have of God: 'There is within the human mind, indeed by natural instinct, an awareness of divinity." John Calvin, *Institutes of the Christian Religion, Vol. 1* (Philadelphia: Westminster Press, 1960), 43.

21 The *imago del* is the biblical teaching that human beings 'by creation uniquely bear the image of God." See Karl Barth, *Church Dogmatics 111:2* (Edinburgh: T & T. Clark, 1960), 324, 327. See also: "The 'image' presupposes certain qualities (rationality and morality), but at the same time transcends them. It points to the very special relationship with God, into which man was created: the relationship of a child who may call God his Father." *Let the Earth Hear His Voice: International Congress on World Evangelization Lausanne, Switzerland,* J. D. Douglas, ed. (Minneapolis: World Wide Publications, 1975), 1011.

22 See Stephen Neill, *A History of Christian Missions* (New York: Penguin, 1964), 478.

23 Although Kenneth Scott Latourette rightly cautions against taking this position too far: "In spite of the intimate connection with the expansion of European, ostensibly Christian peoples, there was less direction and active assistance from the state than in any era since the beginning of the fourth century. The extension was chiefly by voluntary organizations supported by the gifts of private individuals." *A History of the Expansion of Christianity,* Vol. 6 (New York: Harper and Row, 1944), 443.

24 Adolf Harnack, however, gives good expression to the difficulty of ascertaining the causes of Christianity's growth: "It baffles us to determine the relative amount of impetus exerted by each of the forces which characterized Christianity: to ascertain, e.g., how much was due to its spiritual monotheism, to its preaching of Jesus Christ, to its hope of immortality, to its active charity and system of social aid, to its discipline and organization, to its syncretistic capacity and contour, or to the skill which it developed in the third century for surpassing the fascinations of any superstition whatsoever." *The Expansion of Christianity: the First Three Centuries, Vol II* (New York: G. P. Putnam's, 1905), 452-453.

25 One positive way this has been implemented in missions history is the emphasis on the indigenous principle, that is, turning control of the missions operation over to indigenous peoples. See Henry Venn, *On Steps Towards Helping a Native Church to Become Self-Supporting, Self-Governing and Self-Extending* (Grand Rapids: Eerdmans, 1971), 74-78, and Rufus Anderson, *Foreign Missions: Their Relations and Claims* (Grand Rapids: Eerdmans, 1967), 97-102. Several years ago church historian George Marsden, in reference to the problem of the church and secular power, proposed that the church consciously adopt a "policy of inverse use of power": the more secular power a church group accrues, the less it should use it.

26 A principle perhaps first stated inversely by Tertullian: "You choose to call us enemies of the human race, rather than of human error." "Apology," in *The Ante-Nicene Fathers, Vol. III* (Grand Rapids: Eerdmans, 1951), 45.

27 A somewhat unlikely source for this recommendation: William Carey, who said, "it is necessary that we become acquainted with the religious state of the world." Carey himself with his study of the religions of India exemplified this. *An Enquiry into the Obligations of Christians to Use Means for the Conversion of the Heathens* (Dallas, Texas: Criswell Publishers, 1988), 1.

28 Clement of Alexandria made this argument against Greek philosophy: "The word of our Teacher remained not in Judea alone, as philosophy did in Greece; but was diffused over the whole world, over every nation, and village, and town, bringing already over to the truth whole houses, and each individual of those who head it by him himself, and not a few of the philosophers themselves." "The Stromata," *The Ante-Nicene Fathers, Vol II* (Grand Rapids: Eerdmans, 1951), 519-520.

29 See, for example, Claude Levi Strauss, who in *Myth and Meaning* (New York: Schocken Books, 1979) explores indigenous people's rationality.

30 See William Dyrness, ed. *Emerging Voices in Global Christian Theology* (Grand Rapids, Michigan: Zondervan, 1994).

31 The Eastern Orthodox have perhaps kept alive best the full-orbed nature of the gospel vis a vis human nature: "Mission is not only realized 'in the name of the Father, and of the Son, and of the Holy Spirit,' but mainly it is a participation in the life of the Holy Trinity, an expression of this love with all the power of existence, 'with all our hearts and with all our souls, and with all our minds.'" Anastasios of Androussa, "Orthodox Mission—Past, Present, Future," in *Your Will Be Done: Orthodoxy in Mission*, George Lemopoulos, ed. (Geneva: WCC Publications, 1988), 81.

32 *Eusebius. Church History*, Vol. I. A Select library of Nicene and post-Nicene fathers of the Christian Church. Second Series. (Grand Rapids: Eerdmans, 1952, 1890), Vol. I: 169, 224-225.

33 There are many definitions of Christian missions, of course: "The organized effort to propagate one religion among adherents of another." (*Dictionary of Religion*) "Carrying out God's work among people who are struggling to live with dignity and wholeness and in harmony with nature." (*Dictionary of Feminist Theologies*) "The manifestation of God's plan, its epiphany and realization in the world and in history." (*Roman Catholic-Ad Gentes*) "Continuous act by which a Christian or a Christian community proclaims God's acts in history and seeks to reveal Christianity as the true light that shines for every man." (World Council of Churches) "Participation in the life of the Holy Trinity." (Eastern Orthodox) "The effort to effect passage over the boundary between faith in Jesus Christ and its absence." (American Society of Missiology) "To spread the good news that Jesus Christ died for our sins." (The Lausanne Covenant) "One beggar telling another beggar where to get food." (D. T. Niles)

34 This understanding of identity witness has a rich heritage. Consider Bertilla: "Bertilla was an example and model of piety to all. She carefully taught religious customs to her subjects not only through holy speech, but even more through her own sanctity." *Sainted Women of the Dark Ages*, Jo Ann McNamara and John Halborg, eds. (Durham, NC: Duke University Press, 1992), 285-286.

35 In "Holy Scripture, Proclamation, and Liturgy," Ion Bria, says this: "The Eucharistic liturgy is the full participation of the faithful in the salvation brought about by the incarnation of the divine Logos and through them into the whole cosmos. . . . The liturgy is the restoration in Christ of the fallen world." He goes on: "The Holy Eucharist was instituted among other things to proclaim the death and the resurrection of our Lord to church members, nominal Christians, and non-Christians." *Go Forth In Peace: Orthodox Perspectives on Mission*, Ion Bria, ed. (Geneva: WCC, 1986), 29.

36 "All Christians by the example of their lives and the witness of the word, wherever they live, have an obligation to manifest the new man which they put on in baptism, and to reveal the power of the Holy Spirit by whom they were strengthened at confirmation, so that others, seeing their good works, might glorify the Father and more perfectly perceive the true meaning of human life and the universal solidarity of mankind." "Ad Gentes," *Vatican Council II: The Conciliar and Post Conciliar Documents*, Austin Flannery, ed. (Northport, New York: Costello Publishing, 1975), 825.

37 "What is clear is that every Christian was a witness. Where there were Christians, there would be a living, burning faith, and before long an expanding Christian Community." Stephen Neill, *A History of Christian Missions* (New York: Penguin, 1964), 22.

38 Although these critiques are needed and important, they must be balanced by work such as that done by Lamin Sanneh who shows that missionary influence was not just a one way imposition of western culture, but a two-way influence which included good elements of culture exchange on both sides. See, for example, his book, *Translating the Message: The Missionary Impact on Culture* (Maryknoll: Orbis, 1989).

39 "The Church seeks to discover the right way to announce the Good News. She takes her lead from Divine Pedagogy. This means learning from Jesus himself, and observing the times and season as prompted by the Spirit." "Dialogue and Proclamation," in *Redemption and Dialogue: Reading Redemptoris Missio and Dialogue and Proclamation*, William Burrows, ed. (Maryknoll: Orbis, 1993), 112.

40 "Our mission as Christians is to live the faith experience in Jesus Christ, so that we are credible, and our credibility can be evangelizing." Rose Fernando, "God's Love Cuts Across History," *International Review of Mission* 74(1985), 498-501.

41 "We cannot proclaim a reign of justice, love and peace, while at the same time contradicting its inclusive, non-dominating character in our mission practice and structures. If the kingdom is our focus, then a more collaborative, egalitarian, ecumenical effort in mission will be a more compelling witness." Virginia Fabella, "Christology from an Asian Woman's Perspective," in *We Dare To Dream: Doing Theology as Asian Women*, Virginia Fabella and Sun Ai Lee Park, eds. (Maryknoll: Orbis, 1990), 4, 10-13.

42 "The manner of doing mission cannot be separated from the mission itself." Mercy Oduyoye, "Church Women and the Church's Mission," in *New Eyes for Reading: Biblical and Theological Reflections by Women from the Third World*, John Pobee and Barbel von Wartenbert-Potter eds. (Geneva: WCC, 1986), 69-70.

43 "The present ecumenical movement came into being out of the conviction that the division of Christians is a scandal and an impediment to the witness of the church. There is a growing awareness among the churches today of the inextricable relationship between Christian unity and missionary calling, between ecumenism and evangelization." *The San Antonio Report: Your Will Be Done— Mission in Christ's Way* (Geneva: WCC, 1990), 25-35. Excerpted in *New Directions in Mission and Evangelization 1: Basic Statements 1974-1991*, James Scherer and Stephen Bevans, eds. (Maryknoll: Orbis, 1992), 75.

44 Technology is not irredeemably bad, however. As one mission's statement put it, "Despite intolerance and fanaticism, Christians can use the immense potential offered by contemporary technology to witness to and evangelize others." "Final Report of CWME Consultation of Eastern Orthodox and Oriental Orthodox Churches," in *Mission from Three Perspectives* (Geneva: WCC-CWME, 1989), 32-47.

45 "We can hardly commend a man who takes the section of the Lord's vineyard that has been allotted to him for cultivation, and proceeds to treat it as a piece of private property, a domain not to be touched by the hands of an outsider." Benedict XV, "Maximum Illud," *Catholic Missions: Four Great Missionary Encyclicals*, Thomas Burke, ed. (New York: Fordham University Press, 1957), 12-13.

46 This is one of those statements that I have heard Calvin scholars I respect quote, but have never found the reference. I like it. I hope Calvin said it. It matches my understanding of him, if not the caricature often painted of him-which is probably why I hope he said it.

47 Read the rather disheartening account of the mixing of business and ministry by Abbe Migne in R. Howard Bloch's *God's Plagiarist: Being an Account of the Fabulous Industry and Irregular Commerce of the Abbe Migne* (Chicago: University of Chicago Press, 1994).

48 "The prayer 'Come, Holy Spirit' is uttered by those who believe that the world, in spite of technological and scientific advances and pretensions of self-sufficiency, cannot exist or develop its full potential apart from God's presence and action in it. As humanity moves freely towards God, all life begins to be experienced as a communion of love, reflecting the life of the Holy Trinity." *The Holy Spirit and Mission*, George Lemopoulos, ed. (Geneva: WCC-CWME, 1990), 89-100.

49 "It is His will that His Holy Faith should be preached and that the beings He has created and redeemed should know Him and that His predestined ones should be saved and His

Majesty and Your Highness receive great services." Bartholomew de Las Casas in a letter to Philip II of Spain, pleading for the fair treatment of the South American Indians as objects of missionizing activity. *Bartholomew de Las Casas: His Life, Apostolate and Writings*, Francis MacNutt, ed. (Cleveland: Arthur H. Clark, 1909), 222-231.

[50] "All men form but one community. This is so because all stem from one stock, which God created to people the entire earth." "Nostra Aetate," *Vatican Council II: The Conciliar and Post Conciliar Documents* Austin Flannery, ed. (Northport, New York: Costello, 1975), 738.

[51] "We repudiate any symptoms of a religious imperialism that would desire to impose beliefs and practices on others in order to manage their souls in their supposed interests." "The Christian Message," *The Jerusalem Meeting of the International Missionary Council*, Vol. I (London: Oxford University Press, 1928), 400.

[52] Taylor, Charles, "The Politics of Recognition", in Taylor, Charles, et. al. eds., *Multiculturalism: Examining the Politics of Recognition* (Princeton, New Jersey: Princeton University Press, 1992), 27.

[53] "Proselytism embraces whatever violates the right of the human person, Christian or non-Christian, to be free from external coercion in religious matters or whatever in the proclamation of the Gospel does not conform to the ways God draws free men to himself in response to his calls to serve in spirit and in truth." "Common Witness and Proselytizing," *Mission Trends 2: Evangelization*, Gerald Anderson and Thomas Stransky, eds. (New York: Paulist, 1975), 178.

[54] Unfortunately this is still a vision. There is a long history in the church of allowances for coercion. Aquinas and Augustine allowed it in certain instances. Although more recent church documents repudiate these allowances, some still see them as valid. See Thomas Aquinas, *Summa Theologica*, 11:2, Q. 10, Art. 8 (New York: McGraw-Hill, 1964).

[55] Echoing Paul in 1 Corinthians 9:22: "I must become all things to all people in order to save some." In some sense, of course, all means are dependent on an acting God. As the Protestant missionary David Brainerd wrote, "He used me as an instrument, or what I spake as means of carrying on His work. It seemed, as I thought, to have no connection with, nor dependence upon means in any respect. Although I could not but continue to use the means which I thought proper for the promotion of the work, yet God seemed as I apprehended, to work entirely without them." David Brainerd, "The Rise and Progress of a Remarkable Grace" from *Life and Diary of David Brainerd* by Jonathan Edwards (Chicago: Moody, 1949), 224.

[56] "The rise of secular, quasi-religions is one of the most important religious trends of the twentieth century." Chris C. Park, *Sacred Worlds: An Introduction to Geography and Religion* (London: Routledge, 1994), 48.

[57] There is a difference between secularism and secularization. Secularization is a hypothetical process whereby cultural conditions lead to a growth in the understanding of human beings as material and nonspiritual. Secularism, on the other hand, is a well-defined set of beliefs about the ultimate religious issues. Even though secularists deny the existence of God or the gods, their very role as ultimate meaning providers are themselves religious.

[58] Echoing the watchword made current by John R. Mott. *The Evangelization of the World in this Generation.* (New York: Student Volunteer Movement for Foreign Missions, 1995).

[59] "Again and again we have been forced to note that the evils that we face are not the work of bad men only, but of good as well. The gravest of our disasters have been brought upon us not by men desiring to make trouble for mankind but by those who thought they did their best in the circumstances surrounding them. We do not know the man wise enough to have saved the world from its present sufferings-and we do not know the man wise

enough to deliver us now." "A Message to All Peoples," *International Missionary Council Meeting at Tambaram, Madras,* Vol. VII (London: Oxford, 1939), 176.

[60] The big question is whether it is a common search for truth among all the religions, or the recognition that the gospel of Jesus Christ is the single way, with all the religions more or less striving for that standard. This was precisely the nature of the disagreement between William Ernest Hocking (*Re-Thinking Missions: A Layman's Inquiry After One Hundred Years,* 1932) and Hendrick Kramer (*The Christian Message in a Non-Christian World,* 1933), whose two books focused the disagreement over the future trajectory of missions at the Madras missionary meeting of 1938. The question is still with us.

[61] "Evangelization cannot be arrogant, as in the past. It has to be considered as a modest and friendly presence on the part of the churches to discover for themselves the wonder of God's grace in every history, culture, and people, and to celebrate that grace and to give thanks; to be open and accept the other's specific gift of truth and God-experience for their own enrichment and growth; to make available to the other their own specific experience of God, love, and hope as these have entered human history in the reality of Jesus of Nazareth; and to join hands with all who stand for human dignity and struggle together for the liberation of all." *Third World Theologies: Commonalities and Divergences,* K. C. Abraham, ed. (Maryknoll: Orbis, 1990), 209.

[62] "The church is seen, not as a religious assembly, temple, synagogue, or sect which is closed or sacred, but as a part of the world where it joins God's action in becoming a pressure group for change." Letty Russell, *Human Liberation in a Feminist Perspective-A Theology* (Philadelphia: Westminster, 1974), 159.

[63] See John Paul II's exhortation on "The Laity and Other Religions," in *Christifideles Laici* (December 30, 1988). Excerpted in *Interreligious Dialogue: The Official Teaching of the Catholic Church 1963-1995,* Francesco Gioia, ed. (Boston: Pauline, 1997), 99.

[64] The point is subtle. Good deeds on the part of religions don't prove the truth of those religions. But the lack of good deeds should raise real questions about them. "The non-Christian religions can just as well as Christianity show up an impressive record of psychological, cultural and other values, and it is wholly dependent on one's fundamental axioms of life whether one considers these non-Christian achievements of higher value for mankind than the Christian." Hendrick Kraemer, *The Christian Message in a Non-Christian World* (New York: International Missionary Council, 1947), 106.

[65] "Evangelism is supremely God's work in the lives of men, in which he enlists human co-operation." Michael Green, *Evangelism in the Early Church* (London: Houder and Stoughton, 1970), 274. In the mission task of the church, "nothing less than the adequacy of Christianity as a world religion is on trial." *World Missionary Conference Edinburgh, 1910, Vol 1* (New York: Fleming Revell, 1910), 363.

An Evangelical Theology of Service in an Interdependent and Suffering World

Carol J. Birkland

Let's begin with a familiar story.

Because of what he said and the miracles he performed, Jesus and the disciples attracted crowds wherever they went. In the sixth and eighth chapters of Mark they find themselves in the difficult situation of having, over a number of days, attracted a large crowd which shows no signs of dispersing. The problem: the people are hungry and how are they to be fed? Jesus is afraid that if he sends them away without feeding them, they will faint (or worse) on their way home.

The disciples are of little assistance, doing nothing more than asking the obvious question:

"How are we going to be able to feed these people in the middle of the desert when we don't have bread?"

Jesus surveys the situation and then, as was his custom, responds unpredictably. Instead of looking for solutions elsewhere ("Who will go to Tiberias and ask them to send us the bread we need?"), he turns to the disciples and asks: "How many loaves of bread do you have?"

"We have seven," they reply. Seven loaves for 5000 people.

Seemingly not fazed by the apparent lack of available resources at hand, Jesus instructs the people to sit down. Then, taking the seven loaves, he gives thanks for them, blesses them, breaks them, and gives the pieces to the disciples to distribute to the hungry crowd. Someone in the crowd also brought forward a few small fish. After blessing them, Jesus asks that they be distributed as well.

We know the end of the story. After the 5000 ate their fill and departed, Jesus and the disciples were left with seven baskets of leftovers.

Clearly, some kind of miracle had taken place, but it was a miracle that involved Jesus making something out of what, on face value, appeared to be nothing. Considering the scope of the problem he faced, these seven loaves and a few fish could be reasonably dismissed as worthless. However, where others saw nothing of value, Jesus, somehow, recognized potential and possibility and used that to make a miracle.

In this paper, it is my intention to try to address the current status of Christian humanitarian service. Among questions to be asked might be the following: to what extent are Christian service agencies fulfilling the task that Christ set before us to meet human need wherever we find it? Are we providing the kind of assistance that imparts to people the appropriate skills and resources necessary to develop themselves and their communities so that they may actually experience a better quality of life? To what extent do our efforts have "staying power," i.e., are the effects lasting and are people and communities able to improve or expand on them?

After seven years of evaluating Lutheran World Federation development projects and programs all over the world, I have seen much good effort and some success. However, I must admit that in more cases than not, the results achieved have not lived up to our good intentions. In a very general sense, if I were to try to isolate the one factor that has most contributed to failed projects and disappointed people, it would directly relate back to the story of the feeding of the 5000. In short, we have tended to look elsewhere for answers and capacities rather than using first what has been immediately available to us. Additionally, in my view, we Christian service workers have been too concerned with the *what* we have done and not enough concerned with the *how*.

"The poor are look alikes and weak. We know their needs. They need not speak" . . . Robert Chambers

Without a doubt, while church service agencies have provided important and critically necessary assistance to vulnerable and needy people, we, unlike Jesus, have not been particularly good at seeing the potential and capacity that exists in every situation and in every person. We have failed to recognize (or have not taken the time to recognize) the fact that all persons and communities, regardless of their poverty or vulnerability, do possess capacities and abilities. All people have talents and knowledge (yes, even wisdom) which are critically needed in the process of their own development and if we—those who are to assist in that process—fail to recognize or use those capacities, we run the risk of not only failing in our efforts, but even more tragically, creating dependency or killing initiative.

Even if we are able to fulfill our plans and meet our goals, are peoples' lives better in the long run? After we have left, have those we assisted with training and know-how been able to press the agenda forward on their own, to build successes on a foundation we helped them lay? And finally, if we were to return in ten years' time, would there be any evidence that something positive had ever been accomplished?

Over the years churches and church agencies have spent millions of dollars and missionaries and other church workers have spent lifetimes in fulfilling the Christian mandate to feed the hungry and clothe the naked. However, because of who we are, i.e., the products of an economically privileged society that values and rewards quick, decisive action, we have had the tendency to define those we hope to assist in terms of their vulnerable situation. We have had difficulty in seeing anything beyond the poverty, sickness, and hunger. The situation is desperate and hopeless, therefore the people themselves are hopeless and helpless.

Unlike Jesus in the story of the feeding of the 5000, we very seldom looked for, much less ever considered using the resources and capacities that, believe it or not, exist in almost every situation, and in our western urge to "do something" and "do something quickly," we have rushed to prescribe and apply "our" solutions to "their" problems.

The result is that in many cases there has been little "practical fit" between our solutions and their problems. What this has meant is that the problems are "solved" only for as long as we remain in the picture with our skills and our money but as soon as we leave, it is clear that the problem has either not been solved at all or only solved in the short term—in a way, to use current development jargon, that is not sustainable.

Even worse, when we then have proceeded to construct institutional structures around our "solutions," we have been faced with the prospect of being forever responsible for the care and feeding of an institution that, in many cases, has little connection either with the local culture or its supportive capacity.

The other option is to extricate ourselves—as gracefully as possible—in the hope that somehow local people will be able to carry on without us. From my experience I find that because local management has never operated without substantial outside support, they believe that they can continue operations at the same level. Some even take this opportunity to try to expand! With shrinking funding now a reality, what is usually left behind are what the noted development thinker, Robert Chambers, refers to as yet more "rusting relics for archaeological students of error."

It is easy to laugh at the folly of misguided development projects and thankfully most of the legitimately big "white elephants" are the results of government schemes hatched in offices in Oslo or Washington by young, earnest men and women who, armed with the Ph.Ds in Development Studies or Agricultural Economics, are utterly convinced that they have the answers—answers, however, which may have nothing at all to do with realities on the ground.

But backed, as they usually are, by substantial sums of government money, they press on with their plans and projects which, in the end, benefit the subcontractors and procurement officers more than the people themselves. It must be understood: international development aid is a big business in which assisting vulnerable people plays a secondary role to that of making money and career advancement.

However, before we laugh too loudly, we must understand that the real losers in these misguided development schemes are the very people who should have benefited. In many cases they are people for whom failure has become a way of life. The rains have failed, the crops have failed, their cattle have died, and then their children have died. The last thing they need in life is another failure.

If we, the development professionals, fail the worst that can happen is we lose our funding, the project is shut down, and we pack and leave. But local people cannot leave and they are the ones who must confront the dilapidated buildings that we constructed for them (but which they cannot repair) or the rusting machines for which there are no spare parts, and even if there were, there is no money to buy them. I am afraid that what the government agencies have done on a large scale, we church agencies have replicated and unfortunately, in some cases, persist in replicating on a small scale.

Even more insidious are the projects based on free gifts and handouts. I have read many a project monitoring report with notations such as: "Community leaders said, 'You dug the borehole, you put in the head works. Now the pump is broken (or stolen). When are you coming to fix it?'"

How many emergency feeding programs disperse free food with no community studies to find out who is and who is not needy? The fact is that even in some rather bad drought situations, not all community members are equally threatened. Some years ago during a drought, I saw a well-intentioned missionary drive a truckload of grain into a village and everybody just helped themselves—no questions asked. At the time I saw nothing wrong with that. The people were hungry, weren't they?

Who got the food? I would guess that many who really needed it, did not. In drought situations, the most vulnerable are usually the isolated women, children and elderly people who probably had no strength to even walk to the village to collect the food. It is also clear that emergency relief food should be put directly into the hands of those who need it most—again, usually women who will see that children and elderly persons are fed. Unfortunately, it has been the case that the most able bodied, i.e., men, have been known to sell the food and, therefore, it never really reaches those who need it most.

If free food becomes a habit, why is there any incentive at all to cultivate? It is interesting to note that the Government of Eritrea has just informed all international aid agencies (including the LWF) that they must leave the country and most have done so. It seems that Eritrea has looked around and seen in neighboring countries what they believe to be the debilitating effects of long-term international aid. Because of this, Eritrea has decided to forego short-term benefits in favor of constructing, what they hope will be, a self-reliant post civil war society. Without a doubt, this decision will cause problems for Eritrea's citizens and only time will tell to what extent the decision has been a wise one.

There has never been a time, at least in many parts of Africa, when individual and community initiative has had such a chance of really paying off for people. With the opening up of economies and political systems, what is most needed are the kinds of initiatives and projects which understand that sustainable development must take place in the real world. In the real world, like it or not, little comes free. Water is not free and neither is education nor health care. Loans have to be repaid or people lose their credit worthiness.

This does not mean that one simply accepts IMF and World Bank policies that press governments to the wall to repay loans. But regardless of the prevailing neo-liberal economic policy, any kind of development scheme (except in the most dire of disaster/refugee emergency situations) that creates dependency and kills initiative is unacceptable.

Clearly, even if World Bank debt is forgiven (as it should be in many situations) or international terms of trade equalized, it cannot be assumed that benefits will trickle down to the rural poor. Most likely they will not because there is, in every country, a powerful elite who will do everything possible to siphon off the benefits before they leave the capital city.

It is the poor, both rural and urban, who must organize to form what might be called a civil society "critical mass" (some refer to this as "social capital") to *demand* that any benefits are shared with the most vulnerable in society. This is something that no outsider can do. The people, themselves, must do it for themselves. For many this will be a difficult and politically dangerous effort. I do not think it an overstatement to say that unless Christian service agencies can be involved in the kinds of activities that prepare people for this critical struggle, perhaps we should rather do nothing. Certainly, we should not carry on activities that work at cross-purposes by perpetuating a climate of dependence and docility.

I realize that some of what I have written above may be offensive to some. However, it is not meant to denigrate the selfless efforts of dedicated Christians and Christian institutions. It is clear that the whole issue of Christian service—who does it and how it is done—is a complicated one (and certainly too broad for one paper to satisfactorily discuss). It has been said before: there are no simple answers. It is important to remember that good people, thrust into difficult and sometimes dire emergency situations, can only do what they think is best. All of us are only human; we all try to do what we think is best at the time.

However, I feel compelled to be somewhat provocative because I hope this paper will spark discussion. Additionally, it is with more than a little regret that I recognize myself and my mistakes in all that I have written above.

As an evaluator who has come to see evaluation as first and foremost a way of learning lessons, I think that it is incumbent on those of us who are involved in church related service to do just that: clearly look at what we have done, how we have done it, and as a result of the lessons learned, make the necessary adjustments so that mistakes are not endlessly repeated.

In my past travels with evaluation teams to Lutheran World Federation development projects, it did not seem strange to me that we had a tendency to go into a community with what could be called a "shopping list" of possible development activities—everything from water development to income generating schemes. That it would then be the task of "animators" to organize community groups and encourage them to "participate" in one or more of these schemes did not seem unreasonable to me. On the other hand, that it might be possible to go into a village with absolutely nothing other than the desire and commitment to listen to people talk about their problems and then, through a process that they themselves managed, to define what they felt the best solution would be. . . this never crossed my mind as a real possibility.

> *"I am telling you that I have a headache and you keep telling me that I have a footache and you want to force me to take medicine for that."*
>
> . . . quote from a Chadian speaking to a World Bank official

In her recent book entitled *Capacity Building: An Approach to People-Centered Development*, Deborah Eade makes the observation that: "Women and men, however poor or marginalized, always have many capacities, which may not be obvious to outsiders, and which even they themselves may not recognize. It may take time to discover these capacities and potential. But to intervene without doing so is not only disrespectful; it also wastes an opportunity to build on the existing capacities, and—even more importantly—risks undermining them, and so leaving people even more vulnerable than they were before."

All of us who are involved in Christian service work must take Eade's observation seriously and ask ourselves why it has been so difficult for us to see the capacities and potential she talks about. Robert Chambers would say that it all has to do with power and how we, as westerners, evaluate knowledge, i.e., who has it, how they get it, and how they use it.

According to Chambers, in all cultures there are the "Uppers" and there are the "Lowers." Uppers are the powerful and dominant ones in a context while Lowers are the weak and subordinate. In the world of Christian service, we Americans and Europeans are obviously the Uppers and those we seek to serve in developing countries are Lowers. However, it is important to understand that this Upper/Lower configuration also exists within developing countries and in many cases when we "do development," we, as Uppers, may only associate with the Uppers in a given context. For example, when we plan development projects and plans with partner church officials or any local organization's leadership, we have to understand that we are dealing with Uppers and not Lowers, and Uppers in any society do not necessarily represent the best interests of Lowers. In fact, they may operate at cross-purposes. It should never be assumed that they speak for Lowers. Lowers can only speak for themselves.

It has been my observation that in any social context, the more Uppers move up the ladder of professional success, the more they move away from the realities of Lowers. As a result, they (we) become less and less able to recognize and value Lowers' capacities and knowledge.

Because of our history and experience, Uppers believe that knowledge cannot possibly come from below. The only legitimate knowledge is the technical kind that comes from above—imparted by experts who teach in European and American classrooms to which the Uppers from all societies, developed and developing alike, flock to secure their advanced academic degrees.

This statement is not as an indictment of higher education; it is not meant to be anti-intellectual. Rather it is simply a way of describing the reality of how issues of prestige and power combine with western-style higher education to prevent "educated Uppers" from recognizing Lowers' knowledge and wisdom . . . knowledge and wisdom that must be a part of any development process if it is to work and work in the long term.

Not only may Uppers not recognize Lowers' knowledge, they may reject it outright because, if it contradicts or even challenges what they have been taught, it becomes an ego threat as well. When egos are threatened, the result is usually defensiveness and a sheer exercise of power on behalf of the Upper. Chambers puts it this way:

> The Upper rejects discordant feedback. He re-labels the Lower and redefines her reality for her. He seeks to transfer his reality. He wants it to be his reality that counts. What prevents him learning in this case is not professionalism or bureaucracy. It is his dominant behavior, person to person. It is his power.

What then is the response of the Lowers? Strangely, but understandably, Lowers usually play along simply because as the most powerless in the situation, they have no other alternative. Also, Lowers are not foolish. In most development schemes, even the most misguided, there is usually some immediate benefit to be had and Lowers are not going to pass up the opportunity to benefit. Why should they? They are poor and the poor take what they can get when they can get it. Chambers points out that the Uppers in all societies mutually reinforce each other and the Lowers play along . . . so everybody benefits.

Recently, during an LWF Planning Mission to Tanzania, one of the local senior staff told an interesting story. As a Program Coordinator, he and a couple of other local staff had gone out to a village to conduct a routine base line survey on community needs. They drove up in their Land Rover, took their time to get out and walk around with the people, surveying the situation in the village and listening to the villagers talk about what they needed and how the LWF might be able to assist. After a number of such visits, a long list of prioritized needs was drawn up.

However, as time went by and the local staff continued to work with the community, they discovered that this original needs list had little to do with the community's actual needs. The more time they spent in the village (and after the people understood that the LWF was not going to give them all of the things they had put on their wish list), staff realized that the results of the original survey were completely invalid. Why? Finally the truth came out. A leader confessed that when the villagers saw the community development workers drive up in their "big, expensive car," they realized that this was their chance to "get a lot of things." Then when they realized that the LWF was not interested in dispensing free gifts, they got down to the business of really determining what they hoped to achieve.

After recounting this story, the Project Coordinator told me that the lesson he learned was never to send out staff in cars . . . from now on, the approach would be made only on bicycle. One can only imagine what would have happened if a group of well meaning, generous Americans or Europeans had driven up in two or three Land Rovers!

Two years ago I happened to be reading the Annual Report of the LWF Mozambique program. This was a program I knew well because some years before I had planned and participated in a "Planning Mission" to set the program's overall strategy and goals for the next eight to ten years.

What caught my eye was a small, half page story about a meeting with one of the many groups that the community development workers had organized as a way of ensuring community participation in various activities. The idea was the usual one: organize the community into groups and bring them together to discuss their problems. In the language of "Development Speak," what this usually means is that you get the people together as a way of organizing them to "participate" in your plan . . . not theirs.

The Mozambique program is a classic example of the emergency/rehabilitation/development continuum. The people LWF is working with are former refugees repatriated from exile in Zimbabwe. At first the work focused on landmine clearance and rehabilitating infrastructure destroyed during the long civil war, i.e., roads, hospitals, schools, etc. Now, after two years of rather large-scale rehabilitation work, the program's focus was turning more to long-term development work aimed at assisting the returnees to become self-reliant citizens. Components of the integrated rural development program included the usual cast of characters: water development, agriculture, food security, environmental conservation, and income generating projects.

What made me sit up and take notice was that apparently during one of these community sessions, a participant stood up and essentially said, "We don't want what you are offering." What he said was this: "Look, we have been exiles in Zimbabwe for so many years (some people had even been born in exile) and many of us have forgotten how to speak Portuguese, much less write the language. How are we going to be able to go to the market to buy and sell if we cannot speak and write Portuguese? What we really need are language classes. Can you give us that?"

One wonders why, if there were actual conversations about what the people wanted, the issue of language never came up? One can also only marvel at how this person (definitely a Lower) had the courage to stand up in a public meeting and challenge the LWF Mozambican staff (definitely Uppers) to change the program.

It is from reading this exchange that I learned the following lesson: "We know that our work is successful when those we wish to assist are able to tell us that they don't want what we are offering."

The end to this story is that the program was changed. The Mozambican staff had the courage to report to the Project Coordinator who had the courage to report to the Program Director in Maputo that the people wanted language study. To talk of courage here may sound foolish, but remember, we are all dealing with Uppers here whose egos can be bruised when they are told by Lowers that maybe they made a mistake. I am utterly convinced that there have been situations where the local staff person, concerned about being publicly contradicted by a Lower, would simply have dismissed the idea and the program would have continued as before.

Of course, there is a deeper question: why we were wrong in the beginning? It is not that we did not take the time to listen. We did listen, but, I think, we did not actually **believe** that these people were capable of devising and carrying out a situational analysis process that would ultimately provide a solution to practically fit their problem.

Again and again, the principles of Participatory Rural Appraisal have proved that people have the capacity and wisdom to analyze their own problems. Through methods that they themselves create, problems are defined and solutions found. Again, it is the **how,** the process, that is as important, if not more so, than the end result—the **what.**

In order to develop themselves, people need to actually experience a process through which they work to achieve something. Consciousness raising is fine but unless something—some product—is actually produced, it means little. In his book, *Striking a Balance: A Guide to Enhancing the Effectiveness of Non-Governmental Organizations in International Development*, Alan Fowler comments that, ". . . the age of solidarity has come to an end, and the age of pragmatism and efficiency has begun."

Poor people desperately need to succeed. Success may be something as simple as producing an item to sell or learning to read a simple letter. The more we Christian service agencies can stand off to the side and encourage people to get on with this process, the sooner we will begin to see actual positive results in peoples' lives.

Robert Chambers describes the situation well when he writes: "As outsiders most of us dominated. We lectured, holding sticks and wagging fingers; we interviewed impatiently, firing rapid questions; we interrupted and did not listen; we 'put down' the poor and weak. Our reality blanketed that of local people. Our beliefs, demeanor, behavior and attitudes were self-validating. Treated as incapable," he continues, "poor people behaved as incapable. They reflected the beliefs of the powerful. Their capacities were hidden even from themselves. Nor did many outsider professionals know how to enable local people to express, share, and extend their knowledge. The ignorance and inabilities of local people were then not just an illusion; they were an artifact of outsiders' behavior and attitudes, of arrogant and ignorant manners of interacting."

Let's take another example . . . this time an even more difficult one since it involves an emergency. Uppers usually act like Uppers, but in emergency situations they become Super-Uppers. If, according to Chambers, in development work power means getting things done, in emergency work, power means getting things done *fast*.

Over the years the LWF has gained a reputation for a fast, effective operational response in emergency situations. We have had a cadre of experienced professionals with the capability to quickly move into an emergency situation and begin providing assistance. If there was one thing that was understood in these situations it was that local people, i.e., existing community institutions like local non-governmental organizations or churches, had no capacity to assist in the emergency. "If they had capacity," we thought, "why would it be necessary for the LWF to be there?"

While the necessity to move quickly in emergency situations should not be underestimated, it is also clear that in many places where the LWF has operated in an emergency mode, local institutions— including the church—have felt very much pushed aside since it was assumed they had no capacity to be involved.

But here, too, in both emergency and relief situations, we are beginning to understand that not only do local capacities exist but they should and must be tapped in order to do what is possible to give people the confidence and ability to prepare for the time when they will again be faced with an emergency/relief situation.

Mary Anderson, who has done much work in trying to make a link between relief activity and long-term development, has written: "When assistance is provided to people 'to meet their needs' without regard to their existing capacities, very often the capacities that they do possess are undermined and weakened by the overpowering presence of the aid giver. When this occurs, vulnerabilities are often increased rather than reduced by aid. An adequate notion of vulnerability, then, must take account of people's capacities."

It is also clear that how an agency operates and makes decisions in emergency situations will have a major impact on the long-term development work that follows. If peoples' capacities are ignored in the emergency, they will be ignored later on as well. If people become overly dependent in the emergency phase, trying to do good follow-up development work aimed at self-reliance will be difficult or impossible.

If there is one thing that all of us should have learned by now, it is that disasters (especially in Africa) are recurring events and, unless attention is given to building peoples' capacities to prepare for disasters, we face nothing more than a continuing series of desperate scenes on our television screens. One can only watch so many of these scenes before one becomes immune to human misery—it is only a matter of emotional self-defense. From there it becomes easy to begin blaming the victims.

Tanzania, like much of East Africa, has suffered from flooding as the result of El Nino. In January of this year when the LWF planning mission visited the country, one of the major concerns to be addressed was how the local church, the Evangelical Lutheran Church of Tanzania (ELCT) might be involved with the LWF in future emergencies. On a field trip, the planning team visited a flooded area that had been the home of hundreds of sisal plantation workers. It was a pathetic sight to see the people in this desperate situation. The only question they asked was: "When are the lorries coming to take us out of here?" The planning team had to tell them that no lorries were going to come for them since it was almost impossible for Land Rovers to operate on the flooded roads, much less heavy lorries.

During the planning sessions, the team, which included church representation, discussed this situation and decided that what had to be addressed was the root of the problem. Why had these people been flooded out and what could be done to see that it did not happen again? That it would happen again, there was no doubt since the sisal company had decided to house the workers on a flood plain.

In this case, it was decided that the ELCT should take the initiative. As a large and politically influential local institution (many of the flood victims were ELCT members), the church would flex its political muscle by lobbying hard with both the government and the sisal company to relocate the flood victims' housing area to higher ground. All concerned, LWF and ELCT, were convinced about the wisdom of this plan and, particularly for the ELCT, it provided them with the opportunity to use their abilities to address the actual root cause of the problem.

It is clear in any disaster situation, the goal should never be simply one of returning the community to the previous pre-disaster state. This is just setting people up to suffer again. The goal must be to understand why the people are vulnerable and then to do everything possible to help people decrease that vulnerability. In the Tanzanian case it was the very practical task of trying to relocate people off a flood plain.

> *"Strengthening peoples' capacity to determine their own values and priorities, and to organize themselves to act on these, is the basis of development."*
>
> ... Eade and Williams

Christian service agencies—including those related to church mission agencies—have historically been responsible for establishing a number of Christian service institutions—including what eventually became national church structures. Unfortunately, many of those institutions, even after decades of existence, still survive only because of on-going outside financial support with no indication that, at least in their current form, they will be able to operate from a local funding base. Additionally, many institutional decision-making structures are hierarchical and undemocratic in terms of lay and female participation.

It makes little sense to rehash the history of how these institutions were established. The fact is that they do exist; though, with shrinking outside support, it is certain that operations will become ever more difficult in the future. However, what should concern us as Christian service workers is the question of what kinds of institutions (either existing or to be created) will now give people the opportunity to determine their own values and priorities and then collectively act on those principles—both socially and politically.

In the process of encouraging people to diagnose their own problems, prescribe their own solutions, and collectively act on them, the role of institutions is critical. Why? Because when people are given the chance to inter-relate in the context of institutions which are inclusive and democratic, when they are able to learn the political realities of consensus and compromise, they have gone a long way toward empowering themselves to press forward their demands in the political arena where public policy is made. It is in this process that people, who have never before believed that they possessed talent or ability, realize that they do, in fact, have the collective power to make the system work for them.

It is critical for us, the outside agencies, that these kinds of institutions are formed and flourish. Both now and in the future, they will be our partners in a cooperative relationship that brings together efforts at the micro and macro levels. Again, any pressure from the outside to make political and economic changes on the macro level must be matched by local institutions pushing forward the same agenda at the micro level. In short, it is these kinds of institutions which can give vulnerable people the kind of "political savvy" to make their own governments responsible to them.

"Our personal mental frames are made up from our past learning and experiences, and our constructs, beliefs, values and preferences. What we perceive and believe is also molded by ego and power: ego in the sense of personal needs, as for self-esteem, rewarding social relations and peace of mind; and power in our relations with those who are weaker and stronger than ourselves."

... Robert Chambers

Any discussion of the current status of Christian service in contemporary mission must also deal with the issue of money. Who gives it . . . why do they give it . . . and how honest are we as Christian service agencies in what we do to encourage them to give?

Of one thing there can be no doubt. Funds for relief and development work which come from private sources are decreasing and funds coming from official government sources are increasing. This is a troubling development since regardless of what governments say—even the "squeaky-clean" Scandinavians—official government development aid is **always** tied to a specific political agenda.

But back to our original questions: Who gives the money? Without a doubt, especially in terms of private donations from churchgoers, they are people who feel a genuine Christian concern to assist people in need. We need their money. What do we do to get it?

Alan Fowler comments that, "The messages needed to raise money in the North—appeals to pity and compassion . . . are inconsistent with the dignity of the poor and the slow, contextual nature of sustainable development work."

While Fowler's statement may be more applicable to aid organizations not directly related to churches, we must still face the fact that if we actually do the kind of development work which does acknowledge and build on the innate gifts and capacities of those we hope to assist, can we at the same time allow the impression to be perpetuated that these are hopeless, helpless people?

Would any of us take the risk that Fowler points to? He writes: ". . . the re-education needed for the general public to understand that development work in not simply a case of shipping money overseas. Altering the public's perception of what development is about—from quick, cheap and easy to slow, costly and complex—has to happen sooner or later. The trouble is, who will take the lead at the risk of losing market share?"

And what do we do about the fact that many in our constituencies, mistrustful of bureaucracies, believe that they and they alone know best what should be done and are involved in any number of bi-lateral mission/development projects which may not only be misguided but actually inhibit the efforts of others to do the kind of work which encourages self-reliance and is also sustainable in the long run?

In all my years of being involved in church development work, I have only once heard a person say that they would not accept outside funds to support their work. In this case it was an extremely capable and wise young Tanzanian woman who had been able to successfully organize and operate a childcare program without outside assistance. One day she found her project included on the agenda of a group of church development tourists from Germany. The well-intentioned visitors were so impressed with her project that they were ready to make a rather substantial contribution right on the spot. Later she told me that she literally had to beg them *not* to give her the money. "It would only have killed what I was trying to build. It is not just a matter of providing affordable child care," she said, "it is how the project was conceived. From the beginning I wanted the women to know that we were capable of doing something for ourselves and by ourselves."

This colloquium has been given the task of articulating an evangelical theology of service in today's interdependent and suffering world. Having written all of the above, I would say that a possible reference point for such a theology might be found in the story of Jesus' feeding of the 5000. The focus of Jesus' attention in that story were the people themselves and the assets that they, and they alone, possessed. In trying to solve the problem of how to feed them, Jesus first looked to them for the answer.

Perhaps such a theology of service might also consider the fact of creation itself. All that God has created is good. People are part of that creation and in creating human beings, God provided *all* people with gifts and talents. It is true that the world's dark forces have stifled these gifts and sometimes made them difficult to see—to the extent that the people themselves may not know that they exist. However, is it not unreasonable to assume that Christian aid agencies, understanding the goodness of God's creation, must look first to God's creatures—especially the most vulnerable of them—and understand that these themselves have the capacity and wisdom to define their problem and formulate answers? What we must do is help them (and not hinder them) in that important process which, I believe, is the essence of development.

In the Spirit of Jesus:
A Vision Paper on Christian Service and Mission

Mark W. Thomsen

Introduction

The Winter Olympics in Nagano Japan opened with a colorful ceremony. Representatives of the global community who gathered to participate in the winter games marched into the arena clothed in the styles of a multitude of countries. Three billion members of the human family watched via television as the citizens of Japan, through moving cultural symbols, welcomed us to their homeland in the mountain country north of Tokyo. I was mesmerized by the gigantic choir led by the Japanese conductor, who is employed halfway around the world as the director of the Boston Symphony Orchestra. Powerfully, the choir sang "Ode to Joy," with its references to the one human family. Then through the miracle of modern fiber-optic technology the choir in Nagano was joined with choirs from Sidney, Australia, Cape Town, South Africa, London, England, and from the United Nations building in New York City.

The event manifests what is being identified as *globalization,* one global village, created as modern technology compresses time and space. This is the context of mission and service today and the twenty-first century. Robert Schreiter in his recent book, *The New Catholicity*, lists a number of features of this contemporary globalization process:

- A world dominated by one political and national power, the United States of America, since the collapse of the Soviet Union.

- A world in which capitalism and the free market dominate the economic global landscape.

- Instantaneous electronic communication which increasingly weaves the global community into one vast network of relationships.

Mission Voices Form the Center of Power

There are significant consequences for the life and mission of the church emerging from this powerful context. Obviously, globalization has been a phenomenon that has been emerging over hundreds of years; however, that process has led to a point where we in the United States are at the center of world power. In the words of the April 12, 1998 *Chicago Tribune*, the U.S.A. is "Alone at the Top." Furthermore, we are at the center of power precisely at the time when the compression of time and space is accelerating at a breathless pace. This reality comes to expression in a multitude of ways. The simple fact that we as Americans can travel almost anywhere in the world and speak and be understood in English illustrates this phenomenon.

In February, I awoke at 1:30 a.m. one morning to watch, by television, Kofi Annan and Tariq Aziz questioned by reporters from around the world. The news conference held in Baghdad, Iraq was being conducted in English, the international language of contemporary globalization. Reporters from China-TV, Jordanian newspapers, and a host of others asked questions in English. Annan and Aziz responded in English. That phenomenon was made possible by hundreds of years of globalization. Science and technology produced machines that resulted in the British Industrial Revolution. That revolution produced a gigantic economic and military machine which, through developing communication and transportation systems, resulted in the British Empire. The English language began to encircle the globe. The Second World War made possible by incredible innovations in military hardware and communications ended with a British-American victory. At the end of the war, the United States produced and consumed one-half of the worlds total wealth. This economic and military power has led to American domination within the world community. And a news conference in Baghdad is held in English.

Can a church living and working within the center of global power authentically participate in the mission of the body of Christ? History forces us to ask this question since past Christian communities living at the center of world power have failed. The original documents of the Christian community were written in Greek. Greek was the international language of the day, a fact made possible by the victories of Alexander the Great who conquered the "known world." The early church moved out of a small marginal Aramaic speaking Jewish community into the Roman Empire. For over two centuries it was a marginal community, witnessing in the Greek language to their faith in Jesus Christ. They were often persecuted by the established powers for challenging in the name of Jesus the values and customs of the day. However, in the fourth century the Emperor Constantine accepted the Christian faith and Christianity became the religion of the State. It was then through the Greek language of the Byzantine Empire that Christian orthodoxy was imposed upon the inhabitants of the Empire. Christians now persecuted heretics and pagans for their lack of conformity to the new Christian society.

The official language of the western church was Latin. Originally Latin was the international language of the Roman Empire and its legions of fighting men. The early church permeated the Roman world as a community of the marginalized, suffering through two centuries of persecution. When the church began to emerge as a major voice in the West, the military and political power of Rome was collapsing. The church became a power in this political vacuum. Later the Latin church, in cooperation with European ethnic groups and kings, developed into the Holy Roman Empire. The Holy Roman Empire, often with

Mission at the Dawn of the 21st Century

the threat of death, imposed Latin Christianity upon the rest of Europe. In the years following 1492, the "Christian" royalty of Portugal and Spain cleansed the Iberian Peninsula of Muslims and Jews and set sail for America, as well as portions of Africa and Asia in order to conquer the world for Spain, Portugal, the Pope, and Jesus Christ. The brutal destruction of people and cultures is a matter of record. Is it possible for a Christian community at the center of world power to authentically participate in the mission of the body of Christ? If the "sacred" languages of Greek and Latin were transformed from the language of marginalized Christian communities to the language of Christendom's oppression, has it not also happened to the language of English as it became the medium through which the Gospel is proclaimed among the nations?

The history of western imperialism is the history of the intertwining of the Christian witness with the power of western expansion. Within the context of this discussion of the mission of the global church, it is necessary to remind ourselves that western expansionism has always been explosively fueled by white racism which has viewed "non-white" people and their cultures as inferior or uncivilized. There have always been prophetic voices that cried out against this unholy alliance of religion and state, and there have always been Christian witnesses who have been molded by the mind of Christ. However, more often than not, the Christian witness that moved out of the centers of English speaking power have been twisted and distorted by racism, cultural prejudices, and societal values that have betrayed the original witness of the New Testament to Jesus, the crucified Messiah. In his recent book, *Missionary Conquest*, George Tinker has documented the inability of the missionary community witnessing among the native American nations to separate the witness of the Gospel from their cultural values and customs. Tinker notes that John Eliot, the seventeenth century missionary to New England, actually writes that it was first necessary to move native peoples out of their traditional surroundings and into "civilized" towns before they could be prepared for baptism (See Tinker, p. 36).

Evangelical enthusiasts may perceive this warning about unholy alliances as a sign that there are those within the church who have simply lost their missionary nerve. They would say that we must simply accept the fact that the church is always made up of sinners and saints, or are paradoxically both sinners and saints. This is always a fact, so let us get on with the job! Recently I was once again reminded of the horrifying consequences of just getting on with the task. Marc Ellis, author of the recently published book *Unholy Alliance*, is a powerful prophetic voice who speaks from his own isolation within his Jewish community. In addressing a group of Christians at the Lutheran School of Theology at Chicago, he described what he sees as the great tragedy of his own people. The Jewish people, from his perspective, have moved from being a marginalized community within western culture to a major player in world power politics. Much more tragic, they have moved from the indescribable suffering of fiery furnaces where millions of Jewish people were slaughtered in the final attempt to rid the Aryan race of their presence to a "Constantinian" people who now are in the process of oppressing and destroying a Palestinian people. As Marc Ellis concluded he reminded us that the Christian community shares the same kind of history and guilt. He noted that we live after 1492, after the imperialistic conquest, after slavery, after Auschwitz, after Bosnia, after Rwanda, after _____. Fill in the blank.

A number of years ago, Kosuke Koyama told a few of us who were working on a mission statement, that any plans for mission that were to move out from the center of western power into Asia, had to begin with a recognition of the horrors of the past and deep repentance. Within a Christian context, repentance always means a reversal of direction, a move from our road to God's road, from participation in the norms and values of contemporary culture to participation in the mission of God embodied in Jesus, the crucified Christ. That means being called by God into conformity with the humble and vulnerable servanthood of Jesus. It means listening to Jesus as we hear, "Take up your cross and follow me." This "Congress of 98" is called into this reality of the marginalized, prophetic mission of God which flows from the Holy Spirit's witness to Jesus Christ. It must live and think in repentance, and live and think in faith in the God of Jesus. At this conference we must continually ask the question "to what extent is this gathering one more manifestation of a church within the center of global power attempting to speak of truth so easily distorted by the cultural context which insidiously permeates our lives?"

The church at the margins of the power structures may rightfully ask how a church located within a culture where the mission outreach of the Christian community seems to be withering on the vine can speak to the church where evangelical outreach seems to be exploding. Or how can a church saturated with the materialistic values of global capitalism speak to the world about the Holy Spirit, deep spirituality, human dignity, justice, and sacrificial service? Or, as a conference at the University of Chicago heard from James Cone in April, how can a church insidiously divided on Sunday morning by racism, witness authentically to Jesus? Or how can a church so deeply entrenched in western culture recognize the values and possibilities of contextualization in another culture? This is not to say that such a congress cannot say something significant; however, if it does, it must be put in the realm of the impossible possibility of God's miracles. Jesus himself said that even the rich can be saved through the miraculous activity of God. Even a missionary community marked by western imperialism and systemic racism can be used by God to bring forth fruits where once again the body of Christ is alive among the marginalized peoples of Asia, Africa, and Latin America. However, our eyes and ears here must be open to voices from these margins of the power structures where God's truth in Christ is more apt to be manifest than among us. Perhaps the most important point that this gathering can make is that the most authentic voices of the mission of Christ may be found elsewhere hidden as leaven on the continents of Africa, Latin America, and Asia, or within the marginal communities of the United States and Europe.

Mission Out of the Capitalistic World

The collapse of the Soviet Union has meant the end of the socialist-communist experiment. It no longer competes with global capitalism for global influence. This major event at the end of the twentieth century has had devastating economic consequences for the marginalized people of the world because they, as marginalized people, have been further marginalized.

Capitalism and the free market dominate the world. The development of instantaneous, global financial transactions has led to a global economic system that has created a unified and interdependent global market. Global stock markets operate 24 hours a day and massive amounts of capital move from continent to continent in microseconds (over one trillion dollars a day) threatening the financial stability of the most powerful countries. The collapse of the Thai "bat" or the Indonesian "rupiya" threatens the world market. International capitalistic institutions rush to infuse capital funds into threatened countries in order to prevent an international financial meltdown. Countries that are active players in this capitalistic system reap the benefits of being consumers and producers for the world market. Those who cannot compete in selling and buying, as for example Africa, are relegated to the scrap heap of the international system. Senator Paul Simon, speaking to the ELCA Bishops in January, spoke of the extreme difficulty in moving Congress to be engaged creatively on the African continent. Before leaving with President Clinton on his recent trip to Africa, Commerce Secretary William Daley said, "basically Africa is a continent that has been left out of this century."

A powerful symbol of this global marginalization is found in Georgetown, the capital of the tiny country of Guyana on the northern coast of South America. In this small country with a population of 600,000 people there are two huge embassies representing the United States and what formerly was the Soviet Union. This tiny nation was once the focus of international competition between communism and capitalism that resulted in financial aid coming into the country from two giant global sources. With the disintegration of the USSR not just one source of outside revenue and expertise disappeared but two, because world capitalism no longer had any interest in investing in a world where profits, if any, were minimal. Like many countries of Latin America, and most of the continent of Africa, Guyana was written off by the West as an unprofitable region of the globe. Marginalized nations marked by extreme poverty are falling into even deeper poverty.

Dr. Peri Rasolondraibe, Director of the Department of Mission and Development of the Lutheran World Federation, speaks of the "backward countries of Africa." He speaks this way not because he sees the African continent as inferior, but within the international capitalistic system they are powerless and their economies are in reality moving backward. Their international debts often accumulated by irresponsible military regimes borrowing from irresponsible banks from the North are bleeding African nations to death.

Mark W. Thomsen   259

The gap between rich and poor, which has always been manifest in some manner within human society, is now clearly manifest as a growing gap within the global community. According to the World Health Organization there are one billion hungry persons in the world whose calorie intake is not sufficient to enable them to develop to their potential as human beings. Many of them suffer incredible physical and psychological consequences simply because they do not have sufficient food to eat. Thirty-five thousand children under the age of five die every day because of inadequate diets or lack of primary health care.

That is the equivalent of 100 Boeing 747s crashing daily, each with 350 children on board. That daily tragedy does not even register on the horizon of our consciousness. Again the WHO notes that in many Third World countries, maternal mortality is the leading cause of death of woman, claiming the lives of one-fourth to one-half of all women of reproductive age (15-49 years old). There are 20 million refugees within our global life that are separated from their homes by human violence or natural disaster. Most of this human disaster takes place outside the United States and Western Europe. That is accounted for by the fact that the U.S., Europe, and Japan make up 30% of the world's population but produce and consume 80% of the world's wealth. The U.S. with 4% of the world's population has 20 to 25% of the world's wealth. In spite of the wealth of this country, there is, even here in the U.S., a growing gap between the rich and poor. It is estimated that 1 out of 5 children in the U.S. is malnourished.

Mission Voices from the Marginalized

One of the miracles of the twentieth century is the fact that the Christian community is growing at an incredible rate in those regions of the world where there is the greatest poverty. In 1900, 87% of the world's population lived in Europe and the U.S. Ninety-eight years later, 60% of the Christian world lives in Latin America, Africa and Asia. In 1900, there were between three to ten million Christians on the continent of Africa. Today it is estimated that the number is over 300 million. These Christian communities live in the midst of poverty and oppression. Living within this context of poverty, oppression, and marginalization, they read the Bible with different eyes or from different perspectives. Passages which were skipped over by Christians who live within established churches at the center of world power, leap off the page for those who read them with empty stomachs or from within prison walls. This reading of the scriptures resulted in another miracle, a theological miracle called liberation theology, Dalit theology, Black theology, feminist theology, and their encirclement of the globe. The German theologian, Michael Welker, writing in his recent volume, *God the Spirit*, asserts, "every credible act of asking about God and talking about God must confront the challenges and impetuses of these theologies" (See Welcher, p.17).

People living in poverty discovered that the God of the Scriptures and the Father of Jesus is passionately concerned for the poor and the oppressed. In the prophets like Hosea, Amos, and Isaiah as well as in the Law and the Psalms, there was and is a call from God for justice for the poor and the oppressed. Amos shouted that God was not concerned about religious ceremonies and sacrificial rites, but God called for justice, "Let justice roll down like waters and righteousness like an ever flowing stream" (Amos 45:24). Isaiah stated that God was not concerned about penance as sitting in sack-cloth and ashes, but God wanted a revolution in our lives, God wanted the hungry fed and the naked clothed (Isaiah 58: 6-7). Jesus himself said that the final judgment before the Son of Man would reveal that compassionate concern for the hungry, thirsty, lonely, and naked is the most significant factor in life. Furthermore, the Son of Man is so focused upon the suffering ones that the Lord of the universe is passionately involved in their lives and Divine reality shares the pain and the suffering of the least, the most marginalized within the human community. "Inasmuch as you did it to one of the least of these my sisters and brothers you did it to me" (Matthew 25:40).

This biblical call for compassion and justice strikes a resonating chord in the hearts of the oppressed. In many cultures poverty, illness and violent oppression have been signs of God's absence or even God's judgment. This was certainly true in Jesus' own day (Luke 13:1-5; John 9:2). It is precisely for this reason that Jesus told the parable of the rich man and Lazarus (Luke 16:19f.). Poverty was not a sign of the absence or judgment of God. It is why Jesus cried out, "Blessed are you who are poor for yours is the Reign of God," (Luke 6:20-22). In contemporary terms the poor and oppressed are a top priority for God. They are not forgotten and they are not damned! They have a future with God! They too have been created in the image of God, and have gifts and potential that neither they nor their oppressors have dreamed of (Acts 2: 17-18).

In many non-western cultures the biblical message that God's saving activity includes the whole person and the whole community also strikes a sympathetic chord. This is true because these cultures, in contrast to the West, never have separated the human person into a spiritually-oriented soul and a physical body. These cultures have assumed that humans are psychosomatic beings. They presuppose that God will address the whole person. In 1972, the Mekane Yesus Church of Ethiopia developed a document which was addressed to the western churches. That church was disturbed by the fact that there were more financial resources available for relief and development work than for evangelism. This was because many government funds were flowing out of Europe for relief and development that could not be used for evangelistic purposes. They could not understand how one could divide God's work into two compartments. How could you serve the body and not the spiritual life of the human family; and how could you serve the spiritual life of the human family and not serve their physical needs? It is noteworthy that last year the Mekane Yesus Church, which has one of the strongest relief and development programs of any church, grew in membership at the rate of between 20 and 30%. At the present time this church with a membership of over 2 million has a temporary halt to their evangelism program as they are training more people to teach those who desire to be baptized.

Mission Visioning from the Center of Power

What can this conference learn and say in this global context? A few years ago an ELCA staff person was visiting Africa for the first time. She was traveling with a small group of people though Zimbabwe during the time of a severe drought. They saw hundreds of malnourished and starving children along the way. They saw the elderly sleeping away to death under the dust-ridden trees of the countryside. Toward evening entering Bulawayo and driving to their hotel she saw the unbelievable sight of a green golf course with its sprinklers on! That horrifying picture speaks volumes concerning the gap between the rich and the poor. It also is a parable of global life. It says to most of us that in a world of stark contrasts, we live on the global country club and the sprinklers are on! What does it mean to live and view life from this perspective?

First, it means that we have a very limited perspective. If we are to catch a glimpse of God's perspective we must depend upon those who live elsewhere for a glimpses of the whole. The global community has powerfully called to our attention that the whole includes millions of the dispossessed. They have pointed to the Bible, the source of our faith, which proclaims that the dispossessed are a priority for God. Jesus' own ministry focused there. The sick were healed, the blind saw, the lame walked, the lepers were cleansed, the demon possessed liberated, the poor were promised the Reign of God, the hungry were fed and promised that they would rejoice in being filled, and sinners and the morally marginalized were placed center stage at Jesus' dining table. The Third World perspective declares to the churches of the West: "Please take note!" Christian mission that does not prioritize the poor and is not wholistic, is not the mission of the body of Christ. Christian mission that envisions its task from the global country club must focus on its responsibility, its answerability, to the God of the dispossessed. It cannot say, with Peter, that we do not have silver and gold (Acts 43:6). It will have to answer to God who asks, "where is your sister and brother?" (Genesis 4:9).

I would suggest that it may be the grace of God that allows us to participate in this dimension of the mission of the Reign of God. Contemporary church history would indicate that when one analyzes the global church for the gifts to be found around the globe, the western church, does not stand out as having an abundance of gifts in the realm of evangelism, prayer, spiritual healing, or cultural sensitivity. Many, even within the western church recognize that our future as communities of faith may depend upon our openness to receive the gifts of the Spirit from our global companions. Even though we can not claim to be rich in the gifts of the Spirit: faith, love, and hope; living in the country club, we have tremendous resources that could be used to address the problems of global hunger, suffering, oppression, and injustice. The churches of America have access to incredible financial, technological, and organizational resources that can be dedicated to the mission of the body of Christ. However, they must be channeled in the Spirit of the crucified suffering servant who washed his disciple's feet. This is not a simple task for a people who live within a community permeated with the spirit of competitive capitalism. It is almost impossible for a person within this culture to walk with (accompany) persons of another culture without walking over them or in front of them. Once again we live within the promise of Jesus that even the rich can be saved by a miracle of God. Even the members of the global country club through the power of the Spirit can accompany the churches of Africa, Latin America, and Asia in mission. Within the global Christian community they can participate in the wholistic mission of the body of Christ.

With this promise of Christ as our assurance of the possibility of authenticity in mission, I believe that this conference should suggest to western churches that they immediately, as official policy, make concrete plans to double the amounts of money that are being channeled to programs of churches and NGOs which address issues of health, poverty, and oppression. Most of these programs make creative contributions to local communities as they emphasize self-reliance, development of local leadership, community organization, capacity building, and grass roots development in health, education, and agriculture. There is no need to develop new development and relief programs, for there are hundreds of excellent programs available that need further funding. A 1998 UNICEF Report on the World's Children states that progress is being made in Sub-Saharan Africa. The number of children dying before five years of age has changed from one in five (1960) to one in six (1996). What is needed is a commitment of the church to increase funding, to make health and poverty issues as important as issues that deal with pastoral pensions, churchwide medical plans, ecumenical relationship statements, funding of colleges and seminaries, liturgical styles, and numerous other items that receive primary attention within ecclesiastical discussion. This is not necessarily a suggestion to decrease funding for the programs mentioned, but to prioritizing the raising of new money out of our abundance. For example, within the ELCA, the bishops of the church could determine that hunger funds for the year 2000 A.D. will be twenty-five million dollars rather than twelve. This would be a miraculous contribution to the Year of Jubilee that many Christians are celebrating at the end of the second millennium. Jesus said the poor are God's first priority. A church that is not in conformity with this mission of God is out of touch with their master and teacher.

This conference also should recommend that one of the most effective ways of addressing health, poverty, and justice issues is advocacy work at the local, county, state, and national level. There is need for increased funding and staffing at all of these levels. Several major international issues to be addressed relate to capitalism's dominant role around the globe: global debt and its consequences for the marginalized, international trade relationships and their negative effects upon less economically developed countries, and IMF restructuring without consideration for the most poor. These issues must be addressed both from the perspective of protecting the most vulnerable and also seeking to equip marginal nations to participate in the global market system. Other global issues are: justice for the Palestinian peoples, human rights issues in the Sudan, racism, ethnic cleansing on all continents, natural and international disasters, health issues, particularly for woman and children, and the exploitation of children in the work place around the globe.

Poverty issues also plague the United States. The growing gap between the rich and the poor in the U.S. is an incredible tragedy within the most powerful economy in the world. It is a national disgrace. The horrendous inequity between inner city school funding and suburban educational funding in the U.S. is a primary example of this problem (See *Savage Inequality* by Jonathan Kazol). For example, in the State of Illinois two-thirds of the students are funded at $4000 a year and one-third of the students, most of whom live in suburbia, are funded at $12,000 a year. The governor's recent attempt to rectify this situation by moving from a property tax based educational system to a sales tax system was defeated with much of the opposition coming from the wealthy Chicago suburbs. The world and our nation are marked by innumerable forms of evil which create poverty, injustice, and oppression. Within the U.S. context, there is no more destructive power of evil than white racism contributing to the gap between rich and poor. The Christian community corporately and individually is called in this realm of dehumanization to advocate on behalf of life for the dispossessed.

The church is 98.8% lay people who spend over 99% of their time in the world outside the walls of a sanctuary of corporate worship. In contrast to the clergy whose primary call is normally to a ministry of Word and Sacrament, their call is to be light and salt in the secular arena. People are to be fed, the sick are to be healed, the children are to be cared for, youth are to be educated, families are to be housed, society is to function on behalf of the total community, the weak are to be protected, the violent and the greedy are to be opposed, etc. This conference can be a prophetic voice within the church by calling their official spokespersons to lift up the calling of people to service in their daily lives.

The primary calling of lay persons is not to be lay assistants to the clergy in their calling to ministries of the Word and Sacraments; rather it is to see and experience their daily callings within their vocations and avocations in the world. I remember a deputy sheriff, who played lead guitar for a family choir, saying that one could not spend too much time in church since crime was rampant upon the streets. Although the statement was made somewhat in jest, it is a profound truth. The church does not exist for itself. It is called by God for the sake of the world. The church's primary agents for transforming the world are those 98.8% of the community who live 99% of their lives outside "the holy gates" in service of their families, their communities, and the world. The twenty-first century church must ask the question how are the 98.8% of the membership to be better equipped to serve the world, particularly the poor and dispossessed. One will probably hear the question whether lay persons do not also have a calling to witness explicitly to their faith. I can just observe that the deputy sheriff has also been seen praying with rape victims and families of those who have had loved ones die in the violence of our highways.

A number of years ago, a conference on "Justification and Justice" was held in Mexico City. Before the conference began local leaders took the participants on a geographically short but culturally long journey outside the city to see the garbage dumps of that gigantic city. We were driven up a high hill from where we could look across a valley to the burning waste that stretched over hills in the distance. This was a distant perspective from the country club. I remember looking out over the valley and seeing people moving within the wasteland: men, women, and children. There were little shacks constructed within the fire and the smoke and there were families who survived there by sifting through the garbage for things that could be sold in the market. What kind of inner strength did it take to survive there? I remember Bishop Sheen writing years ago that some people did not have to believe in hell, because they lived in it. As I stood there as a distant country club observer, something within me said that Jesus was not a fellow observer! Jesus was over there in the fire and the smoke. Jesus was looking through the garbage as suffering participant. The cross is planted deeply in the garbage dumps of the world, and if we are to serve Jesus we need to take up our crosses and follow him into the pain and suffering of the world. We are to be present there that we might participate in God's Messianic mission on behalf of life.

Mission Within One Vast Network of Global Relationships

The disciples of Jesus Christ are called into the life transforming activity of the kingdom of God. The twenty-first century context for that mission is marked by global religious pluralism. As members of the western world, we were separated from this religious diversity. Engagement with people of other faiths took place in Asia or Africa. That has always been a characteristic of the life of the Christian communities upon those continents.

However, today as time and space are compressed, it is a reality for the whole global village. There are approximately 1.8 billion Christians around the world, 1.1 billion Muslims, 800 million Hindus, 300 million Buddhists, 200 million followers of Traditional Religions, 1 billion persons for whom the sacred is irrelevant, and countless other smaller groups. The vast network of global relationships have made the world of religious pluralism a reality in our own time and space. Within the city of Chicago there are 350,000 Muslims, 170,000 Hindus, 130,000 Buddhists, and 260,000 Jews.

It is essential to recognize that all attempts to address health, poverty, and justice issues on a global scale must be done ecumenically and in dialogue with the many faith communities. The biblical faith calls us to common visions and tasks on behalf of life.

This is not a new vision of relationships within religious pluralism; however, it has often been a hidden vision. It is a vision that has biblical roots. First, the biblical tradition affirms that God is the creator of all reality and every human is created in the "image of God" (Genesis 1:27). This theological concept affirms that humanity has the potential for relationships with God and in some way has the possibility of imaging God and participating in the creative work of God. Proverbs 8 portrays God working with Wisdom at God's side. Proverbs then notes that when rulers judge righteously it is because wisdom is woven into the fabric of reality. Paul in Romans 2 writes that all humanity is accountable to God, not just those who have encountered the Scriptures because God has woven into the fabric of every human being a sense of right and wrong, a sense of the God-intended life. Therefore, people may be found guilty or excused on the day of judgment. Jesus himself sees the Wisdom of God within the created order. I think that it is very striking that one of the most radical statements of Jesus, "love your enemy," is rooted not in the covenant or in the law, but in creation. God makes the sun to shine and the rain to fall on the good and the evil, therefore one is to be perfect in love as God is perfect (Matthew 5:4). Also it is striking to observe that when Jesus tells a parable to image the good life within Kingdom reality, Jesus tells a parable of a Samaritan who is filled with compassion and risks his life to serve a member of the Jewish community. This was a Jewish community who despised him as heretical foreigner, as someone outside the Reign of God.

This faith perspective sees God present and at work throughout all creation and in every human being. Whenever a Muslim mother nurses her child and loves that child into life it is a manifestation that God's love and wisdom have been woven into creation. Whenever a Buddhist artist paints the beauty of nature, a secular engineer creates a life sustaining structure, a Christian politician enacts legislation that will protect the weak from the greedy and the powerful: There the wisdom and grace of God are present in the fabric of creation. This means that even though God's intended plan for life is distorted by sin, it is still present and again and again breaks into historical reality. That reality is present within every human and every culture whether religious or secular. It is there to be engaged with and cooperated with. It is a global reality calling for common visions and efforts on behalf of life.

The gospel of Jesus Christ also calls us into that reality of life-affirming and transforming service. Speaking from the Lutheran tradition, the gospel proclaims that one is justified by grace through faith. One's relationship with God is sheer gift; therefore one is totally free to be about God's work in the world. One is free from the impossible struggle of self-salvation, and free to be a fellow servant of Christ in the suffering and pain of the world. Earlier we noted that service for the marginalized as whole persons was at the center of Jesus' own servant ministry. When the early church, in its struggle with Gnosticism, proclaimed that the Father of Jesus *created* the world and Jesus' mission was the *incarnation* of the mission of God, they were asserting that God in love intended life to bubble out of the desert of the flesh and blood world. The sick were to be healed, lepers cleansed, the lame walk, the blind see, and the marginalized placed center-stage. Creation was not to be devalued or denied. Rather creation was to be transformed! The future whether this side, or the far side, of death was to be a new creation. Miracle of miracles, sinners were to be forgiven and those who fought to destroy the work of God were still loved and called to return to the Messiah's banquet in which the Master poured out his own life blood for the sins and the transformation of the world.

Such a vision of God's mission within religious pluralism compels the Christian community into relationships with people of other faiths. This God-intended engagement will mean experiences of friendship and mutual enrichment. However, that engagement must be centered in the possibility of the various communities focusing upon the brokenness and the suffering of the human community. The question must be, "How can we find common visions and tasks on behalf of life?" World history is replete with examples of how religious plurality has resulted in death and destruction. We pray that the twenty-first century will be marked by visionary people who will recognize the life enhancing possibilities of interfaith religious relationships and find within their own traditions, values, and directions which will make common visions and efforts on behalf of life possible. As Christians we pray that we might be grasped and empowered by the Spirit of Jesus.

This essay is dedicated to Eva Leo, a lay woman and artist,
who knew and lived God, Jesus, compassion, and justice.
Good Friday, April 10, 1998.

The Status of Global Mission Structures

Duain William Vierow

Introduction

Since New Testament times, the manner in which mission was structured has been vital to the communication of the gospel. For example, missionary bands were responsible for much of the early success of Christian mission. As time progressed, such structures were multiplied and became more complex. They have been influenced by contemporary society as well as tradition, by charismatic individuals as well as ecclesiastical hierarchies, by theology as well as politics and by finance as well as prayer.

Throughout mission history structure has been a crucial factor in Christian mission, at times assisting in the effective communication of the gospel and at other times hindering it. Structures for mission have made a significant difference. So our consideration of mission structures is not just an academic exercise or ecclesiastical aerobics to appraise the past, it is vital to the future mission of Christ!

The Crisis of Mission

Echoing a common assessment, Barrett and Reapsome state that current mission efforts are "in a mess" (1988:65). This crisis in Christian mission has lasted at least three decades.

How did this happen? Scherer states: "The Christian missionary movement today is in a state of crisis because the larger community of faith of which it is a part is also in a prolonged state of crisis" (1987:21).

The old missionary order has been hit by several blows, including:

- the dismantling of the colonial framework under which the Gospel was proclaimed to much of the Two Thirds World;
- the decline of "Christendom": that perception, if not reality, of the dominance of the Christian faith and its institutions since the time of Constantine;
- the loss of political influence and status of the West;
- the revival of other major religions and their support for mission outreach;

- the movement toward a truly global community with the need for inter-dependency;
- a shift in the global axis of Christianity with the majority of Christians now in the Two Thirds World;
- the decline of faith in the One Third World;
- a growing negative attitude toward missionary activity both outside and inside the community of faith;
- a lack of clarity in purpose and theology of mission, with a misunder-standing of what constitutes authentic mission in today's world.

Missions have moved from having problems to being, in the minds of many, a problem. The whole effort is being questioned by many, particularly in the West. A concrete expression of the current crisis is the declining of financial support in many Mainline denominations.

The church and her mission now face a crisis because of the massive changes that have transformed modernity. In the process the church has shifted from the center of culture to the margins and now finds herself labeled "irrelevant" by much of society. Western Christian missionary structures are, in some measure, products of modernity that have impacted, for ill as well as good, the church and her mission. Denominational structures have by-in-large reflected corporate structures of society. Are we now able to accept the challenge of embracing a new mission paradigm and transforming structures to facilitate it?

Reviewing the Past

Bosch (1992) follows the historic-theological subdivisions suggested by Hans Küng in describing six major paradigms of Christianity. The last of these, the "emerging ecumenical paradigm," is our major concern in the present status of global mission structures. But it is preceded by three other paradigms that are relevant to our consideration, for each has had a significant impact on mission in the second half of the twentieth century. Much of this section is an attempt to summarize Bosch's treatise (ch 7-9) with a focus on structures.

1. The Medieval Roman Catholic Missionary Paradigm

Although shaped during the Middle Ages, this paradigm has continued to influence Catholicism through much of the twentieth century. The basic structure for mission was the institutional church, with support and close ties to the state. The church, as a powerful and privileged organization, and the bulwark of western culture and civilization, came to use methods of coercion to facilitate conversion. The close identity with colonialism in Africa, Asia, and the Americas provided unique privileges and opportunities for mission. The biblical motif seemed to be Luke 14:23 "compel them to come in," and the goal of missions to expand Christendom.

The Monastic Movement provided a less ambivalent vehicle for mission. The mission dimension, not self evident early in the movement, gradually became so through the attitude and activities of the monks. Their powerful witness had a profound effect on those who observed. "Their implicitly missionary dimension began to spill over into explicit missionary efforts" (Bosch 1992: 233). Monasticism became a powerful model that had a profound impact on missionary activity and is the forerunner structure for later sodalities of mission.

Since the Second Vatican Council, the Roman Catholic understanding of mission has undergone a profound change.

2. The Protestant Reformation Missionary Paradigm

The primary missionary text of this paradigm in its many forms is Romans 1:16, the Gospel "is the power of God for salvation to everyone who believes." The Reformation paradigm did not break with the medieval Catholic paradigm totally, but did differ markedly. Justification by faith was the theological starting point, with a rediscovery of the priesthood of all believers and the centrality of scripture as primary cornerstones of faith. Reformers were preoccupied with addressing the fundamental problems of the church. In the process they seemed indifferent to mission and certainly toward developing new structures for mission. There was little mission activity for two centuries. Lutheran orthodoxy as a whole failed to catch the vision for mission. The belief that any mission activity had to be done in conjunction with the state, a carry over from the medieval period, and that the state was an agent in mission, made world mission nearly impossible for the Northern European Protestant world.

Anabaptists held views that more readily allowed them to respond to mission opportunities. They did not adhere to territorially circumscribed parishes and ecclesiastical leaders tied to it as did Lutherans, thus expanding the potential for mission far beyond traditional boundaries. They also insisted on absolute separation of church and state.

Pietism, with its warmth and emphasis on personal experience, reinstated the biblical call to proclaim the Gospel of redemption to all. Rejecting the cold, cerebral faith and institutional church, as well as the close connection between church and state, Pietism made an abiding contribution to the development of mission as a necessary part of the Christian life. True believers were distinguished from formal church membership. Emphasis was on individual decisions for conversion. The church was neither the bearer nor goal of mission. Structures for mission also broke from the traditional patterns of the time. Following the pattern of the apostles, small missionary bands were sent out to the ends of the earth to establish provisional Christian communities. While there was accommodation to the state, mission efforts were viewed as separate.

Dutch and Anglo-Saxon Calvinism were more successful than Lutheranism in keeping the missionary spirit alive. Puritanism in England became a catalyst for some mission activity. These efforts, however, were all undertaken within the framework of colonialist expansion.

During this era, the goal of most mission effort was renewal, with the church as the reforming community.

3. The Enlightenment Missionary Paradigm

A continuation of the Protestant paradigm, the Enlightenment profoundly influenced over 200 years of history, including religious life and mission expansion. The full impact of the Enlightenment was delayed in North American Protestantism. Rationalism gained the upper hand of European Protestantism.

In the mid 1700's the American colonies were impacted significantly by the First Awakening which combined experience with scripture, laying the foundation for later missionary activity. Toward the end of the eighteenth century the Second Awakening spawned a missionary spirit that became a passionate cause for American churches. Those touched by revival were anxious to share the faith with the world and banded together for the sake of mission. A new volunteerism was evident in the forming of interdenominational mission societies that sent missionaries abroad. Support and candidates came from those having a burden to share the good news that was Christ centered, but clouded by western imperial and Enlightenment ideas.

The ecumenical climate declined in the mid-nineteenth century. The rise of denominationalism was seen, for example, in the move toward Lutheran Confessionalism and the establishment of distinctly denominational societies. These also were not at first directly attached to the denominational structures, but were independent societies led by those willing to make an extra commitment. Protestant missions gained momentum at the close of the century with the rise of imperialism.

There has been an astonishing growth of mission agencies of all kinds over the past 100 years, including agencies known as "faith missions." These represented an adaptation of the earlier volunteer societies. Volunteers were challenged to go overseas without any financial guarantees. Unfortunately preparation for service was often lacking.

The modern evangelical missionary movement reflects an impatience and mistrust with the cumbersome machinery of the institutional church, therefore the structures formed were separate from the denominational church organization.

There are several texts that have been used in developing a biblical motif for this era, but the one that appears to be more prevalent was the Great Commission in Matthew 28:18-20. During this era the centrality of the missionary task became evident again in the life of the churches. Sometimes mission agencies clouded their efforts by viewing mission as a civilizing process.

These three paradigms have made a lasting impression on the structuring of mission in the emerging ecumenical paradigm that Bosch labels as "postmodern."

Our Inheritance

In order to better understand the present and plan for the future, it is helpful to review the past. Reviewing historical trends and influences is useful toward a realistic appraisal of where we are today.

My own mission understanding and involvement have been influenced by numerous avenues of missionary development. The personal convergence of these realities, I believe, is similar, yet unique to what others have experienced.

In part, I am a product of the old missionary age, identified closely with a truncated view of mission as the activity of western pioneers going to the underdeveloped and needy in "foreign" lands. My heritage includes a pioneering Lutheran pietist missionary to the Diaspora in North America, Henry Melchoir Muhlenberg, as well as Father J. C. F. Heyer, who was part of the confessional resurgence of the nineteenth century and the first American Lutheran pastor to be sent to India under the auspices of a Lutheran mission society. In my youth and early education, occasional visiting missionaries on furlough and those who were my teachers were closely tied with the old thinking and structures of mission. The life and commitment of Albert Schweitzer touched me deeply. Missionaries appeared to be "heroes" of the faith who left the comforts of the West to go to those abroad who lived in difficult circumstances and spiritual darkness. The first mission magazine I read regularly, entitled *The Foreign Missionary*, did little to change that impression.

These images were changed as I learned of a far more complex and challenging missionary enterprise. I witnessed a swing from the monolithic approach to mission to the diversity that characterizes today's mission agencies. The Lutheran tradition (United Lutheran Church in America, Lutheran Church in America, and Evangelical Lutheran Church in America) to which I am connected moved from a world mission structure that was an autonomous, free-standing agency to incorporation in our denominational structure as a division of the national church.

I considered joining a non-Lutheran mission service agency (American Friends Service Committee) for a term as a lay missionary. After nearly twenty years of missionary service with my denomination (1960-1979) I considered overseas ministry with the World Mission Prayer League, a Lutheran missionary movement (para-church structure). When I was called to overseas service it was by the Board of Foreign Missions of the United Lutheran Church in America (later LCA) which had started outreach among the Chinese in Malaya. Soon after I was seconded to work with the Church of Sweden Mission (who had taken over a mission effort in South India orphaned by the Leipzig Mission) among Tamil Indians (Diaspora Christians and Hindus who had immigrated to Malaya under British rule, mainly as indentured laborers). These two groups (Indians/Swedes and Chinese/Americans) attempted to establish a single national Lutheran church, but even with the intervention of the Lutheran World Federation were not able to do so. The insurmountable hurdle appeared to be the Episcopal office, whether or not it would be necessary to have apostolic succession. Each went on to establish independent national bodies. The Evangelical Lutheran Church in Malaysia and Singapore worked primarily among Indians and the Lutheran Church in Malaysia and Singapore primarily among Chinese. I worked with both of these churches during the 1960s and 1970s and was assigned positions by their leadership (three terms of service with ELCMS and one with LCMS).

The Ecumenical Movement captured my interest in seminary. En route to my first term of service, I met Dr. Visser T'Hooft , General Secretary of the World Council of Churches, on a visit to its headquarters in Geneva. While serving in Malaya/Malaysia, I was active in the regional Council of Churches, facilitated and pastored the first ecumenical congregation (Anglican, Methodist and Lutheran) in the country, and participated in the first national ecumenical youth gatherings. Dr. Franklin Clark Fry, President of the Lutheran World Federation and chair of the Central Committee of WCC spent time with our missionary group en route to New Delhi and the merging of the International Missionary Council and WCC in 1961. The start of work among the Chinese by the ULCA involved a type of comity arrangement with other Conciliar churches. While doing language study in India, I observed further the results of earlier comity agreements there and attended dialogues between Lutherans and the Church of South India. My final term in Malaysia I coordinated a national church growth program that included outreach planning with eighteen different church and para-church groups, Conciliar and Evangelical.

My initial missionary training at the School of World Mission in Maywood included courses from R. Pierce Beaver, dean of American missiologists, and James A. Scherer, dean of American Lutheran missiologists. But it was also my privilege to study under several well-known missiologists at Fuller Theological Seminary School of World Missions. I found much common ground in the theology and practice of mission among Conciliar and Evangelical scholars. In Malaysia, I was involved with theological education planning and teaching in traditional, extension, and self-reliant training programs for lay and clergy. This included establishing a lay training program by extension and teaching in a school where students worked to provide for their needs as well as studied theology.

After returning to North America from missionary service, I served for fourteen years in parish ministry with local congregations, which brought me again to the realization that the congregation is the basic unit for mission and must be considered in any concerted global mission effort. I served for two years in a deployed staff situation working with several LCA Synods in the

Upper Midwest area, assisting with planning, structuring, and training for effective global mission interpretation.

My missionary service was directly effected by a variety of mission structures including sending agencies, indigenous churches and international organizations. These have shaped my personal missionary service, but more importantly, they have impacted the fulfillment of the missionary mandate around the globe. I have been blessed with a rich heritage. The church and all of us associated with her are blessed with a rich heritage of mission activity. Not all of our heritage, however, is honorable. But to the degree that it has been faithful to the Gospel, we surely can and need to celebrate.

Relationships of mission agencies and the manner in which they are structured is largely the result of choice (and sometimes accident) governed by denominational ties, larger international gatherings and movements and traditional patterns. My heritage includes the following developments that have also influenced the structuring of global mission.

1.   The three-self formula (self-propagating, self-governing, and self-supporting) continued to be utilized (although in somewhat altered form) as a model for mission planning and implementation for much of the twentieth century.

2.   The decline of Conciliar Protestantism and the general failure of commitment to global mission was primarily due to the crisis of purpose and identity within mainline denominations.

3.   The rise of church growth has impacted denominational as well as parachurch organizations.

4.   The impact of liberation theology and the resulting development theology with its strict separation of evangelism and development enabled the global church to examine critically mission practice.

5.   International gatherings and organizations from Edinburgh to St. Paul have done much to shape the structuring of mission. These gatherings, Conciliar, Evangelical, and Catholic, have kept the overriding concern for mission alive.

6.   The convergence of these three movements in the theology and practice of mission has been startling and changed each toward a healthier and more productive global strategy.

7.   Theological and missionary training, both in the One Third and Two Thirds Worlds have provided mission leaders for structures at all levels with an understanding of the nature of mission.

8.   Church organizations and societies have been effective instruments in lifting up the call of mission among church members.

It is also my heritage to grapple with mission in today's world, seeking to define mission in a manner that is faithful to scripture, yet planning and carrying out mission (including structuring) that remains true to the message but is understandable in the contexts of contemporary mission and best facilitates the work of the Spirit in mission.

Each of us has been blessed accordingly with a mission heritage (some of which is common) which has had a profound influence on where we are and how we approach global mission today. Understanding that heritage is crucial to evaluate critically the present and plan for the future.

Trends and Issues

Many have written of trends and issues that impact today's mission milieu. Not all are quite as dramatic as the call for a moratorium on the sending of western missionaries at Bangkok in 1973, but are perhaps more significant and need to be considered in the development of mission structures for the 21st century. Due to lack of space, I focus on a few I consider key for the global community, the global church, and the North American Christian community.

Trends
1.*Global Community*

We are a global community that shrinks as technologies of communication expand. As we are influenced by events in other parts of the world, the sovereignty of the nation state is eroded. People are embracing global perspectives on life, or at least must react to what is happening on the world scene.

The greater our awareness of global realities the more apparent becomes the widening gap between rich and poor. Bonk comments: "Global poverty is an acute material problem, no doubt; but western affluence is a profoundly spiritual one" (1993:307). He believes it is at least as difficult for the West to overcome our affluence as it is for those in poverty to overcome their poverty. He goes on: "Unless we come to see our western world through the eyes of Jesus and the writers of Scripture, we will continue to excuse the personal and collective covetousness that has made us 'great'." The poor are chosen to play a role in the global community that will challenge the church at its very core.

The rise of other world religions has been a global trend that continues to gain momentum. Islam is perhaps the most aggressive in extending the faith, but others have been actively growing as well. Religious pluralism is a characteristic of modern societies, along with a growing fundamentalism in world religions (most notable in Islam). Accompanying this has been a resurgence of cultural traditions and identity.

This, along with the continuing population explosion in much of the Two Thirds World, has resulted in a rapid growth of those who have not been exposed to the Christ event. The number of non-Christians is growing at an unprecedented rate. Christians have remained about one third of the world's population throughout the past millennium.

Another trend that is particularly evident in international circles and visible globally is the increased role of women in the public arena. Effective partnership with women will be important to the future of mission.

2. Global Church

A major demographic of our age is the shift of the center of gravity of the world's Christian population to the South and the Two Thirds World. The vitality of the church and of mission activity has also shifted. International church leadership positions are being filled by persons from the TwoThirds World, providing vision and challenge for the global community of faith.

Closely tied to a revisioning of mission has been the realization that Christ's mission is on all continents and the need for witness in the One Third World is every bit as crucial as the Two Thirds World.

Equally dramatic has been the rise of Two Thirds World mission agencies. Keyes has documented this phenomenal growth of nearly 14 percent per year with 1,094 mission societies (excluding Catholic and Orthodox) sending 35,924 cross-cultural missionaries in 1988, far outnumbering western agencies. (1993:190) Siewart and Valdez estimate that there are about 50,000 Protestant missionaries from the Two Thirds World working cross-culturally (1998:43). India alone has over 200 societies. While some of these are attached to denominational structures, most are free standing para-church movements.

The rise of Pentecostal/Charismatic Christians is another phenomena of this age. These believers have increased 130 fold in this century and now comprise 26 percent of all Christians (ibid.,33).

An encouraging statistic is that the percentage of Christians active in mission is at an all time high of 36 percent (ibid.). There is a surge of lay persons embracing global mission today.

3. Church of the West

The crisis of mission, due in part to the crisis of the Christian community in the West, has already been documented. Regarding evangelization, Scherer observes: ". . . the will to accomplish it simply does not exist in most of our western churches." Many, especially mainline churches, appear to be hanging on and "make relatively small plans"(1987:21). Our communities of faith need to recapture the theme that the church is an instrument of God's mission.

Engel comments: "We cannot accept the growing pattern of American church withdrawal from the world scene. We are developing a world view which cannot be defended scripturally, and it is no little wonder that vitality is draining so rapidly from our churches" (1996:132). He believes a root problem is the churches are too frequently pre-occupied with institutional and program concerns.

This crisis has its consequence in the decline of fund raising, which places fiscal restraints on what can be accomplished. The church's rank and file have concerns about the structure of fund raising. Members want to know where funds are to be expended.

The decline of long-term missionaries is partly due to finances, but also to other factors (e.g. governmental limits). The numbers of those who make a life time commitment to serve among a people, to understand the culture, to learn the language, and to serve at all costs are dwindling.

The dramatic increase in short-termers is a fact of recent times. While many so called missionary trips appear to be closer to a travel tour than a missionary encounter, countless numbers who have participated have been excited about mission and their witness, especially among youth. Benefits to the overseas Christian community may be limited. Those who go for an extended period (three months to two years) can make significant contributions in specific areas of need. These developments, however, do not and cannot replace the important role of the long-term missionary.

Given the decline of vitality and funds in the West, there has been a movement to start new missionary societies. While most of these are independent many have denominational loyalties. In the 19th century, missionary societies were formed in part because the churches were unwilling to take up the responsibility for the missionary mandate. This appears to be a strong motivation today also. However, the entrepreneurial nature of these groups is a continuing concern.

Issues

Arising from these trends are issues that need to be addressed in strategizing structures for global mission. I raise these in the form of questions.

1.   How do we make sense of the Gospel in this postmodern world? How do we communicate in ways and words that hold meaning and are yet true to the Gospel in each culture? How do we share salvation history and such basic doctrines as justification by grace through faith? Is there a way of approaching this issue that will assist structures for mission?

2.   How can we globalize the church? Globalization is not owned by missionaries, mission agencies, or institutions of higher learning. How do we enable church members to see and think globally, to see themselves as players in the global mission of Christ? With the shrinking of the globe, and the rise of religious pluralism and world religions, can we help people to be globally sensitive, yet theologically sound and challenged to be involved in reaching those without the Gospel?

3.   What is the role of theological education in preparing leaders of mission communities? So often those associated with the preparation of leaders in mission have been on the periphery of the conversation. When I attended seminary in the 1950's, any mission focus basically depended on individual charismatic teachers who had a passion for mission. In the United States over

the past twenty years, I have witnessed significant changes in Lutheran theological education from a basic maintenance (professional care taking) emphasis to a clear, missional focus (seminary as a school of mission). If mission is the basic reason for the existence of the church, how can our seminaries not be centers of missionary training? This is just as true in the Two Thirds World as in the West. Gifts need to be cultivated for mission. Each faculty member and student needs to be a global citizen. The study of sociology and anthropology in ministerial training would help equip persons for dialogue in the world, as well as assist in spiritual formation.

4.   How do we address the need to reach those populations now beyond the reach of most of the agencies with which most traditional structures cooperate? There are at least two billion people who have yet to hear clearly the claims of the gospel. Over 1.1 billion people have little chance to hear the gospel unless someone goes specifically to their people group. Five hundred people groups have never heard the good news. Yet only 4,000 of the 332,000 missionaries globally are deployed to evangelize among them. Only 1.2 percent of mission agency funding and missionaries go to these unreached peoples (Siewart & Valdez 1998:43). How can we structure and develop links so that the vision presented by the New Testament is not just a dream, but a serious mandate? It is time to get back to the specificity of mission.

5.   How do we harness mission forces for the conversion of the West? Van Gelder, raising Newbigin's question, "Can the West be converted?" goes on to summarize the answer given by Newbigin in this way: ". . . if we were to take this task seriously, it would require of us that we develop a paradigm of mission to North America which is fundamentally different from the operational missiologies of denomination building, culture caretaking, privatized faith, church renewal, church growth, and church effectiveness which have been or are now at work" (1994:334). Surely our overseas brothers and sisters in Christ will need to help us in this task. Indeed, they could well be the catalyst for conversion.

6.   Does our ecclesiology serve Christ's mission?   Van Engen believes that the ecclesiology of churches stemming from the Reformation is an obstacle to mission today and pleads for a new mission oriented ecclesiastical paradigm that is dynamic, constantly changing and growing. He writes of the new paradigm of ecclesiology as an "emerging" reality which "becomes in fact what it is in faith" (1991:59).

7.   What is the role of the local congregation in global mission?   The thinking that has dominated much of the 20th century, that the national church and its agencies did mission (especially overseas) for the whole church, is now being replaced by a new understanding that the local congregation is the primary unit and agent for mission. Participation in God's mission is the task given to each Christian in baptism and belongs to all local congregations. Martinson writes: "Every Christian community has a mission that begins lo-

cally and does not stop till it embraces the world" (1998). The local church, wherever it may be, is the primary structure for mission. Yet so often they appear unable to act decisively. While most North American mission agencies are struggling to grow, mega-churches are becoming their own sending agencies or joining forces with others in special alliances.

8. What part can we expect and encourage the churches and mission agencies of the Two Thirds World to play in the global fulfillment of the missionary task? If all Christian communities are both givers and receivers of mission, we need to strategize so that true giving and receiving can happen with integrity. Why is it that non-western agencies are sending missionaries at a rate four times higher than the West? The passion and witness of overseas Christians are desperately needed by the churches of the West. We acknowledge that they are in many cases the stronger and more experienced partner in witness to the Gospel. They have distinct advantages in mission activity in the Two Thirds World in that they are more able to reach areas closed to activity by western agencies, are often culturally closer to those to whom they go, and can carry out mission at a fraction of the cost of western agencies .

They, like western agencies, will make mistakes and face many of the same problems. Perhaps supporting them in their efforts with encouragement and training will be our greatest contribution to mission. Western agencies need to see themselves as partners, even junior partners, not as controllers. The time has come to cut all strings that have limited our overseas partners, acknowledging their leadership, accepting their decisions, and setting them free to be the leaders of mission internationally This will require humility as well as trust by western agencies. Keyes believes that the next phase of world missions will become a movement centered in the Protestant Two Thirds World and be as dramatic a shift as that from Catholic to Protestant in the eighteenth century.

9. I repeat a question raised by Scherer: "What structures of mutuality and partnership are needed?" (1987:237) Are there limits to cooperation? If so, what are they? Can Christians of differing national denominational and theological backgrounds work together in witness to the Gospel, theological education, or service? How can we best practice equal decision-making and representation with churches on other continents? Should bilateral structures be kept or discarded? Perhaps foremost we must remember that we are partnering people, not just structures.

10. Finally, there is the important issue of who controls the funds and how they are spent? True partnership in mission implies mutual trust, even a willingness to risk for the sake of the potential benefits in fulfilling the missionary task. Often joint consultations and strategy sessions have limited outcome partly because funds imply dominance. A manner of developing a common pool absolutely free of psychological as well as implied dominance is necessary.

Present Mission Structures

MARC's latest *Mission Handbook* has more than 360 pages describing over one thousand U.S. and Canadian Protestant global mission agencies. There are myriad possibilities of categorizing these agencies.

Ralph Winter has characterized mission structures as falling into two basic categories: modalities and sodalities (1974). Modalities are patterned after the New Testament church (earlier synagogue) where all believers gathered. In time these were clustered under a governmental system similar to that of the Roman government. Modalities are those structures formed out of commitment to Christ in baptism and follow the traditional pattern of diocesan Christianity. Mission Sodalities were patterned after the early missionary bands organized out of believers committed to a specific task, e.g. evangelization. This structure was seen most clearly later in monastic orders. A distinguishing characteristic of a sodality is that it is a group of workers who have made a second decision to serve in a special cause. These two types of structures have been present in the community of believers from the New Testament period and both have greatly assisted in the expansion of the faith. I use these two broad categories below.

For the purpose of providing some common ground for discussion, I briefly summarize several major sub categories as I perceive them, describing one in each category that may be familiar to most, focusing on those that are Lutheran. Basic information on several of these is from the *Mission Handbook*.

Modalities

These agencies are part of the denominational structure and governed by constituent representatives. On behalf of member congregations they recruit and send missionaries to various global locations in a variety of ministries. Funding comes from congregational benevolence offerings and in some cases through special appeals or direct missionary support. One of the difficulties with this type of structure is that local members feel distant from the mission effort.

1. *Mainline*: The Evangelical Lutheran Church in America, Division for Global Mission dates from 1842 and has an annual income of about 23 million dollars. The current Director for Planning and Evaluation has summarized its structure as follows:

The Evangelical Lutheran Church in America (ELCA) mandates that the Division for Global Mission (DGM) shall "be responsible for this church's mission in other countries and shall be the channel through which churches in other countries engage in mission to this church and society." Through its global mission program the ELCA relates to approximately 70 companion churches globally. In pursuing the ELCA's mission, DGM works through approximately 427 missionary staff including 275 compensated, 116 volunteer and 36 global mission associates. Forty-seven churchwide staff in Chicago is divided among general administration, overseas, international personnel, finance, international scholarships, development, planning and evaluation, and Global Mission to the ELCA (GMELCA) departments. GMELCA channels the companion churches' witness to ELCA congregations and involves the ELCA constituency with the global companion churches. Its methods include popular Global Mission Events which address the challenge of global mission to ELCA members and the Companion Synods Program which links ELCA synods, congregations, and individuals with global companion churches (Reko 1998).

Basically a staff-driven operation, it has a governing board elected from its constituency.

2. Pentecostal: Assemblies of God, General Council Division of Foreign Missions. Stated purpose: ". . . to . . . evangelize the spiritually lost . . . establish indigenous churches . . . train national believers . . . show compassion for the suffering. . . ." Founded in 1914, it has an annual income of about 115 million dollars. They send over 1,500 long-term missionaries and 2,750 short-term missionaries to over 100 countries. The home office staff number over 100.

3. Evangelical: Evangelical Free Church Mission was founded in 1887, has income of over 10 million dollars and sends 275 long-term and 500 short term missionaries. These are engaged in church planting, theological education, TEE, evangelism, and leadership development. Emphasis is on discipling new believers and incorporating them into congregations.

4. Service Agency: Lutheran World Relief was founded at the conclusion of World War II as a Lutheran relief agency, primarily in Europe. It has become global, continuing to focus on relief, now expanded to agricultural programs, community development, and leadership development. With an annual income of about 22 million dollars, it provides services on behalf of constituent churches to specific areas as need arises. Unlike sending agencies, it has few persons overseas, but a home office staff of 23.

Sodalities

These agencies are usually supported by a group of persons and congregations who have made a separate commitment to the specific cause of the agency, providing funds and serving as volunteers (including a governing body) and personnel to serve. Funds are usually given above and beyond regular church benevolence. The majority of these are of evangelical tradition.

1. Denominational Related Sending Agency: World Mission Prayer League (WMPL) is a Lutheran missionary movement (society) of about 6,000 members in the United States and Canada. It sponsors 130 long term missionaries (half of whom are non-North American persons serving in their home countries) in 15 countries and has an annual (basically unsolicited) income of about one and a half million dollars. The income that comes in for missionary support is shared equally among its total staff, with a strong reliance upon prayer support and response to need. WMPL seeks to serve in areas not served by denominational mission groups and utilizes primarily the talents of lay persons.

2. *Interdenominational Sending Agencies*: Campus Crusade for Christ was founded in 1951, has an income of nearly 55 million dollars and a missionary force of about 665 long-term missionaries and 1,300 short term. It is an interdenominational agency of evangelical tradition engaged in evangelism, training, video-film production and distribution, youth programs, and small group discipleship. It has a home ministry staff of over 5,000.

3. *Denominational Related Service Agencies*: Global Health Ministries has emerged in the last 20 years as a Lutheran assisting agency dedicated to support the need for quality health care in the Two Thirds World by providing project financial assistance, shipping urgently needed medical supplies, recruiting personnel, and funding the training of national health care givers. It has partnered with the Evangelical Lutheran Church in America in many health-related projects. A small staff coordinates efforts and a significant voluntary force.

4. *Interdenominational Service Agencies*: Heifer Project International, was founded in 1944 and has an income of five and a half million dollars. It is of ecumenical tradition and engaged in agricultural programs, development, extension education, technical assistance, and training. The home ministry staff numbers about 100. Overseas staff are primarily nationals serving in their own countries.

5. *Denominational Specialized Ministries*: Lutheran Bible Translators is engaged in Bible translation, linguistics, print and non-print media, literacy work, and missionary training. It was established in 1964 and has an annual income of over two million dollars. Long term overseas personnel number about 40 with more nationals assisting in their own countries. Its home ministry staff numbers twenty-one.

6. *Interdenominational Specialized Ministries*: Wycliffe Bible Translators USA is of evangelical tradition engaged in Bible translation and related ministries. Its purpose is ". . . to integrate Scripture translation, scholarship and service so that all people will have access to God's Word in their own language." They have a long-term missionary force of 2,450 and a home ministry staff of 950. It was founded in 1934.

These ten categories are representative of most, but by no means all North American mission agencies. A growing number of new agencies are more entrepreneurial in character, usually with charismatic leadership.

Recent Models

In the current crisis there is a clear challenge to create innovative and relevant new approaches in structuring for mission. There are several recent models that appear to have potential. Their number and variety are notable. Van Beek (1992) provides a summary report of several. I've chosen a few and added several to highlight in six categories.

1. First Steps in North-South Relationships

Representatives of partner agencies from the Two Thirds World on the boards of North American agencies have been controversial, bringing accusations of tokenism in the "business as usual" atmosphere. There are several agencies, however, that have moved beyond this approach toward the beginning of an attempt to be inclusive with broad representation and shared decision making.

The Methodist Church Overseas Division in the United Kingdom has formed regional "round tables" with partner churches with the expectation that these would be instruments for shared decision making on priorities and resources. Similar efforts have been made by several North American agencies.

The United Board for Christian Higher Education in Asia, a long established agency concentrating on assistance in higher education, has established consulting groups from the various areas of Asia who function like a foundation in the disbursement of grants by established criteria.

In the Netherlands there is an experiment known as Andersom, meaning "the other way about." Various Dutch church agencies have joined together in inviting persons from the South for an extended period of at least six months. During this time they work on specific tasks within the organization, providing opportunity for reflection and dialogue on priorities, relationships, and methods.

A bold step was taken by Norwegian Church Aid, a development agency of the churches of Norway. They invited a select team of five from Africa, Central America, and Asia for a critical evaluation of the agency. The team offered specific concrete recommendations. Norwegian Church Aid has given testimony to the impact of the review.

2. European Societies

Two long-standing societies have recently reconstituted. In 1971 the Paris Missionary Society dissolved and The Evangelical Community for Apostolic Action (CEVAA) was created. Churches in Africa, Madagascar, and the Pacific became equal partners with churches in France, Switzerland, and Italy. This was a significant breakthrough in modern missionary relationships.

A second and similar renewal came when the Council for World Mission (CWM) was formed from the London Missionary Society. This is worthy of note because the old society had been integrated as a council within the church structure. Van Beek comments on a conceptual difference between CWM and CEVAA. "The later perceives itself as a community of sharing for mission. The sharing of partnership is not an objective in itself but a means at the service of the common objective of the community, which is to be in mission. CWM puts more emphasis upon the sharing among its member churches and the self-reliance of each one of them. The partnership has an enabling role. In a sense, CWM, as the overarching body, could disappear once it has fulfilled its role of enabling the churches to be themselves fully in mission"(1992:418).

The Basel Mission Society adopted a new structure with four continental entities, each with its own executive body and staff.

3. Reorganized U.S. Denominational Agency

The Southern Baptist Convention International Mission Board is the largest Protestant denominational mission agency in North America. It is associated with the Southern Baptist Convention. It has recently changed its name and reorganized in a significant restructuring to focus more clearly on reaching previously unreached people groups. The new paradigm includes choosing "regional leaders" instead of area directors with a focus on leadership and strategy rather than management and administration. These staff persons will also rotate assignments and be overseas as well as at home base. Administrative responsibilities will be delegated to others on each regional team.

4. Churches in the Two Thirds World

There have been some notable attempts by southern churches to address common issues faced by mission agencies. We note three.

The Mekane Yesus Church of Ethiopia addressed the issue of the division of the "spiritual" and "developmental" aspects of mission. The 1972 statement objected to the imposition of criteria separating the two, arguing that they could not and should not be separated. The Church has made consistent efforts to bring evangelization and development agencies together.

The United Church of Christ in the Philippines took a bold step in establishing their own criteria for partnership. Participation in mission is viewed as a mutual process among equal partners, whether from the North or the South.

The Evangelical Lutheran Church in Tanzania has been among the leaders in the South to initiate a thorough study process that has led to a purposeful sharing with churches of the South (e.g. Malagasy Lutheran Church) as well as the North.

5. U.S. Lutherans

Among North American Lutherans the Lutheran Church Missouri Synod (LCMS) perhaps has the most innovative structure. LCMS documents describe how Recognized Service Organizations (RSO) and Mission Societies

(MS) partner with the LCMS. An RSO "fosters the mission and ministry of the church, engages in program activity that is in harmony with the programs of the boards of the Synod, and respects and does not act contrary to the doctrine and practice of the Synod"(1997). They are independent and receive no support from LCMS. Mission Societies relate to LCMS World Mission in two ways. Those with service agreements exist solely to help LCMS and designate funds for specific areas of work. An MS with a statement of partnership does not exist solely to help fulfill LCMS World Mission program and priorities. They partner with LCMS for mutual benefit and to advance the mission. There may be a sharing of funds and programs as agreed upon.

Among groups that have bonded together in support of mission, the Lutheran Order for Discipleship is worthy of note. A brochure describes it as "a community of lay people, pastors, missionaries and theologians committed to the mission of the church, the Lutheran Order for Discipleship seeks to provide assistance within the structures of the church. Members agree to a pattern of scripture study, prayer and financial support; volunteers provide service at subsistence levels so that the mission and outreach of the gospel can continue to grow locally, nationally, globally"(1993). The Order does not act as a sending agency.

6. New Congregational Partnerships

There has been a trend toward the clustering of like-minded congregations, especially mega- congregations, both along and across denominational lines, in support of select mission efforts. Emphasis is on direct involvement in projects that are known by members. One such clustering, spearheaded by Robert Schuller, Churches United in Global Mission, has participation from a variety of denominational congregations.

Siewart & Valdez (1998:57) give several examples of local churches that work closely with their denominational boards in long-term programs. Many local churches are taking a more active role in program planning and missionary deployment decisions with the agencies through which they support missionaries.

Lutheran Health Care Bangladesh (LHCB) was formed in 1992 by a consortium of congregations in Minnesota committed to work among Muslims. A health care facility for women and children has been built and staffed by US and national personnel in Dumki, a small rural town in southern Bangladesh. About twenty-five Lutheran congregations have become members, providing support for this ministry to several villages.

Several mega congregations have direct involvement on their own, supporting missionaries with several organizations and even preparing persons to serve overseas. North Heights Lutheran Church in St. Paul, Minnesota is a notable example.

7. International Interdenominational Networks

There is a growing number of international networks partnering for the sake of mission, usually with a particular emphasis. Examples are the International Fellowship of Third World Mission Theologians, the Oxford Conference on Christian Faith and Economics, and Centers for World Mission. The Adopt-a-People program has called attention to unreached peoples and enlisted support.

Observations

There is a clarion call for a change in the traditional twentieth century paradigm of western agencies. The legitimacy of hierarchical and highly institutionalized organizations is being questioned. The current crisis in mission will continue in the West as we face this postmodern age. While structuring will continue to be a crucial factor in the fulfillment of mission, how that structuring is done will be vital.

Myers believes, ". . . we will have to set aside our beliefs in centre-driven organizations. We will have to learn to trust those on the front lines. We will have to define new roles for the centre, so that the front line becomes the centre with the former centre redefined in a supporting role"(1992:406).

North American mission agencies would be wise to explore the following ideas.

1. Mission agencies need to pay attention to what congregations are communicating. The increasing disregard for denominational structures implies that ecclesiastical nationalism is not working. If congregations are the basic structure for mission, then broader mission structures must tune in to why increased numbers of congregations are functioning independently. While denominational agencies experience funding problems, there is much activity and sufficient funding for direct global mission efforts in congregations. They feel separated from central agencies. The old order where the national structures speak and act for its membership is dying. National agencies have a unique opportunity to reorganize to address these phenomena. Congregations need services that assist them with training and enable them to do mission work effectively, making wise, informed decisions. Mission outreach will continue to be a major concern for a minority of church members. Congregations have the best opportunity to make that minority as large and strong as possible. Deployed national staff could provide helpful services.

To do this, Myers states ". . . we will have to ask a new set of questions about the role of the centre in management. Instead of asking how it should direct and control, the post-modern centre will ask how it can add value. We will learn to celebrate the fact that those who do the ministry at the grassroots, the local congregations, the development workers, the itinerant evangelists are the centre, not the periphery" (1992:406).

2. Structures need to be effective in assisting all Christians to become global citizens. There is little faith today that national and international struc-

tures do well that which has to be done locally. But members would be truly impoverished if we are not informed and exposed to global realities. As Siewart and Valdez observe: "Our structures are not keeping up with the changes in the contexts in which they work. The Christian church needs to work away from its hierarchical past and move toward fostering twin citizenship, helping us be citizens of our local churches and their contexts on the one hand, and citizens of the global church and the world on the other" (1998:50). We cannot expect to be effective in our global witness if our people are not globally aware and committed to mission. The whole people of God are needed to fulfill the whole mission of God.

3. Agencies could be more effective by moving beyond partnership to networking, where function can rule structure, rather than the other way around. Martinson argues that "the practice of Christian mission needs to move beyond a centrally controlled and bureaucratically defined mission pragmatics to a diversified model that includes mission as joint venture, intersection and parallel presence and in which networking becomes the modus vivendi." He continues: "Rather than centralized bureaucracies there should be dispersed networks that fit the communication realities of our day. And, rather than centers of control in a top-down fashion mission agencies should serve to consult, inform, inspire and connect, functioning differently at different levels, letting the energy of local communities of faith take shape in any number of ways, in many manners of configuration" (1997). Skreslet also makes a case for networking, focusing specifically on NGOs as a model. Such an approach would be more dynamic and open up the opportunity for more local communities to be directly involved.

4. North American agencies could benefit greatly by embracing their brethren from the Two Thirds World. Scherer provides us with food for thought. "As current structures tend to maintain the dominance of wealthy western partners, do not express the international and inter-racial character of mission, and are therefore inadequate for expressing oneness in Christ, high priority should be given to designing structures for sharing mission resources and engaging in joint planning on a regional, national and local basis. This is especially necessary in the case of western sending agencies and growing churches of the two-thirds world" (1987:238).

Siewart and Valdez comment: "We need to develop an inter-continental conversation that helps identify the gifts God has placed in each continent for the well-being of his global Christian community. Not every continent has the same things to offer" (1998:50). Adding value to our diverse experiences will enhance our understanding and practice of mission. Avenues for equal partnerships need to be formed. The churches and agencies of the Two Thirds World should be coveted partners for mission in North America. A new cooperative effort could greatly assist us in reaching the unchurched. North American agencies could be of great assistance in encouraging Two Thirds World churches to send missionaries by supporting the training of persons in specific activity and in fostering tent-making.

Allowing the Spirit to speak, we will together discover different ways of relating to different people around the globe. The call to reach those billions of persons beyond the reach of a viable Christian community will require careful joint planning and reallocation of funds to pioneer areas.

5. Do all possible to encourage seminaries in making mission the heart of their life as well as curriculum. Meeting the rise of world religions and the decline of Christianity will be a major challenge in North America. The Two Thirds World calls us to join hands in a global effort to share the Gospel. This will not be done unless the leaders of our congregations are prepared to be leaders of mission communities, providing clear preaching and teaching of Christ's mission to the world and enlisting response to the call of the people of God to be persons ever reaching beyond themselves. Our congregations will not be centers for mission unless their clergy are leaders for mission.

6. Open up closer lines of communication between diverse agencies, especially between modalities and sodalities. Existing side by side with little communication and sometimes suspicion, there is much to be gained in sharing ideas and strategies. It will take this kind of cooperative, joint effort to meet the challenges of the twenty first century. No longer can we have the luxury of working only with those who are close members of the family. It will take the gifts, ideas, and resources of all mission agencies in concert to fulfill Christ's call to mission.

The call and opportunities for mission are as great as ever. Mission structures will continue to be important in the fulfillment of Christ's mission. By God's grace we must move boldly and decisively into the twenty first century!

For Further Reading

Amaladoss, Michael

1991 "The Challenges of Mission Today," in *Trends in Mission: Toward the Third Millennium.* Edited by William Jenkinson and Helene O'Sullivan. (Maryknoll, NY.: Orbis Books), 359-397.

Barrett, David B. and James W. Reapsome

1988 *Seven Hundred Plans to Evangelize the World: The Rise of a Global Evangelization Movement.* (Birmingham, AL: New Hope, 1988).

Bellagamba, Anthony

1992 "Megatrends Affecting the Church and Its Mission," in *Mission and Ministry in the Global Church* (Maryknoll, NY.: Orbis Books: 1-16).

Bonk, Jonathon J.

1993 "Mission and the Problem of Affluence," in *Toward the Twenty-First Century in Christian Mission.* Edited by James M. Phillips and Robert T. Coote. (Grand Rapids: Eerdmans. 295-309).

Bosch, David J.

1992 *Transforming Mission: Paradigm Shifts in Theology of Mission* (Maryknoll, N.Y.).

Camp, Bruce K.

1995 "A Theological Examination of the Two-Structure Theory," *Missiology* 23 (2): 197-209.

Collins, Travis

1995 "Missions and Churches in Partnership for Evangelism: A Study of the Declaration of Ibadan," *Missiology* 23 (2): 331-339.

Engel, James F.

1996 *A Clouded Future? Advancing North American World Mission* (Milwaukee: Christian Stewardship Assoc.)

Green, Robin

1991 "God is Doing a New Thing: A Theological Reflection on the Practice of Partnership," *International Review of Mission* 318: 219-229.

Judd, Stephen P.

1992 "Towards a New Self-Understanding: The U.S. Catholic Missionary Movement on the Eve of the Quincentennial," *Missiology* 20 (4): 457-468.

Keyes, Larry E. and Pate, Larry D.

1993 "Two Thirds World Missions: The Next 100 Years," *Missiology* 21 (2): 187-206.

Lutheran Church–Missouri Synod

1997 Documents describing the relationship of LCMS World Mission with Recognized Service Organizations and Missionary Societies, and Missionary Advisory Committee.

Lutheran Order for Discipleship

1993 Interest Brochure and "Statement of Purpose and Membership Expectations."

Martinson, Paul Varo

1997 "The Soul of China and The New Missionary Pragmatics," MS.

1998 "Social Capital and the New Missionary Pragmatics," *Word and World*, Spring 18(2):155-165.

Motte, Mary

1995 "World Mission Conferences in the Twentieth Century," *International Review of Mission* 334: 211- 222.

Myers, Bryant L.

1992 "A Funny Thing Happened on the Way to Evangelical—Ecumenical Cooperation," *International Review of Mission* 81: 397-407.

Phillips, James M. and Coote, Robert L., editors.

1993 *Toward the Twenty-First Century in Christian Mission* (Grand Rapids: Eerdmans).

Pobee, John

1992 "Equipping People of God for God's Mission Today," *International Review of Mission* 81: 21-31.

Reko, Karl

1998 Correspondence dated March 18.

Duain William Vierow

Scherer, James A.

1987 *Gospel, Church and Kingdom: Comparative Studies in World Mission Theology* (Minneapolis: Augsburg).

1997 "Faithful to the Fundamental Task: Mission in the LWF" in *From Federation to Communion: The History of the Lutheran World Federation* (Minneapolis: Fortress Press. 145-178).

Scherer, James A. and Bevans, Stephan B., editors.

1992 *New Directions in Mission and Evangelization I: Basic Statements 1974-1991.*

1994 *New Directions in Mission and Evangelization II: Theological Foundations* (Maryknoll, N.Y.: Orbis).

Shenk, Wilbert R.

1992 "Reflections on the Modern Missionary Movement: 1792-1992," *Mission Studies* 9 (1): 62-78.

1993 "Mission Strategies," in *Toward the Twenty-First Century in Christian Mission.* Edited by James M. Phillips and Robert T. Coote (Grand Rapids: Eerdmans), 218-234.

Siewart, John A. and Valdez, Edna G., editors.

1998 *Mission Handbook: 1998-2000* (Monrovia, CA: MARC).

Skarsten, Trygve R.

1980 "Free Movements in American Lutheranism," in *Movements in the Church: A Journal of the 1980 ALMS Theological Conference.* Edited by Duain W. Vierow (Minneapolis: Affiliation of Lutheran Movements), 12-34.

Skreslet, Stanley H.

1995 "The Empty Basket of Presbyterian Mission: Limits and Possibilities of Partnership," *International Bulletin of Missionary Research* 19 (3): 98-104.

1997 "Networking, Civil Society, and the NGO: A New Model for Ecumenical Mission," *Missiology* 25 (3): 307-319.

Van Beek, Hubert

1992 "New Relationships in Mission—A Critical Evaluation," *International Review of Mission* 81: 417- 434.

Van Engen, Charles

1991 *God's Missionary People: Rethinking the Purpose of the Local Church* (Grand Rapids: Baker).

Van Gelder, Craig

1994 "Defining the Center—Finding the Boundaries: The Challenge of Re-Visioning the Church in North America for the Twenty-First Century," *Missiology* 22 (3): 317-337.

Vikner, David L.

1974 "The Era of Interdependence," *Missiology* 2 (4)

Winter, Ralph D.

1974 "The Two Structures of God's Redemptive Mission," *Missiology* 2 (1): 121-139.

1998 *Organizing for Mission.* Part of a Manuscript for publication by William Carey Library: Pasadena.

Impending Transformation:
Mission Structures for a New Century

Stanley H. Skreslet

The relationship between mission structures and theology is complex. Mission structures are a kind of "theology on four wheels," enfleshed demonstrations of a theoretical orientation to the world. As such, they are contingent and secondary, depending upon theology to suggest their proximate uses and ultimate purposes. They are also vulnerable to critique in a way that theology is not, because they are concrete. Mission structures necessarily entail the application of human institutional forms. Structures devised for mission will thus always be susceptible to the same faults and distortions that beset their secular counterparts.

Though limited in these ways, mission structures are nevertheless crucial. They are windows that allow one to peer closely at the underpinnings of a given theology of mission. They make manifest the actual direction one's missiological thinking is likely to run in practice. In fact, mission structures can lay bare assumptions about human nature and one's understanding of God's purposes with such clarity that words may no longer be able to cover them up. Mission structures are critical tools, therefore, not least because without them no theory of mission has a chance of ever becoming more than unincarnated mutterings, words without effect in a world that expects action.

Andrew Walls has shrewdly observed that the structural mainstay of modern Protestant missions, the voluntary association or mission society, got its start just as missiology entered into an entirely new theological phase. From the beginning, it seems, William Carey recognized that new instruments would be required to accomplish the ambitious agenda he laid before the Christian public in his 1792 *Enquiry.* Thus, in acknowledgment of the close connection between theology and mission structures, Carey addressed not only the world's need and the church's call in his proposal but also the "means" by which the heathen might be converted and the "practicalities" of future missionary endeavors.[1] A similar awareness may be detected at work behind the theological ferment of the early 1960s. Hans Küng, for one, understood all too clearly that a thoroughgoing theological aggiornamento in the Roman Catholic Church would demand that familiar institutional assumptions and forms be reexamined. An early contribution of Küng to this effort was *Strukturen der Kirche*, published on the eve of Vatican II.[2] Coincidentally, and in precisely the same theological atmosphere, ecumenically inclined Protestant theologians embarked on a major three-year study entitled "Missionary Structure of the Congregation." This too was an attempt to reflect on the need for institutional change in light of a shift in theology, represented in the integration of the World Missionary Council and the World Council of Churches at the New Delhi WCC Assembly in 1961.

Mission Structures and Historical Contexts

If the preceding comments are well founded, then one should expect effective mission structures to have theological integrity. That is, they should be able to express institutionally genuine insights that theology has discovered in the abstract. Long experience of the church in mission warns us, however, that validity in a purely theological sense is never the only issue. To be truly suitable, mission structures must also be culturally appropriate and right for their age.

Thanks to David Bosch, it is now commonplace in missiology to speak of this generation as the beginning in earnest of a new age in the history of humankind. Intellectually, this is a time of transition, in which the West seems to be passing from the certainties of Enlightenment thinking into an extended period of cultural crisis. Geopolitically, the customary ways by which the world's nation-states have related to one another have been knocked hard by a realignment of the superpowers. Economically, new patterns of global capitalism have emerged with the power to affect for good or ill (or both) the life of virtually every person on the planet.

Perhaps the most fundamental shift to have occurred in the late twentieth century revolves around the issue of cultural identity. Conventional boundaries of language and distance are rapidly collapsing, throwing traditional notions of social reality into disarray. It is not only that a globalized economy is reaching into and tying together the fates of far-flung communities. Nor is it just a matter of one particular language, English, positioning itself to become the next millennium's lingua franca. There is also a widespread diminishing of confidence in local wisdom, as invasive new sources of authoritative information (like CNN) become available throughout the world. One may also perceive in our time a loosening of the ties that used to bind extended families and specific places closely together, as increasing numbers of people migrate in search of opportunity or to flee some danger. There is also a kind of reconfiguration of priorities taking place in countless households and communities worldwide in the face of overwhelming economic pressures introduced from without by the logic of a market-driven global economy that relentlessly sweeps everything before it.

Not surprisingly, these and other changes have affected the ways in which late twentieth century people have taken to organize themselves socially. New patterns of institutional life have moved to the forefront, while other previously vital structures have faded in importance. It is not possible here to describe these adjustments in any depth, but a few observations may be offered to suggest what the church's present context seems to be saying about effective organizational structures.

Numerous social commentators have pointed to the phenomenon of decentralization as a distinctive mark of economic and political activity today. This trend may be seen, for instance, in the push to privatize many of the functions that used to be performed by governments. In like fashion, huge corporations, many of them multinational attempts to straddle whole industries or sectors of the economy, are spinning off parts of their businesses in an effort to focus on core interests.

New businesses, too, are likely to be conceived as small, agile units that can respond quickly to changes in taste or economic conditions. Mobile and nimble, they need not be anchored to one physical location or bound to produce forever the same goods or services with which they were first identified. The most successful of these tend to rely on technological adroitness rather than on the sheer weight of massed labor or material resources to dominate markets. For these companies, careful market research is necessary in order to identify ever-larger groups of potential customers. Rigid command hierarchies and inflexible work rules are giving way to models of teamwork, even in the old, downsized entities that are left following corporate restructuring.

What might an ideal corporate structure look like today? For some very good reasons (not least among them a ledger showing some $36 billion worth of business annually), Robert Kaplan, writing in the *Atlantic Monthly,* has recently lifted up the engineering firm of Asea Brown Boveri (ABB) as an example of organizational approach that closely fits the demands of our age. All of the characteristics highlighted above—teamwork, attention to market forces, technological acumen, and so forth—are there, but it is the loosely knit web of tightly focused subunits that Kaplan highlights. ABB encompasses some 1,300 independent companies, spread out over 140 countries, which are linked together in an "umbrella" corporate structure. "Decentralization," says CEO Percy Barnevik of ABB, "goes hand in hand with central monitoring."[3] In Kaplan's view, this kind of industrial enterprise aptly illustrates the shape of a successfully globalized corporation that is likely to survive and thrive well into the third millennium.

Tried and Still(?) True Structures

The potential universe of structures for mission is already vast. For centuries, and without apology, the parish was the church's basic unit of evangelism and mission. On a larger scale, but in a similar manner, the diocese was used to extend the geographic reach of the institutional church. As bold new ventures *in plantatio ecclesiae* were initiated in the Age of Discovery, variations on a theme were introduced for Catholic missions, such as the apostolic vicariate. In time, these would be emulated by Protestant denominations that devised overseas equivalents of domestic judicatories. What all these structures have in common is that they are decidedly ecclesiocentric.

The bishops and clerics of the early and medieval church did not do their missionary work alone. Equally important, and in certain situations far more effective than the regular clergy, were the great missionary monks. In the West, at least from the time of St. Columbanus and his fellow fish itinerants, examples abound of monastic outreach to village communities that lay outside the urban areas where the church first took root. Eventually, monastic orders devoted to missionary witness would spearhead the church's expansion into many new areas outside of Europe. Again, well-known Protestant equivalents lie at hand, in the nineteenth century's ubiquitous private volunteer organization, for instance, and the more recent founding of sodalities through which mainline Protestant energies for mission might be focused.

A wide variety of other key mission structures also rose to prominence in the course of the modern missionary movement, some of which continue to be of great use for Christian witness. These would include the thousands of schools, hospitals, and institutions of higher learning that were founded around the world in the nineteenth and early twentieth centuries by mission agencies and non-western national churches. Standing next to these were countless attempts to foster cultural advance in a broader fashion, not a few of which were sponsored by institutions like the local YMCA chapter. The crucial mark of all these structures at their inception was a desire to engender and sustain a movement in non-western cultures toward "civilization" and "uplift."

In the wake of the Second World War, a different set of emphases took hold in western mission circles, and the leading institutions of the day illustrate the shift well. Ministries of charity, supported by theologies of "disinterested benevolence," were pushed aside by efforts to foster self-help. This approach did not preclude churches from participating in the huge tasks of relief and disaster assistance that war and periodic catastrophes still made necessary, but another kind of mission objective emerged as primary: development. Mission organizations restructured themselves in order to respond accordingly, seeking new ways to make material aid, technical expertise, and encouragement available to church partners and new nations. For these ventures, human need was the presenting problem, but the form of the response was influenced to a great degree by a secular ideology of modernization that had insinuated itself within the western churches.

Within this context, short-term mission programs began to take on a new importance as structures for mission. Technicians, it was recognized, did not need to commit to a lifetime of mission service. A more efficient use of their knowledge might see them brought in temporarily, say at the planning and training stages of a development project, after which national workers would assume responsibility. The same could be true for teachers of English and other European languages, who came to be thought of as another kind of specialist with skills that could help Third World people take advantage of all the West's technical resources.

A final category of structures already in place, which nevertheless promises to continue as a vital part of Christian mission in the future, consists of those associations and groups through which many Christians around the world are now working to effect social change and to influence political policies. Here one would include the burgeoning number of church-related, nongovernmental organizations (NGOs) that have sprung up in ever-greater numbers in the 1990s.[4] In the West especially, NGOs often take the form of political action committees that advocate in the halls of power on behalf of the marginalized. These might be closely defined groups (political refugees from a particular area, for instance) or broader classes of people (like the homeless or persecuted Christians). For many NGOs, their chief goal is to gather comprehensive amounts of information on a select number of topics (like the environment or human rights) and then to make this information available to international organizations, governments, the churches, and other nongovernmental actors. In some places, base ecclesial communities fulfill many of the same functions undertaken by NGOs.

Incipient Outlines of the New

One should expect that all, or nearly all, of the structures mentioned in the previous section will continue to be part of the churches mission in the next century. Based on what was presented earlier with respect to historical contexts, however, these organizations will not likely stay fixed in just these configurations or remain bound to the precise terms of their current mission statements. Rapid change in institutional life is a symptom of our age. Therefore, the conditions of late twentieth century life, some of which were described above, are sure to shape these institutions as they continue to evolve, just as they will influence the creation of new structures for mission. In this section, an attempt will be made to characterize these institutions of the future, both the newly created and remodeled, based on what is now known about the context in which they will emerge.

Three attributes in particular suggest themselves to me as likely characteristics of the next millennium's mission organizations:

Niche oriented. As the world's complexity continues to increase, mission organizations, like businesses, are becoming more specialized. Few new organizations will attempt to mount the kind of comprehensive enterprises that defined earlier Protestant denominational approaches to mission. Instead, a particular service or form of mission tends to predominate, and the structure devised to present this good work will often be tightly focused as well. It also seems that some older institutions, which at one time did try to field sweeping programs of mission, are being pressed by circumstances to restrict their primary emphases to just a few areas.[5] In this respect, moves to narrow the reach of some existing mission organizations may be a symptom of a larger adjustment taking place at the denominational level, among Protestants at least, away from a centrally managed, hierarchically arranged corporate model and toward a more flexible, decentralized approach to organizational structure.

Any attempt to survey the current field of mission work around the world is sure to turn up an astonishing variety of organizations that have mobilized in response to an equally diverse collection of needs and objectives. Many groups specialize in mission outreach to particular countries. Others concentrate on whole regions, language families, and/or specific non-Christian populations. Some aim to facilitate interfaith encounter and dialogue, while others restrict themselves to activities that correspond more closely to traditional notions of evangelism. In this latter case, some novel ways have been developed to address a familiar objective, as with the growing frontier mission movement and the concern many groups have for "unreached" peoples.

A newer category of mission organization that seems to be expanding rapidly in the 1990s is what might be called an outsourcing instrument for congregational mission. The model and, perhaps, the originator of this approach on a large scale was Habitat for Humanity, on whose building projects thousands of church mission teams have worked over the past decade or more. Many other organizations have sprung up recently with a similar role in mind, hoping to make available to congregations ongoing ministries of service or proclamation in which visiting groups can participate for a week at a time. The advantages of this approach for youth directors and pastors with a desire to involve their young people and adults in mission outreach are obvious: remote sites are offered for Christian service that have their own infrastructure already in place. Advertisements and promotional materials for these ministries often highlight their exotic locale.[6]

The "information agent" is yet another type of niche-oriented mission structure that has flourished at the end of the twentieth century. Here might be included organizations devoted to the task of gathering and analyzing mission information, an activity that David Barrett has dubbed the science of "missiometrics."[7] Others might try to combine information gathering with a desire to influence public behavior, especially with respect to issues of justice, in the manner of an NGO like Amnesty International or Greenpeace. Yet other organizations within this category, if one may be allowed to stretch the limits of the type somewhat, might specialize in recruiting (of teachers, for instance), facilitating communication between missionaries, and supporting constituencies (as the Mission Aviation Fellowship does), or performing fund-raising services on behalf of other mission organizations.

Networked. No more powerful demonstration of the power of networking need be cited than that offered by the International Campaign to Ban Landmines, headed until recently by peace activist Jody Williams. In just over fourteen months, an informal coalition of some 250 organizations scattered around the world but linked by computer managed to persuade a majority of the world's countries to initial a formal treaty that commits them not to use, produce, or export antipersonnel land mines. For their effort, the coalition and its chief organizer were jointly awarded the Nobel Peace Prize in 1997. The land mines campaign was remarkable not only for its outcome but also because it was conducted without a formal organizational structure, an office, or even a staff. The key element that made its success possible was the concept of networking.

Networking is a virtue whose stock has risen considerably in the postmodern era. It is very likely to be an element assumed by many mission structures in the near term. An obvious reason for this is the degree of specialization that seems to characterize so many mission organizations already. In many cases, networking will make it possible for highly specialized mission structures to coordinate their work and to complement each other. This, then, may turn out to be a way to recapture in the next century a measure of the comprehensiveness that tends to be sacrificed when mission is pursued by thousands of niche-oriented organizations.

Technologically adept. Since mission is essentially a matter of witnessing to the gospel of Jesus Christ, it only makes sense that faithful Christians and their organizations will want to make full use of all the tools of communication that God's providence has placed at their disposal. In the next century, as now, many of these tools will be technologically based.

It is possible to see already how technological devices like the computer have begun to alter the way many mission organizations function. Electronic mail now links all but the most isolated places to everywhere else, providing assistance to missionaries far from home and timely information about their work to supporting constituencies. Satellite broadcasts of Christian programming are able to reach into the heart of non-Christian populations, whose governments may have blocked access previously. Desktop publishing is lowering dramatically the cost of producing high quality materials that are attractive and informative. Those involved in what is called non-residential missionary service depend heavily on technology to conduct research and to communicate with nascent groups of believers among whom they cannot live.

Other benefits of advanced technology may not be so obvious. If the example of the landmines campaign is an indicator of what is to come, perhaps computers and other telecommunication devices will also render superfluous or much less important the idea of a fixed headquarters location, at which all key staff are required to work together. This could make it much easier to assemble multinational teams of mission coworkers, a goal that has often been voiced in the postcolonial period but seldom realized because of the expense and disruption to family lives that long-term relocation requires. Technological aids to communication may also make it possible for highly specialized agencies offering unique services to a worldwide community of mission organizations to achieve the economies of scale that might be required for their viability.

Congregational Missionary Structure(s)

All of the mission structures discussed up to this point have been extracongregational. This reflects the persistent inclination of many mission practitioners to favor parachurch structures over the local church as frameworks for their labor, a trend that seems certain to continue. An orientation in this direction could be a cause for concern, especially if it obscures the fact that groups of believers, whether assembled as formal congregations or more simply gathered together, are, in truth, the most basic means of mission at the disposal of the gospel. This, in my view, was among the most profound insights of the Second Vatican Council, which reclaimed for the twentieth century a vision of the local church as the fundamental expression of the church universal.[8]

In the coming century this perspective may become even more vital than it is now. A future marked by increasing numbers of technologically linked but narrowly conceived mission structures will need healthy congregations that can reach out to near neighbors with the fullest possible witness to the gospel. As useful as they may be, mission structures that concentrate on the delivery of ancillary services to the church cannot replace witnessing communities that worship together and, in fact, must assume them as the primary means by which the good news of Jesus Christ is made known to the world.

There is at least one more reason why the congregation ought not to surrender its primacy in mission to parachurch structures. It is that these organizations are inherently entrepreneurial in a way not true of congregations. To be sure, local churches also have bottom lines to respect, overhead expenses to meet, and membership concerns, but still they find their essential identity in language that identifies them as signs and "sacraments" of the gospel, as the "body of Christ" and the "people of God." Extracongregational organizations, in contrast, are more naturally viewed as an instrument or tool. As such, they must swim more directly in the hazardous waters of the marketplace, in competition with each other, and in the delivery of some services (like the brokering of intercultural living experiences to short-term mission participants), they must contend with a vigorous assortment of secular alternatives.

Having underlined the importance of local congregations to the world mission of the church, one is reluctant to leave it at that, without having said anything specific about how this particular structure might be helped to become a more effective agent of missionary service and outreach in the coming century. A final point of the present discussion will take up this concern.

Most local churches (among Protestants, at least) have in their organizational framework a committee within whose brief is lodged the task of "mission." It is not unusual for the profile of this committee to be quite modest. More prominent, as a rule, are those parts of the local church's governing structure that have charge over Christian education, worship, and pastoral care. In most congregations, the mission committee is given each year a rather small portion of the church's total budget, which the members are free to allocate as they wish. This money is essentially a fund for grant making, and the mission committee is expected to administer it on behalf of the congregation in a responsible manner. Typically, they will decide to use it in support of persons serving in mission outside the local community or give it to one or more service projects that might be local, national, or international.

One has to wonder if this is really the only, or best, way for a structure nominally assigned responsibility for mission in the local church to carry out its work. What does it mean when the mission committee is effectively denied meaningful contact with the greater part of the church's budget? An important assumption about the nature of mission could be at stake here. By restricting the work of the mission committee in this way, local churches may be saying that mission is a peripheral undertaking, a mere adjunct to other, more consequential functions of the church.

An alternative approach might attempt to reposition the mission committee (or its equivalent) nearer to the center of the local church's life. Reconceived in this way, the mission committee would be expected to reflect on *all* the activities and major decisions of the congregation, asking how each contributes to the great ends for which this community has come into being. This is not unlike what strategic planning committees do, but the work would be joined on a continuing basis.

The mission committee is also a natural point of contact between the congregation and what is happening around it in mission. Neighboring communities of faith, specialized mission organizations, civil society groups whose objectives complement those of the local church, other parts of the world church—all these just begin to indicate the complex web of relationships that might be constructed in support of the local church's missionary outreach. A mission committee that seriously probes existing relationships and creatively explores new forms of missionary partnership could be transformed into a kind of missiological gyroscope for the congregation, a means of theological navigation that tries to take into account what may lie over the immediate horizon. With constant change and rapidly shifting circumstances likely to define every local church's setting in the twenty-first century, this kind of structural help could be critical.

Notes

1 Andrew Walls, "Missionary Societies and the Fortunate Subversion of the Church," *Evangelical Quarterly* 88 (1988): 141—55; reprinted in Andrew Walls, *The Missionary Movement in Christian History: Studies in the Transmission of the Faith* (Maryknoll, N.Y.: Orbis Books, 1996), pp. 241-54.

2 Published in English as *Structures of the Church* (New York: Nelson, 1964).

3 Robert Kaplan, "Was Democracy Just a Moment?" *Atlantic Monthly* 280 (December 1997): 72.

4 In two recent articles, I have explored this kind of mission structure in more detail than will be possible here. See my "Networking, Civil Society, and the NGO: A New Model for Ecumenical Mission," *Missiology* 25 (July 1997): 307-19, and "Emerging Trends in a Shifting Global Context: Mission in the New World Order," *Theology Today* 54 (July 1997): 150-64.

5 Such would seem to be the case in my own denomination, the Presbyterian Church (USA), which used to be a model of comprehensiveness in its approach to mission. The impossibility of maintaining such a broad design in the late twentieth century has contributed, in my opinion, to a new strategy that emphasizes certain activities within the larger agenda (like short-term missions, development, and education), while letting go of others as primary objectives (like direct evangelism and medical work). In a textbook illustration of the phenomenon described here, other institutions related to the PCUSA but outside the official denominational structure have gained increased prominence by specializing in these "neglected" areas (e.g., the Outreach Foundation and the Medical Benevolence Fund).

6 This impression is formed on the basis of a small mountain of materials that have come my way from these ministries over the past year through the mail, visits to the web sites of many of these same organizations, and a look at the way they present themselves in publications like the *Great Commission Opportunities Guide*, an annual compendium of mission opportunities published by the Real Media Group (whose own web site is denominated www.GoYe.com). "Exotic" may mean anything in this context from Colorado mountains to the tropics.

7 See David B. Barrett, "'Count the Worshipers!' The New Science of Missiometrics," *International Bulletin of Missionary Research* 19(1995):154-60.

8 As in *Lumen gentium* 26: "This Church of Christ is really present in all legitimately organized local groups of the faithful, which, in so far as they are united to their pastors, are also quite appropriately called Churches in the New Testament."

This essay first appeared in the *International Bulletin of Missionary Research*, January 1999. It is reprinted by permission of the *International Bulletin of Missionary Research*, © 1999, Overseas Ministries Study Center.

Missiology and Mission in Theological Education

Craig J. Moran

The purpose of this paper is to provide an overview of the current state of missiological education in North American institutions of theological education and to raise some of the questions that have been asked about its means and goals. This "status report" will necessarily be couched in general terms because the vast range of diverse practices prevalent in those institutions makes it impossible to attempt a detailed inventory at the level of the concrete and particular. Although such a treatment will inevitably overlook some important matters and distort others, it is hoped that a degree of abstraction will nevertheless help clarify some issues regarding the teaching of missiology today in a way that is provocative and serves as a stimulus for further discussion.

J. Dudley Woodberry, in his concluding chapter to *Missiological Education for the 21st Century: The Book, the Circle and the Sandals*, helpfully describes six methods of missiological education: apprenticeship, monastic orders, universities, self-standing seminaries, Bible colleges and institutes, theological education by extension, and postdenominational megachurches (Woodberry *et al.*, 274-276). It is beyond the scope of this paper to touch directly on all these models. For our purposes it seems most useful to focus on missiological education in the seminaries, and in the course of examining the advantages and disadvantages of training in that context, at least allude to a few of the reasons why some might feel that one or more of these other alternatives are either better in serving the cause of mission, or provide a needed corrective for existing seminary programs in the new circumstances which confront and challenge the life of the Church (for a description of these circumstances and how they influence our understanding of mission today, see Neely, 273- 276).

The problems related to the role of missiology in seminary theological education has a long and varied history that we cannot go into here (for a useful description of this history see Hogg, "The Teaching of Missiology: Some Reflections on the Historical and Current Scene"). Nevertheless, the central question of this brief paper, that of the potentially problematic relationship between missiology and mission, can best be illustrated by reference to a historical example. Roger Finke and Rodney Starke, in *The Churching of America. 1776-1990: Winners and Losers in Our Religious Economy*, describe changing attitudes toward evangelism in the 19th century Methodist Church stemming from the introduction of increased seminary education for clergy. As Finke and Starke note, "The training of clergy had gradually shifted from an informal apprenticeship program in the local circuits to a formal education at the national seminaries" (Finke and Starke, 155). The result of this movement toward increased control of clergy and higher education, which was in fact supported by the clergy because it enhanced their status and economic position, was a turn away from the vigorous methods that Methodists had used successfully for church growth in the past such as revivals and camp meetings. The correlation between higher education for clergy and a decline in ardor for evangelism is succinctly expressed in a quote describing the changes at the famous Ocean Grove Camp Meeting that occurred over the decades in which rigorous academic training gradually became more prominent:

> In 1872 the report from Ocean Grove to the *Guide for Holiness* had been, "Multitudes were sanctified wholly and many sinners were born into the Kingdom"; and in 1878, "Nearly six hundred . . . in converting, sanctifying and reclaiming grace." In 1894, however, the report said, "Several persons were at the altar and some were converted" (156).

Finke and Starke point out that this trend continued throughout the first part of the twentieth century, and refer to a talk given in 1939 by Charles Schofield, president of the Iliff School of Theology, in which he attempts to argue in favor of increased evangelism, but in which he can only conclude that "Evangelism is no longer *the* mission of the church . . . and the clear boundaries between Christian and non-Christian have faded" (159). Although Schofield ends with a call to evangelism, Finke and Starke note, he can no longer tell his seminarians whom to evangelize or how.

It is, of course, impossible to draw a direct correlation between the demands of a rigorous, professional education for clergy and a decline in commitment for mission among those who receive such an education. But the above example does at least raise the question of the relation between the goals of theological education, including the teaching of missiology, and missionary activity, and leads us to wonder whether or not they are entirely complementary. Perhaps the best way to summarize this issue is to refer to the distinction Norman Thomas makes between maintenance and mission (Thomas, 1990, 17-19). Thomas contends that considerations introduced by globalization in theological education force us to confront key questions related to the purpose of theological education and its connection with mission. When the purpose of theological education becomes the maintenance of the church, he implies, then the impulse for mission is either lost or diminished. Here, it seems to me, the purpose of theological education needs to be evaluated to determine if it is conducive to the mission of the church. Prior to any consideration of the place of missiology in the curriculum, the content of mission courses or appropriate pedagogies is the question whether theological education in our seminaries and related institutions is entirely consistent with a call to mission.

Mission at the Dawn of the 21st Century

The Role of Missiology in Theological Education

Before we begin our brief discussion of theological education and mission, however, it is necessary to raise a number of issues that require more reflection. The first of these concerns the definition of missiology. James Scherer has noted that the quest for a definition of this term remains elusive, in part because of different perspectives among those who teach the discipline and in part because of its uncertain relationship with the goals of theological education (Scherer, 509). Another significant reason for confusion over the meaning of missiology is the corresponding uncertainty over the meaning of mission. Working toward a more adequate understanding of missiology, then, would involve a consideration of its role in theological education and an examination of its relation to mission. Perhaps one way to approach these two issues is to examine them in the light of general categories drawn from the current debate on the means and goals of theological education. Since missiology is, after all, an element of theological education, it should not be surprising that the categories that define this debate can be applied specifically to reflection on its meaning and purpose.

David Kelsey, in his well-known and provocative book *Between Athens and Berlin: The Theological Education Debate*, describes two fundamental models for theological education. The first he calls the "Athens" model, a means of "culturing" the soul *(paideia)* with the goal of "character formation"(Kelsey, 6). This model is characterized by "a movement from source to personal appropriation of the source, from revealed wisdom to the appropriation of revealed wisdom in a way that is identity forming and personally transforming"(19-21). This kind of theological education focuses on the student in that its purpose is to help the student undergo a deep kind of formation. The relationship between student and teacher in this model is indirect, for the teacher only teaches "by providing a context in which the learner may come to that combined self-knowledge and God-knowledge that is a 'personal appropriation' of revealed wisdom" (20). Teachers are qualified, not only by extraordinary learning, but also by the personal gifts necessary to serve as a "midwife" for the students in their quest for wisdom.

In the "Berlin" model, which is based on the educational style developed at the University of Berlin in the ninteenth century, theological education is "a movement from data to theory to application of theory to practice" (22) and combines *Wissenschaft* for critical rigor in theorizing, and "professional" education for rigorous study of the application of theory in practice. This model of theological education tends to be oriented toward "the truth about the origin, effects, and essential nature of 'Christian' phenomena" (24). As such, it focuses on the "professional" education of leaders whose purpose is to nurture the health of the church. The relation between teacher and learner in this model is basically that of "a researcher who needs the student to help achieve the goal of research in a cooperative enterprise"(24).

The question for our immediate purposes is which of these models most accurately reflects the teaching of missiology in our seminaries and their related institutions?

Missiology and the Seminary Curriculum

The impression that a significant proportion of missiological education is done according to the "Berlin" model is verified by a quick look at catalogues of seminaries offering degrees in missiology, such as Trinity Evangelical Divinity School, Westminister Theological Seminary, the Columbia Biblical Seminary and Graduate School of Missions, and the School of World Missions at Fuller Theological Seminary. No one would deny that elements of "Athens" are present in these programs, just as no one would deny the importance and effectiveness of what is taught. The point, however, is that these examples of excellent missiological education strongly emphasize a thorough academic training in a wide variety of topics with the goal of providing professional training in the discipline. All these programs obviously assume a rigorous academic program intended to produce either skilled and knowledgeable missionaries or academically qualified missiologists capable of reflecting on the meaning of mission as well as serving the mission needs of the church. These programs, in short, provide a "professional" education in that those who successfully meet their requirements qualify for certain positions in mission agencies or academic settings (as one student is quoted as saying in the Trinity Evangelical Divinity School Catalogue, "Having a degree from Trinity will open a lot of doors with different mission agencies", 169). The statement from Fuller probably sums up the purpose of the different degree programs in missiology by referring to a commitment to "academic integrity, professional training and ministry maturation" (Fuller, 120).

The MA Degree in Missiology at Westminister Theological Seminary in Philadelphia, for example, is explicitly described as a "specialized professional degree," and requires Hebrew, Greek and basic classes in Bible and theology in addition to courses specifically designed for Urban Mission. The final requirement, described as a "Ministry Project," needs to be approved by the Practical Theology department before it is defended before the urban ministry faculty team (Westminister, 57-60). Here, clearly, is an example of an admirable program that combines professional training with specific mission activities, and which is set up to meet strict academic standards in the "Berlin" style.

This general characterization of missiology is also evident in the on-going controversies over the place of missiology in the seminary curriculum. David Bosch has described three possible responses to this problem, all of which place missiology within a program for theological education dominated by what Edward Farley calls the "clergy paradigm." According to this paradigm, mission has been considered to be on the periphery of the church—as such, it has neither contributed to the "theoretical" aspect of theology nor to the "practical" component of this education which concentrated on ministry as service to the institutional church (Bosch, 490). When missiology has received attention within the curriculum, there have been three ways of relating it to the other disciplines:

(1) appending it to one of the existing disciplines, usually practical theology, a strategy which, as Bosch notes, means that it becomes "the study of the self- realization of the church in missionary situations" and has clear links with the training of the pastorate;

(2) advocating the introduction of missiology as a theological discipline in its own right, a strategy which led to missiology's development as a mirror image of the other theological disciplines and resulted in its becoming "a science of the missionary, for the missionary"; and

(3) incorporating missiology into the other theological disciplines so that the missionary dimension is introduced into the entire field of theology, a strategy which, while theologically sound, often led to neglect by teachers who were not sufficiently aware of the missionary dimension of their subjects.

In each of these three possible roles for missiology in the curriculum, the professional training for clergy is assumed to be the goal of theological education, and the problem for missiology really becomes clarifying its role in the professional education of pastors.

The interest in globalizing theological education over the past decade has given new prominence to the issue of missiology's role in the seminary curriculum, and it is not entirely clear that missiologists have successfully met that challenge. As Norman Thomas noted at the beginning of the discussion of globalization in 1989:

> Missiologists whose discipline has been marginal in the theological curricula find it difficult to contemplate a future in which the missiologist may become the catalyst/enabler of significant changes in theological education (Thomas, 1989, 107).

It would be interesting to discover whether missiologists have, in the intervening years, divested themselves of this timidity, or whether they still feel most comfortable at the periphery of theological education. This is not a challenge that can be confronted only through curriculum reform or by adding new degree programs, important as these may be, but a challenge that also requires a thorough re-evaluation of the goals of theological education in light of missiological concerns.

The Goals of Missiology

The observation that most contemporary missiological education is done according to the Berlin model is also borne out by an examination of the diverse goals that are pursued under its various guises. Charles Van Engen describes the current state of missiology by positing a spectrum ranging between the poles of Specialization and Integration. The Specialization pole is characterized by a commitment to action, and defines mission in terms of action and goals, emphasizes results, is task-oriented, and stresses strategies and methods (Van Engen, 212). The organization most representative of this perspective is the Institute of Church Growth at Fuller Seminary, which suggests that missiology is to be considered as a specialized topic that is only minimally integrated into the rest of the seminary's curriculum. Van Engen points to Donald McGavran's understanding of mission being the clearest example of this position: "an enterprise devoted to proclaiming the good news of Jesus Christ, and to persuading men and women to become his disciples and responsible members of his church" (215). To this end, then, missiological research and education is intended to mobilize Christians for active participation in this task as missionaries dedicated to church growth.

At the other end of the spectrum Van Engen places the Integration pole, which is characterized by reflection on mission in a theological context. In this view, mission is defined by concepts, emphasizes understanding and new insights, and is oriented to past and present "mission studies" (212). Van Engen does not offer an example of this extreme, but we do not have to look far to find one. Bosch points out, for example, that theology in general, and missiology in particular, are not proclamations of the message, but are "reflection on that message and its proclamation." He continues, "Missiology cannot, as such, issue in missionary involvement. . . a missionary vision is *caught,* not *taught"* (emphasis in original, Bosch, 498). In this view, then, the primary task of missiology is to perform a "critical function" in regard to other theological disciplines. As Bosch notes:

> . . . missiology acts as a gadfly in the house of theology, creating unrest and resisting complacency, opposing every ecclesiastical impulse to self-preservation, every desire to stay what we are, every inclination toward provincialism and parochialism. . . (496).

At the Integration end of the spectrum, then, the stress is on the interplay of missiology with the other theological disciplines without overt concern for direct missionary action. The goal of missiology at this extreme is to serve theological reflection. This is the position that Andrew Walls advocates when he calls for a depth of scholarship in mission studies "which engages with all the existing theological disciplines and in doing so enriches them" (Walls, 150).

A moderate position between the two poles would attempt to combine both theological reflection with mission activity. One example of a missiologist who typifies this position, according to Van Engen, is Johannes Verkuyl, for whom missiology's task is "to investigate scientifically and critically the presuppositions made of structures, methods, patterns of cooperation and leadership which the churches bring to their mandate" (214). This rigorous academic work, however, is not to be done only for its own sake, but is to serve the cause of communicating the Christian message, proclaiming the Gospel to non-Christians and planting and nurturing the growth of the church. As Verkuyl notes, "Missiology may never become a substitute for action and participation" (214).

There are significant differences among the various positions located on Van Engen's spectrum, and he points to the "dynamic tension" among them. Nevertheless, he does hold out the possibility that they can be combined in a more comprehensive approach to missiology. As he asks, referring specifically to the tension between the Institute of Church Growth and the School of World Mission at Fuller Seminary:

> Is there a way to affirm the whole of the continuum—to continue to be the ICG/SWM, both institute and school? Is there a way whereby the ICG/SWM can serve mission agencies who want professional training for their personnel within their own individual agendas and missional tasks (especially in relation to church growth); and at the same time serve the world church, which needs teachers of reflective missiological integration, related to the larger missiological academy, and participating in global missiological theorizing? (218)

He thus expresses the need for a "full-fledged missiology" that would combine the integrational and activist poles, and would "emanate in biblically informed and contextually appropriate missional action" (221). I would suggest that what makes it possible for Van Engen to imagine a combination of these two extremes, despite their radically different goals, is that they share a common ground in "Berlin"-type schooling. This, of course, is not a criticism, but simply an observation that despite the diversity of goals in missiological education, the different forms that missiology takes tend to fall into the same pedagogical category and therefore also have many characteristics in common. These characteristics would include not only what is taught and how, but who is qualified to teach and who the intended audience might be.

Further Issues in Missiological Education

To identify these broad similarities in contemporary missiology is not to gloss over the very real questions that need to be discussed, such as "What is the place of missiology in the seminary curriculum?" and "What is the goal of missiology? Action? Reflection? Or some combination of the two?" These questions obviously require our immediate and undivided attention. However, to categorize the teaching of missiology in this way has the benefit of making us aware of a broad range of concerns about its limitations and results that can be raised from beyond its prevailing methods and goals.

The Students

The first issue is whether this style of missiological education serves the cause of mission by reaching the people most suited for the work that needs to be done. Woodberry observes that theological schools need to make a decision whether their "calling is to train the masses of missionaries or educate the elite, the leaders and educators" (Woodberry, 271). Ralph Winter notes that "Education is thus not merely a matter of the right curriculum but the right students. It is more crucially a matter of *whom we are training than what we are teaching"* (emphasis in original, Winter, 184). The right students, in Winter's view, are, in many cases, lay people who have great leadership potential, but no access to formal seminary training. Winter puts the basic question this way, "Do we have to choose between (1) untrained but gifted leadership and (2) less gifted but academically qualified people?" (183) Unless seminary education reaches those who have the gifts to lead congregations, evangelize and work in cross-cultural mission, Winters would say, its quality and content will be irrelevant—it will never have the results that its proponents are hoping and praying for. This leads Winters to conclude that unless seminaries find new ways of making what they teach "accessible to the full spectrum of believers, the greatest leadership potential of the church cannot be harvested..." (184).

Concern for spreading mission training to as many Christians as possible was, and continues to be, an important cause underlying the growth of Bible colleges and institutes. Kenneth Mulholland points out that these institutions had their beginnings in the great evangelical awakenings of the ninteenth century and in the vocationally oriented educational currents prevalent in the first part of the twentieth century (Mulholland, 51). These Bible schools were characterized by their accessibility—as Mulholland notes, "They aimed to train all whom God was leading into active Christian service regardless of educational level, chronological age, gender and life circumstance" (45). That accessibility and mission were primary goals of the Bible schools is corroborated by James Bergquist. In an unpublished paper entitled "The Bible School Movement in the Postmodern Era: Where Should We Be Positioned?", he maintains that the identity of the Lutheran Bible Institute of Seattle was strongly influenced by strains of continental Lutheran pietism which "spawned a whole array of social service institutions and stressed an active role for the laity, an emphasis which contributed greatly to later Protestant volunteerism" and "awakened Lutherans and Protestants to global mission." Bible schools, such as LBIS, were formed to express these impulses, which were not supported by the dominant non-Pietist Lutherans who established seminaries and colleges (Bergquist, 6). Clearly, the founding of Bible schools, such as LBIS, was to make training for mission available to as many people as possible, including many who, for one reason or another, were not qualified for a seminary education.

Closely related to this discussion is the choice Norman Thomas poses between "Clericalism or Shared Ministry?" Thomas, like Winter, suggests that the current methods of theological education in North America may not be the most suitable ways of serving the needs of mission throughout the world, either because they fail to recognize the important role that laity are assuming in mission and evangelism, or because they do little to make themselves accessible to those who do not fit preconceived notions of what a church worker or a missionary should look like. Thomas points to both the "declericalization of parish ministry" and the "deprofessionalizing of global mission" that is occurring in churches around the world, and argues that these movements will force

"North American seminaries to rethink their role in equipping the people of God for their several ministries" (Thomas, 1990, 21).

Here Winter's fundamental question of whom we should be trying to reach with missiological education is pertinent. If our view is limited to just those individuals who have the means and qualifications to come to the seminary with the intention of becoming parish pastors or who are seeking some other form of professional theological training, then perhaps we are not reaching the right people with our efforts. It may be, then, that other models of missiological education which are more accessible to greater numbers of people, like the Bible schools, extension programs or training based in congregations, would be more conducive to the practice of mission than formal instruction in missiology at a high academic level.

One more issue needs to be raised here. When we discuss the question of who we should be educating for mission, it is important to take into account the large number of international students who have come to our institutions for training in missiology. The presence of these students greatly enriches our classes and our communities, but we need to ask ourselves a number of difficult questions: are we adequately providing them with the training they need to return to their home settings for work as missionaries or mission teachers? What kind of special attention do these students require? To what degree do we expect them to fit into our existing programs? Are we getting the students who will benefit most from this kind of education? These and many related questions will need our careful consideration in the future.

Pedagogy

A second issue concerns the form of pedagogy appropriate to missiology. Within the "Berlin" model, the goal remains the acquirement of knowledge suitable for the specific purpose of serving the church in a professional capacity, and this goal governs who is qualified to teach and the nature of teacher-student relations. We are justified in asking whether the methods consistent with this goal are capable of serving the broader concerns of mission. Darrell Whiteman, for example, in his discussion of "The Role of the Behavioral Sciences in Missiological Education," maintains that an important purpose for employing the behavioral sciences in missiological education is to help us be aware of the ways we and our message have been influenced by our own culture:

> . . . we need to have the blinders of our own culture removed so that we understand one another better. Missiological training informed by insights from the behavioral sciences can help us make that cross-cultural conversion so that we can be God's people in the world, sharing God's love and grace across all social, cultural, and economic barriers (143).

No one can dispute the important role that the behavioral sciences play in helping us to understand the contexts in which the gospel is to be preached and realizing our own limitations. Nevertheless, we can wonder if they can deliver on all that they promise. Whiteman is assuming that these sciences are value-free and beyond cultural conditioning, and so can be used as neutral tools with which to criticize ourselves and our culture. But if those sciences are seen as being products of the culture they are intended to criticize, then that criticism is either compromised or has the unintended effect of reinforcing one's commitment to that culture.

The broader question being pursued here is whether a pedagogy associated with a professional education of the "Berlin"-type tends to perpetuate itself so that the student trained under this system is predisposed to consciously or unconsciously assume a certain relationship to others in the work they embark on after completing their studies. Marc S. Mullinax, for example, questions whether these styles of pedagogy can achieve the radical implications of globalization, which require that the student be "culturally dislodged, so that one can hear, include and most importantly become, a student and colleague of the Other" (Mullinax, 33) and "experience the world of those traditionally defined as Others in order to become explicitly accountable to them" (35). The underlying question is not just what kind of information needs to be transmitted to make a person a qualified missionary or missiologist, but what personal qualities are we trying to inculcate and what kind of person do we foresee embodying our vision of mission. Are classical academic pedagogies consistent with the formation of people who will do "mission in Christ's way"? Or do they propagate personal characteristics and certain kinds of relationships which are not consistent with this image?

It is important to note that when discussing the effect of higher academic standards on motives for participation in mission and evangelism, we are not just speaking of the curriculum and the stringency of standards, but also of the culture of the institution. A recent study of two seminaries entitled *Being There: Culture and Formation in Two Theological Seminaries*, has highlighted the importance of an institution's culture for the formation of students for the ministry. Among the study's conclusions is the observation that students are most strongly affected by the examples set by the faculty, both in and out of the classroom, and by their encounters with the seminary administration. This suggests that whatever the stated goals of the institution may be or however strongly worded the school's mission statement, unless the faculty and administration embody a commitment to mission, in word and practice, the message is likely to go unheard:

> Our study suggests that curriculum change alone will not produce changes in what students believe, in how they act, and perhaps even in what content they have appropriated at sufficient depth to make a long-term difference in their capacities and aptitudes. These are shaped, we have concluded, by formal "symbolic vehicles of meaning" (Carroll, 270).

One example cited in the study involved the discrepancy between one seminary's commitment to the poor, a commitment evident in the seminary's

Mission at the Dawn of the 21st Century

life in many ways, and the unforgiving collection practices of a new Financial Director. Talking and teaching about mission are not enough; it is just as important, if not more so, to be aware of the subliminal messages students are receiving from a variety of sources outside the classroom, and to promote an institutional culture that not only supports commitment to mission, but also is as consistent as possible with the gospel message we are called to embody and disseminate.

The Role of Spiritual Formation

The final area of concern is the role of "formation" in missiological education. The issue here is whether the "Athens" model has anything to offer missiological education and whether the two models of theological education can be combined in some way. Mary Motte, in her article on "A Roman Catholic Perspective on Missiological Education," recognizes the need for social analysis in missionary education, but points beyond it to the necessary dimension "spiritual formation" brings to the training process. It is this "formation" which leads to discernment of the "signs of God" in a situation, and which provides both the guide to, and the goals of, action. As she notes:

> It is not a question of providing a clear recipe for action, but rather of enabling a missionary to enter into a dialogical process with adequate missiological resources that will permit further discernment about how to proclaim the reign of God in a given place and time (Motte, 80).

The neglect of such formation will result in a lack of Christian identity in the work undertaken and an incapacity to identify the missiological questions in today's context. "Formation" is thus essential, Motte maintains, to the development of skills without which the missionary task can easily become directionless and pointless.

In the same way, Robert Schreiter has pointed out that to focus too heavily on culture and the dynamics of cross-cultural communication, a necessary and important task in the education of missionaries and missiologists, can lead one to neglect important aspects of one's faith life:

> Cultural sensitivity can become an excuse for not examining the depth and intensity of one's own commitment to Christ and thus a way to avoid the demands of mission or the stringency of sustained dialogue. Likewise, acute cultural sensitivity may end up affirming patterns of sexism, racism and classism . . . (Schreiter, 125).

The School of World Mission and Evangelism at the Trinity Evangelical Divinity School offers, in its own words, "outstanding training in intracultural and cross-cultural evangelism and discipleship" (Trinity, 169). These are essential tasks, but, as Schreiter suggests, to concentrate only on them may lead one to overlook personal faith issues as well as concerns with justice and reconciliation, and it is for this reason that "formation" becomes a necessary aspect of missiological education.

It is important to note that the concept of formation is not entirely absent from the rigorous academic and professional training advanced by the "Berlin" model. Kelsey points out that this model for theological education also speaks of the need for "character transformation," but warns us against assuming that formation in this sense is the same as that assumed by practitioners of the "Athens" model. Kelsey points out that "formation" from the perspective of the "Berlin" model assumes the "ideal" of the Enlightenment view of humanity in which the "characteristic defining human being is reason's capacity to test and if necessary correct any and all 'intuitions'" through its capacity for disciplined and orderly critical inquiry. This is in contrast to the "Athens" view that the defining human characteristic is the "capacity of reason in intuitive, cognitive judgment to apprehend the ultimate principle of being and of value—that is, God." From this perspective, this intuitive knowing provides the foundation for all other knowing. The point here is that both the Berlin and the Athens models speak of the need for "formation," but both come to that term with different anthropological assumptions. For "Berlin," a human being is defined by their critical reason; for "Athens," a human being is defined by a capacity for a direct apprehension of God (Kelsey, 26-27).

Given this fundamental difference, the question arises as to whether they can be combined. Woodberry, for example, refers to the need to incorporate spiritual formation into missiological education. He points to three goals for such education, spiritual formation, graduate or undergraduate education, and ministry development, and calls us to face "the challenge to keep in balance the inherent tensions, among the spiritual, the academic and the practical" (Woodberry, 271). Kelsey, however, warns against the assumption that this kind of balance can be easily achieved. He notes that "the best that can be hoped for is an unstable truce, constantly threatening to break down into educational incoherence," and goes on to explain:

> . . . if the goal of one pole of theological education is cultivation of capacities for *Wissenschaft,* and if the goal of the other pole is cultivation of faith's *habitus,* theological education ends up with two overarching goals and is inherently incoherent (228).

In short, we cannot simply assume an easy compatibility between a professional program of missiological education and the different needs and methods of a program stressing the cultivation of a missiological *habitus.*

The discussion of the role of spiritual formation in missiological education has been expanded by some missiologists to envision the shape such training would assume. Barbara Hendricks and Thomas E. Clarke, for example, suggest that such training would include self-knowledge based on psychological resources, initiation into varieties of prayer experiences, an authentic experience of basic community and what they call "an internship in nonviolence" (Hendricks and Clarke, 210). Other theologians have written about the needs of theological education in a way that raises questions for the teaching of missiology as well. Craig Dykstra does not rule out the need for ordered learning in the cultivation of *habitus,* but also calls for a learning that involves "affections, judgements, perceptions, intentions and bodily experiences and movements." As he points out, this takes us beyond curriculum reform into an area where the formation of self and community requires a reformulation of "imaginative, aesthetic and linguistic learning" (Quoted in Chopp, 17).

Vague as these proposals may seem at this stage, it will be necessary to explore and experiment in order to determine how they can be incorporated into theological, and specifically missiological, education. Consideration of these matters opens up a new dimension in discussions of missiological pedagogy. As Rebecca Chopp admits, "To limit ourselves to curriculum reform without asking other substantive questions about how we teach, what we teach, whom we teach, and where we teach is simply to keep rearranging and redecorating the deck furniture on an unsteady, if not already sinking, Titanic" (17).

Conclusion

Chopp's comparison of the contemporary state of affairs in theological education with the Titanic may be overstated, but her quote does point out the necessity to reconsider such education in the light of unprecedented circumstances. This is even more true in missiology, where the adjustment to a new situation is just as pronounced, and where fundamental questions, such as the role of missiology in theological education and its relation to mission, have received such a variety of conflicting answers. The discussion of these fundamental questions needs to continue, even if no resolution is immediately in sight. As part of this conversation, we need to discuss some of the related issues raised above: What is the goal of missiology? What is its relationship with mission? Who should we be teaching and how is the best way to reach them? What teaching methods best serve the unique needs of mission training? What role, if any, should "spiritual formation" (or *habitus, paideia,* "practice") play in this training? This, of course, is only a sampling of the questions that will need to be considered as missiologists converse about the future of their discipline in a radically changing world.

References

Bergquist, James A. "The Bible School Movement in the Postmodern Era: Where Should We Be Positioned?" Unpublished Manuscript, 1996.

Bosch, David J. *Transforming Mission: Paradigm Shifts in Theology of Mission* (Maryknoll, New York: Orbis Books, 1991).

Carroll, Jackson W. *et al. Being There: Culture and Formation in Two Theological Schools* (New York: Oxford University Press, 1997).

Chopp, Rebecca S. *Saving Work: Feminist Practices of Theological Education* (Louisville, Kentucky: Westminister John Knox Press, 1995).

Columbia Biblical Seminary and Graduate School of Mission. *1995/96 Academic Catalog* (Columbia, S.C.).

Evans, Alice F., Evans, Robert A. and Roozen, David A., eds. *The Globalization of Theological Education* (Maryknoll, New York: Orbis Books, 1993).

Finke, Roger, and Starke, Rodney. *The Churching of America. 1776-1990: Winners and Losers in Our Religious Economy* (New Brunswick, N.J.: Rutgers University Press, 1992).

Fuller Theological Seminary. *Catalog 1994-1995* (Pasadena, CA).

Hendricks, Barbara, and Clarke, Thomas E. "Spiritual Formation for Mission," in Phillips and Coote, eds., *Toward the 21st Century in Christian Mission*, 203-217.

Hogg, William Richey. "The Teaching of Missiology: Some Reflections on the Historical and Current Scene," *Missiology* 15.4 (October 1987): 487- 506.

Kelsey, David H. *Between Athens and Berlin: The Theological Education Debate* (Grand Rapids, MI: William B. Eerdmans Publishing Company), 1993.

Motte, Mary. "A Roman Catholic Perspective on Missiological Education," in Woodberry, *et al*, eds.,*Missiological Education for the 21st Century*, 76-82.

Mulholland, Kenneth. "Missiological Education in the Bible College Tradition," in Woodberry, *et al.*, eds., *Missiological Education for the 21st Century*, 43-53.

Mullinax, Marc S. "Globalization's Definition Proceeds from Its Modeling," *Theological Education* XXX (Autumn 1993): 33-45.

Neely, Alan. "The Teaching of Missions," in Phillips and Coote, eds., *Toward the 21st Century in Christian Mission*, 269-283.

Phillips, James M., and Coote, Robert T. eds. *Toward the 21st Century in Christian Mission.* (Grand Rapids, MI: William B. Eerdmans Publishing Company, 1993).

Scherer, James. "Missiology as a Discipline and What It Includes," *Missiology* 15.4 (October 1987): 507-522.

Schreiter, Robert. "Globalization as Cross-Cultural Dialogue," in Evans, *et al.*, eds., *The Globalization of Theological Education*, 122-133.

Thomas, Norman. "From Missions to Globalization: Teaching Missiology in North American Seminaries," *IBMR* 13.3 (July 1989): 103-107.

___"Globalization and the Teaching of Mission," *Missiology* 18.1 (January 1990): 13-23.

Trinity Evangelical Divinity School. 1994-95 *Catalog and Application* (Deerfield, IL).

Van Engen, Charles. "Specialization/Integration in Mission Education," in Woodberry, *et al*, eds., *Missiological Education for the 21st Century*, 208-231.

Walls, Andrew F. "Structural Problems in Mission Studies," *IBMR* 15.4 (October 1991): 147-155.

Westminster Theological Seminary. *Catalog 1994-1996* (Philadelphia, PA).

Whiteman, Darrell. "The Role of the Behavioral Sciences in Missiological Education," in Woodberry, *et al.*, eds., *Missiological Education for the 21st Century*, 133-143.

Winter, Ralph D. "Missiological Education for Lay People," in Woodberry, *et al.*, eds., *Missiological Education for the 21st Century*, 169-188.

Woodberry, J. Dudley. "Till the Final Book is Opened in the Final Circle," in Woodberry, *et al.*, eds., *Missiological Education for the 21st Century*, 271-276.

Woodberry, J. Dudley, Van Engen, Charles, and Elliston, Edgar J.,eds. *Missiological Education for the 21st Century: The Book, the Circle and the Sandals* (Maryknoll, New York: Orbis Books, 1996).

Toward the 21st Century:
Educating People for God's Mission

J. Dudley Woodberry

To acquire a vision for educating people for God's mission as we enter the twenty-first century we need, first, to ascertain a biblical vision to give us direction and the educational values to guide and propel us in that direction. Secondly, we need to discern the emerging contexts in which education and ministry will take place. Finally, we need to look at the implications of the first two for the content and form of our education.

Biblical Vision and Educational Values

We start with biblical vision and educational values since they provide focus and continuity irrespective of the changes in our contexts that we envision or encounter.

Biblical Vision

A biblical educational vision for mission might be summarized as *equipping leaders to incarnate the gospel of God's reign among all peoples.* "Equipping" involves mentoring in being (character formation), knowing, and doing, in a way that empowers others. "Leaders" refers to various levels of leaders, as well as a spectrum from mid-career, proven leaders to emerging leaders who are being helped to discern and develop their gifts. "To incarnate the gospel" emphasizes both character formation to live out the gospel and the need to do so in a specific cultural context in a form that make a dynamically equivalent impact to that which it had in first century Palestine. "The gospel of God's reign" expresses a "kingdom missiology" which holds firmly to the necessity of conversion and church planting while recognizing that the good news applies to all of life, and God's reign through his Spirit extends beyond the church. "Among all peoples" refers to the crossing of barriers to plant culturally relevant, multiplying churches among every grouping of people whether defined by religion, ideology, ethnicity, or culture. The educational process involves the interaction of the learner (what she/he brings), the word (with a resultant theology of mission), the world (as understood through the behavioral sciences), and the church (with the lessons of mission history and church growth).

Educational Values

The values that drive missiological education tend to be couplets that are in creative tension with the balance and emphasis being influenced by the context and desired outcomes. They are:

evangelistic passion	—	holism of the gospel
evangelical	—	ecumenical
contextual	—	global
learning from history	—	preparing for the future
academic quality	—	practical engagement
excellence	—	empowerment
recognized standards	—	flexible
strong center	—	extended partnerships
stable	—	responsive to opportunities
integrated programs	—	modular offerings
mentoring individuals	—	equipping the many

Emerging Contexts

We need to look into the future to try to discern the contexts in which mission and education for mission will take place, noting, in both the world and North America, those current trends that may be expected to continue and new ones that can be anticipated. As the values have been seen to be bipolar and in tension, so most of the world trends are bipolar. In most cases one pole, such as globalization, is dominant, but the other, in this case regional or ethnic resurgence, is also present. Having identified the trends, we must note their implications for education for mission, and each educational institution or organization then needs to prioritize which implications should most involve their energies.

World Contexts

The global megatrends will impact all the variables that constitute relevant missiological education.

General

Global trends like the population explosion, accelerated change, and globalization are too pervasive to fit into any single categorization such as political or economic.

Population explosion in developing world, stagnation in the developed

The world population is mushrooming. By the year 2000 it will be 6,236 million (Johnstone 1993, 22; Barrett 1999, using U.N. statistics gives slightly lower figures). By 2025 it will be 8,312 million, led by Asia with 4,939 million followed by Africa with 1,510 million, Europe with 743 million, Latin

America with 706 million, North America with 375 million, and Oceania with 39 million (Myers 1997, 29).

The annual growth rate of the Southern Hemisphere will far outstrip the North (Johnstone, 22-75), which in turn will retain much of the wealth. The population doubling time of many of the poorest countries will be 31 years. The Chinese, already 20 percent of the global population, have 50 million outside mainland China and 150,000 students in the United States. India is not far behind China and growing.

Over a billion will need cross cultural witness to understand the gospel. Most are in the 10-40 window (10 to 40 degrees latitude in Asia and Africa), where 86 percent of the unreached people groups, a majority of Muslims, Hindus, Buddhists, and Marxists, and 80 percent of the poorest live.

Implications for education:

a. The population explosion necessitates a focus by educational institutions on the equipping of the leaders or the *leaders of the leaders* as the best way to multiply effectiveness.

b. The location of the majority of the unreached suggests that North American institutions should be involved in:

- overseas *partnerships*
- locally *affordable distance learning*
- consultations with other institutions to see that between them each major *cluster of unreached peoples* (e.g., Chinese and Indians) has one or more *programs tailored to their specific needs*.

2. Accelerating change, except for small pockets

Apart from some marginalized pockets, the pace of change is increasing across the board—demographic, technological, economic, political, and social. This leads to uncertainty, information overload, hesitancy to make long-term commitments, and difficulty in making plans.

Implications for education:

a. The pace of change necessitates

- *research* to ascertain *significant trends*
- *instruction* on *current trends*
- maintaining *stability in missional focus and values* while being *alert and flexible to change paradigms*
- providing *continuing education*, web-based where helpful.

b. The information overload requires the equipping of students to *discern significant knowledge from information*.

3. Globalization and localism

The accelerating change involves the compression of time and space in a shrinking world of rapid communication and travel. National boundaries and oceans are not significant barriers in the global market and city where financial markets and multinational businesses are linked, western culture and English are the medium of understanding, and governments strive for a New World Order. At the same time there are centrifugal forces away from globalization to various localisms that seek to retain or forge ethnic or religious boundaries. These range from nostalgia to conflict.

Implications for education:

a. Globalization provides a climate and opportunities for

    - *networking* with mission educational institutions and agencies for *cooperative education*
    - *internet* and *email research* and *education*
    - teaching students *internet literacy*
    - training in the teaching of English as a second language (*TESOL*) and other *tentmaking entrance strategies* for creative access countries

b. The erection of ethnic and religious fundamentalist barriers provide challenges for research and instruction to

    - facilitate *understanding* of these groups
    - facilitate *reconciliation* through conflict resolution and ministries for trauma
    - understand how militant forms of ethnic and fundamentalist resurgence lead to *receptivity* to the gospel when Christians are present.

Religious and secular

The religious and secular trends are paradoxical. Secularization and the religious resurgence increase together as do pluralism and the conflict of civilizations with religious roots.

4. Increase in secularization and religious resurgence

Secularization has been progressing since the Enlightenment and has led to the post-Christian west, especially in Western Europe. The religious resurgence has been largely a reaction to the loss of religious and traditional values that has accompanied secularization and, in countries that have been under Communist domination, a reaction to the bankruptcy of atheism.

Islam is the fastest growing world religion in percent of growth, though more people become Christians every year. Islam's growth is primarily by birth rate but also by conversion in Africa, especially since 1974, when the

Muslim World League began organized efforts to propagate the faith. Hinduism has experienced resurgence both in the often militant Hindu nationalism in India and in the more pluralist form in the New Age movement in the West.

With the decline of Communism, Buddhism, often blended with Taoism and Confucianism, has experienced resurgence in China, Mongolia, Cambodia, and Vietnam, as well as the United States. The same failure of atheistic Communism has led to the growth of animistic tribal religions in the emerging ethnic nations of the former Soviet Union and the Eastern Block, and the decline of Christianity in Europe has led to the increase of animistic magic.

Implications for education:

a. Secularization in the post-Christian, and sometimes postmodern, West requires that more attention be given to *missiology for western culture.*

b. The resurgence of world and tribal *religions* necessitates that at least certain schools or centers do research and *training for ministry to adherents of each.*

c. The linkage between secularization, the rise of religious fundamentalism, and the receptivity to the gospel engendered by militant expressions of the latter call for *research* and interpretation of the interrelationship.

d. The chaos that has resulted from the flood of missionaries entering former Communist countries encourages attention to *priorities and cooperation in mission.*

5. An ethos of pluralism and conflict

On the one hand, the shrinking of the globe and the migration of peoples have created a pluralistic world—not only in the sense that many religions live side by side, but philosophically that all are to be accepted as different facets of truth. On the other hand, beside this tolerant, accepting attitude is what Samuel P. Huntington has called "the clash of civilizations"—that is, the clash of civilizations or cultures where religion is often the greatest influence. He names eight: Western, Orthodox, Latin American, Chinese, Islamic, Hindu, Japanese, and African. As a foretaste of the coming conflicts he shows how more of the 59 major conflicts in the world in 1993 were between civilizations rather than within them (1996).

Implications for education:

a. The attitude of pluralism which has sapped missionary motivation needs to be addressed in courses on the theology of mission to *define the uniqueness of Christ* and *how the Spirit of God works* beyond the direct witness of the church.

b. The prominence of the world civilizations demands that among the mission study centers and training institutions there be those that focus *research and education on each major civilization.*

Political

Political trends like other trends are full of paradoxes: a multipolar world with only one superpower, political boundaries breached by the forces of communication and economics, and political instability after the cold war.

6. Multipolar unstable world with the end of the cold war

The collapse of Communism left only one superpower, but it also reduced the pressures to base political alliances on a relationship with one of the superpowers or a non-alligned block. The globalization of communications and trade has made alliances possible that ignore ideology or contiguity of land. The collapse of Communist control also let loose ethnic rivalries. The cold war was replaced by ethnic wars. Some 50 ongoing wars have swelled refugee ranks to 47 million (Myers, 18, 44).

Implications for education:

a. Educators must keep *alert* to discern the changing alliances and *flexible* enough to adopt to the *new opportunities* for mission that they provide.

b. The unrest calls for training in *relief and development* and *trauma ministries* that are sensitive to spiritual need while not exploiting human misery for spiritual ends.

c. The conflicts raise the need for attention to *issues of peace, justice, and conflict resolution*.

7. Closing front doors, opening back doors

An increasing number of countries have restricted access to traditional missionaries. Yet at the same time such phenomena as the globalization of the economy and the Trojan horse of Hong Kong slipping behind the bamboo curtain have opened the doors for bi-vocational missionaries.

Implications for education:

Educational institutions must *equip bi-vocational missionaries* by *intensive courses* and web-based and other *distance learning* throughout the world.

Social and Cultural

Globally societies and cultures are in crisis with the transitions and stresses of moving from the agricultural to the industrial to the information age, of the homogenizing force of western culture against the separating forces of ethnicities and civilizations, of urbanization, and of the changing roles of different segments of society.

8. Postmodern society has impacted but not replaced modern and traditional societies

The wave of postmodernism has joined modernism and traditionalism. Or from another perspective, the information age has joined the industrial and the agricultural. Yet in each case all three remain with their interacting tensions.

Implications for education:

a. Attention needs to be given to contextualizing the gospel for each audience.

b. Attention needs to be given to the *needs* and *increased receptivity* to the gospel of *people in transition*.

9. Homogenization and separation of cultures and civilizations

Western culture, together with the English language and popular music is homogenizing particularly the culture of youth in urban settings. At the same time we are experiencing the resurgence and clashing of ethnic cultures and the major world civilizations of which Huntington speaks.

Implications for education:

a. The homogenizing effect of western culture raises the opportunity to train students in *TESOL* as a means of entry and ministry and the need to learn from *those successful in ministering in western cultural contexts*.

b. The resurgence of ethnic cultures and civilizations raises the need to *equip Christian leaders* from these groups for mission and equip others with *cross-cultural skills*.

10. Urbanization, involving mixing and fragmentation

The world is increasingly becoming urbanized. By 2015, 17 of the 21 cities of over 10 million will be in the Two Thirds World (Myers, 41). With urbanization come the problems of the ghettoization and marginalization of the poor and some ethnic groups. Yet most major ethnolinguistic groups are found in the cities, and people who have recently moved to cities have proved to be more receptive to the gospel than they have been previously or will be later. Both have implications for mission planning.

Implications for education:

a. All schools of world mission will need *urban programs*.

b. Attention will need to be given to *community development programs*.

c. Church growth principles will need to analyze how urban situations affect *approaches to people groups* and the *timing of receptivity*.

11. The enlarging and restricting of women's roles

Even as women are acquiring increased opportunities and expectations in both the secular and religious world, they are being forced into more restrictive roles in other contexts by either government edict, as in the Taliban-controlled areas of Afghanistan, or by social pressure in places of Islamist resurgence. Except in life expectancy, women in the developing world lag behind men significantly in literacy, school enrollment, and the labor force (Myers, 46).

Implications for education:

a. In the light of the enlarging of various women's roles, this needs to be *reflected in mission school faculties.*

b. In the light of the restricting of women's roles in some contexts, women students may need to learn to

  • *give up some of their rights* for Christ's sake in order to identify with other women

  • be *sensitive agents of change* also for Christ's sake.

c. In the light of the lag of women behind men in areas such as education, many missionaries need to acquire *basic skills in teaching reading* to women.

12. The developing world gets younger while the developed world gets older

Birthrates are low, and life expectancy is increasing in the developed world while the population is burgeoning in the Two Thirds World. Currently one-third of the world is under 15 years of age, with 85 percent of these children in the developing world (Myers, 40).

A global youth culture is developing—non-Christian, united by MTV, rejecting the past, and focusing on the now.

Implications for education:

If we do not provide equipping in *international youth ministries,* our students will increasingly be ill prepared for the largest and growing segment of the developing world.

Economic

Contrasts abound in the economic trends—an increasingly global economy with regional power blocks, resource relocation with concomitant chaos, and a widening gap between the rich and the poor.

13. Globalization and regionalization of economies

The collapse of state socialism in the areas formerly dominated by the Soviet Union and its modification in China has left a worldwide market capitalism. At the same time regional power blocks are being formed in Europe with the Common Market and the Euro, North America with NAFTA, East Asia, China, and the Muslim nations. Increasingly economy rather than politics determines alliances, making new bridges for Christian contacts.

Implications for education:

The new bridges for witness that the economic alliances are providing raise the need for

- the *missiological training of global Christian businesspersons.*
- education in the *use of money to effect* such *Kingdom goals* as the betterment of people's quality of life.

14. Resource relocation with resultant shifting economic strength, chaos, and potential for interrelated collapses

In the 1970s wealth shifted to the OPEC nations, largely Muslim, then in the 1980s to the Pacific Rim, which in the late 1990s has experienced decline. The capital flowing to Southeast Asia dropped from $93 billion to $12 billion from 1996 to 1997 (Garten 1998, A19). African economies have largely been in decline, exacerbated by strife and drought, except for pockets of new wealth from, for example, oil in Equatorial Guinea. The shift in wealth has allowed countries like Korea to expand their missionary force, though recent financial reverses have made this more difficult. Chaos results from economies in transition, where $1.5 trillion in foreign exchange dealings take place every day, much instantly with a computer keystroke (Garten, A19). The tightening web of interconnection of the global market means that instability in one area can affect the whole.

Implications for education:

a. The shifting economic strength allows *strengthened regions to assume a greater proportion of the cost* of missiological education.

b. The potential for the rapid collapse of regional economies

- argues against multinational schools basing *too much of their financial base on one national group.*
- encourages *flexibility* to adapt to rapidly changing conditions.

c. The financial chaos and potential for collapse encourages training for rapid deployment of relief *and development.*

15. A widening gap between the wealthy and burgeoning poor

The gap between wealthy and poor is both between regions and within regions. The Northern Hemisphere overpowers the Southern in per capita GNP, with North America, Germany, and Japan monopolizing almost half the world's income. The richest 20 percent of the world have 85 percent of the global income. In parts of Latin America the income share of the richest 20 percent of the population is 15 times that of the poorest 20 percent (Myers, 22-24, 47).

The poorest are marginalized. The combined national debts of the developing world are $1.8 trillion (Myers, 24). Yet with global trade, electronic knowledge, and communications in other hands, they have little chance to escape from poverty. By 2025 it is estimated that more than one-fourth of the world will be in poverty. Eighty-five percent of the poorer countries are in the unevangelized world (Myers 25, 41). It is the Pentecostal and charismatic churches that have mushroomed among the poor in regions like Latin America and helped them raise their standard of living.

Implications for education:

The extent of poverty requires that mission education

- highlight a *theology and ministry* of serving *with and for the poor.*
- teach the use of programs and money in a way that will *empower and enhance the condition of the poor* without creating dependency.

Technological

New technology has put most of the world on the information superhighway.

16. Information and communication explosion, while pockets served less

Most of the world is on the Internet, and much of what remains has e-mail. Only Africa has major areas off the highway. The new technologies provide opportunities for consultation and collaboration between missionaries, crossing boundaries into "closed" countries, computer assisted translation, and resources by CD-ROM and desktop publishing. At the same time some strife-torn or marginalized areas have deteriorating communications.

Implications for education:

a. New technologies present the challenge to help students

- be *computer literate.*
- make *technology a servant* rather than a master.
- learn to *discern useful knowledge* from information.

b. Distance education can be enhanced by *Web-based interactive instruction* that is supplemented by on-location mentoring and fellowship.

Ecclesiastical and Missional

In both the church and its mission there have been major changes in the vitality of regions, branches of the church, and forms in which mission is expressed.

17. Shift in geographical and vital center of gravity of the church from the West and North to the East and South

While Christians remain about one third of the growing population of the world, much of the church in the West, especially in post-Christian Europe, has been in decline. The center of gravity of the church moved from the West in the early 1970s. By 1985 non-western Christians began to compensate for the decline in the West and by the year 2000 will represent more than two-thirds of Christians (Johnstone 25).

The largest number of Christians in Asia is in the Philippines (61 million), China (61 million), India (33 million), and Indonesia (25 million). The largest Christian minorities of the larger countries and administrative districts are South Korea (35 percent), Hong Kong (14 percent), Indonesia (13 percent), and Singapore (12 percent) (Myers, 35).

Implications for education:

The shift in the center of gravity of the church calls on western/northern institutions to

- *partner with overseas institutions* and agencies to provide what they need and want, especially in countries or localities with the maximum potential for missionary outreach.
- *develop distance learning*, with interaction, to provide the desired education in students' ministry location.
- increase *funding for international leaders who need specializations* best obtained in the West/North.
- with sensitivity to the "brain drain," *appoint international faculty* to bring relevance to the world scene and insights for witness in the post-Christian West.
- expand the *study of world and tribal religions*.

18. Increased diversity and unity as western mainline Protestant churches decline and the more evangelical, charismatic, and postdenominational ones multiply, often in new forms

During Christianity's decline in the West, evangelical growth has been slow in the West but significant in the non-west. With over half of Christians now in the non-western world, 77 percent of these non-western Christians are expected to be evangelicals by the year 2000. The growth is even greater among Pentecostals and charismatics, since they now represent more than half the evangelicals (Johnstone, 25-26).

Also among the evangelicals are growing numbers of postdenominational or "new apostolic" churches. Many of the independent or indigenous churches in Africa, for example, could also be considered evangelical or charismatic. They have their own indigenous or more charismatic worship forms. Many of the leaders of these growing churches have little formal education.

The increasing proportion of Christians who are evangelicals coupled with the networking organizations like the Lausanne Committee, AD 2000 and Beyond, the World Evangelical Fellowship, and INTERDEV have brought greater unity and cooperation in the diversity.

Implications for education:

a. The *growth of Evangelicals and Pentecostals/Charismatics, especially overseas*, means that schools of world mission have a lot to *learn from them*.

b. The indigenous worship forms call for education in *ethnomusicology and worship*.

c. The *low formal education* of many of the *leaders* of growing churches means that educational institutions must be *alert and flexible to work out educational programs tailored to them* as they see the need for more depth.

19. Indigenization and internationalization of mission

As Christianity has globalized, indigenous missions have sprung up around the world. South Korea, for example, has well over 5,000 missionaries. This year the Two Thirds World will send more cross-cultural Protestant missionaries than the West. Mission teams are being comprised of personnel from different nationalities and different sending agencies. In some cases North Americans are supporting Christian missionaries from another country to go to a third country.

Implications for education:

The indigenization and internationalization of mission requires that mission schools in the West

- equip students to *remain learners who are flexible and empower others.*
- present *varieties of models of mission.*
- equip students with *specializations to complement* other team members.
- *partner* with international mission institutions and agencies.

20. Declining mission interest and confusion in some circles while increased interest and confidence in others

There has been a decline in world mission interest and activity in mainstream Protestantism. One cause has been theological—a turn toward universalism and away from a view of the lostness of those without Christ, a focus on dialogue but not on evangelism, a healthy broadened view of the gospel to include human rights and ethics but where evangelism unfortunately has gotten diffused, and the view that "the church is mission" which should make mission central but which further diffused evangelism.

Another cause was not giving adequate attention to the millions who still required cross-cultural evangelism when missions were turned over to national churches. Sociologically when ethnic conflict began to involve sending churches, their enthusiasm for cross-cultural mission waned.

Some of the same influences and results are also found among conservative evangelicals. Some evangelicals are allowing, for example, that salvation does not depend on the respondent knowing specifically about the historical Jesus. Such attitudes can lessen the sense of urgency of mission (Covell 1991, 12-17). There has been a decline in applications for career service in many traditional evangelical mission agencies like Wycliffe Bible Translators.

At the same time there is increased interest, focus, and optimism concerning mission in other circles. Since 1975 the number evangelized (i.e., having an opportunity to understand the gospel) has outstripped the number of non-Christians, though the percentage of Christians has remained about one third of the world. The remaining task is clearer. Through the Adopt-a-People Clearing House, the remaining major unreached ethnolinguistic groups are known and are being adopted by churches and missions.

Through the efforts of the Lausanne Committee for World Evangelization, AD 2000 and Beyond, and the World Evangelical Fellowship coordinated efforts are being made in church planting, especially in the 10-40 window (Africa and Asia between the 10th and 40th degree latitude) with considerable church growth. Clear planning is being done with optimism as was evident at the Global Consultation on World Evangelization in Pretoria in 1997 under the auspices of AD 2000 and Beyond.

Implications for education:

a. The theological confusion in the church demands the clear enunciation of a *theology of mission* that deals with issues such as the *uniqueness of Christ* and the *condition of humans* who have not heard of Christ.

b. The *guidelines for honoring and empowering national churches* while not neglecting *unreached people groups* nearby will need treatment in *theory of mission* classes.

c. Educational institutions need to complement the cooperative efforts in mission by *partnering with other institutions* abroad and in North America.

21. Decline in traditional mission models and rise of new

There has been a general decline in traditional career missionaries provided by churches, educated in seminary or Bible college mission programs, and sent by denominational or interdenominational mission agencies. Instead, more are going as short-termers as a result of the current ethos of short-term commitments, family considerations, finances, or the increase of countries closed to traditional missionaries. These short-termers are often specialists rather than generalists, tentmakers, volunteers without normal pay, retirees, or nonresidential missionaries facilitating others to enter restricted countries. Some go to focus on specific concerns like prayer, peace and justice, or religious liberty. Others go as career missionaries but leave prematurely because of such family concerns as education of children or personnel conflicts (see Taylor 1997).

For many missionaries local churches provide their own training and serve as the sending agency. Many new multidenominational or nondenominational agencies have arisen that are quite entrepreneurial and also provide their own training like Youth with a Mission, Operation Mobilization, Frontiers, Campus Crusade, and Pioneers.

Implications for education:

a. The growth of short-term missions calls on schools of mission to
   - provide *intensive modular training* for those who do not want an extended degree program
   - *integrate short-term mission experience* into the equipping of pre-service students.

b. The high attrition rate of career missionaries demands that schools address such issues as *family concerns* and *conflict resolution*.

c. The growth of the prayer movement raises the need for *discerning guidance on biblical prayer*.

d. Since churches, often with little experience, are providing their own missionary training, schools need to seek ways to *train the trainers* or provide *intensive training for the churches*.

e. Likewise schools should seek to *train the trainers* in the new mission agencies and/or *contract with them to provide training* in specific areas.

North American Contexts

North America, of course, participates and will participate in the world trends; so there is no need to reiterate what has been said above other than to highlight how some of them are manifested in the North American context.

1. Erosion of Christian and traditional values despite religious observances

The secularization of modernity ushered in the rejection of traditional and religious authority, and postmodernity brought a lack of confidence even in reason and facilitated the fragmentation of society (trends 4 and 8). The result is the rise of antisocial behavior in crime and drug use, the breakdown of the family, the decline of voluntary associations, and the increase of self indulgence in the "now generation." At the same time church attendance remains relatively high, and eastern religions like Buddhism and Hinduism or their ideas in New Age thought are on the increase.

Implications for education:

Schools must increasingly apply the skills of cross-cultural mission in a *missiology for western culture*.

2. Increasing mosaic of cultures coupled with isolationism

This increase is a result of political instability (trend 6) and the attempt for economic and social betterment (trend 15), but it brings the peoples and religions of the world to our doorstep. Metropolitan areas, as the name implies, gather many peoples. At the same time the United States became more isolationist with the evacuation of troops from Somalia and with the skepticism among the boomers of the value of such ventures.

Implications for education:

a. Schools must equip students for *cross-cultural ministry in North America*

b. *"Cross-cultural" mission needs to be redefined,* since it is no longer necessarily "foreign" mission. On the one hand, cross-cultural mission can take place in North America, and a foreign student can come here, minister among his or her own people, and not be cross-cultural.

3. Decline of congregational involvement in foreign missions with increased involvement in their local context

This shift in mission emphasis is an expression of the decline of traditional models of mission and the rise of new (trend 21) and the confusion and decline of foreign mission interest in some circles, with increased confidence and interest in others (trend 20). It also expresses increased focus on the local context (trend 3). What makes it significant here is the dominant role that North America has had in providing personnel and funds for foreign mission in the past. Yet the donor base is graying, and the majority of the growing churches in North America are ethnic churches which, except for the Koreans, have not had a major interest in foreign mission.

Implications for education:

Schools need to *equip churches for local mission* and use this as a <u>bridge for their involvement globally</u>.

4. Increase in evangelical mission faculties while some mainline Protestant seminaries have trouble finding professors of mission

This again is a reflection of the decline in traditional models of mission and the rise of new (trend 21) and the confusion and decline in mission interest in some circles with increased interest and confidence in others (trend 20).

Implications for education:

The increase in North American evangelical mission faculties when even many evangelicals are bypassing the traditional missionary establishment suggests they

- look for ways to *partner with each other* to avoid unnecessary duplication.

- find ways to *train the trainers* and *contract with the local churches and new mission structures* that provide training for the new breed of missionary.

Resultant Education

Missiological education for the future must be focused by a biblical vision, driven by values such as those suggested and be relevant to future trends to the extent that we can discern them. Each institution, however, will need to prioritize the values and implications of the trends for the learners they have and the purpose of the institution, since a given institution can only do a limited number of tasks well. I shall indicate how some of the educational implications of the trends relate to the components of a missiological program. (For a description of the components, see Elliston 1996, 237-256).

Learner Selection

The above trends suggest the following learner selection for North American schools of mission:

1. *International students* should
   - be selected by *demonstrated leadership in ministry contexts*
   - be preferably *leaders of leaders*
   - be brought to North America only for *equipping or specialization not available* in their homeland
   - be in *strategic roles or locations*
2. *Proven leaders* with *inadequate formal education* should
   - be treated *flexibly*
   - be offered what will *deepen and enhance their ministry*
3. *North American students* can be
   - *pre-service*
   - *short-term*
   - *bi-vocational*
   - *career missionaries*

Content

Since the purpose of mission education is equipping disciples as leaders to make disciples, the content should foster being, knowing, doing, and impacting others.

1. The *core competencies* must include the interaction of
   - *Word*—a biblical theology of mission
   - *World*—help from such behavioral sciences as anthropology to understand cultures and how to communicate between them
   - *Church*—lessons from mission history and church growth
   - *Learner*—what she/he brings and how to *develop as a leader*

2. Other *general competencies* the trends suggest are
   - leadership
   - research methods
   - computer literacy
   - models of mission
   - family concerns
   - conflict resolution
   - discernment in prayer
   - ethnomusicology and worship
3. All *schools of the future* should *include* studies on
   - urban ministry
   - international and community development
   - Islam as the major non-Christian religion
   - international youth ministries
4. *Partnering schools between them* should *include* studies of
   - the major *unreached peoples and civilizations,* including western
   - world and tribal religions
   - secularism, modernism, and postmodernism
   - empowering the poor
   - global economics for Kingdom ends
   - TESOL and literacy
   - Bible translation

Location

With the geographical and vital center of gravity of world Christianity in the non-west, North American schools of mission need to adapt.

1. North American institutions can train North Americans and a few internationals on their central campuses, but for most international students these institutions will need to develop *overseas partnerships* where
   - *local persons have control* to the extent that *accrediting organizations,* if applicable, allow
   - *local faculty* are used to the *extent possible*
   - *costs* are determined by the perceived value and the students' and community's *ability to pay*
   - students can *remain in ministry*

- local churches, mentors, and school community can facilitate *spiritual formation*
- *local institutions* and agencies are encouraged to *cooperate together*

2. North American institutions will increasingly need to develop *delivery systems* for *distance education*:
   - *interactive web-based education*, CD-ROM, teleconferencing and interactive video at the learners' levels of capability
   - supplemented by on-location *mentoring* and a *community* for fellowship

No matter how sophisticated the possibilities are, ultimately the purpose of missiological education is to equip Christ's disciples to make disciples among all peoples. Therefore, it must always include the model of the Master Teacher, incarnating the gospel in a particular cultural context so that others might do the same.

References

Barrett, David B. and Todd M. Johnson

    1990   *Our Globe and How to Reach It: Seeing the World Evangelized by AD 2000 and Beyond* (Birmingham, AL: Women's Missionary Union).

    1999   "Annual Statistical Table on Global Mission: 1999," *International Bulletin of Missionary Research*, 15, No. 1 (January), 12-17.

Covell, Ralph R.

    1991   "The Christian Gospel and World Religions: How Much Have American Evangelicals Changed?" *International Bulletin of Missionary Research*, 15, No. 1 (January), 12-17.

Elliston, Edgar J.

    1996   "Moving Forward from Where We Are in Missiological Education," *Missiological Education for the 21st Century: The Book, the Circle, and the Sandals*. J. Dudley Woodberry, Charles Van Engen, and Edgar J. Elliston, eds. (Maryknoll NY: Orbis Books), 232-256.

Garten, Jeffrey E.

    1998   "Adrift in the Global Economy" *New York Times* (May 11), A19.

Huntington, Samuel P.

    1996   *The Clash of Civilizations* (New York: Simon and Schuster).

Johnstone, Patrick

    1993   *Operation World*, 5th ed. (Grand Rapids, MI: Zondervan Publishing House).

Myers, Bryant

    1997   "The New Context of World Mission," *Mission Handbook: 1998-2000*, John A. Siewert and Edna G. Valdez, eds. (Monrovia, CA: MARC), 5-56.

Taylor, William

    1997   *Too Valuable to Lose: Exploring the Causes and Cures of Missionary Attrition* (Pasadena CA: William Carey Library Publishers).

Information Technology and the Communication of the Gospel

John A. Siewert

Introduction and Background

This paper was written as a "status paper" for the Information Technology and the Communication of the Gospel work group at the Congress on the World Mission of the Church. The assigned purpose was to "outline where we seem to be [in world mission] at this moment in terms of the use of information technology in the communication of the Gospel." Due to the restricted length of the paper, it deals with the most well known facet of information technology (IT), the Internet. Current uses of the Internet are reviewed in relation to missionary sending/support activities (initially modeled in Acts 13:1-3) and by those sent to "make disciples of all nations, . . . teaching them to obey everything that I [Jesus] have commanded . . ." (Matthew 28:18-20).

Given the overall purpose of this paper, the examples of IT activities discussed are drawn from a broad spectrum of world mission and support activities. It is not the purpose to indicate strengths and weaknesses of the ways IT is used but to highlight "what is." The reader also needs to keep in mind this paper was for a meeting about world mission. On the World Wide Web (the Web) there is much about religion and a wide spectrum of ideas about God (see *God on the Internet* by Mark Kellner, *www.markkellner.com*), significantly less about Christianity, and relatively little of substance about the Christian world mission.

Since there are Website references throughout this paper, readers with access to the Web can also view illustrative and other additional materials. However, the paper does stand on its own for those not wishing to also view "live" examples. Some of the Websites may have been further developed and expanded since this paper was written. Therefore, the Web references have given an expanded meaning to the guidelines of the Congress committee who asked that the status papers show where we seem to be "at this moment." This was the case for the original users of the paper who received it well in advance of the Congress and even more so for current readers after the Congress.

What eventually became the Internet got its start in 1969 as a USA Government project known as ARPAnet. The new packet switching technique used enabled network resources to be shared more efficiently than the older circuit switching technique. It also allowed segments of the network to operate independently without a central physical facility. Throughout the 1970s and 1980s various developments made the Internet easier to use by non-specialists. A major advance took place at the University of Illinois in 1993 with the development of the "browser," a graphical user interface to the Web with "point-and-click" features.

Time magazine had a July 1994 cover story entitled "The Strange New World of the Internet" which, along with other media, brought the wonders of the Internet to the attention of the general public. In the Christian press, *Christianity Today* in April 1995 had a cover story entitled "Cybershock: Can the church keep pace with the new information culture?" by Timothy C. Morgan with reporting and sidebar stories by Helen Lee. The October 1995 *Christian Century* had an article by John Ottenhoff (*www.alma.edu/Academics/English/ ottenhoff/ottenhoffs*) "The World Wide Web: Taking the plunge" (*www.alma.edu/Academics/English/ottenhoff/plunge*).

Even before the Internet became popular, the mission community was using it. On home leave from Africa, missionary Richard Chowning hooked into the computer center at Abilene Christian University in Texas. His article "Missions and Information Technology" in the April 1994 issue of the *Journal of Applied Missiology* (*sam.acu.edu/academics/missions/jam/techno.htm*), tells how he and other missionaries took advantage of improved communications from their networked PCs. Erkki Sutinen wrote an article in the October 1994 issue of the *International Review of Mission*, describing how computer networking was increasing mission interest in Finland at the support level: "In conjunction with the Internet . . . the Freenet bulletin board gives information both on missionary work in various countries and on current issues. . . . As a worldwide net the Internet discussions are frequently quite personal and profound."

Electronic Mail (E-mail)

E-mail is an early aspect of IT that has become well known and continues to grow in use. The advantages of e-mail go beyond the benefits of message transmission to many places in the world within minutes at a low cost. Along with a host of other features, one can quickly "cut-and-paste" parts of previous correspondence, include immediate copies to others who may need to be aware of the communication, quickly attach other computer files, etc. However, since standard e-mail documents are restricted to plain text, messages look like they were composed on an old typewriter without the benefit of contemporary font styles, bold or italicized type, etc. But it is still very readable and speeds the flow of communication and collaboration, enabling group objectives to be accomplished more effectively. Organizations that standardize on high level packages, such as IBM/Lotus NotesMail software, can incorporate more readable type styles and formatting, as well as graphics, for a more effective communication medium.

By the early 1990s, mission agencies such as World Radio Missionary Fellowship, Southern Baptist International Mission Board, World Vision, Wycliffe Bible Translators, and others were using software packages such as cc:Mail for daily, or more frequent, e-mail exchange through telephone connections. As commercial e-mail services such as CompuServe became available overseas, they were, and still are, also used by quite a number of mission agencies.

The greatest impact of e-mail and other Internet communication forms has been the increased information flow among missionaries, field offices, home offices, local churches and individual prayer and financial supporters. This has led to more informed prayer, strategic planning, decision making, and associated activities. The organizational culture and management style of an organization is a significant factor in how much impact e-mail and other IT technologies can have on increasing the overall effectiveness of an organization. In terms of gaining flexibility and lowering costs, a missionary with a large USA board has written that "e-mail has more than revolutionized our office communications here in Buenos Aires. Probably 95% of all mail sent/ received from our [USA] home and [Ecuador] administrative area offices is through e-mail." Another mission agency reports that the speed, accessibility, closed conferencing, and lower costs of e-mail have enabled their international leadership team to have greater discussion of issues beforehand and "arrive to strategy meetings much better prepared."

In terms of individual missionaries using e-mail, the ministry situation, personal style, national relationships, etc., have much to do with the difference it can make. Recently a person with over 40 years of experience in overseas ministries, USA pastorates, and theological education expressed his view from Central Europe. He is involved in church leadership development and had recently became a personal user of e-mail. He said, "I've gotten online and am now communicating with church leaders in Siberia [where he had taught short courses the previous November], Moscow [where he taught in March], Kinshasa [where he had taught and served in the 60s and 70s], and Israel [where he served in the 70s and 80s], and with USA churches. What a difference e-mail makes!!!" But the effects of e-mail go beyond internal organizational activities and are changing the context in which mission takes place. Mark Elliott, editor of the *East-West Church & Ministry Report,* who has served in teaching posts in Russia, has pointed out that e-mail was a factor in helping to spread the truth during the critical early days of the Communist abortive coup attempt in 1991. Regarding the recent Russian law restricting religious freedom, Elliott writes in a Fall 1997 editorial about international pressure and wonders "if e-mail may make it difficult, if not impossible, for local Russian authorities to engage in religious repression without word reaching the whole country and the West in record time."

But there are some aspects of e-mail that have raised questions in the missions community. Andrew Schachtel, an area director of the international evangelical mission Interserve (*www.interserve.org*) in Cyprus, explained in an article why he sees e-mail as a mixed blessing. "I wonder if e-mail will make it harder for new cross-cultural workers to 'let go' of their own cultures and integrate well into new ones." Schachtel, who describes himself as "a frequent and enthusiastic user of e-mail," warns missionaries that "unless e-mail is used with discipline, it may become a strong electronic umbilical cord to our mother culture, so that we log on religiously each morning and evening to all our friends 'at home'" (*GO* magazine, First Quarter 1998).

Some smaller agencies have found it more effective to use an outside provider for all their e-mail services. Large agencies sometimes find it advantageous to use a service provider for part of their e-mail network. More than 150 mission and other Christian agencies use e-mail services from Mission Aviation Fellowship (*www.maf.org*). MAF's Information Technology Division (*www.xc.org*) provides e-mail, e-conferencing, Web-hosting, and other IT services such as radio and satellite links for telephone, voice, and e-mail.

E-Mail Newsletters, E-Mail Conferences, and Websites

These three aspects of the Internet are grouped together because they are often used in conjunction with each other.

E-mail newsletters are transmitted to one's e-mailbox directly from the publisher, and can go to a few or thousands of recipients. There are no postage costs or other mailing costs, if the computer equipment and Internet connection already exists. Some e-mail newsletters have an associated e-mail conference for those wanting to discuss subjects raised by the newsletter articles.

E-mail conferences route e-mail messages to all participants who in turn can easily respond with comments through their PC's reply function. In an unmoderated conference the response is immediately delivered (posted) to all subscribers. In moderated conferences, messages are reviewed for relevancy and appropriateness before being posted. One can always "unsubscribe" to a conference and no longer receive postings. Conferences usually include some "lurkers" who read postings but rarely, if ever, respond. Conferences may be closed, that is, restricted to a certain group. Among other features of e-mail conferences are digest version files where all messages posted during a week or month are stored in a shortened form to be retrieved by new subscribers or others wanting to see the discussion flow of select time periods. Conference topics may be on a general subject like historical mission research, a specific focus like the evangelization of a particular people group, or a closed conference of an organization's planning group. Key to a conference is the moderator/coordinator.

Websites can serve as newsletters, conferences and general information servers and in other ways. Most e-mail newsletters and conferences also have descriptive and other information on a related Website. In the early stages of an organization's Website development, content is usually much like conventional printed magazine pages. This can be created with a wordprocessor such as WordPerfect and converted to the HyperText Markup Language (HTML) required by the Website. As communications and IT staffs of an organization become more experienced in the new media, the interactive capabilities of the Web are usually put to better use and new kinds of content and format presentations are added. To ease the implementation of Web presentations, Web authoring tools, such as Microsoft's FrontPage, are available. FrontPage is the leading IT tool of this type among mission organizations.

There was a PC-based means of sending messages through telephone connections before the Internet become available to the general public. It is known as a bulletin board system (BBS), and also has computer file exchange and other features. The convenience and availability of the Internet and Web replaced BBSs for the most part. An early BBS network was established among several denominations in the late 1980s by Ecunet, a coalition of denominations. Now based on the Internet (*ecunet.org*), its member networks serve broad purposes.

IT has brought a new dimension to communications between missionaries and their support group. From countries where a reasonable e-mail connection is available, "as-it-happens" letters may be e-mailed directly from the field and read by a personal support group within minutes. For a broader distribution where some editing may be needed, a single copy can be e-mailed to a USA distribution point and then distributed. It can reach those with e-mail within a day or two, and for those with only postal mail connections within a week.

Some organizations take missionary communications to another level utilizing the Web (see the Newsstand section of *www.bgc.bethel.edu*). IT tools enable the quick conversion of the plain text of e-mail into a more graphically appealing look, including pictures if available, and placed on a Website within days for wider distribution beyond the e-mail and postal versions. In such an atmosphere of immediacy, newsletters usually take on new meaning.

A good example of expanded mission information sharing and cooperation through the various forms of the Internet is Brigada (*www.brigada.org*), designed by Doug Lucas as a "gateway to missions networking." There are now over 9,000 subscribers to the weekly e-mail newsletter *Brigada Today*. All one needs to do to subscribe is send an e-mail to *hub@xc.org* with the words "subscribe brigada" (without quotes) in the body of the message. There have been as many as 100 different Brigada e-mail conferences going at the same time with people from all over the world participating. These range from specific interests such as praying for the Yanadi people in India, to general subjects such as travel advice and tips. The current conferences are listed on the Brigada Website and can be subscribed to with a single e-mail command.

World mission organizations using all aspects of the Internet for communication with supporters, home staff, missionaries, and national partners is increasing steadily. The following are a few examples: AD2000 & Beyond Movement (*www.ad2000.org*), American Baptist Churches International Ministries (*www.abc-im.org*), ABWE (*www.abwe.org*), Caleb Project (*www.cproject.com*), Evangelical Lutheran Church in American Global Mission (*elca.org/dgm*), Presbyterian Church (U.S.A.) Worldwide Ministries (*www.pcusa.org/pcusa/mission.htm*), SIM (*www.sim.org/sim.html*), and World Vision (*www.worldvision.org*).

Websites from Non-Western Countries

The India Missions Association (IMA) comprises about 100 national Indian mission agencies. Their Website (*www.inmissions.org*) gives data on India in terms of ethnic, linguistic, and postal code categories. For example, IMA has compiled data on the 953 castes and tribes in India, of which nearly 204 are "totally unreached." IMA also lists on their Website individual categories (*www.inmissions.org/send.htm*) of Christians who could be helpful in the work of missions in India. These include physicians, teachers, and development project designers among others. Also a category that may come as a surprise to North Americans: "Software professionals to set up multi media, WAN, mainframe, etc." They also have a weekly e-mail newsletter covering salient events in India. To be added to their list, see *www.inmissions.org/ frmmail.html*.

In Latin America there are several mission and evangelism agencies with Web sites in Spanish, Portuguese, and English for information sharing and other communication. One of them, Comibam Internacional (*www.comibam.org*), has extensive information about missionaries sent from Latin America to other parts of the world and cross-cultural mission work within Latin America. This information is presented in various forms including full-color materials that can be downloaded to one's PC and used with presentation software such as PowerPoint.

Among other non-western Websites useful to USA world mission agencies is the Amity News Service of the China Christian Council (*www.hk.super.net/ ~amityhk/home.htm*) and Antioch City, fulfilling its 1994 vision of "creating an electronic network of information, riding the Internet, for the body of Christ to access" (*www.antioch.com.sg*). Leading English language newspapers from other countries, like the South China Morning Post (*www.scmp.com*) and the India Times (*www.india-times.com*) are useful for those preparing to go there.

Conferences and Other Activities Focusing on It and World Mission

Global Mapping International (*www.gmi.org*) was involved in the early development of IT applications to assist in world evangelization. Their first training conference in September 1987 included workshops on computer-based mapping, research databases, and electronic networks. They continue to conduct technical training seminars in the USA and Third World and recently instituted the GMI Research Fellow program that provides a formal affiliation with recognized scholars pursuing research in areas central to the GMI mission "of giving Christian ministries access to mission information."

The International Conference on Computing and Missions (*www.iccm.org*) is an annual gathering that first met at Taylor University in Upland, Indiana in June 1989. It is primarily a community of Christian IT practitioners who meet to learn from each other about advances in technology and mission computing opportunities. The 1998 sessions from Abilene Christian University in Abilene, Texas were available to remote participants with RealPlayer software through live video webcasts. These continue to be available on their Website.

One of the first organizations to share missions information online was the Southern Baptist International Mission Board. In July 1989 they made available their World Evangelization Database in Videotex format. Today their Global Research Office (*www.imb.org/missionaries/globalresearch*) functions as the internal strategic information center within their Office of Overseas Operations and continues to make available key global information that can be viewed online or downloaded into one's PC.

In June 1995 the Committee on Common Witness held a conference on Christian advocacy, communications and missions entitled "The Global Information Infrastructure, The Justice Agenda, The Churches." This brought together 100 church leaders, communications specialists, and industry representatives in Washington D.C. at Catholic University with its up-to-date digital computing facilities. Featured were demonstrations and panel discussions on the global impact of IT. One of the ongoing efforts discussed at the conference was Worldwide Faith News (*www.wfn.org*), an online "searchable data base of official full text news releases and other documents, including policy, from the news offices of the national and world faith groups." This went online later that year on December 24, 1995.

The Overseas Ministries Study Center (*www.omsc.org*) in November 1995 hosted a week-long seminar on "The Missionary Journey on the Information Superhighway." This was followed by a 2-day study group of senior mission leaders on the theme "The Information Superhighway: Which Way for Christian Missions?" This brought together those on the forefront of mission IT applications with senior mission leaders from a wide spectrum of affiliations to consider world mission and IT.

The most far-reaching use thus far of IT for expanding participation in a missions conference event and encouraging ongoing worldwide mission initiatives is most likely the Urbana 96 World Mission Convention for Students (*urbana.org*). InterVarsity Christian Fellowship sponsored the event at the University of Illinois in Urbana-Champaign, Illinois, December 27-31, 1996. There was no shortage of participants at the site as over 19,000 gathered in the huge Assembly Hall with live video fed to a nearby auditorium for several hundred that wouldn't fit into the meeting hall. Still pictures, text, and some live audio and video went out on the Web. It is estimated that thousands participated remotely through the "Urbana Live" webcasts. Perhaps more importantly were the ongoing connections through the Web after the convention for the 9,873 who at the convention committed or recommitted themselves to mission service ranging from summer involvement to life work as a missionary.

New organizational forms have been created to help meet the technical needs of the IT challenge. An example is the International Christian Technologists' Association (*www.gospelcom.net/icta*). ICTA is activating a global network of Christians working in IT fields to assist the church in implementing behind-the-scenes technology that can be used to further the kingdom of God through improved communications and information sharing among global ministries.

Catholic Information Technology Initiatives

NewTech 98 (*www.newtech.org/proceedings_en.htm*) was a Catholic-sponsored conference attended by Catholic Church leaders from around the world as well as participants from various Catholic communications and educational institutions. From the IT industry, there were experts from companies such as Microsoft and IBM Global Services. The opening speaker was Archbishop John Foley, president of the Pontifical Council for Social Communications in Rome. His topic, "Announcing the good news to a new millennium: the new media and the task of evangelization," framed the purpose of the conference.

Workshops and presentations were given by leaders of several highly visible Catholic projects. Franciscan Sister Judith Zoebelein led a work group session that dealt with practical issues in Website development such as navigation, structure, content organization and security. Sister Zoebelein is technical director of the Internet Office of the Holy See, and has responsibility for the overall direction of the Vatican Website (*www.vatican.va*). Pope John Paul II gives strong support to such projects, recently saying that "with the advent of computer telecommunications . . . the church is offered further means of fulfilling her mission" (*Christian Century*, Dec. 17, 1997).

A session on adapting the new technologies for evangelization was led by Brother Woodworth, a Benedictine monk leader of the nextScribe Studios (*www.nextscribe.org*), described as a "highly focused world-class endeavor . . . in the technological, creative and managerial state of digital content creation." One of their projects is tracking the state of current technology and trends to understand "the differences in technological access by geographical, cultural and other demographic criteria, in order to assist the development of content for targeted audiences."

Mission, Evangelism, and Information Technology

Does IT have a role in the communication of the gospel in direct evangelism? Can the online medium help persuade people to make a life change? In April 1997, ninety-one people gathered in Naperville, Illinois for the Internet Evangelism Consultation (*www.wheaton.edu/bgc/ioe/Inevco/ summaryreport.html*). Many attendees were already involved in some facet of evangelism and the Internet. For an example see the article by Tina Kirsch about Christianity Online in the April 1998 issue of *World Evangelism* Magazine (*www.lausanne.org/we498/498kirsc*). The purpose of the consultation was "to explore ways the awesome potential of the Internet can be harnessed to the task of communicating the Gospel of Jesus Christ to a lost world."

SOON Gospel Literature based in the U.K. sees the Web as a means of extending their outreach. They are an evangelistic literature ministry using direct mail and other means to distribute their free quarterly small-type one-page *SOON!* magazine. It has short stories of general interest that usually end with a Christian message. Besides English, it is also printed in seven other languages. A free Bible course in simplified form is offered. *SOON!* is now on the Web (*soon.org.uk*) as "an easy-English web magazine" and being accessed "from every part of the world." The Web enables them to do more things than were possible on two sides of a sheet of paper and with the potential of a larger audience. They have found "internet evangelism exciting, rewarding, and challenging" (*www.brigada.org/today/articles/web-evangelism.html*).

Some, however, feel that life-changing decisions will not be made in response to online communication, and that referrals over the Internet for personal counseling will not be heeded. Reed Jolley, in his essay on "Apostle to Generation X: C. S. Lewis and the Future of Evangelism" (in *C. S. Lewis: Lightbearer in the Shadowlands*, edited by Amgus J. L. Menuge), says that Generation X, roughly those in their twenties and early thirties, "feel the heavy weight of living in a technological society. Though, in increasing numbers, they 'surf the net,' chat on their cellular phones, and send e-mail, they sense their depersonalization in our 'accelerated culture.'" Jolly doesn't see the Internet having a role in evangelizing the X Generation. In his opinion, "if we desire to reach Generation X for Jesus, it will not be through a modem. E-mail will make few disciples of Jesus Christ. Only a more personal model will suffice."

The Expanding Electronic Networked World: One of the "New Facts" of Our Time

The late missionary and church leader Lesslie Newbigin, a man with profound global vision and understanding, said there are unusual times when the church "faces a radically new situation, and nothing will suffice save radical rethinking of the nature of her mission. Such rethinking must include both a realistic understanding of the new facts with which mission has to deal, and a humble return to the source of the mission of the Gospel. It must take both the Bible and the daily newspaper seriously" (*The Theology of the Christian Mission*, ed. by Gerald H. Anderson).

There are reasons to believe we are now facing such a radically new situation on several fronts and that the emerging "networked world" enabled by IT is one of the significant new facts of our time. With the rapid spread of PCs, fiber optic cable, communications satellites, etc., the Internet is increasingly becoming accessible around the world. The immense effect of this on the lives of people everywhere and its potential for expanded communications is constantly being reported in the daily newspapers and other media. Should some rethinking of the nature of the world mission of the church be taking place? On the basis of the almost complete lack of articles and study papers in church journals and other forums where the role of IT in world mission could be discussed, the answer seems to be "no." However, there are a few activities that indicates some discussion is taking place. What may be needed is broader participation. Perhaps the fact that one of the eleven work groups here dealt with mission and information technology is a promising sign. Somehow, it isn't hard to think that the one who by example pushed the church into using the printing press centuries ago, and for whom the seminary that hosted the congress is named, took note of this congress.

More Radical
than the Reformation

J. Martin Bailey

Background

My thesis is simple. The church and the Christian mission are at the threshold of a new era. The Christian community faces challenges unmatched in its history since the Protestant Reformation of the sixteenth century. How it responds to the new circumstances in the remaining years of this decade and in the early years of the new millennium may well determine the character and effectiveness of its witness for the next several centuries.

Just as Martin Luther's Reformation spread because of the introduction of moveable type for printing[1], twenty-first century Christianity will be stimulated and changed by new communication technologies. These new technologies are even more radical in their character, and will be more revolutionary in their impact, than was Gutenberg's printing press.

The structures and relationships that characterize the contemporary church were formed in the late 1800s and were modified in the period following World War II. During the formative period in the nineteenth century, the churches of North America and Europe generally adopted or accepted national identities; their synods and general assemblies were national, rather than local or regional, in scope. This also was the period when national churches in the West "sent" missionary representatives "into all the world." Then, in the post-colonial period that followed World War II, most of the churches in Asia and the Southern Hemisphere (whom we called "younger churches") became autonomous; they began to relate to other national churches as partners.

During those two periods, communication was essentially as it had been at the beginning of the Christian era. Like St. Paul, church leaders and missionaries commonly traveled from nation to nation by ship and sent long letters filled with questions and instructions or admonitions. Picture, for example, John R. Mott or Archbishop William Temple, embarking on one of their voyages, with trunks filled with books to occupy them during the long "crossings." Wrapped in lap robes, and seated on deck chairs, they read and wrote volumes. In those days, church leaders in the United States and Canada criss-crossed the continent by railroad—glad to take advantage of special clergy rates. (One of my mentors tired of that seemingly endless travel and yearned for what he called "ITP"—instantaneous transmission of personality.)

Changes began in the 1960s and accelerated dramatically in the last two decades—changes that already are reforming the church. Air travel, direct-dial telephones, and fax machines launched a revolution in travel and communication. An "ecclesiastical jet set" established personal ties that enabled a new kind of Christian community. The relationships between overseas missionaries and their sponsoring congregations "at home" also began to change.

Now at the end of the century, computers equipped with modems, linked through telephone lines and geo-synchronous satellites, have become not only the arteries of transnational business but also the effective instruments of religious interaction in the global church. As we move into the third millennium since the birth of Jesus, the world is as different from the days of Dietrich Bonhoeffer and Amsterdam as from those of St. Paul or the Council of Jerusalem. How our churches will meet this challenge is not yet clear. As William Temple once called the ecumenical movement the "great new fact of our time," new technologies are certain to create a qualitatively different kind of Christian community.

The question is *"What will the church by the side of the information superhighway look like and how will it function?"*

Some Theological Assumptions

I am convinced that the Pauline image of the body of Christ will be more apt than ever. As "one body with many members," we will certainly know one another better and rejoice and suffer with one another more frequently. The etymology that links communion, communication, and community will have new, and perhaps even more dramatic, poignant, and current illustrations. This leads me to identify several theological assumptions.

1. *Contemporary communication technologies are a gift of God for the people of God.* The origins of these powerful media lie in the creative energy of an omnipotent and communicating God. The history of the faith could well be recalled as the history of communication. From the early oral tradition through the teaching ministry of Jesus, from the development of the biblical canon to modern telecommunications, human beings have sought to record and to share their religious insights. Those whose imaginations have led to the cybernetic revolution have discovered how to use and harness natural phenomena energized by the Creator and offered freely to all who are created in God's image.

2. *For Christians, Jesus is both the model of communication and the subject of communication.* As the World Association for Christian Communication declared in 1986 in its *Christian Principles of Communication,* "Jesus announced the coming of God's Kingdom and commissioned us to proclaim the good news to all people. . . . Hearing the Good News, living by it and witnessing to it, is the basic calling of all Christians."[2] WACC also affirmed that "Christ's own communication was an act of self-giving. He 'emptied him-

self, taking the form of a servant' (Philippians 2:7). He ministered to all, but took up the cause of the materially poor, the mentally ill, the outcasts of society, the powerless and the oppressed. In the same way, Christian communication should be an act of love which liberates all who take part in it."[3] The invitation to the Congress on the World Mission of the Church properly insisted that the church must function "under the theology of the cross and with a spirit of global collaboration."[4]

Communication is more than technology. As the General Board of the National Council of Churches declared in November 1995, it is "more than gadgets and machines."[5] As the church looks at contemporary media, it needs to be clear about the content of its proclamation and to claim (i.e. redeem) the technology as a medium through which the full Gospel may be announced.

3. *The Holy Spirit works among us, constantly communicating God 's love and often surprising us, as all things—including the church, the community, and the media—are made new.* The WACC pointed out that "it is this Spirit that can change the Babel of confusion into the Pentecost of genuine understanding" and that because the Spirit "'blows where it pleases,' (John 2:8) no one, neither church nor religious group, can claim to control it."[6]

Constant, rapid changes in the technologies of communication surround us and change us. This technological change is a significant part of the environment in which the church is called to communicate the gospel.

4. *The church, through which the gospel is communicated in word and action, is at once the living body of Christ and a model of community.* In both of these aspects the church relies upon and uses the arts of communication its proclamation takes many forms—each a kind of communication: worship, preaching, service, the written word. Each of these can be electronically mediated. Its proclamation also involves its own lifestyle—its sense of being a community, its actions in a suffering and hungry world. The church, whether local, national, or global, communicates powerfully to the world because it is a unique kind of community. That modeling is often described and shared through the media.

As the church models its own sense of being, it will affirm in words and practice that true community is open, democratic, and participatory. It not only invites others to join its life but affirms that God's love is inclusive and enables human beings to live together in justice, equality and peace. As it tells its own story and advocates for others it will find that the new technology can be helpful and can stimulate creativity.

5. *Contemporary media of communication are not inherently evil or sinful.* Although much of the content of television, movies and the Internet lacks "redeeming social value" and is often destructive of human community, the media themselves are potentially as positive as they are negative. Still, the church needs to recognize that, as William Fore and others have pointed out, the media are radically reshaping contemporary society. The NCCC General Board acknowledged that the media have become "both a producer and definer of culture."[8] The General Board called on Christians to confess their own complicity as media consumers without whom destructive programming would not exist.

6. *The new media should be utilized by Christians as they seek to witness to the gospel of Christ and also should be shaped and held accountable for more constructive programming and content.* The media offer an enormous potential to the church as it seeks to tell its story and extend its witness. They are indeed a gift to be used. In addition, the church has a mission to those who labor within the communication industries and needs to advocate for responsible media choices.

Thus as the church reviews its deepest convictions and as it refines its mandate for mission, the principle of communication is both an article of faith and the object of responsible mission activity.

Some Characteristics of the New Communication Technology

William Fore has described the astonishing pace of change in the ways human beings communicate. The earliest writing probably took place around 3500 B.C. Block printing originated in Rome about 131 A.D. The first newspaper was published in Amsterdam in 1621, the first magazine in London a century later. Photography and the telegraph appeared as late as 1839 and 1844. The balance of the nineteenth century saw the invention of the telephone, the phonograph, the linotype, motion pictures, and wireless telegraphy (radio) in quick succession. The first radio broadcast, less than 80 years ago, was followed by television, sound movies, and a massive electronic computer (in 1946 at the University of Pennsylvania). However, Fore's book, *Mythmakers: Gospel. Culture and the Media,*[9] published in 1990, omitted mention of the fax machine and the modem; they were not yet important. He mentioned X-rated videos but said nothing, then, about the Internet!

The marriage of the computer and the telephone has been revolutionary. Virtually every institution or business now utilizes a Website—even newspapers, radio programs, and television networks—to say nothing of local libraries and the IRS! The rapid pace of contemporary technology, as well as its omnipresence, are only two of the most obvious characteristics of what was once called "computer-aided communication" but what has become a medium in its own right. One television commentator refers to the "ubiquitous computer" pointing out that computer chips already are being installed in a wide variety of everyday products and appliances.

Some of the other characteristics of computer-driven communication are particularly significant for the church's mission. They include the following:

1. *This form of electronic communication facilitates contact across geographic boundaries.* Although there is reason to be concerned that the Internet is still inaccessible to the world's poor, computerized communication is by far the fastest and least expensive way to communicate globally. There are, of course, remote areas where telephone lines are unavailable. But even that limitation is being overcome with direct- to-satellite connections and by linking a battery-powered, laptop computer to a mobile phone. Some mission agencies are already placing dishes capable of transmission and reception in the hands of missionaries who work at a distance from the nearest city.

This phenomenon of the last half of the 1990s has closed a significant geographical gap for industry, education and the church. Such international inclusivity has itself begun to change the character of the Christian mission, particularly the relationships between headquarters staff and mission workers and between sponsoring local churches and mission workers.

2. *Computer-driven communication is inexpensive, immediate, and flexible.* Aside from the initial cost of a computer and modem, messages sent in this manner are frequently much less expensive than what is commonly called "snail mail." Even the cost of computers adequate to access the World Wide Web have come down in cost so that many households have more than one. In North America and Europe it is not uncommon for children to learn to type at the computer and to correspond with international "pen pals." Transmission is virtually immediate; it is not unusual for persons half a world away to exchange several messages in the course of a day—or even in the course of an hour.

When there is less sense of urgency, another advantage is that such communication can be "time-shifted," i.e. persons need not be available at the same moment in different time zones to make communication quick and easy. There are numerous other "advantages" as well. For example, individuals who receive a document in this manner are able to edit or "massage" the material in their own computers before printing and distribution.

3. *There is a degree of privacy in such transmissions that is often not available by fax or regular mail.* Hypothetically, computer-driven communication is subject to monitoring by, say, a government bent on eavesdropping or censorship, at least when standard telephone lines are used. The fact is, however, that transmissions are so rapid and are now so numerous, that such monitoring is unlikely. The other privacy option is within an office or church. Fax machines are typically used by several persons and mail frequently is sorted and opened by a staff person. E-mail, on the other hand, most commonly involves a personal inbox on a computer and there are several levels of passwords possible to protect privacy.

4. *The word "interactive" describes not only the way in which an individual can request and receive data from a computer (either at hand or through telecommunications) but also the relationships between persons and groups.* Thus computer-driven communication is often "participatory" and encourages the sharing of ideas and concepts. John Bluck, who teaches pastoral theology and communication at Knox College, Dunedin, New Zealand, asserts that "the basic, non-negotiable premise of human communication is that it is dialogical, two-way, respecting the receiver as much as the sender and able to reverse those roles."[10] His book, *Beyond Technology,* was prepared in 1984 before the word interactive had come into common parlance. That word, however, describes what Bluck believes is basic to human communication.

Bluck's book was developed following the Vancouver Assembly of the World Council of Churches. That assembly received a statement, "Communicating Credibly," that included these words: "At its most effective, Christian communication is person-to-person communication, like Jesus conversing with Nicodemus or the Samaritan woman. At its most effective it is what comes out of authentic experience. It shares one's own life with others, as Jesus did. It empowers people to tell their stories, as happened in the case of Zacchaeus. It builds community, as it did in the early church."[11] More than most other forms of electronic media, computer-driven communication can facilitate person-to-person communication, even though people may never meet and even though they may be thousands of miles apart. It is ironic but true.

5. *Interactive communication is, by its nature, non-hierarchical, perhaps even anti-hierarchical.* One of my own early experiments with this medium was to invite laypersons (including youth!) and clergy from many denominations to become aware of and involved in the issues before the NCCC's General Board. Issue papers were made available on line and debates were summarized as the meeting progressed. Individuals were invited to send comments to members of their church's delegation. This, of course, threatened some church leaders; it seemed to change the rules of the game. Today it is quite commonplace for local Christians to be in direct contact with their missionary representatives overseas, effectively cutting the mission boards "out of the loop."

In addition, the style of computer-driven communication is generally informal, commonly brief and to the point, and utilizes friendly, personalized conventions. Typically the sender and receiver write, read and reply to mail (significantly called "notes") themselves, no longer relying on dictation to a secretary and office procedures that now seem cumbersome.

There are both positive and negative aspects of such a situation. The point is, however, that the relationships between church and mission representative are changing.

6. *Electronic communication, often involving networks of persons around the world, facilitates ecumenical communication.* In its infancy, Christians who experimented with Email flocked together across denominational lines. Networks like "Ecunet" were developed to facilitate both intra-denominational and interdenominational communication.

Besides being less formal, electronic mail can be transmitted to multiple addresses. This quickly led to wide networks of persons interested in particular topics or concerns. These networks often included individuals on several continents prompting a global and ecumenical experience.

How the Church Can Utilize Computer-Driven Communication

These new media can and should be used by the church in a number of ways:

1. *For Administration.* Perhaps most obviously, church offices already are using the Internet and private networks to improve their administrative work. Office procedures are quicker, more accurate, and more easily retrieved. Internally, the staff of a church or agency can keep in contact with each other and their staffs by computer. The laptop is becoming "standard issue" and executives who are unable or unwilling to use a laptop on the road are few and far between. Use of such equipment will continue to grow as new uses are developed.

2. *For Research and Planning.* Mission agencies and churches will increasingly utilize computer databases as they plan programmatically. Specialized databases will be developed and mission workers and partner churches overseas will be invited to contribute to the data pool—using computer-driven communication. Although "numbers aren't everything," they are important factors and the development of alternate ways to look at budgets and programs through computer models will grow in the church as it has in business.

3. *For Evangelism.* Already creative Websites are being developed by congregations, denominations, agencies, and overseas churches. These present many direct and indirect ways to proclaim the gospel to those who have not heard and who just may be more open to the Christian story when they find it on the Internet. Two illustrations will suffice. Developed by the American Bible Society as a major database, every congregation in the country now has an opportunity to post a "home page" at the site known as "Houses of Worship." The format calls on each church to state a number of things. Two seem particularly significant. Each church posts directions by which a visitor may find the house of worship and each congregation is asked to identify its particular mission objective.

The other illustration is personal. Some time ago I was in an ecumenical setting where we were talking about the Internet. We shared our business cards. At the time my E-mail address was <mbailey@cc.huji.ac.il>. My new friend was immediately excited. Responsible for the Website for the organization Jews for Jesus, he was eager for an explanation of my Internet address. It seems that his Website received more "hits" from "cc.huji.ac.il" than any place else. He was thrilled to learn that my internet service provider was Hebrew University Jerusalem Israel, an academic institution in "il", the country designation for Israel. I could tell him that his site was more significant than he knew, for missionary activity by Christians is forbidden in Israel.

4. *For Education.* There are many educational applications already and more creative approaches will soon follow. Particularly intriguing and significant, I believe, are opportunities for "distance learning," in which serious students are led through a course of study by a teacher or professor at a distance. Several seminaries are experimenting with this. Some use a period on campus followed by interaction between the faculty and student and sometimes among students in an on-line seminar.

I sat one day while a professor opened his E-mail and responded to several students. "You must get weary of that kind of interruption," I said. "On the contrary," the professor said. "These are very serious students. And, in the long run I spend less time with each—but in every case it is more quality time. When you send and receive an E-mail message, you get right down to business. And often rather than speaking 'off the top of his or her head' the student has taken time to think his question or proposal through."

As audio and video contact on the Internet become more common, and as networking options are opened, classroom or seminar opportunities for students in relatively remote places will become available and desirable.

5. *For Service.* The service ministries of denominations were among the first to see the value of rapid information sharing and response. News of natural disasters or some new evidence of human aggression often reaches mission agencies first through Internet contact. Assessments can be made and contacts made in appropriate places. One only needs to see the way in which the staff of the World Council of Churches uses computer-driven communication to appreciate the potential for quick and appropriate response that the Internet provides.

6. *For Advocacy.* Similarly with their advocacy ministries, a number of denominations are able to make an effective witness by the use of E-mail. One of my own interests when I was living in Palestine and now that I am home has been the inadequate and biased news coverage of Israel's occupation of Palestinian lands and cities. I was encouraged, recently, to learn that one active American of Arab descent had single-handedly had an impact on the coverage of National Public Radio. He listened avidly to NPR's coverage of events in the Middle East, and almost daily sent an E-mail comment. Sometimes he praised the reportage. Other times he pointed to errors and furnished additional information. The NPR office acknowledged that this one individual had become "a force to be reckoned with—he helps keep us honest."

E-mail also furnishes a relatively easy, rapid way to write to legislators and to submit letters to the editor. A number of periodicals not only welcome such submissions but indicate the E-mail address of the respondent. Furthermore, networks of persons who share a concern are being developed in some denominations, with updates and suggestions being transmitted by E-mail. Some committees within the NCCC's Church World Service and Witness Unit keep in touch with each other using online communications.

7. *For the Promotion of Its Mission.* Increasingly denominational mission agencies are helping to keep their members and local churches up-to-date on the activities of their organization by posting information on the church's Website and by sending E-mail messages when the occasion warrants. As new developments materialize in the audio and visual transmission of material, these efforts will be appreciated even more. Direct contact between overseas mission representatives and local churches are being encouraged in some communions.

There must be many more examples of ways in which the church's mission is being strengthened through the use of computer-driven communication.

Recognizing and Overcoming Inherent Problems

It is important to acknowledge that there also are problems. These need to be recognized for what they are and appropriate steps taken to lessen their impact or to overcome them completely. I mention a few:

1. *The impersonality of the medium.* At best, computer-driven communication is impersonal and lacks the warmth of the human touch. Although there are exceptions and although some persons clearly respond better to the unthreatening atmosphere of the computer screen, electronic communication is impersonal. Technologically, advances are being made to add voice and sight contact to electronic communication. The limitations persist, however.

Those who wish to work at on-line relationships have been able to achieve some significant breakthroughs and these are to be encouraged. One young couple, separated by educational and vocational circumstances for over a year, told me of their experience. Each worked with a computer and so it was possible for them to be in touch electronically several times a day. I was surprised to hear both husband and wife indicate that it was E-mail that kept them sane and together. Their most significant conversations were online. "It gave us an opportunity to think clearly about what we were saying to each other; we took pains not to hurt each other by a casual remark that could be misunderstood."

2. *The medium is used most heavily by young people; the church is dominated by older folk.* Most of us "old-timers" don't use the Internet as effectively as we might, but in the church at least, there seems a lack of concern for reaching and enabling participation by younger men and women. This is an area in which I believe the church needs to be intentional about change.

3. *Globally, the English language dominates the electronic media.* Among some Christians in other parts of the world, this has the effect of disenfranchisement. For all, it reveals a lack of cultural sensitivity and minimizes the ethnic contributions of others. Several Websites have been built in more than one language and the home page offers hypertext links among the various language possibilities. The problem, of course, is not limited to electronic communication. Greater sensitivity and new approaches are needed to assist churches that worship in a language other than English to use their own tongue on their own Websites and in their own E-mail. The church will do well to watch and encourage developments in electronic translation.

4. *Ownership of electronic media is also an issue.* Clearly the Internet and other E-mail systems are owned, operated, and managed by wealthy institutions that seek a profit—sometimes unscrupulously. The church needs to be sensitive in its use of such media, understanding of those who are further isolated in society by these circumstances, and articulate in seeking to interpret their concerns to the owners and managers. The church is in a position to advocate for the poor and oppressed, not only in the society as a whole but particularly among those who control the electronic media.

In all that it does in response to the challenges of the new communication technologies, the church and its mission agencies need to listen for the movement of the Spirit and to walk humbly into the future expressing love for the God of mercy and doing acts of justice.

Notes

[1] Printing from moveable type was relatively new when the Reformation began. Recognizing its potential, Martin Luther published thirty books and pamphlets between the years 1517 and 1520. According to Elizabeth Eisenstein, Protestant clergy "viewed printing as a providential device which ended forever a priestly monopoly on learning, overcame ignorance and superstition . . . and, in general, brought western Europe out of the dark ages." *The Printing Press as an Agent of Change* (New York: Cambridge University Press, 1979), page 305.

[2] Quoted from *Statements on Communication by the World Association for Christian Communication* (London: WACC, Revised Edition 1995), page 5.

[3] Ibid., page 5.

[4] Invitation letter from Roland E. Miller, dated February 17, 1997.

[5] Quoted from "Violence in Electronic Media and Film," a Policy Statement of the NCCCUSA, approved on November 11, 1993, and published in *The Church and Media* (New York: NCCC Communication Commission, 1997), pages 7f.

6   Op. cit., page 5.

7   Fore, William. *Mythmakers: Gospel, Culture and the Media* (New York: Friendship Press, 1990), pages 29f.

8   Quoted from "The Churches' Role in Media Education and Communication Advocacy," a Policy Statement of the NCCC adopted by the General Board on November 16, 1995 and published in *The Church and Media* (New York: NCCC Communication Commission, 1997), page 32. See also "Global Communication for Justice," a Policy Statement adopted on November 11, 1993.

9   Op. cit., pages 34-35.

10 Bluck, John. *Beyond Technology* (Geneva: World Council of Churches, 1984), page 8.

11 Op. cit., pages 84f.

CONGRESS
PRESENTATIONS

A Friendly Observer's View of North American Global Mission Responsibility Today

Chee Pang Choong

A "friendly observer"? More than a friend: an immediate beneficiary of North American global mission.

I am extremely grateful to the organizers of "The Congress on the World Mission of the Church" for the wonderful opportunity to participate in this great event. Professor Roland Miller first mentioned this congress to me in Bangkok in the summer of 1996. A year later his kind invitation came with a request to give a thirty-minute "reflection" on the topic "A Friendly Observer's view of North American Global Mission Responsibility Today." Like John Wesley at a small Moravian meeting in Aldersgate Street in London on 24 May, 1738, while listening to the reading of Luther's preface to Romans, my heart also felt "strangely warmed" when I first read the proposed topic of my reflection. "Strangely warmed," because I felt greatly honoured to be regarded as "a friendly observer" of North American Global Mission. This was so particularly because I had attended quite a number of "mission" conferences both regionally and internationally when the North American Global Mission of the past was severely and often unduly criticized by some participants, especially those from "the South." In fact, in terms of my own "conversion" experience as well as those of my family members stretching over three generations, I would like to gratefully and proudly regard myself as far more than just a "friendly observer." An "immediate beneficiary" of the North American global mission would be a more truthful and accurate description of my position, as I openly testified in my keynote address at the Ninth Assembly of The Lutheran World Federation in July 1997 in Hong Kong. The executive of this congress has described the congress as "A Major Reflections on Mega Issues." I will try to be faithful to this general theme of our congress in my reflection.

Reference to some of the points raised by three "friendly" observers of North American mission: "Letter from Africa" (Tokunboh Adeyemo), "Letter from Asia" (Vinay Samuel), "Letter from Latin America" (Valdir Steuernagel) in Mission Handbook *(MARC, 1993-95).*

In the MARC *Mission Handbook* (1993-95), I found three letters on North American mission, one each from Africa, Asia, and Latin America. The African Letter, while appreciative of North American Mission enterprise in the past in Africa, was very critical of its close link with western colonialism, especially its failure to separate the church from the state in southern Africa. The rapid numerical growth of the Christian population has also not been matched by strong discipleship and well planned educational programmes. It expresses deep concern over recent aggressive Muslim attempt to Islamize the whole African continent. It also sees a disturbing tendency in some mission agencies to replace the proclamation of the Gospel and discipling with "development" programmes. The Letter from Asia by Vinay Samuel focuses on the vital issue of "Gospel and Culture" in the Asian contexts together with its many other related concerns. The Latin American letter observes that there is now no real distinction between mission "nearby and far away" or between mission "there and here." It points out that "mission frontiers" are not only geographical, but also socio-economic. All three letters emphasize the importance of exploring new concepts and styles of partnership in mission. These and other issues raised in the letters are clearly relevant to the reflection and serious thinking of this congress.

Mission: A Holistic Approach

The personal

There are three aspects in my holistic approach to mission. I would like to begin with the personal aspect because it was through my personal encounter with the living God in my own conversion experience and subsequent pilgrimage existentially that I have come to appreciate the socio-political as well as the creational-cosmic aspects of the Christian mission. In our many mission activities today, the emphasis is often on and the attention is often given to "programmes" and "projects" resulting, unwittingly, in the neglect of the truly *personal* needs and concerns of those whom we intend to serve and help. "Globalization," "modernization," and "industrialization," etc. mean that our human society has become increasingly impersonal, resulting in the loss of the individual man or woman in the mighty ocean of humanity. It is therefore of vital importance that we take the individual being, whether a man or a woman or a child *personally* and seriously in all our mission efforts. Here I have no new theology to offer except to return to the old biblical understanding of the *imago Dei* which would constantly remind us of the worth, dignity and freedom of the individual person created after the *image of God*. The individual person, despite his or her creatureliness and falleness, is *still* the image bearer of the Creator-God.

A recent close encounter with two Chinese intellectuals separately reassured me that a sincere seeker can still find meaning and fulfillment in the One who is "the ground of our being."

a) Some months ago while lecturing in a top university in China, I was introduced to a doctoral candidate who had just had a "conversion" experience. There was nothing particularly *dramatic* about her pilgrimage to faith: regular and private Bible reading and prayer, occasional participation in worship service in a local church near her university, etc. Then one Sunday, after a worship service, she just returned to her university dormitory and the Holy Spirit simply convicted her of her sin and her need of Christ. She responded with a clear conviction and accepted Christ as her Lord and Saviour.

b) A good friend of mine from the same university was lecturing in Singapore as a visiting professor at a local university. His wife has been serving with an international organization in Europe with a very handsome income. She is accompanied by their two sons who are studying in a noted university in Europe. To many of their colleagues back in mainland China this is just dreamlike. I was therefore most surprised when he recently confessed to me that he has been haunted lately by a rather mysterious kind of feeling—the felling of sheer emptiness and meaninglessness. "If I ever became a serious believer," he said, "that religion must be Christianity." And my response to him was: "Well, my dear friend, I think you are not too far from the kingdom of God."

The socio-political

Our globe is not just a world of living beings and non-living things. It is also a "jungle" of multiple and complex structures and systems. We human beings and other creatures are paradoxically, served and enslaved by these structures and systems at the same time. One of the main reasons why environmental issues, such as deforestation in Mexico, Brazil, Indonesia, and China cannot be effectively dealt with, is precisely because the structures and systems in these countries have been built, maintained, manipulated and selfishly exploited by people in high places.

As a community called to witness, the church is expected to be an active and dynamic entity. As such, the church must set an agenda for herself instead of just passively responding to an agenda set by the world. Many in the church today feel rather strongly that the church has given in too much to the world and has thus lost her initiative and leadership in many crucial areas. They therefore suggest that the church should stop this disturbing trend with all the resources at her disposal and set her own agenda. This concern is apparently legitimate and laudable. However, there are also those, while not denying the legitimacy of this concern all together, somehow feel that the suggestion is just too idealistic, if not somewhat presumptuous. The reality perhaps lies somewhere between the two positions. To simply allow the world to dictate and set the agenda for the church would be tragic and ultimately defeatist and suicidal. As a living entity engaged in witness and service the church must consciously and actively set a certain basic agenda for herself and respond realistically and courageously to important socio-political issues raised by the world at the same time. However, the degree of interest and intensity with which we individually respond to them, and the order of priority that we give them, may be quite different due to the diversity of our socio-politico-cultural backgrounds and contexts. For example, concerns for human rights and gender issues may have far greater priority in the developed regions of the world, especially in the post-modern North than in the South. On the other hand, the problems of poverty and suffering and the challenge of non-Christian religions and cultures could be far more pressing for the smaller churches in the South. As such, bread and butter, rather than ideologies, evangelism rather than academic religious dialogues, may occupy higher priority in the member churches of the South.

The creational-cosmic

Scientists who are seriously engaged in space research have certainly made some very remarkable discoveries in recent decades for which we ought to be grateful. Yet many questions and mysteries remain unanswered regarding the universe. So far, the *only* planet that is inhabited by humans and hosts of other living beings that we know for absolute certainty is still *our* planet—*our* globe, which is the "earth" of our Christian confession: "I believe in God the Father Almighty, Maker of heaven and earth". But *this* globe and *this* earth, and not just something else in the remote outer space, is now universally acknowledged to be in great crisis, ecologically as well as environmentally. However, this crisis must not be treated in isolation from other equally serious crises, crises that are socio-politico–economic as well as human and personal. Because all these crises are interrelated and interwoven so that one is bound to affect the others whether directly or indirectly. As such, the "curse" that was brought upon the earth because of Adam's sin (Geneses: 3:17) should no longer be regarded as "poetic imagery" or the language of "myth." No, it is neither "poetic" nor "mythical," it is, unfortunately, very real and concrete, just as human sinfulness and its many outward manifestations are concrete and real. It was Isaiah and other prophets of old, who clearly remind us of the vital link between sinful human behaviour and the pollution of the earth:

> Behold, the Lord will lay waste the earth and make it desolate,
> and he will twist its surface and scatter its inhabitants. . . .
> The earth shall be utterly laid waste and utterly despoiled;
> for the Lord has spoken this word.
> The earth mourns and withers,
> the world languishes and withers;
> the heavens languish together with the earth.
> The earth lies polluted
> under its inhabitants;
> for they have transgressed the laws,
> violated the statutes,
> broken the everlasting covenant.
> Therefore a curse devours the earth. . . .
> (Isaiah 24:1, 3-6; Cf. Hos.4:1-3; Jer.12:4, 11)

The picture that Isaiah paints for us is indeed gloomy. The Apostle Paul also takes up the theme of the suffering of creation in Romans 8:18-25. The most revealing thing about this section is that St Paul is *not* talking about the suffering of creation in isolation, but in *solidarity* with the whole of humanity in the hope that both humanity and the rest of the created order may obtain liberty or redemption together:

> I consider that the suffering of this present time are not worth comparing with the glory that is to be revealed to us. For the creation waits with eager longing for the revealing of the sons of God; for the creation was subjected to futility, not of its own will but by the will of him who subjected it in hope; because the creation itself will be set free from its bondage to decay and obtain the glorious liberty of the children of God. We know that the whole creation has been groaning in travail together until now; and not only the creation, but we ourselves, who have the first fruits of the Spirit, groan inwardly as we wait for adoption as sons, the redemption of our bodies. For in this hope we were saved. Now hope that is seen is not hope. For who hopes for what he sees? But if we hope for what we do not see, we wait for it with patience. (*Romans 8:18-25*)

This message of *hope*—humanity and the whole of creation *suffering together in hope*—must be loudly and clearly proclaimed in our Christian mission today.

"A crisis of degradation is [indeed] enveloping the earth. Never before have human beings wielded so much power over creation," warns Calvin B. De Witt, editor of the book *The Environment and the Christian* (Grand Rapids, 1991) and Professor at the Institute For Environmental Studies, University of Wisconsin. And what threatens the survival of humanity and the earth are not imaginative, but concrete: global toxification, atmospheric contamination, cultural subversion, land exploitation, species extinction, soil destruction, waste mismanagement, modern science and technology, the myth of unlimited economic growth, over-consumption and population growth.

The task to effectively deal with the whole ecological crisis is dauntingly hard and seemingly insurmountable. And human beings "formed of dust from the ground" are in desperate need of something, no less than that of a heavenly vision and mission, for inspiration and perseverance to take on the task. It is my conviction that a biblical hope for the redemption of the creation is a solid basis for ecological concerns and commitment. *Nature and humanity do have a shared destiny.*

The Topic and Its Basic Assumptions

Although this is a "Congress of the World Mission of the Church," I am glad that the topic that has been assigned to me has a clear geopolitical focus, namely, North America. Yet, in my reflection, North America, unique as it is, will not be taken as an entity in isolation, but in the context of a *global* vision missiologically. Unlike many skeptics and cynics even within the church who think that the days of North American mission are well over, it is my conviction that in this modern and post-modern era North American mission in fact has a greater role to play although its style and form of operation may have to be modified, even drastically changed in response to a rapidly changing globalized world. It is in this context and assumption that I talk about North American global mission responsibility. In terms of North America's mission responsibility, especially stewardship and accountability, I subscribe to the most basic and obvious biblical principle, that is, "To whom much is given, much is required." North America has indeed been blessed with much, perhaps far too much, in comparison to most other regions in the world. As such, her responsibility is correspondingly great and heavy. Not only should her commitment to global mission be strong, her sense of stewardship and accountability must also be equally compelling.

The clash of civilizations and the remaking of world order

Modern mission thinking and strategy, since Edinburgh, 1910 have consistently been influenced and shaped by changing world conditions and trends. This is only natural since the Christian message, although itself unchanging, could only be proclaimed and communicated effectively when all the essential dynamics of the world were clearly understood, firmly grasped and taken seriously. Here I refer to some of the dynamics which have been singled out in Professor Samuel P. Huntington's "clash of civilizations."

The hypothesis of Professor Samuel P. Huntington

Professor Samuel P. Huntington's article, "The Clash of Civilizations?" appeared in the 1993 Summer issue of *Foreign Affairs*. He is the Director of the John M. Olin Institute for Strategic Studies at Harvard University as well as the president of the Harvard Academy for International and Area Studies. He also served, among other posts, on the National Security Council under the Carter administration. It is therefore important not to regard him as a mere academician. In his 1993 summer article, Huntington states:

> It is my hypothesis that the fundamental source of conflict in this new world will not be primarily ideological or primarily economic. The great divisions among humankind and the dominating source of conflict will be cultural. Nation states will remain the most powerful actors in world affairs, but the principal conflicts of global politics will occur between nations and groups of different civilizations. The clash of civilizations will dominate global politics. The fault line between civilizations will be the battle lines of the future (p.22).

According to Huntington's classification, there are seven or eight world civilizations: Western, Confucian, Japanese, Islamic, Hindu, Slavic-Orthodox, Latin American, and possibly African civilization. He gives *six* reasons as to why civilizations will clash. Here are four of them:

First, differences among civilizations are not only real; they are basic. Civilizations are differentiated from each other by history, language, culture, tradition, and most important, religion. . . . Over the centuries . . . differences among civilizations have generated the most prolonged and the most violent conflicts.

Second, the world is becoming a smaller place. The interactions between peoples of different civilizations are increasing; these increasing interactions intensify civilization consciousness and awareness of differences between civilizations and commonalties within civilizations.

Third, the processes of economic modernization and social change throughout the world are separating people from longstanding local identities. . . . In much of the world religion has moved in to fill this gap, often in the form of movements that are labeled "fundamentalist." Such movements are found in western Christianity, Judaism, Buddhism, and Hinduism, as well as in Islam.

Fourth, growth of civilization—consciousness is enhanced by the dual role of the West. On the one hand, the West is at a peak of power. At the same time, however, and perhaps as a result, a return to the roots phenomenon is occurring among non-western civilizations. . . . A West at the peak of its power confronts non-wests that increasingly have the desire, the will and the resources to shape the world in non-western ways (pp.25-28).

Looking at these as well as other reasons, Huntington thinks "that the paramount axis of world politics will be the relations between 'the West and the Rest'. . . a central focus of conflict for the immediate future will be between the West and several Islamic–Confucian states" (p.48).

Christendom, the West, and the rest

Hungtington claims that it is not his intention "to advocate the desirability of conflicts between civilizations." His article only sets forth "descriptive hypotheses as to what the future may be like." However, it is evidently his intention to want the West to seriously consider the implications of his "descriptive hypotheses" for their policy. He concludes his article with the following advice to the West:

In the longer term other measures would be called for. Western civilization is both western and modern. Non-western civilizations have attempted to become modern without becoming western. Todate only Japan has fully succeeded in this quest. Nonwestern civilizations will continue to attempt to acquire the wealth, technology, skills, machines, and weapons that are part of being modern. They will also attempt to reconcile this modernity with their traditional culture and values. Their economic and military strength relative to the West will increase. Hence the West will increasingly have to accommodate these non-western modern civilizations whose power approaches that of the West but whose values and interests differ significantly from those of the West. This will require the West to maintain the economic and military power necessary to protect its interests in relation to these civilizations (pp. 48, 49).

In his 1996 book, *The Clash of Civilizations and the Remaking of World Order,* Huntington "expands on his [Summer 1993] article, explores further the issues he raised then, and develops many new penetrating and controversial analyses . . . showing not only how clashes between civilizations are the greatest threat to world peace but also how an international order based on civilizations is the best safeguard against war" (see book jacket). One of the "many new penetrating and controversial analyses," as far as I can see, is clearly the subject on "Chinese Hegemony." It is Huntington's belief that "China's history, culture, traditions, size, economic dynamism, and self-image all compel it to assume a hegemonic position in East Asia." (p. 229). In fact, China is already "acting in classic fashion as a regional hegemon" (p. 230). Confronted with this assertive role of China, the rest of the world, especially the West, led by the United States, could either try to contain/counter-balance the rising power of China, or simply accept this perceived inevitable reality. Left by itself, the rest of east and southeast Asia, including Japan, is more likely to opt for "bandwagoning" rather than "balancing" the power of China (pp. 229-238) Huntington agrees with Lee Kuan Yew of Singapore that if China maintains its unity and growth for the next 30 or 40 years, it is going to be, not just another big player, but "the greatest player in the history of man" (p.231).

One may not agree with Huntington's hypothesis, and some scholars, both American and non-American, have even considered it "dangerous," but his idea certainly has ready takers, especially the right-wingers.

Huntington's message is obviously for all readers. However, reading between the lines, one seems to get the impression that the writer has a compelling sense of urgency to want to get his message of warning across particularly to his western compatriots: "The survival of the West depends on Americans reaffirming their western identity and westerners accepting their civilization as unique not universal and uniting to renew and preserve it against challenges from non-western societies" (p.21). "In the clash of civilizations, Europe and America will hang together or hang separately"(p.321).

Implications for Christian identity in the non-western world as well as for North American global mission because of Huntington's understanding of the western civilization in relation to Christianity has serious implication for Christian identity in the non-western world as well as for North American global mission.

To begin with, "the West" for Huntington, "includes Europe, North American, plus other European settler countries such as Australia and New Zealand." "The West," which is now led by the United States, is understood by him as referring "to what used to be called 'western Christendom' " (p.46). While this may be true historically it is rather disturbing to observe that throughout the book the term "western" or the "West" is used rather broadly or loosely as a synonym for "Christian" or "Christianity." Because by identifying "the West" too closely with Christianity, Huntington has in fact deliberately or unintentionally confirmed or deepened the already common impression and prejudice in the non-western world that Christianity is a *western* entity rather than a *cross-cultural* and *universal* religion. This immediately creates an *identity crisis* for Christians in the non-western world, especially in Asia, where virtually all major world religions — Hinduism, Buddhism, Christianity, and Islam have their origin and roots. Even Huntington himself repeatedly states that "religion is a central defining characteristic of civilizations" (p.47). To which civilization, for example, does a *Chinese* Christian belong? Strictly speaking, a Chinese Christian will have difficulty identifying himself with Confucian civilization although he can conscientiously subscribe to certain Confucian thinking, especially in the ethical area, because as a way of life the Confucian world view is essentially humanistic and self-sufficient. It admits no sin and is not aware of any need for "salvation" in the common religious sense. It is generally understood that traditional Chinese culture or civilization actually consists of 3 major streams—Taoism, Confucianism, and (Chinese) Buddhism. And after nearly 50 years of continuous communist rule, one should perhaps even add Marxist-Leninist-Maoist ("Dengist"?) to the 3 traditional streams of Chinese culture or civilization. The matter of civilizational identity now becomes the more difficult and complicated for the Chinese Christian since Taoism and Buddhism are religious systems and communism is atheistic. Yet he cannot belong to Christianity *civilizationally* speaking since there is no *Christian* civilization in Huntington's classification, unless the Chinese Christian wants to identity himself with the western, Slavic-Orthodox or Latin-American civilization. If not, he is lost. The case becomes even more serious for the Indian and Indonesian Christians since Hinduism and Islam are *both* religions and civilizations.

When using the term "the West" or "western" to refer to what used to be called "western Christendom," and when regarding "the West" as representative of Christianity, Huntington seems to have failed to recognize the very important fact the Christian population or "map" world wide has changed significantly since the end of World War II. Indonesia, for example, has a population of nearly 200 million. Although it has the largest Islamic community in the world, the Christian population (including Roman Catholics) is estimated, in non-government circles, to be around 20% of the total population, that is, around 40 million. As such, the *Christian* population of Indonesia is far more than the national population of Canada. Similarly, the *Christian* population in mainland China or Korea today is believed to be as big, if not in fact bigger, than the *national* population of Australia.

I attended the 9th Assembly of the Lutheran World Federation which was held in Hong Kong from July 8 to 16, 1997. The Lutheran World Federation has a total membership of about 60 million, representing 122 member churches from 68 countries of all continents. The 9th World Assembly this year was also the 50th Anniversary of the founding of the Federation. The shift of leadership from the North to the South in the last 20 years has been quite consistent and impressive. After the disintegration of the old "Christendom" in the Post-Christian and Post-modern era, the West itself has already rejected much that is *Christian* in their private, familial and social life, resulting in a very serious and disturbing crisis of faith. As such, the West, as a demographic block, is evidently not adequate to represent Christianity. For years I have been trying very hard to convince my part of the world that it is a very serious mistake or misunderstanding to identify the West with Christianity without much qualification. In a small way I think I have succeeded doing so when an influential Chinese daily in Singapore, the *Lianhe Zhaobao*, last year (June 1997) commented quite extensively on my paper that was presented at an International Symposium which was jointly sponsored by the National University of Singapore, and the International Association for Confucian Studies, with a prominent headline, "The West is inadequate to represent Christianity." It was a symposium on "Confucianism and World Civilizations." The title of my paper (in Chinese) is "A Critique of Huntington's Understanding of Confucianism and 'Chinese Hegemony'."

Huntington and other scholars are certainly right in their observation that as the process of globalization continuous, there is also, paradoxically, a keen desire on the part of many in the non-western world to return to their own cultural roots and become increasingly more confident and assertive about those resources and values they find in those roots.

I personally have no knowledge about the religious affiliation, if any, of Huntington. Whatever the case may be, in the eyes of his readers, especially those who are in the non-western world, he is clearly and rightly identified as a key spokesman for the West. And since he identifies the western civilization so closely with Christian religion, his position is quite commonly regarded as a *Christian* position, and not just as a *western* position. This is at least the unmistakable impression I have after reading those materials on Huntington in Asia, especially those that are written in the Chinese language. This is in fact very understandable since Asians, including those elite who have been educated in the West, and are supposed to know better, are still quite accustomed to identify what is *western* with Christianity. As such, it is difficult to expect the common people in the street to be able to distinguish what is *western* from that which is genuinely *Christian*.

In recent years there have been quite a lot of controversies, debates, and quarrels between China and the United States over democracy, human rights, and freedom. Similar situations are also found between Singapore and the West, including Australia. Although the debates etc., are between nations, it is not uncommon, however, for them to be perceived, interpreted, understood or misunderstood in cultural or civilizational terms, i.e. as the "clash of civilizations." The Sino-American debate thus becomes a "clash" between the "Sinic" (or "Confucian") and western, or *Christian* civilizations. And for those of us who are Asian Christians and are already lost in our civilizational identity, whenever the "Christian" West gets bashed up or criticized we feel the hurt and bear the pain for Christianity. The problem and challenge that we encounter are certainly not academic but profoundly *existential*. The question of Christian identity is not just an Asian issue, but a global one. It deserves further inquiry and in-depth study, because it has profound implications for the mission and life of the church.

North American Mission and North American Culture

The Rev. Elizabeth Beissel in her greetings to the participants of our mission congress on Tuesday night (June 23) at the Central Lutheran Church used three key words to describe contemporary American society: Secularism, consumerism, and pluralism. One of the congress background papers by Alan Neely, "Religious Pluralism: Threat or Opportunity for Mission?" asks "what will be the theological and missiological response of us to the presence of peoples of other faiths in this land [America]?" and "What is the legitimate role of religion in public life?" Although Christianity continues to be the majority religion, at least nominally, in America, strong religious conviction, especially *Christian* conviction, strangely enough, is very unpopular in society. On my way from Singapore to St. Paul, Minnesota, I came across an interesting, but disturbing essay in the June 15, 1998 issue of the *Time* magazine, entitled "Will it be coffee, tea or He? Religion was once a conviction. Now it is a taste." by Charles Krauthammer. Here is an excerpt:

> In ancient times, they asked, "Who is your God?" A generation ago, they asked your religion. Today your creed is a preference. Preference? "I take my coffee black, my wine red, my sex straight and my shirts starched. Oh yes, and put me down for Islam."

According to Chesterton, tolerance is the virtue of people who do not believe in anything. Chesterton meant that as a critique of tolerance. But it captures nicely the upside of unbelief: where religion is trivialized, one is unlikely to find persecution. When it is believed that on your religion hangs the fate of your immortal soul, the Inquisition follows easily; when it is believed that religion is a breezy consumer preference, religious tolerance flourishes easily. After all, we don't persecute people for their taste in cars. Why for their taste in gods?

Oddly, though, in our thoroughly secularized culture, there is one form of religious intolerance that does survive. And that is the disdain bordering on contempt of the culture makers for the deeply religious, i.e., those for whom religion is not preference but a conviction. Yale law professor Stephen Carter calls this "the culture of disbelief," the oppressive assumption that no one of any learning or sophistication could possibly be a religious believer—and the social penalties meted out to those who nonetheless are.

Every manner of political argument is ruled legitimate in our democratic discourse. But invoke the Bible as grounding for your politics, and the First Amendment police will charge you with breaching the sacred wall separating church and state. Carter notes, for example, that one is allowed to have any view on abortion so long as it derives from ethical or practical or sociological or medical considerations. But should someone stand up and oppose abortion for reasons of faith, he is accused of trying to impose his religious beliefs on others. Call on Timothy Leary or Chairman Mao, fine. Call on St. Paul, and all hell breaks loose.

It is really incredible that such could be the situation in a society which is supposed to be "Christian," although it is certainly not the whole picture of the American society. Nonetheless the situation is serious enough to call for some deep thinking missiologically.

A mistake of the past? Christianization = Westernization / Civilization

From about the end of the eighteenth century, through Edinburgh 1910, until around the end of second world war, for about one hundred and fifty years, during the heyday of western imperial and colonial powers, it was common for the western church to take on the whole mission enterprise as a "white man's burden." Moreover, when no clear-cut separation was made between "church and state" and between "Christ and culture," biblical evangelization became "Christianization," and westernization was often thought to be the only way to true "civilization," excepting perhaps Japan, after the Meiji Restoration. This close identification between the Euro-American mission enterprise and western powers has certainly marred and distorted the image of western mission in the non-western world and the effect of which can still be clearly perceived and deeply felt in many parts of the South even in our days of globalization. If that was indeed a mistake of the past, important lessons could still be learnt so that, hopefully, history might not repeat itself.

A temptation of the present? Christianization=Americanization/ Modernization

After the collapse of the Berlin Wall and the disintegration of the former Soviet bloc in the 1980s, America has now become *de facto* the only superpower of the world, which is sometimes dubbed the neo-colonial or imperial power. America's "interference" in regional as well as in domestic affairs of other nations; her "control" and "manipulation" of world economy and market; her self-appointed role as the sole guardian, defender and interpreter of universal human rights and freedom etc. are often cited as clear examples.

Whatever the case may be, the rich and powerful "Uncle Sam" does face a *real* temptation. In terms of the global mission enterprise, there is a *real* temptation, consciously or unconsciously, for North American Christians to treat their mission outreach as a kind of "Christianization" campaign. Moreover, since things "American" are so attractive, effective, and successful, Americanization is not uncommonly regarded as the fastest track to modernization. This naturally leads to my next point which is the greatness of the American nation: asset and/or liability in global mission?

The greatness of the American nation: asset and/or liability in global mission?

The greatness of America as a nation is such a blatantly clear reality that both her friends and foes alike simply have to accept it. But is this greatness an asset or a liability in her global Christian Mission? Or both? According to one statistic, the United States accounts for one quarter of the world's total income. This is just in sheer economic terms. In addition to this are the vast resources that this great nation has been blessed with, especially in human resources. Christian mission is primarily and ultimately a "faith" venture that depends on divine power rather than human might. Yet for great and sustainable mission programmes to be initiated and effectively carried out, vast resources, both financial and human are needed. Here the greatness of the American nation is obviously an asset. But, paradoxically, North America's greatness, not just in terms of financial and human resources, but also in political, military and other powers, can also be a liability in her global mission. *First*, there is the problem of "image"—especially in the way that the outside world perceives North American global mission *in relation to* her greatness. The tendency here is for the outside world to view and interpret North American global mission as an *extension* of North American interest and influence, even "aggression," socio-politically as well as religio-culturally, not unlike the way they used to perceive the western missionary enterprise in the old colonial and imperial era. It requires a great deal of concerted and conscious effort to constantly dispel such a misconception. *Second*, there is the problem of mentality and attitude on the part of those North Americans who are involved in mission. The obvious danger here is to forget that our global mission is essentially and ultimately a "spiritual" (not in the narrow sense) matter, so that all the vast resources that we have been blessed with should be gratefully received and wisely utilized as means only. These resources, great and precious as they are, must never be allowed to become the object or basis of our faith and trust. It is in God and God alone we trust. I hope that Americans have not forgotten what is clearly printed on the "Federal Reserve Note" of the United States: "*In God We Trust.*"

How "Christian" is the American society: the challenge of home mission?

I personally do not think that there is any society or nation today that can truly be called a "Christian" society or nation. However, whether we like it or not, for whatever reasons, the North American society is somehow perceived by many in the outside world as rather "Christian," at least more "Christian" than most other nations, including those in Europe. This is an "image" or "perception" problem. I would like to think that this is a burden as well as a challenge to North America, especially to the Christian church. It is a "burden" because humanly speaking, no society can actually live up to such an expectation—to be a "Christian" society in the true sense of the world. It is a "challenge," especially for the Christian church, because being regarded somehow as a "Christian" society is a kind of compliment. That is, people seem to have some kind of high regard for the North American society. Perhaps people have been rather impressed by the general civility of the North American society, its system of government, its rule of law, the transparency of the public office, the freedom of speech and the press etc. which people might rightly or wrongly attribute to "Christian" roots and origin? But how "Christian" is the North American society in reality? As an "observer," I dare not ever attempt to answer. But it does call for in-depth heart—searching for the North American Christians who take the moral as well as the socio-political implications of the gospel of incarnation seriously. It certainly has vital bearing on and serious implications for North America's mission abroad. Because not only does the North American church do a lot of "preaching," national leaders of the United States and its policy makers are constantly involved in the same exercise, such as superimposing certain cherished American principles and (Christian?) values, like human rights, freedom, and democracy *universally* and *indiscriminately* upon others. But does the preacher practice what he preaches? And people do naturally expect the preacher to set his own house in order first . As such, the "home mission" of North America is just as important as the global one. It is also an "image" problem and ultimately a matter of creditability.

What are "our [America's] most basic values"? (reference to President Bill Clinton's commencement speech at Portland University on Saturday, June 13, 1998)

More than a week ago I read with great interest in the *Los Angeles Times* the commencement speech of President Bill Clinton which was delivered at Portland University on Saturday, June 13, 1998, in which he advised immigrants to "honour our laws . . . embrace our culture . . . our most basic values." What laws, what cultures, and what basic values are the President talking about? What are their essential nature and character? "Christian," "pagan," or a mixture of both? When virtually everything and anything that is closely connected or remotely related to the sex scandal of the President —the most powerful leader on earth—has been openly discussed and relentlessly exposed to the horror and utter dismay of the average person in the States and abroad, are there still any "basic values" left? Even if they still exist, how seriously can people take them? Certainly not the skeptics and cynics. Nor should anyone forget that it is a *Christian* President who is on trial. Even if this simple fact is no longer significant in the mind of the Americans, it is certainly very important in the eyes of the *moralistic* non-Christians world-wide who have been following the trial through CNN and other media coverage. I have no particular intention to single out President Clinton like this. In fact as a fellow mortal and fallible human being myself, I have a lot of sympathy for the President who happened to be a "college-mate" of mine at University College, Oxford, although we were in College at different times. I do not think that the President is necessarily more guilty or morally worse than many other world leaders and politicians in the area of private life. It is the American media, in particular, that has made him appear in such bad light through its relentless scrutiny and excessive coverage and exposure. I am inclined to think that if some national leaders, whether of the North or the South, were brought under similar scrutiny, President Clinton may well appear rather saintly by comparison! Whatever the case may be, unfortunately for the President and for the United States, the harsh reality remains. A case like this unfortunately does occur in a supposedly "Christian" society. No one should be judgmental and self-righteous. But it does have implications for North America's mission both at home and abroad. For it is the very business of Christian mission to be profoundly concerned with life and life-style, both private and public, not just theologically or missiologically, but also *existentially*.

Global Mission and Global Partnership:
No paternalism, no dependency, but fellowship and mutual accountability

The concept of "partnership in mission" which is clearly biblical, has gained considerable acceptance and popularity in the church universal for about thirty years now. But what about actual practice? How do our mission agencies in Chicago and other places relate to our "mission partners" abroad? Are they truly being treated as "partners"? Even in the best of our intention, do we not consciously or unconsciously display an attitude that is still rather paternalistic? In our generosity and eagerness to help, do we not continue to inculcate in the mind of our poor partners abroad a mentality of dependency? Have our missionaries who serve in those partner-churches or organizations abroad been promoting an education of responsible stewardship and self-reliance effectively? How are our mission policies formulated, priorities set, and decisions made? Has there been sufficient consultation involving all the parties and partners concerned in the whole process? Or do we just "inform" our partners abroad either directly from our home office or through our area or field directors and secretaries *after* our policies have already been formulated, priorities set and decisions made? Over the years have not our partners abroad learnt to read our mind so well that they will only request funding for projects which our mission board at home *likes* and not what the partner-church abroad most urgently *needs*? I raise these questions not in the spirit of criticism, but as one who has been dealing with quite a number of mission agencies, including those in the United States, for well over twenty years now. I raise them for *our* reflection and thinking *together* and I sincerely believe that I would have done even a poorer job as "a friendly observer" of North American global mission responsibility should I fail to pose those questions before this very distinguished gathering.

There is an explicit emphasis on "responsibility" in the topic that has been given to me. I would like to conclude by reiterating the biblical principle which I have stated earlier: "To whom much is given, much is required."

Scenario 2000:
World Evangelization Review

Tom Houston

Sheep Without Shepherds

Recently the picture for looking at World Evangelization has been the "Harvest." The emphasis has been on numbers. I want to take another metaphor, which comes from the passage that gives us the "Harvest." Jesus speaks in Matthew 9:36 of the crowds whom he saw as being "worried and helpless, like sheep without a shepherd." He tells the disciples to pray for workers. We think he was talking about harvesters and I am sure he was. He was also talking about shepherds. When he proceeds immediately to send out the twelve he says, "Go to the lost sheep of Israel." He saw them going out as "shepherds"(Matthew 10:5).

The idea of people being like straying sheep and Jesus as the shepherd is mentioned several times in the New Testament. The roots of this picture are in the Old Testament. It is a strong metaphor not a sentimental one. Kings, princes, nobles,—the civil leaders—are all called shepherds. Jeremiah actually distinguishes them from priests and prophets who are the "spiritual" leaders (Jeremiah 2:8).

The picture is used by the prophets of the exile. The nation state of Judah was disintegrating. The civil and spiritual leaders of Israel had massively failed their people. If we summarize from Ezekiel 34 and the other passages.

> The lost were not sought and found.
> The weak were not strengthened.
> The sick were not healed.
> The wounded were not bound up.
> The hungry were not fed.
> Those in danger were not rescued.
> The straying were not brought back.
> The strong were not watched over.
> The sheep died and were consumed.
> The sheep were just not known.
> The shepherds gained at the expense of the sheep.
> The flock was scattered.
> The flock was divided

It is a terrible indictment. Two remedies are promised.

God would give them a king like his servant David to be their one shepherd (Ezekial.34:23, 37:24). This is what Jesus claimed to be in John 10.

God would also give them "shepherds according to his heart who will feed them with knowledge and understanding" (Jeremiah 3:15, 23:4). This is behind the Pastor/Teachers of Ephesians 4:11. The Old Testament background implies that it is not only pastors in the church that are God's provision. As well as Christian pastors, They are:

> Teachers in classes.
> Councillors in local Government.
> Heads of departments.
> Sisters in hospital wards.
> Ministers in national government.
> Employers in business, etc.

If we see the world as being "Sheep without Shepherds," it gives us a more holistic perspective. It is a message not just for church and mission executives. It is message for every leader, of even a few people, because the challenge of sheep without shepherds is all around us. It shows us all as accountable to the Great Shepherd for the state of the flock. It keeps the cross in the picture because the good shepherd gives his life for the sheep.

The Depletion of the Flock

David Barrett's figures show that the overall percentage of those who say they are Christians in the world today is about the same as in 1900—34%. It has fluctuated during the century, rising a little until 1914, then going down until the 1970's and recovering again today. At present he shows the percentage increasing at about 0.1% per annum.

That enables us to count on a gradually improving situation, take heart from it and work from there.

There have, however, always been questions about these figures. They depend on the definitions, sources and statistical methods used. If you vary the definitions etc., you can get different results.

In 1997, in the *World Churches Handbook*, Peter Brierley has gone inside some of the figures used by David Barrett and Patrick Johnstone. He has reproduced the figures of the denominations, country by country that Patrick Johnstone uses in *Operation World*. If we use the picture of "Sheep without Shepherds," the churches are a more appropriate place to start because it shows how the "enfolding" of the sheep is progressing.

Peter has presented the figures comparatively over the years 1960-2010. These show that as a percentage of the world's population, the Christian community is declining.

In 1960 it was 30%.

In 1995 it was 28%.

In 2010 it is projected to be 27%.

This is not such a rosy picture of world evangelization. The ninety and nine in the fold may be being depleted. There are several comments to be made.

Countries with a Lutheran Church

In 53% of the countries that have a Lutheran Church, the forecast is of decline in the overall percentage of Christians in the populations. In another 30% the situation is static. Only in 17% of these countries are the churches experiencing overall growth.

The picture in the Lutheran churches is more encouraging. 60% are growing. 22% are static. 19% are declining.

The growth is mainly in Africa, Asia, and Latin America and the size of the growing churches is often small. The three continents account for just over 11% of all Lutherans. In Europe, the heartland of Lutheranism, and where 67% of Lutherans are, most churches are static or declining. There is growth mainly in former Communist countries and there the numbers tend to be very small. In North America, where 20% of the Lutherans are, the numbers are just about static.

These are only projections based on known statistics. It could turn out differently, but that will depend on the blessing of God on the work of the shepherds and their effectiveness in bring lost sheep into the fold.

People Who Say They Are Christians

Evangelicals always have problems with statistics that count all the people who say they are Christians. We are aware that there are goats as well as sheep in the fold and that the judgement will sort us all out.

Churches Getting Smaller

A closer look at the numbers reveals something else. Despite the decreasing overall global percentage, the number of churches is growing. The average size of each church in 1960 was around 1,000. By 2010 it will be 670. So, the folds are increasing faster than the flock.

This true with Lutherans. The average church in 1960 had 658 members. In 1995 this had dropped to 483. By 2010 it is forecast to have dropped again to an average of 413.

There has been a great emphasis recently on church planting. We need to ask, however, whether this is always a wise strategy if it results in a smaller total number of Christians in more churches. In some places like New Zealand, some church planting is beginning to be seen as dissipating effort and weakening the churches.

Tom Houston

Wandering Sheep

There is a lot of movement between and away from churches.

In Latin America there is a massive movement of people from being, at least nominally Roman Catholic to Evangelical/Pentecostal churches. 75% of all Protestants in Latin America are Pentecostal. There is growing evidence, however, of another spiritual movement as people return to the original church —mainly Catholic—or even depart from all organized Christianity. In a 1989 survey of Costa Ricans, nearly as many said they used to be evangelicals as currently identified themselves as such.[1] Even within Pentecostal churches there is much splitting of churches and movement from one to the other.

In 1988, Barrett reported that there were six times as many post-Charismatic Catholics as current Charismatic Catholics and his figure for Protestants was 1.8 times as many. This tends to indicate that there are Christians who are revitalized through contact with the Charismatic emphasis and want to come back and serve in their own churches with the benefit of what they have experienced. Others end up totally disillusioned with Christianity.

In South Africa, there is a remarkable transfer-taking place between the main line denominations that are linked with missionary founded denominations and the burgeoning African Independent Churches.[2]

	1950	1980	1991
Denominations	75-80%	52%	41%
Independent Churches	12-14%	27%	36%

This trend is repeated also in many countries of Africa, south of the Sahara, but at a slower rate.

We called this section "wandering sheep" but we need to ask if the sheep are the main cause of the wandering. Ezekiel and Zechariah thought that the shepherds were responsible for this phenomenon. Some shepherds starve or neglect their sheep and they wander off to survive. Others are sheep stealers who rob other congregations and then feed off the sheep. Jesus calls them thieves, robbers, strangers and hirelings and not shepherds (John 10:1-13).

Wolves Among the Flock

With the development of independent nations in the Third World, and the move from Modernism to Post Modernism in the West, Christians can expect to have a lot more serious competition from other faiths than they have experienced in the earlier part of this century.

Non-Trinitarian Churches

Jesus told us that the wolves would include false Messiahs. We have an increasing number of active, heretical groups who are growing in the world. The one we know best is probably Jehovah's Witnesses. They are everywhere and growing even where the church is not growing.

The Moonies (The Holy Spirit Association for the Unification of World Christianity) are well known and are now the largest "Christian" denomination in Japan. They effectively target people in power through programs, conferences, and publications and have a large financial empire.[3]

The Church of Jesus Christ of Latter Day Saints is active and growing. *The World Churches Handbook* gives their figures for 95 countries, all of them growing.

Many of the African Indigenous churches are non-Trinitarian and they are making strides also.

Non-Christian Religions

A new feature in our context, is the aggressive return to the battle of the non-Christian religions. This is strikingly presented in a book called "The Revenge of God" by Gilles Kepel.

The emergence of fundamentalism and militant Islam was a striking feature of the 1970s and 1980s. There was the Iranian revolution under the influence of the Ayatollah Khomeini. The political emergence of the late Zia ul-Haq in Palestine. The Muslim resistance movement in Afghanistan. The impact of Shi'ism in the Middle East and the development of an Islamic resurgence in Malaysia. They changed the atmosphere in the world of religion.

Christians in Taiwan are reporting a very strong resurgence of Buddhism in their country in the nearly 9,000 temples but also by more sophisticated methods in the cities.

In Japan, a quarter of the people are adherents of new religions and 100 new groups are founded every year. The largest of these is Soka Gakkai (Society for the Creation of Value) officially established in 1951. It is a lay Buddhist movement with roots in the past. By 1974 it claimed 7,500,000 families and now has 17 million individual members in Japan.[4]

In India there is a Hindu revival backed by strong political parties and Christians in some places are put more and more on the defensive. Hindus also have their missionaries in the West.

Then there is a move back to the older traditional religions. Much of this goes under the name of New Age. Often, as in Scandinavia, there is a return to their pagan religion that antedated Christianity. In the CIS with the relaxing of Communist controls, the resurgence of all kinds of religious ideas is as prominent as the renewed interest in the Christian churches. There is a widespread preoccupation with the occult, which seems also to be a reversion to pre communist ideas and practice. It is featured prominently on television. There is a strong showing by Macamba in Brazil.

There is anecdotal evidence that there is a reversion to various forms of secret societies that ask for loyalty on pain of death. The economic side of this is often in the rise and spread of different mafias. There are, however, places where political control is sought or maintained by these means.

From these sources Christians experience persecution, economic and occupational discrimination, second class citizenship, imprisonment, torture and death. These are the kind of birth pangs that will lead to the growth of the church if only we are ready for them.

Paul, in Acts 20:28-31, says it is the task of the shepherds to watch and guard against the wolves that will come and attempt to destroy the sheep. Can we seriously think about world evangelization without having strategies that deal with such opposition?

The Sheepfolds

Jesus said. "There shall be one fold and one shepherd" (John 10:16) The church is the instrument of God's purpose for the whole world. Globalization is the process by which the world is now becoming more and more one place. Globalization, for good or ill, is affecting all structures including those of churches and other Christian institutions.

The whole balance of forces in the Christian enterprise has shifted. In 1900, according to Barrett, 83% of all Christians were Europeans or Anglo Saxons with only 17% in the other parts and of the other peoples of the world.

By 1990 the European Anglo Saxon figure was 42.5% and the rest of the world 57.7%. By any account, this is a remarkable demographic shift and represents a great globalization of the Christian gospel.

Trends within secular globalization are reflected in the way Christians are organizing themselves today.

Large Organizations

Business has thrown up the large multinational and transnational corporations like IBM, Siemens, ICI, Toyota, and Hyundai. These are often displacing the national corporations of the past both public or private.

David Barrett estimated that in 1991 there were 33 Christian agencies with an annual budget of over $100 million per year. Some of these are recent and expanding. Others are historic, centralized, bureaucratic, denominational structures that are declining.

Small Organizations

Small businesses have been proliferating that can do work more economically than the larger companies.

There is also a proliferation of new churches and Christian organizations. In 1993-4 the amount of money coming to parachurch agencies in the world surpassed, for the first time, all the money coming to all the churches. The gap is increasing now every year. It is a fruit of the current emphasis on individual autonomy in society. Barrett estimated the parachurch agencies in 1991 as 22,000.

New Industrialized Countries

Formerly undeveloped countries in South and East Asia and Latin America, have developed very rapidly in the last 20 years. We only need to mention Japan, Hong Kong, Singapore, Thailand, Malaysia, and now China to think of the term East Asian Tigers even if currently they are in difficulty. Brazil, Argentina, and Chile show the same trend in Latin America.

Parallel to that there has been the very rapid rise of Third World missions. Missionaries from India, Nigeria, Korea, Brazil and the Philippines, etc. were 36,000 in 1988. By AD 2000 it is expected there will be 150,000 Third World Missionaries in the fields. This too is globalization.

New Players

Globalization has led to direct intervention in international trade by new players who find a product and sell it.

Since 1970 there has been a significant increase in the phenomenon of the local mega-church with memberships of more that 5,000 and, in a few cases, more than 100,000. Their financial strength is making it possible for them to train and send out their own missionaries assisted by all the immediacy of inexpensive travel and modern communications. They are bypassing the missionary societies.

Displaced Peoples

Increased and less expensive travel is part of globalization. Some are economic migrants fleeing poverty for a better life. Some are traveling for international trade and commerce. Others are refugees from famine or political oppression. There are now significant and growing immigrant communities in many countries.

These migrations of people have led also to the beginning of the mobilizing of Christians in the Diasporas of peoples who are now scattered all over the world. These also are producing transnational structures that will be increasingly significant for world evangelization.

1. The Overseas Chinese have the Chinese Coordinating Center for World Evangelization. They now have 49 chapters located in many countries and are thinking and planning and praying both for their host countries, their countries of transit and mainland China when it may be open to them again.

2. The Jews have the Lausanne Committee for Jewish Evangelism. They have fostered the unity of the Jews and those who work among them since 1980.

3. The South Asians are mobilizing from what used to be called the subcontinent. In 1991/2 South Asian Concern was started in UK. In 1994 the launch of NACSAC (North American Consultation of South Asian Christians) took place in Chicago. They have organized in Kenya and the Philippines and have hopes of doing so in South Africa and other places.

4. The Arabs: In 1992 The Arab World Evangelical Ministers Association (AWEMA) was formed. They now have committees in 22 countries and are seeking to network between churches in the Middle East, North Africa, and the rest of the world.

5. The Philippines. There are 4 million Philippinos scattered throughout the world. They formed the Filipino International Network in 1995. They have imaginative programs for becoming intentional in using their "scattering" to further the gospel.

I can only list the rest: the Japanese, the Koreans, the Cambodians, the Vietnamese, Russians, Ukrainians, Armenians, the Francophone Africans in France, Anglophones in England, and Luzophones in Portugal.

I believe that all these scatterings of people are part of God's plan for world evangelization, both of the homelands and their new host countries. This is not an easy concept and it will not be an easy process to relate to them. Yet they have much in common and they could help one another and together become a tremendous force for the gospel.

Strategic Alliances

Strategic Alliances are the new way of doing business. They are formed and disbanded in a great variety of ways to make the best of the skills and know how of every conceivable kind of entrepreneur.

This is now being paralleled in Christian organizations. INTERDEV has been concentrated on forming strategic evangelism partnerships and there are Lutherans in some of them.

Some of these are vertical partnerships with more than 20 or 30 organizations with different skills working together to reach a region or a people. They include local churches, Bible translators, literature people, broadcasters, relief and development agencies, Bible correspondence courses, and all the services needed to win and disciple a people for Christ.

These are mostly targeted on inaccessible peoples in North Africa or Central Asia. Some of them are horizontal partnerships where all the people in one field get together like the various agencies related to Bible translation, like educators, administrators, trainers, publishers, linguists, anthropologists, marketers, etc.

In both horizontal and vertical partnerships the personnel are both local and global, each making the contribution that they are gifted to make.

In all these ways national, denominational, and institutional boundaries are being eroded and penetrated without anyone being able to prevent it. New forces are at work and old controls are crumbling. The old sheepfolds are hardly recognizable and the mixing of the flocks is having its own fruitfulness.

Storms and Earthquakes

The Nativity Story describes shepherds keeping watch over their flocks by night. The sheep can be exposed to storms and natural disasters. It is the shepherd's responsibility to be there for the sheep. There are already some storms raging and signs that others may break soon.

The countries of the CIS (Commonwealth of Independent States) are already in a storm of economic hardship and political and religious uncertainty. The new freedoms are challenging the shepherds who learned to operate in a different world under Communism. Restrictions will come from Central Governments and from local officials.

Here and in many places, the adjustment of economies, as they become market driven, will mean trial and hardship for many believers and those among whom they witness. Many will lose jobs and become unemployed. The gap between rich and poor will increase and even the safety nets that were in position will have larger holes and more people will fall through. We may look at it from two angles.

The countries with the lowest GNP per capita are all in Africa. They are seriously deficient in caloric intake by the population. Many of them have had civil wars or are in serious political crisis. They all have churches. There is a particular challenge on their pastors and on us as those who profess to be their partners to be ready for crises of poverty.[5]

Six of the countries with the biggest gap between the income of the top 20% and the bottom 40% of the population are in Latin America. Six are in Africa. In both we see the continuing footprint of colonialism giving way to an elite in independence that has taken over from the colonial elite. These too have churches of both the poor and the rich, and the shepherds, spiritual and secular, will need to be ready for very human crises in the days ahead.[6]

We can anticipate something of an economic and political earthquake in North Korea. Our friends in South Korea pray fervently and often for the reunification of their divided country. The events in East Germany in 1990 indicate that such a reunification is not easy and the economic and ideological gap between the two Koreas is much greater.

We must anticipate change in China. When or how it will come we do not know. We do not know if it will be a peaceful transition or one fraught with internal strife. We have no patterns in previous experience or in history, anywhere in the world, of churches growing so rapidly in a situation of restriction, oppression, and yet astonishing economic growth and then able to come out to the wider church in the world. One of the largest flocks in the world will suddenly or gradually be linked with the one fold of the one shepherd. They have so much to teach us, learned in the fires of persecution. They have had such a different experience. They have such human resources. It cannot but be dramatic and disturbing when this link up takes place.

Indonesia and Nigeria are the two places where there is a significant and growing Christian presence in a predominantly Muslim nation. We can be sure that Islam will contend furiously to reverse this situation. Political changes will provide the backdrop for this clash.

The Middle East will also see storms. We need to keep our eyes and our prayers on the goals of the turning to Messiah of his ancient people, the Jews and the discovery of their Prophet and Savior, Jesus on the part of the Muslims.

We are not yet finished with the Balkans. This too is a front line and we are not promised fair weather. Our capacity as ministers of reconciliation will be tested to the uttermost in these situations fraught with ethnic and religious strife.

We need to prepare also for onslaught of Post Modernism in the West. I think we have only begun to see the destruction and moral decay that will assail our western societies, unless we are better able by the relevance of our witness and the quality of our lives, individual and corporate, to show a better way. The Gospel and Culture project on both sides of the Atlantic is working away at the intellectual groundwork for a Christian comeback.

Let me end this section by warning that we also may have to deal not only with thunder and lightning storms but also with a drought of motivation. Jesus warned that when the Son of man comes, he may find little faith on the earth. Apathy is often a more difficult factor to fight off than persecution. I am concerned that we should be ready to deal with the disillusionment that may well set in after the passing of the millennium fever. It is only two years away. Many of peoples' dreams and goals will remain unrealized and it will be more difficult to fight off the pessimism and cynicism of unmet expectations.

Fresh Pastures or the New Frontiers

I want to end by reminding you of the pristine new fields of Albania, Mongolia and Nepal. Christian witness was resumed in Albania in 1992. It too has been an example of different organizations working together well. It received a major setback in 1997 but there is still a lot of hope. Christian work began in Nepal in the mid-1950s. In Mongolia in 1989 there were fewer than 10 Christians. Yet today there is a church of maybe 100,000 in Nepal and 3,000 or 4,000 in Mongolia. Each has its share of problems.

Each is a symbol that the world is continuing to be evangelized and fresh fields opened up to the influence of the Savior and the work of the Holy Spirit.

Conclusion

I have tried to survey our world for you and speak of its evangelization under the picture of Sheep without Shepherds. I believe that the most striking lesson that comes out of all of this is the need for us to develop under-shepherds that are like the Good Shepherd. He will give them the lost to find, the sick to tend, the wandering to recover, the wounded to heal, the hungry to feed, the straying to recover, those in danger to rescue, and the scattered to bring together in the shelter of the fold.

Notes

[1] Nunez, Emilio and Taylor, David. *Crisis and Hope in Latin America: An Evangelical Perspective* (Pasadena, CA: William Carey, 1996), p. 463.

[2] *International Bulleting of Missionary Research,* January 1997 (Vol.21 No.1): p. 8.

[3] Robertson, Roland and Garrett, William, eds. *Religion and Global Order* (New York: Paragon House, 1991), pp. 201-220.

[4] Robertson, Roland and Garrett, William, eds. *Religion and Global Order* (New York: Paragon House, 1991), pp. 183-199.

[5] Bellamy, Carol. *The State of the World's Children 1997* (Oxford Union Press), p.80-81.

[6] Bellamy, Carol. *The State of the World's Children 1997* (Oxford Union Press), p.82-83.

Countries (Alphabetized in Continents)

Lutheran Countries	Christians growing as % of pop.	Lutherans growing	Lutheran Countries	Christians growing as % of pop.	Lutherans growing
AFRICA (23)			MIDDLE EAST (2)		
Angola	yes	yes	Israel	static	static
Botswana	no	yes			
C.A.R.	yes	yes	EUROPE (35)		
Cameroon	no	yes	Austria	no	no
Chad	static	yes	Belarus	no	no
Congo (PR)	no	yes	Belgium	no	no
Cote d'Ivoire	no	static	Bosnia/Hertz.	no	static
Eritrea	no	yes	Croatia	no	no
Ethiopia	no	yes	Czech Rep.	no	yes
Ghana	no	yes	Denmark	no	no
Liberia	no	yes	Estonia	yes	yes
Madagascar	no	yes	Faeroe Isles.	static	static
Malawi	no	yes	Finland	no	yes
Mali	static	yes	France	no	static
Namibia	static	yes	Germany	no	no
Nigeria	no	yes	Georgia	static	static
Sierra Leone	static	yes	Greenland	no	yes
South Africa	no	no	Hungary	yes	yes
Swaziland	no	yes	Iceland	static	yes
Tanzania	no	yes	Italy	yes	yes
Togo	static	yes	Latvia	yes	yes
Zambia	no	no	Liechtenstein	no	static
Zimbabwe	static	yes	Lithuania	yes	yes
			Luxembourg	yes	static
ASIA (17)			Moldova	yes	yes
Bangladesh	yes, just	yes	Netherland	static	no
China (PROC)	yes	yes	Norway	static	static
Guam	static	static	Poland	static	yes
Hong Kong	yes	yes	Portugal	static	static
India	static	yes	Romania	static	no
Indonesia	static	yes	Russia	static	yes
Japan	static	yes	Slovakia	no	no
Jordan	no	static	Slovenia	no	no
Kazakhstan	no	no	Sweden	no	static
Korea S.	static	yes	Switzerland	no	static
Malaysia	static	yes	U.K	no	static
Myanmar	static	yes	Ukraine	yes	yes
Philippines	static	yes	Yugoslavia	static	static
Singapore	yes	yes			
Sri Lanka	no	yes			
Taiwan	static	yes			
Thailand	yes	yes			

Mission at the Dawn of the 21st Century

Lutheran Countries	Christians growing as % of pop.	Lutherans growing
LATIN AMERICA (19)		
Argentina	no	no
Bolivia	no	yes
Brazil	no	yes
Chile	no	static
Colombia	static	yes
Costa Rica	no	static
Ecuador	no	yes
El Salvador	no	yes
Guatemala	no	yes
Guyana	no	yes
Haiti	no	yes
Honduras	no	no
Nicaragua	no	?
Panama	no	yes
Paraguay	static	yes
Peru	static	static
Suriname	no	no
Uruguay	yes	yes
Venezuela	no	no
NORTH AMERICA (4)		
Canada	no	static
Puerto Rico	static	yes
USA	no	static
Mexico	static	no
OCEANIA (4)		
Australia	no	yes
New Zealand	no	static
Papua New Guinea	static	yes
Virgin Islands	yes	yes

Countries growing	Yes = 17 (16%)
	Static = 31 (30%)
	No = 55 (53%)
Lutherans growing	Yes = 62 (60%)
	Static = 31 (30%)
	No = 19 (18%)
100% = 103 Countries	

Tom Houston
June 4, 1998

The Mission of the Church Today in the Light of Global History

Andrew Walls

The twentieth century has been the most remarkable of all the Christian centuries since the first. Within it, the composition of the Christian church, ethnically and culturally, has changed out of recognition. On the one hand there has been a great retreat from Christianity. That retreat has been centered in the West, and especially in Western Europe, where active Christian profession has dramatically receded during the century. At the same time, there has been a massive accession to Christian faith. One has to go back many centuries for any parallel to the number of new Christians and new Christian communities. This accession has taken place outside the West, in southern continents, including many areas where, before the present century, Christians were few in number. At the beginning of this century, some 83% of those who professed the Christian faith lived in Europe and North America. Now, some 60% (probably) live in Africa, Asia, Latin America, or the Pacific Islands, and that proportion is rising every year. The center of gravity of the Christian church has moved sharply southwards. The representative Christianity of the twenty-first century seems set to be that of Africa, Asia, Latin America, and the Pacific region. These areas look destined to be the launch pad for the mission of the church in the twenty-first century.

To considered that mission in the light of global history – six continents and two thousand years, to take only the Christian centuries – is hardly a task to be undertaken in half an hour. The most that is possible is to point to some recurrent features which seem to have characterized Christian history in its first two millennia which may give some clues to the essential nature of Christian faith and, thus, of Christian mission. Three are suggested here. They are:

1. The spread of Christianity has not been progressive, but serial.

2. Christian faith involves translation, cultural as well as linguistic.

3. Christianity is about conversion.

The Spread of Christianity Has Not Been Progressive, but Serial

Long ago, Kenneth Scott Latourette pointed out that the history of Christianity has not been one of steady progress, let alone of resistless triumph. There have been periods of advance, but also periods of recession, or falling back, of withering and decay. Islam can make a much better claim than Christianity for progressive expansion, for steady numerical increase and geographical growth. Generally speaking—there are some exceptions—land that became Islamic have so far remained Islamic. The Arab lands seem now so inalienably Muslim that it is hard to remember that the Yemen was once Christian territory. Contrast Jerusalem, home of the first Christian church, or Syria and Egypt and Asia Minor and North Africa, which one provided the brightest examples of Christian devotion, scholarship, and witness. Or take my own country, where John Knox and John Wesley once preached, now full of unwanted churches turned into furniture stores, garages, or night clubs.

In each of these latter cases, a place which had been a Christian heartland, a shining center of Christian devotion and activity, ceased to have this function; the light burned down or burned out, and the candlestick was taken out of its place. But in none of these cases did this decline mean the disappearance of the Christian faith or the end of Christian witness—rather—the reverse. By the time the Jerusalem church was scattered to the winds, the gospel had taken hold in the Hellenistic world of the Eastern Mediterranean. When the literate civilization of the Roman Empire broke up, the gospel was making its way among the barbarians north and east of that empire. And as the modern recession began to accelerate in Europe and to wash into North America, the churches of Africa, Asia, and Latin America began to come into their own. The Christian story is serial, its center moves from place to place. No one church or place or culture owns it. At different times different peoples and places have become its heartlands, its chief representatives. Then the baton passes on to others. Christian progress is never final, is never a set of gains to be plotted on the map. The rhetoric of some of our hymns, and many of our sermons, about the triumphant host streaming out to conquer the world is more Islamic than Christian. Christian history reveals the faith often withering in its heartlands, in its centers of seeming strength and importance, to establish itself or begin its margins. It has vulnerability, a certain fragility, at its heart; the vulnerability of the cross, the fragility of the earthen vessel.

Christian Faith Involves Translation, Cultural as Well as Linguistic

Our faith depends on the Word made flesh, God made human. One way of looking at this is as a great act of translation: in the Incarnation, God is translated into humanity, the whole meaning of God is expressed in human categories, as though humanity is the receptor language into which God is translated. But when God became human, it was not as generalized humanity, but as a particular person, a person living in a particular culture at a particular time, the culture of a Palestinian Jew of the first century. The only humanity we ever know is culture specific, reflecting the customs and language of a particular time and place. The cross-cultural spread of the Gospel leads to Christ being received by faith in other cultures, and thus successively retranslated into the customs and languages of those peoples. The extraordinary thing is that this process of re-translation constantly reveals new truths about Christ. To take the most obvious example, to be seen within the New Testament itself: The first believers were Jews who saw Jewish history, tradition, and belief. But when they came to share that faith with Greek-speaking Gentile Peoples, they found it was of little use to talk of Jesus as Messiah. The word meant nothing to Greeks, and needed endless explanation. They had to translate, to find a term that told something about Jesus and yet meant something to a Greek pagan. According to Acts (chapter 11, verses 19-21), they chose the word *Kyrios*, "Lord", the title that Greek pagans used for their cult divinities. Jewish believers (and the action was taken by Jewish folk) had long thought of Jesus as Messiah. For them, the word, standing for a rich, pregnant concept, indicated the ultimate significance of Jesus. Greeks could readily think of "the Lord Jesus." This was a rich concept, too, but it gave a new dimension to thinking about Christ. Translation also raised questions, awkward questions that a Jew would never ask. Jewish believers could readily use a phrase like "Jesus is at the right hand of God." The significance of that statement was well understood by the Sanhedrin: using it brought Stephen to his death. But a Greek would be puzzled by such a phrase – did it really mean that the transcendent God had a right hand? What Greeks wanted to know was the relationship of that ultimately significant Christ to the Father. Thus, inevitably, the language of ousia and hypostasis enters. Were Christ and the Father of the same ousia? Or different as to ousia? Or similar in ousia? To find out meant a process of exploring what Christians really believed about their Lord, using the indigenous methods of Greek intellectual discourse. It was a long, painful process; but it issued in an expanded understanding of who Christ is. Christian theology moved on to a new plane when Greek questions were asked about Christ, and received Greek answers, using the Greek scriptures. It was a risky, often agonizing business, but it led the church to rich discoveries about Christ that could never have been made using only Jewish categories such as Messiah. Translation enriched; it did not negate the tradition.

Similar developments can be traced in later Christian theology as new questions have arisen as a result of the gospel crossing cultural frontiers. We are now at the threshold of a time when new questions will be asked about Christ, arising from the attempt to express Him in settings that are dominated by the venerable traditions of Asia and Africa. If past Christian experience is anything to go by, this can only enrich the church's understanding of Christ and lead to new discoveries in theology.

Christianity Is About Conversion

The theme of conversion, of turning to Christ, is closely linked with the previous theme or translation. God is the great Translator. In Christ, God is translated into humanity, so that we look at that human being and say "This is what God is like." If the idea of translation expresses something of the saving activity of God, the idea of conversion may express the proper human response to that activity.

Conversion means turning. Conversion to Christ is turning towards Him. There is a vital difference between converts and proselytes. Long before the time of Christ, Jews had designed ways of welcoming Gentiles who recognized the God of Israel and wanted to serve Him in the community of Israel. Proselytes, as such people were called, were circumcised, were baptized, thus symbolically washing away the dirt of the heathen world, and entered into the life of Israel by seeking to obey the Torah. It would have been very natural for that first, entirely Jewish, community of believers in Jesus to maintain this venerable system. But the great council described in Acts 15, which considered how Gentiles who believed in Jesus should be introduced into the community, deliberately rejected the time-honored model of the proselyte. It was an astonishing decision. Hitherto all believers in Jesus had been circumcised and kept the Torah, just like the Lord Himself. It was the standard lifestyle for believers. But the early church decided that Gentile believers in Jesus – ex-pagans, remember, without the lifelong training in doctrine and morality that Jews had – should not be circumcised, should not keep the Torah, and should be left to find a Christian lifestyle of their own within Hellenistic society under the guidance of the Holy Spirit. They were not to be proselytes, but converts.

This distinction between convert and proselyte is of fundamental importance. If the first Gentile believers had become proselytes, living exactly the style of life of those who brought them to Christ, they might have become very devout believers indeed, but they would have had virtually no impact on their society; they would effectively have been taken out of that society. In fact, it was their task as converts to convert their society; convert it in the sense that they had to learn to keep turning their ways of thinking and doing things – which, of course, were Greek ways of thinking and doing things – towards Christ, opening them up to his influence. In this way a truly Greek, truly Hellenistic type of Christianity was able to emerge. Not only so, but that Hellenistic Christianity was able to penetrate the Hellenistic intellectual and social heritage. Hellenistic thought, Hellenistic social and family life, and Hellenistic civic organization were challenged, modified, and put to new uses —but from the inside, by people whose own inheritance they were.

Conversion means turning. It is not about substituting something new for something old—that is the proselyte model, that the early church might have adopted but deliberately abandoned. Nor is it a matter of adding something new to something old. It is much more radical than either. It is the steady, relentless turning of all the mental and moral processes toward Christ. In other words, it is *turning what is already there*; turning to Christ the elements of the pre-conversion setting. Origen puts it beautifully, with a little vouch of his own special sort of exegesis. How is it, he says, that the Israelites were able to make the cherubim and the other gold adornments of the Tabernacle, when they were in the wilderness? The answer is that they had previously spoiled the Egyptians. The cherubim and the vessels were made from Egyptian gold, and the Tabernacle curtains of Egyptian cloth. It is the business of Christian people, he goes on, to take the things of the heathen world and to fashion from them things for the worship and service of God.

Together, these three features of global Christian history may give us some hints for Christian mission today. The serial nature of Christian expansion has taken its heartlands away from the West, and into the southern continents. The translation of the faith into new cultural contexts, and the new questions to which that process gives rise will expand and enrich – if we will allow it – our understanding of Christ. And Christians everywhere, including those who live in the Mammon-worshipping culture of the West, the last great non-Christian culture to arise, are called to the relentless turning of their mental and moral processes towards Christ. In the process, and in the fellowship of Christ, we may notice that the Tabernacle is now adorned with African gold, and hung with curtains of Asian cloth.

The Mission of the Local Congregation

Timothy F. Lull

We are edging close to the end of the century and to the end of the millennium. Christians know that this is an artificial moment and no cause for either jubilation or alarm. But, despite such disclaimers, we Christians share with everyone else the strong interest in looking back at these past hundred years (which we can imagine with a little help from family memories) and the unusual experience of trying to comprehend the end of these thousand years (a period of time almost beyond imagination, even for the historian).

So I'm going to use that special interest in the future of the church that feeds off this arbitrary and artificial moment—Century's End and Millennium's End—as an occasion to invite you to think about the future of the church. Such thinking is always worth doing if we undertake it in the right spirit. And I want to think tonight not just about the church in general, but about the corner of the church I know best, the future of the North American local congregations. Readers from other parts of the world may well find what I say puzzling or familiar, and my fellow North Americans may have quite different analysis. But if we take this as an occasion for considering our call, with due humility, we may all benefit whether or not we agree on what is happening and what I propose needs to be done.

I've mentioned undertaking this in the right spirit. For Christians that means remembering at every stage of a discussion of the future of the church our confession that the Holy Spirit is Lord of the church, that it is the Spirit who calls, gathers, enlightens, sanctifies, and preserves the church. It is a regular work of the Spirit to surprise human expectations and overturn human plans (this is, I think, the theme of the whole book of Acts), even those made with great good intentions by the church's own leaders. So we could consider this essay under the rubric of Paul's invitation to bear with him in a little foolishness (II Corinthians 11:1). Let's try to imagine the emerging future of the church, not to get it under our control, but rather to see how we might get ourselves under its control, in line with the coming kingdom of God as the Spirit wills it for us.

I want to begin by discussing four trends that are shaping the future of the church for North American congregations. Though I speak as someone knee-deep in Lutheranism, I think all of these apply to most Protestant communities and even most Roman Catholic parishes. The ways that we deal with them may be shaped for good or ill by what is left of our confessional particularity, but the trends themselves are major factors that all of us must respond to in some way.

The passing of Christendom. In more and more places in North America, active church-going Christians will live as a minority in the population in the new century. This trend is nothing new, being long developed in Europe— first in the Protestant North, and then, since Vatican II, in many traditional Roman Catholic countries as well. The change is coming quite unevenly in various parts of North America, most strongly in the West, but everywhere today in urban areas. This change brings a special sense of threat to many Christians in North America. Many members feel that they remember better days for the church, larger crowds, more influence, fewer financial problems. We live increasingly among neighbors who feel no pressure toward religious affiliation, and many children of religiously active parents are not churched in any active way.

There are opportunities in such a transition, as has been pointed out especially in the recent writings of Canadian theologian Douglas John Hall.[1] But wherever Christendom has thrived until quite recently, there tends to be deep discouragement at its passing. It takes a great shift in attitude to avoid depression and discouragement, and a genuine theological vision to see opportunity rather than decline. But in these changes Christians are being forced to the mission question if they are to have a future at all. How can we make our appeal without the benefit of a position of privilege or advantage? [2]

The unchurched as formerly-churched. The local mission task is greatly complicated by the fact that so many of those who are outside the church were, at one time in their lives, church members. It is a great challenge to take the Christian story to those who have never heard it; it is a double challenge to convince those with earlier and negative experience of the Christian community to give the church another try. I often encounter such persons on my travels, these casualties of Christianity, and their stories deserve our attention.

This scar tissue among former church members (many of whom continue to consider themselves Christians) is one of the reasons that simple appeals to hospitality are inadequate. Creating a climate of welcome is a foundational task for mission-readiness, but even the warmest and most-welcoming church will not easily receive a visit from those whose memories of the church are of law, judgment, or even boredom. One does not have to take all of the complaints of the formerly-churched at face value; they may or may not represent a fair evaluation of the communities which they seem to describe. But the impression that religion is a source of strife, of judgment, of exclusion, or even of obscure and unhelpful dogma is a challenge that few local communities have really pondered. Does anything in our parish life and public witness challenge their perception of the church as a negative institution?

Residential religious pluralism. Our congregations live surrounded by neighbors who practice many forms of Christianity, and by those who have no formal religious affiliation at all. But a new factor in recent decades is the presence of adherents of the major world religions in many local communities —especially metropolitan centers. The world mission is now a local mission in our cities, and even to some extent in smaller towns, as ones' neighbors and coworkers may be Muslim, Buddhist, Hindu, or adherents of other traditional non-Christian religions. Most North American Christians have not yet completely mastered the art of living in a neighborly and well-informed way with Jews. But now Jews may seem like close or familiar neighbors as Christians encounter more distant neighbors, many of whom are not likely to join our churches whatever the mission strategy.

Religious pluralism is nothing new, and the history of Christianity is full of diverse strategies for dealing with this diversity—from sympathetic dialogue to harsh intolerance. But the new factor for many North American Christians is the proximity of these other options, which is why I call the new situation an experience of residential pluralism. When people are coworkers, when children attend school together, when intermarriage looms as a real possibility, then the confident sense of living as a Christian in a Christian culture is deeply challenged. I see many more signs of conflict at this point than evidence of local congregations dealing positively with how to live together in this new situation. The minimal first step would be opportunities to learn more about the religions of these neighbors, but few of our congregations have an effective parish education structure for adults that could take up this teaching challenge.

The ambiguity of new technologies. The other striking change that is influencing all aspects of life, including the religious, is the pervasive presence of new technologies. It is far from clear what the long-term influence may be from the presence of computers, the Internet, satellite television, and all the other media that make local communities less isolated than in the past. In one way these diverting opportunities may drive us all into solipsism, or at least into pervasive isolation with such virtual opportunities. In another respect, these technologies offer a great possibility for the reconnection of the church, with support and resources becoming available to the local congregation not simply through vertical church governance structures, but now through complex patterns of free-sharing and purchasing of services. [3]

There may be deeply negative aspects of this new technology, especially if the continuing explosion of possibilities drives a fresh wedge between the rich and the poor. But there are also reasons to be hopeful that this set of new possibilities will be affordable enough to be a powerful new tool for the sharing of the Christian message, even as printing turned out to be a driving force for the Reformation of the sixteenth century. I see some signs that our churches are confronting this opportunity more energetically than they faced the visual revolution at the beginning of the century (which so many Christian groups never explored). Our symbolic world is now largely shaped by movies and television from which religion is fundamentally absent. May it not be so with the new world of the Net!

You may have your own list of trends, and these four are simply meant to begin to illustrate the new challenge and new opportunity that is before local communities. For the church to have a future there must be mission, and the mission in this setting must be more than passing on the faith to one's own biological children. There is still a story to share and many near us with whom to share it. There will be new possibilities to use technology to share ideas and resources and to overcome the discouragement of isolation. Will local communities have the courage and the vision and the faith to take up the challenge?

At first glance the prospects are not terribly encouraging. It isn't hard to list factors that indicate that congregations may not take up the missional challenge or may not be very successful if they attempt some new approach. The overwhelming reality for many established congregations is their basic comfort with their current life, even in a situation of moderate decline. In many places it is still possible to squint a little and believe that Christendom is still present or easily recoverable. In other locations current patterns of mobility lead to church growth with or without a local missional strategy. But in most communities the task of outreach is hard, and there is enough awareness of this to make congregations slow to set out on what is always a very challenging road.

This hardness is partly a function of religious competition, of the scar tissue of the formerly churched, of the increasing presence of non-Christian alternatives. But the challenge to local mission is also a matter of local attitude. Far more is required for successful mission work than an open door and a little publicity. Real mission work requires two things that are extremely challenging to most North American congregations that I know — a genuine interest in others who are quite different from ourselves (whether that be in culture, in language, in race, in social class, or ethnic background) and a genuine willingness to change the way we do things so that a new form of church life may develop appropriate to the new mix of peoples in a congregation.[4]

Mission work also requires a cadre of adult leaders who are deeply grounded in the Christian story. Here the long-term weakness of our parish education comes back to haunt us. Lutherans, for example, have put most of their energies into teaching children and confirming youth, but the cutting edge need is an expanding core of adult members articulate enough about their faith to make a public witness in the world—in their vocations and their civic life, as well as at the church. Mainline Protestants who were once quite good at Christian education, now need remedial help both from evangelicals (with their successful and attractive patterns of teaching the faith) and from Roman

Catholics (who have great strength in their rite of adult initiation, which is an empowerment for discipleship both to those who join the church as adults and those who participate as their sponsors).

If there were consensus about the centrality of this missional task, mainline churches could call on their cadre of highly trained clergy to play a strong part in the renewal of parish education as equipping for witness in the world. But most clergy strike me—understandably—as having become such generalists (in terms of feeling responsible for meeting all needs within the congregation) that it is difficult for them to have the passion to set priorities and the discipline to stick to them even in the face of resistance. I fear that many pastors find the pressure to be "an employee" of the congregation almost irresistible in the end, so that unwillingly they become chaplains to the needs of dues-paying members. This means the almost sure defeat of any missional strategy, since there is never much time or energy left once all the chaplaincy to those on the membership rolls has been completed. Synodical structures often function unwittingly to urge pastors to "keep everyone happy" as a response to the complaints they receive.

But the most formidable obstacle to renewed local mission may be the general comfort level, the affluence of most North American Christians. Some waning of missional fire is inevitable for people who learn to live and work in complex systems in which one cannot lead with one's faith enthusiasm without being seen as intolerant. But much of the waning of missional fire comes from our own complex and conflicted commitments. The comforting preaching which most of us expect and which many of us offer to these congregations does little to press us to examine whether we have found real happiness, real peace, real joy in lives which are formally Christian, but in a carefully controlled way so that little ever emerges to challenge our many forms of business as usual. It is at this point especially where we hope both to walk with Jesus and to preserve a very peculiar, complex, and expensive way of life, that we may not be able to proclaim an authentic missionary gospel to each other. We may have to depend on those outside this "way of life" to challenge our sense of whether, as Kierkegaard put it, we can both bear the cross and have happy earthly lives.[5]

When we list merely human factors, it isn't hard to pile up an impressive list of obstacles to the renewal of local mission. We quickly get ourselves so discouraged that our doubts might become self-fulfilling. Then we are good as predictors (since pessimism about the future is always a way to avoid disappointment). But we turn out to be very poor Christians, letting our real fears overcome the even greater reality of the promise of God. The repeated pattern in church history is one of God's using unlikely persons to accomplish wonderful things. Perhaps our fears about the future are just one half of the situation; perhaps they ignore signs of how great a renewal may already be stirring in our midst.

Here the theology of the cross can function in a helpful way for those who understand it well. The theology of the cross in this instance is not an understanding of how Christ's saving death benefits us as the clue to the hidden and surprising ways that God always works in the world. The theology of the cross refuses to take either human reports of success or failure too seriously; rather it reminds us that all attempts to know "how we are doing"—statistical, theological, or whatever—are only reports of surface phenomena. God's standards are not the world's standards; the faithful person or community often appear to be despised and rejected. Our God is as likely to be encountered in a still, small voice, or a seed growing silently, as in reports of thousands converting or cathedrals being built.

The theology of the cross does not give us a mission strategy directly, but it warns us, for example, against reading the Book of Acts with an overly intense focus on numerical success. It invites us to think less about ourselves and rather to wonder what God might be doing in the current situation. It warns us against seeing the end of Christendom as defeat, and against restorationist schemes that promise to get everyone back in the church through better preachers, better speaker systems, new forms of worship, or a negotiation of theology according to current market needs.

So let us follow the advice of Pope John XXIII and try to discern for a moment the positive signs of the times. What might be happening among us already that would be promising for the cause of local congregations taking up the missional challenge with new energy and new hope? The signs will be ambiguous, of course, for they are signs rather than proofs since they are able to be read in more than one way.

I can think of three factors, three current developments, that may open the ground for a new approach:

Spiritual hunger. One widely noted feature of the North American culture is a great spiritual hunger. This hunger stems from the fact that our version of the "happy earthly life" has not been altogether satisfying. Some of this is no doubt superficial—consumerism now turning its never satisfied appetite to the religious realm for one more product to buy. But much of this is a sober recognition that persons have not found happiness in their work, in their families, in their community activities. Many of our churches have had little to offer to seekers both inside and outside the church. Yet there are more recent signs of vitality in small groups, in retreats, and in a desire to learn about Jesus—some of it even driven by curiosity about the Jesus Seminar.

This continuing interest in spirituality—a trend that has not gone away—could be the occasion for a renewal of the church's teaching of adults. Those who have ventured into non-church expressions of spirituality have probably learned there that short cuts and bargains are unlikely in this realm. There may be new willingness from some to commit to those forms of study and discipline that could build up a cadre of committed Christians—not just clergy

Mission at the Dawn of the 21st Century

—who would be capable of making a public witness in the world. Any hope for public impact of our mission in a society as complex as ours cannot be left to professional religious leadership but must be a shared mission, one which makes its impact both through the work and teaching of the church but also the vocational witness of its members.

Shared leadership. This growing core of persons—some clergy, some part-time or diaconal church workers, many laity whose primary commitment is to work in the world—could form a critical mass in many congregations to overcome the resistance to mission and articulate together a new vision of the task of the church in that community. Seminaries need to struggle—as some have notably—to produce leaders in mission, and especially pastors who can articulate a theology of mission, a sense of global-connectedness, and who hold a vision that will not be easily dislodged by resistance and inertia. But pastors cannot do it alone. The move from chaplaincy to mission will be more likely to be a sustained vision if it is not seen as the "idea" of professional leaders, but rather as the task to which God calls the whole community.

The task of shaping and sharing a vision together is far more arduous than that of hiring someone to do it for us. Bishops, call committees, and busy laity will be tempted to simplify this process by trying to find that dynamic, even charismatic, pastor who can light or re-light the missional fire in the people. "You lead us and then, when the time is right, we'll do something about mission." But the time for doing something about mission never seems to come, the community's ownership of that vision is very thin, the multiplying effect is minimal, and the probability that the vision will fade with the departure of the leader is very great. No one leader, however well trained at even the finest seminary, has all the gifts needed to lead a reluctant community from passivity into mission and to sustain it through the many struggles and setbacks along the way. (For interesting analogical examples of shared leadership on such a hard journey, see the interlocking roles of Moses, Aaron, Miriam, and a number of others in the story called Exodus).[6]

Generational discontinuity. This conference has expressed some anxiety about the age of those attending. Where are younger people in this Congress on the World Mission of the Church? We know that young North Americans are very globally conscious; their wonderful opportunities for travel and even their Web- surfing reinforce their sense that they live in the global village. Perhaps it is not surprising not to find them here in large numbers; they have other opportunities they might understandably prefer to spending the week theologically.

It could be that one era of missional commitment in the church is coming to an end. There is certainly a break with the generation of those shaped by Vietnam and its aftermath, my own generation, as a matter of fact. However much we may have recovered from the suspicions of those years of too close a connection between mission and empire, there is still something of a shadow for people my age, even though we too, in our own ways, are pretty active in that global village, especially as business becomes more international.

Global mission may be one area of the church where leadership continuity is both unlikely and not to be desired, where discontinuity might lead to fresh vision. Perhaps part of what God is calling us to in this congress is a new start, a real jump of leadership from those who remember the powerful thrust for world mission from the last golden decades of Christendom to those who will build a very different set of connections—more inter-faith and ecumenical than denominational, more high-tech, more willing to work with capitalism without forgetting questions of justice.

So it may be in many of our parishes. Our normal tendency is to continue the old forms of ministry, largely chaplaincy to members, while trying to start something new, but in many places this will be impossible. The clash of different visions of the church will be too hard for many of the traditional members, and is likely to frustrate the full flowering of the new life and new mission as persons from different cultures or classes or generations form the new congregation. Most of us have a prudent desire for maximum continuity, and in the human realm generally that may serve well. But it may also frustrate or even make impossible the missional renewal of the local parish.

A discontinuous jump in leadership is always a risk (and of course total discontinuity is highly unlikely). But at the heart of good missional theology is always a powerful experience of letting go. Those who would authentically share the gospel with others must be those who have experienced it as free, radical, and surprising gift. It can never be our possession or even "our cause." When that gift experience is strongly focused, then every Christian baptism is a miracle, every sharing of faith is a moment of witness, every gathering for worship an unlikely assembling by the Holy Spirit of people who have not chosen each other as community, but have found each other in the church— that surprising and inevitable byproduct of telling the story of Jesus.[7]

I don't expect that I have persuaded you. Discerning the signs of the times, especially the positive signs, is a very complex art, and one in which I am less skilled in than the listing of obstacles or in summarizing theological difficulties. We so often lead with our fears lest we be disappointed. But for people of faith the bottom line is that the Holy Spirit is always up to something. The changing nature of the world has brought the world community to our doorstep in North America. Can all of that have been—theologically— just an accident or for nothing? I believe that there will be a future mission of the local congregation because I confess that God wills for the church to abide, even though there is no promise that it will always thrive.[8] If I have stirred up even a glimmer of hope in you, then we have done well to bear with each other in this bit of foolishness.

Notes

1. While Hall has addressed this in many of his books, his fully developed treatment in the third volume of his systematics is an outstanding presentation of the new situation and its theological implications. See Douglas John Hall, *Confessing the Faith* (Minneapolis: Fortress, 1996), especially chapters 4 and 5.

2. Another seminal theological resource is found in the last volumes of Karl Rahner's *Theological Investigations*, in which he tries to cheer European Catholics (and others) past their discouragement with the collapse of Christendom to see new possibilities. See especially *Concern for the Church-Theological Investigations XX* (New York: Crossroad, 1981).

3. On a recent trip to South Africa we had occasion to spend a day in a poor township in Port Elizabeth as guests of a local Anglican clergy couple. We were shown the newly built church—the pride of the whole community—and its wonderful furnishings for worship. Then we were shown into a locked and very secure room where I expected to find some communion ware or liturgical robes. Instead the treasury contained four computers — a resource for the young people of the township to be able to learn how to use them and access the internet. The possibilities for that poor community to be linked to the whole Christian world show us one way that this new technology might develop.

4. "How many Lutherans does it take to change a light bulb?" (long silence) "Change?" The painful joke reflects the fact that Lutherans (and many others) would rather sit in a darkness to which we have grown accustomed than adjust to the new and radiant light.

5. Beyond the scope of this address is the helpful way in which any contacts that the local community can forge with global Christianity can help us know that "outsider" perspective and be challenged by it. This is especially the case in contacts with so-called "Third World" Christians, but it can happen even when we see the struggles of Europeans churches today. Here the ELCA's program of partnering synods with local judicatories around the world is really visionary and bearing good fruit.

6. The goal is to develop in every congregation a committed core of clergy and laity that together are articulate enough about the faith to make an effective public witness in the world. One precondition for the core to emerge is a strong program of parish adult education. Another, beyond the scope of this paper, is the transformation of the attitude of clergy about how leadership and transformation take place. A hopeful sign, in those churches ordaining women, is that many ordained women bring a different sensibility to this question of parish leadership.

7. At this point in the delivered address I added a "fourth" sign of the times concerning the political crisis about the Presidency and the credibility of leaders in light of sexual and other scandals. My suggestion was that this uproar, which is seen as very negative, could actually be a teaching moment, an opportunity for Christians of all political persuasions to think more deeply about leaders, about sin and forgiveness, about our far from perfect "American way of life." I was not interested in making a point for or against President Clinton but showing one more way in which the theology of the cross encourages us to look "beneath the surface." I see little evidence that any of the churches seized this opportunity, if one was ever there. Perhaps the terrain was too inescapably (and emotionally) political for such reflection to take place.

8. We could pay more careful attention to the wording of the *Augsburg Confession*, opening of Article VII: "It is taught among us that one holy Christian church will be and remain forever." See Tappert, ed., *Book of Concord* (Philadelphia: Fortress, 1959), p. 32. Our current upheavals are an occasion to understand these words as confession of faith rather than sociological prediction.

Contributors

J. Martin Bailey, Upper Montclair, NJ

Retired. Consultant in Communication to the Middle East Council of Churches

Carol J. Birkland, Geneva, Switzerland

Secretary for Planning, Monitoring, Evaluation, Lutheran World Federation, Department for World Service

Allan R. Buckman, St. Louis, MO

Director for World Areas, Board for Mission Services, Lutheran Church-Missouri Synod

Chee Pang Choong, Singapore

Professor, Trinity Theological College, Singapore and Visiting Professor, Beijing University, China.

James F. Engel, St. Davids, PA

Distinguished Graduate Professor in Economic Development at Eastern College and Founder and President of Development Associates International.

Paul Gifford, London, United Kingdom

Lecturer, Department of Study of Religions, School of Oriental & African Studies, University of London

Roger E. Hedlund, Chennai, India

Managing Editor, *Dharma Deepika*; Director, Churches of Indigenous Origins in India Project

Tom Houston, Oxford, United Kingdom

Retired. Minister at Large, Lausanne Committee for World Evangelization

Timothy F. Lull, Berkeley, CA

President, Pacific Lutheran Theological Seminary

Rafael Malpica-Padilla, Chicago, IL

Program Director for Latin America and the Caribbean, Division for Global Mission, Evangelical Lutheran Church in America

Paul Varo Martinson, St. Paul, MN

Professor, The Fredrik A. Shiotz Chair in Christian Missions and World Religions, Luther Seminary

Roland E. Miller, St. Paul, MN

Retired. Formerly Visiting Professor of Missions and Director of the Islamic Studies Program, Luther Seminary

Craig J. Moran, St. Paul, MN

Associate Professor of Mission and Director of the Global Mission Institute, Luther Seminary

Mary Motte, North Providence, RI

Director, Mission Resource Center, Franciscan Missionaries of Mary

Terry C. Muck, Austin, TX

Professor of Religion, Austin Presbyterian Theological Seminary

Alan Neely, Raleigh, NC

Retired. Luce Professor of Ecumenics and Mission, Princeton Theological Seminary

C. Rene Padilla, Buenos Aires, Argentina

President of the Kairos Foundation in Buenos Aires, Argentina and Editor of "Iglesia y Mision" Quarterly

Lamin Sanneh, Hamden, CT

Professor of Missions and World Christianity, Yale Divinity School and Professor of History, Yale Faculty of Arts

James A. Scherer, Oak Park, IL

Retired. Emeritus Professor of World Mission and Church History, Lutheran School of Theology at Chicago

Israel Selvanayagam, Bristol, United Kingdom

Methodist Church World Church Lecturer at Wesley College Bristol, and Queen's College Birmingham

John A. Siewert, Monrovia, CA

Technical Director, Global Information Sharing Program, World Vision International-Marc Division

Stanley H. Skreslet, Richmond, VA

Associate Professor of Christian Mission, Union Theological Seminary and Presbyterian School of Christian Education

James J. Stamoolis, Wheaton, IL

Executive Director of the Theological Commission of the World Evangelical Fellowship

Wayne C. Stumme, St, Paul, MN

Retired. Coordinator, Church and Labor Concerns, Institute for Missions in the USA

Mark W. Thomsen, Wheeling, IL

Director of Graduate Studies at Lutheran School of Theology at Chicago and Visiting Professor of Mission

Duain William Vierow, Lady Lake, FL

Retired. Consulting Director, Global Mission Institute, Luther Seminary

Andrew Walls, Edinburgh, Scotland, United Kingdom

Professor and Curator, Centre for the Study of Christianity in the Non-Western World, University of Edinburgh, Scotland

J. Dudley Woodberry, Pasadena, CA

Professor of Islamic Studies, School of World Mission, Fuller Theological Seminary